TIBETAN BORDER WORLDS

This interdisciplinary study is the outcome of a journey through lands but dimly known and books long shelved for posterity. In this innovative work, the first geohistorical analysis of a Himalayan community, Wim van Spengen explores both the area under investigation, and the wider subject of the place of regional geography within the larger geographical discipline. He argues for a historicizing regional geography, maintaining that geography has much to gain by a regional point of view in which the historical experience of social groups is thoroughly embedded. In *Tibetan Border Worlds*, van Spengen combines history, geography and ethnology and interweaves levels of analysis to set a new standard for writing regional geography based both on fieldwork and on an exhaustive survey of the literature, in an approach that is very much informed by *Annaliste* ideas of structural history, particularly the geohistory of Braudel.

The focus of the study is the Tibetan and Tibetanized border populations in the little known Himalayan high-valley of Nyishang in West Central Nepal close to the Tibetan border. There, a group of traders have greatly extended their external relations over the past century in the form of long-distance trade ventures, thereby thoroughly changing the internal conditions of socio-economic organizations in their home district. The object of the study is to establish whether larger geohistorical processes of structural change may be conceptualized in such a way as to link structuration at the level of the localized social group to the dynamics of the wider regional setting. The approach includes the geographical analysis of culture, a sorely neglected theme in modern studies. Among the subjects dealt with are the geopolitics of Tibet, Tibet as a culture region, the monastic imperative, the traditional barter complex, the ecclesiastical state and trade, the decay of traditional valley life, and the Golden Triangle and Indo-China.

In the course of the work, van Spengen accounts for the rise of the Nyishangba as international long-distance traders through a structured geohistorical description. He demonstrates that in contrast to much formal theory, in which structure is thought of as given, the structure of a particular geohistory only arises while unfolding. Structures in this perspective are not seen as static and durable, but as variable and concordant with historical change. They only acquire meaning through the particular geohistorical experience of social groups. This implies a long-term rather than a short-term perspective on societal change, and a concern with how society becomes or has become, rather than with what society is now. Thus, geohistorical inquiry is the search for structure in societal flux and, in terms of regional geography, the identification of a particular regionality. As van Spengen concludes, the structural imagination of the regional geographer is needed, in order that we may better understand the world in which we live. This unique and challenging work is essential reading for geographers, historians, sociologists and anthropologists who seek to advance the understanding of society in times of change, and to find new ways of writing 'structured narrative' set in a wider regional context.

Contents: 1. Structural imagination in regional geography. 2. A short geopolitical history of Tibet. 3. The regionality of Tibet. 4. The geohistory of Tibetan trade. 5. The Nyishangba of Manang. 6. The emergence of long-distance trade ventures. 7. Post-1962 developments. 8. Structured flux and hidden vistas. Appendix I: Authors, texts and audiences. Appendix II: Fieldwork and its burning questions. Appendix III: Customs exemption for traders of Manang. Glossary. References. Index.

THE AUTHOR

Wim van Spengen holds a BA and MA in Human Geography from the Free University, Amsterdam, and a PhD in Human Geography from the University of Amsterdam. His main research interests are the political and social geography of Inner Asia, particularly Tibet and the Himalayas. He is currently a member of staff at the Social-Geographical Institute, University of Amsterdam.

TIBETAN BORDER WORLDS

A GEOHISTORICAL ANALYSIS OF TRADE AND TRADERS

Wim van Spengen

KEGAN PAUL INTERNATIONAL
LONDON AND NEW YORK

First published in 2000 by
Kegan Paul International
UK: P.O. Box 256, London WC1B 3SW, England
Tel: 020 7580 5511 Fax: 020 7436 0899
E-mail: books@keganpau.demon.co.uk
Internet: http://www.demon.co.uk/keganpaul/
USA: 562 West 113th Street, New York, NY 10025
Tel: (212) 666 1000 Fax: (212) 316 3100

Distributed by
John Wiley & Sons
Southern Cross Trading Estate
1 Oldlands Way, Bognor Regis
West Sussex, PO22 9SA, England
Tel: (01243) 779 777 Fax: (01243) 843 302
E-mail: cusservices@wiley.co.uk

Columbia University Press
562 West 113th Street
New York, NY 10025, USA
Tel: (212) 666 1000 Fax: (212) 316 3100

The publishers with to acknowledge the generous support provided for this volume by the Netherlands Organization for Scientific Research (NWO).

Printed in Great Britain

This book meets the requirements of ISO 9706: 1994, Information and documentation – Paper for documents – Requirements for permanence

ISBN 0-7103-0592-3

British Library cataloguing in Publication Data
A catalogue record for this book is available from the British Library

Library of Congress Cataloguing-in-Publication Data
A catalog record for this book is available from the Library of Congress

CONTENTS

FIGURES

ACKNOWLEDGEMENTS

This study is the outcome of a journey through lands but dimly known and books long shelved for posterity. To gain entrance into these lands and to get hold of the often very rare literature, not to mention the ideas contained in it, one has to rely on the experience and assistance of others and it is only fair to acknowledge so.

First of all, I should like to thank Prof.Dr. G.A. de Bruijne of the Department of Human Geography at the University of Amsterdam, who over the years has shown his total confidence in this research project. Many words of thanks too, should go to Prof.Dr. A.W. Macdonald of the Laboratoire d'Ethnologie et de Sociologie Comparative at the University of Paris X, who in his further capacity of Director at CNRS of a major Himalayan research committee supervised the work of a Dutchman, encouraging him to press on with his Tibetan and Himalayan interests.

I should also like to take the opportunity of thanking Prof.Dr. J.C. Heesterman of the Indological Institute (Kern) at the University of Leyden, who has stood by me near the beginning and the end of this project, read the manuscript carefully and assisted twice in securing a research grant.

I am further indebted to Prof.Dr. H.H. van der Wusten, Department of Human Geography, University of Amsterdam, Prof.Dr. H.W. van Schendel, Institute for Modern Asian History, University of Amsterdam, and Dr. D. Kooiman, Department of Social Anthropology at the Free University of Amsterdam, for offering valuable criticism on a final draft of the manuscript. In addition, Dr. P.H. Streefland of the Royal Tropical Institute in Amsterdam should be mentioned here for his help in obtaining a research grant at the very beginning. Prof.Dr. A. Buttimer, Department of Geography, University College Dublin, showed her appreciation of this 'humanist' project, by her assistance in securing a further grant. Linguistic advice on the glossary has generously been provided by Dr. Th. Damsteegt, Dr. R. Huysmans, and Dr. P.C. Verhagen of the Kern Institute, University of Leyden.

In this connection, I am extremely grateful to the Netherlands Foundation for the Advancement of Tropical Research (WOTRO) for making available a grant in order to enable me to carry out fieldwork in Nepal within the context of this study. The necessary funds for a period of library research in Paris, as well as a publication grant, were provided by the Netherlands Organization for the Advancement of Pure Research (NWO).

I should also like to thank my departmental colleagues Dr. J. Mansvelt Beck and Dr. J. Markusse for moral and technical support, as well as Dr. O.G. Heldring for his rigorous thinking with regard to chapters 1 and 3. In addition, my respect goes to Dr. Ph. Sagant (Paris) for a very stimulating discussion, and to K. Buffetrille and N. Daum (both of Paris) for friendship and practical support.

With regard to the fieldwork proper, I should like to express my sincere gratitude to His Majesty's Government of Nepal for granting a research permit. Further, I am greatly indebted to Dr. Harka Gurung for his unfailing assistance and courteous guidance in Kathmandu. A special word of thanks goes to Harka Bahadur Thapa for his competent and loyal assistance in the field. Useful advice was offered to me by Prof. D.B. Bista and Dr. L. Stiller, S.J., of the Centre for Nepal and Asian Studies, Tribhuvan University, Kirtipur, the social and economic historian M.C. Regmi, as well as Prof.Dr. Ch. von Fürer-Haimendorf, distinguished anthropologist at the University of London. My gratitude also extends to the inhabitants of Nyishang, and especially those of the village of Braga, who offered hospitality to an inquisitive stranger, and took his cultural maladjustment for granted.

Technical assistance in preparing the manuscript for publication was given by J. ter Haar and N. van Betlehem (maps), and my friend P.J. McKenna ('polishing the English').

Last but not least I should like to thank Tiny for her constructive help and technical assistance, as well as Merlijn and Roeland for their patience during periods of absence and absent-mindedness.

[illegible] grant which provided by the Netherlands Organisation for the Advancement of Pure Research (ZWO).

I [illegible] also [illegible] to the [illegible] departmental colleagues Dr. [illegible] Book and Dr. [illegible] for useful and [illegible] support [illegible] Dr. [illegible] Hadding [illegible] [illegible] specific [illegible] and [illegible] [illegible] Dr. [illegible] provided a very stimulating discussion and [illegible] [illegible] for practical help, for [illegible] and practical support.

[illegible] I [illegible] to express my sincere gratitude to [illegible] [illegible] a [illegible] Professor [illegible] is [illegible] to Dr. [illegible] for his [illegible] [illegible], and [illegible] [illegible] for his [illegible] [illegible] [illegible] [illegible] [illegible] [illegible] [illegible] [illegible] [illegible] [illegible] [illegible] social and economic [illegible] [illegible] [illegible] [illegible] [illegible] [illegible] [illegible] [illegible] [illegible] [illegible] and [illegible] [illegible] [illegible] [illegible] and [illegible] [illegible] [illegible].

[illegible] [illegible] [illegible] [illegible] [illegible] [illegible] [illegible] and my friend [illegible] [illegible] [illegible].

[illegible] [illegible] I should like to [illegible] [illegible] [illegible] [illegible] [illegible] [illegible] [illegible] [illegible] [illegible] their [illegible] [illegible] [illegible] [illegible] [illegible].

1

STRUCTURAL IMAGINATION IN REGIONAL GEOGRAPHY

There is a splendid and at the same time telling scene in Pasolini's 1970 film 'Medea', where Jason and his Argonauts steal the Golden Fleece from the Black Sea kingdom of Colchis. The act of stealing and the way in which the army of king Aietos sets out to pursue the intruders reflects the triumph of a calculated barbarism over a complacent archaic symbolism. While Jason and his men make off as quickly as possible with the fleece, the Colchian king is caught in a web of ancient ritual without the performance of which no successful pursuance can be possible. The whole episode leaves the impression of two utterly incomparable worlds. Its *mise-en-scène* highlights the historical nature of the encounter by showing the superiority of new technological equipment, the power of a magic unknown, and the disrespect for ancient values in the face of the holiest. The historical act of desecration heralds a new era, in which the cosmo-royal 'structures' of Colchis will never be the same. It sparks off a sudden consciousness that Colchis is not the only kingdom in the world. Ultimately it is an image of breaking the cultural *cloisonnement* of the classical world prefiguring the rise of a Hellenic empire in which alien cultures do not die but 'like old soldiers simply fade away'.

It is the structural implication of the historical event in the above metaphor which has been made into the point of departure for this study. Colchian culture after the Argonaut incident must be 're-written' to incorporate the terms of a past event. In doing so it creates a new structural awareness of the outside world. From now onwards Colchians interpret their lived experience in relation to a wider geohistorical setting they have come to know by the historical agency of a neighbouring human group. Such an interpretation sets the stage for further acts and new structural developments, which may be analytically brought together under the provisional label of 'a process of geohistorical structuration'.

From idea to thesis

'Structuration'. That was not quite the way in which I phrased the problem some ten years ago when I embarked upon the study of the Nyishangba of Manang, a group of Nepalese traders in the Tibeto-Himalayan border world. Rather, the scientific air at the time was laden with ideas about an all-embracing and all-penetrating capitalist world-system (Wallerstein 1974a, 1974b, Wolf 1982) and for a short time I believed that regional groups answered only the dynamics of higher-level induced processes of capitalist penetration. Nevertheless, as a specimen of those thrice-happy mortals for whom the study of geography began well in advance of the spatial, behavioural and radical shock waves that swept much of the Dutch geographical discipline in the late 1960s, it soon became increasingly difficult to adhere to mechanistic and unilineal interpretations of human society. Having been educated as a freshman with Jean Gottmann, Pierre Gourou and Xavier de Planhol, it was but a matter of time before I realized again the historical nature of human life in its non-deterministic form. At about the same time I rediscovered the regional geographic tradition in human geography, especially in its French guise. Ann Buttimer's *Society and milieu in the French geographic tradition*, 1971, but only read in 1979, sowed the seeds for my return to a more historical and regionalizing human geography. In addition, I discovered the French Annaliste historian Fernand Braudel through the writings of the Dutch anthropologist Anton Blok (1977) and the historian Wesseling (1981). The Annales movement, which rose to prominence after World War II, stood for an interdisciplinary kind of structural history, seeking to explain the stiller waters that run deeper than the ordinary political event. It propagated a multi-level explanatory history, in which political heroes were made subordinate to deep-seated social and economic structures. However, all these new ideas needed time to ripen and for the moment I felt quite comfortable in the shelter of Wallerstein's all-embracing world-system theory. The intellectual appeal of grand explanatory frameworks like Wallerstein's is that all societal developments seem to fit an apparent logic, which makes every bit of information fall directly into its place. Logical minds are therefore irresistably attracted by their systemic elegance, not to mention their seductive qualities, but as with all seductive objects, it needs time to distance oneself from them.

Thus, the theoretical state of mind with which I left for Nepal in 1981 to study the Nyishangba of Manang, was one of emphasis on the effects of external relations on internal conditions (Van Spengen 1987:132), supplemented by a growing awareness of the geohistorical particularity of the group studied. The Nyishangba of Manang, an ethnic group of Tibetan cultural affinity, proved to be a compelling subject in this respect. Chosen at the instigation of the Nepalese geographer Harka Gurung, the Nyishangba turned out to represent a rural community that had greatly extended its external relations over the past century in the form of long-distance trade ventures, thereby thoroughly changing the internal conditions of socio-economic organization in their home district.

Notwithstanding my flirtation with world-system theory, I came to consider the Nyishangba of Manang as a singular instance of geohistorical particularity not to be found elsewhere. True enough, it was a geohistorical particularity which had taken into account the importance of external relations but it did not yet fully appreciate the idea that there might be structurally comparable ethnic groups within the geohistorical setting of the Tibetan borderlands. However, by the time of publication of the Nyishangba monograph (Van Spengen 1987) the first signs of a more balanced interpretation of their geohistorical experience became visible by its reference to a few other Nepalese communities of Tibetan cultural background, sharing likewise experiences. But when it came to an explanation of it all, structural-historical processes at the level of the Nepalese state proved at least as important as the aggregate life-path experiences of the members of the ethnic group concerned. Beyond Nepalese state formation loomed the wider regional setting of Tibet, in between the Chinese and Indian world. It made me realize that if I wanted to give more meaning to the Nyishangba case, I would have to search for higher-level explanations, partly in terms of the regional characteristics of a cultural Tibet and its related border worlds and partly at the still higher level of geopolitical and long-term economic change.

This heralded a new phase in my investigations. It forced me firstly, to look for a conceptual framework that would incorporate both structural explanations at different levels of analysis and an appreciation of the geohistorical particularity of human lived experience and secondly, to study a substantial number of books and articles about the Tibetan culture world, especially in its regional geographic manifestations. The first line made me pick up a thread which I had left unfinished a few years earlier, that of studying the place of regional geography within the history of the geographical discipline. The second made me indulge in a vast but scattered travel literature on Tibet, satisfying boyhood dreams of adventure but at the same time stretching the reading capacity of a single individual to the breaking point. As I have always been convinced of the historicity of human life, it should come as no surprise that I turned towards the French *géographie humaine*, especially in its Vidalian form. Here I found a truly human geography, in the sense that the lived historical experience of culturally disparate groups ultimately decided on the form of a particular regional life-style. The great regional monographs above all, written by a second generation of Vidalians in the period 1900 to 1940, proved a lasting source of inspiration. Soon my interest focused on the life and work of one of Vidal de la Blache's most gifted pupils, Jules Sion (1879-1940). Here was a figure of marked individuality in French academic geography of the time, who produced some fine regional work in which a fully matured Vidalian tradition was welded into the promising enterprise of the new Annales history movement. The fortunate outcome was a strongly historical infusion of Sion's regional work (Van Spengen 1988).

Perhaps no geographer who ever lived was more convinced of the necessity of blending the geographical enterprise with insights from history, sociology, ethnography, and social and cultural psychology than Jules Sion. Emphatically arguing in favour of interdisciplinary dialogue, he supplemented the basically materialist Vidalian tradition with the idea of a cultural superstructure as embodied in social habit and human mentality. At the same time he stressed the need for historical depth in regional studies, thereby remaining true to the historical bent of a first generation of Vidalians. Towards the end of his life Sion became increasingly drawn into the Annales movement. This was focused in a group of historians who published the *Annales d'Histoire Économique et Sociale*, a journal of an interdisciplinary character. Through his friendship with the brilliant historian Lucien Febvre he acquainted himself with the basic tenets of the 'new' history as propounded by the Annalistes. This was not an illogical move. The new history as developed by Febvre, and in particular Marc Bloch, was closely related to the new geography envisaged by Vidal de la Blache two decades earlier. In fact, Febvre and Bloch as the two founders of the *Annales d'Histoire Économique et Sociale* discovered the social sciences through geography in their early years at the *École Normale Supérieure* in Paris. For a geographer like Sion it was but a small step to take part in an academic movement which was pervaded by geographical concepts taken from the Vidalian tradition. Explicit adoption of the comparative method by the Annalistes reinforced Sion's preference for careful thematic work in regional geography (Van Spengen 1988:159-160, 162).

This panegyric on Vidalian regional geography and one of its leading figures should not blind us to its shortcomings. Though historical in orientation, the *tradition vidalienne* is also imbued with ideas of a societal totality, a functionalist analogue ultimately traceable to the vitalism of the late nineteenth century. Its shared rhetoric has been correctly identified as 'organic-humanistic' (Kinser 1981:72, Berdoulay 1982:581). As such it stresses the harmony of community life and milieu, as becomes visible in places and regions having a personality of their own. The resulting explanatory description is therefore synthetic rather than analytic. What is generally lacking are penetrating questions that lay bare the structural characteristics of local change, hint at higher levels of explanation and inspire conceptual thinking beyond the pale of the peasantry. It is the merit of Jules Sion and his fellow travellers in the early Annales movement to have sensed these questions towards the end of the 1930s.

Sion, Febvre and to a lesser extent Bloch, each in his own way, were key figures in the process of cross-fertilization between geography and history during the Interbellum. It initiated the full flowering of the Annales movement after World War II, and found its most telling expression in the *oeuvre* of Braudel, notably in his work on the Mediterranean. It has been argued that the conceptual novelty of Braudel's early work lies in its programmatic interweaving of geography and history and less in its attempt at a structural analysis of political history, that is the search for deeper levels of explanation than the mere configuration of political events

(Kinser 1981:77). If this is true, it is to the conceptual framework of Braudel's geohistory that we must turn in order to reap the full benefits of his thinking. It is one way of heeding the criticism that Vidalian regional geography is synthetic rather than analytic. The affinities between the historical geography of the *tradition vidalienne* and the geohistory of Braudel are beyond doubt. But as Peter Burke has pointed out correctly 'one result of the rise of Braudel's empire (...) was the decline of historical (regional) geography as a discipline in the face of competition from historians' (Burke 1990:103). Together with the spatial-analytical turn in geography in the 1960s, it sealed temporarily the fate of a more regionalizing geography, notwithstanding intermittent attempts at rehabilitation (Sautter 1961, Mead 1963, Fisher 1970, Paterson 1974).

The challenge of the old-style *géographie humaine* surfaced again and was partly met by the 'humanist' movement in geography in the 1970s and 80s (Kouwenhoven 1979). Humanism in geography was in essence a reaction to the reductionism and determinism of the spatial-analytical mainstream, and perhaps the teleology of the radicals. The humanists, by contrast, stressed complexity and individual originality. As the existential lifeworld of men and women (Buttimer 1976:279ff.) and their *espace vécu* became once more central to the endeavour of a geography 'with a human face' (Sanguin 1981:575), history and regional geography came back into focus. It is not without reason that one of the first programmatic readers to summarize the humanist tradition in geography contained Harris's contribution on 'The historical mind and the practice of geography' (Ley and Samuels 1978:123-137), as well as Buttimer's 'Charism and context: the challenge of *la géographie humaine* (ibid.:58-76). The *former* contribution emphasizes the importance of the 'historical mind' for practitioners of geography. This is an intellectual disposition towards the contextual rather than the law-finding. Too strong an emphasis on formal rules of selection in methodological procedures precludes the appreciation of the historicity and contextuality of human geographical life (Harris 1978:125-126). The *latter* one is an apology for a *géographie humaine, style vidalien* and its enduring message of the primacy of human historical action in a 'total' geographical milieu (Buttimer 1978:73).

The issue of contextual knowledge is taken up again by Barnes and Curry in their seminal article of 1983. It makes the point that contextualism as a synthetic-descriptive rather than an analytical approach, must begin not with a denial but with an affirmation of a complex and richly-textured world. In doing so, a degree of intricacy is taken for granted, an inherent contingency which escapes formal theory and therefore probabilistic-predictive argument (Barnes and Curry 1983:468-469). So far, so good. But the question remains to what extent a humanist conception of geography will allow for a certain structural boundedness of human agency. After all, the quality of individual originality and existentiality as the hallmark of humanist geography can never be equated with the unrestrained will of human beings. That would leave the world inexplicable.

What is important to note here is that originality, as the individual's power of independent thought or constructive imagination, is embedded in cultural traditions, laden with inherited value orientations and corporealized in the structural setting of a given society. Dominant value orientations do shape human action as much as the structural nature of the spatial-temporal world in which the actors are set. The question thus becomes one of how much structure we can discern in the interactional process of actor-bound value-orientedness and geohistorical context.

In fact, Harris had already anticipated this question by referring to Braudel's *Méditerranée,* as an example showing the way by which a humanistic geography might learn from the writings of a historian steeped in the geographical tradition of Vidal de la Blache. However, Harris's invocation of Braudel's brilliance (1978:136) is hardly for the reason I should have wanted. In stating that 'it is Braudel's learning we lack, not his method' (idem) he fails to recognize the structural characteristics of Braudel's work that give order and meaning to the lived experience of human groups figuring in the latter's narrative. A good example of such a structural account is Braudel's exposition of banditry as to be found in his *Méditerranée* (1966, vol.II, 83-92). Banditry is being portrayed there as a complex outcome of a geo-historical process in which cultural tradition, the absence of state power in peripheral areas and the shifting coalitions between lords and outlaws, all interact to produce a kind of shadow struggle for political and economic power that runs parallel to the higher concerns of state expansion and contraction.

Braudel, in a way, prefigures the social science attention for structure in relation to human action as surfaced in the course of the 1980s. The tension that logically exists between static societal structures and human historical action was theoretically overcome by the introduction of the concept of 'structuration' by the British sociologist Anthony Giddens (1979, 1984). For Giddens there is no structure-actor dualism. Rather, structure is reproduced by human agency, or, phrased differently, may be seen as both mediator and result of social practice (Giddens 1984:XIX-XXI). Although Giddens stresses the process nature of 'structuration', it remains to be seen how useful the concept will be in the explanation of concrete situations. Though correct in his understanding of structuration as a basically historical process, he fails to appreciate the full weight of a particular geohistory. Structuration is not only 'bounded contingency' (Gregory 1981: 3-5), but also identifiable cohesiveness in concrete space and time. In that sense, Braudel's structural geohistory is preferable to the abstract conception of historical structuration as introduced by Giddens. What lacks in the latter's conception of time is that of a specific historicity, an identifiable sequence of events. On the whole, however, Kirby is undoubtedly correct when he writes, 'Interestingly, debates within the social sciences seem to be catching up with positions outlined by Braudel nearly thirty years ago' (Kirby 1986:211), but, as I would like to add, have not yet fully integrated the Braudelian message into their discourse. It is therefore Braudel's geohistory rather than Giddens's social theorizing that has been taken as a point of departure for this study.

One may ask what the point is of all these disciplinary and theoretical profundities within the context of this study. After all we should avoid a situation in which theory becomes the weapon of argument. Basically, the above thoughts serve the purpose of tracing a genealogy of ideas relating to the possibility of a historizing regional geography. It is my conviction that geography as a discipline has much to gain by a regional point of view in which the historical experience of human groups is thoroughly embedded (cf. Van Paassen 1957, 1976, 1981, 1982, 1991). In line with the above considerations, I should like to bring history back into the geographical mould, not in the sense of a historical legacy shaping the geography of the present, but of a living 'historical' present that is forever constructed and reconstructed in a Giddensian sense. The inseparability of geography and history, as for example given form in the *oeuvre* of the Annales movement, lies at the heart of such a timely counterstream answer to the long-lingering anti-historical assumptions of the more extreme forms of geography-as-chorology. It is the structural implication of the historical event in the Colchian metaphor as presented at the beginning of this chapter which points the way to a regional geography which has found a middle ground between historicist and fully structuralist approaches (Blok 1977:78-80, Baker 1984:9, Sahlins 1985:vii, 72, Pudup 1988:378-379, Pred 1990:1, 6, Entrikin 1991:86). The implications of the above argument for the styling of this study may be summarized under the headings of explanatory form, the role of critical 'time-space edges', and the nature of structuration as conditioned by a particular regionality.

It is contrary to both Annaliste spirit and Giddensian social science logic that historical regional life is reduced to a single structural framework obeying formal explanatory rules. Rather the process of structuration gains form through the descriptive interweaving of historically acting human groups and the particular space-time contexts of which they are an integral part. This awkward sentence only wishes to convey the message that from the viewpoint of the regional geographer structured description may be as good as any formal theory of regional structure, because it leaves room for the appreciation of the geohistorical particularity of human life. However, the imaginative description of this process of geohistorical structuration is not based on wholesale eclecticism or the personal whim of the mediating author. Rather his writing resembles the playing of a game of chess, in which the rules structure the game but do not pre-determine its actual move order. Even the general notions of strategy and tactics only acquire meaning in the context of a specific game which is *einmalig*. In that sense structured description is no longer suspect in an epistemological sense and in fact has never been (Harris 1978:128-132, Pickles 1985:112, Clifford and Marcus 1986:2, Driver 1988:501-502, Entrikin 1991:102-108; cf. Den Hollander 1967:1-32). Over the past years, writers have come to emphasize the narrative quality of description (Reck 1983:8-12, White 1984:8-10, Clifford and Marcus 1986:100,121, Van Maanen 1988). Entrikin even goes so far as to speak of 'narrative synthesis' as the ultimate goal of regional geography (1991:128) but I do not like the term, because it tends to obscure the structural characteristics around which regional life takes shape. I would prefer the label 'structured narrative', thereby allowing for the innate geohistorical 'boundedness' of human-lived experience.

The process of structuration is perhaps best made visible at the level of the human group, because the unifying relationship which defines the group transcends individual action, which, though not unimportant, lacks a common and therefore structural focus. This unifying relationship may be found in a common regional provenance and perhaps a shared cultural tradition. These relationships are long-lasting and may colour any new paths of geohistorical structuration a group is bound to follow (cf. Tonkin et al. 1989). Such a new path is seen here as a structurally identifiable chain of geohistorical action set within the parameters of higher-level societal change. It is in this way that the Nyishangba of Manang are being portrayed in the second part of this study. Their long-distance trade ventures gain descriptive form through a structured narrative making visible a juxtaposition and a sequence of geohistorical action possessing a distinct identity of its own.

Beyond the level of the human group, the larger-scale structures and processes that are transforming regional societies are far more difficult to grasp and I think we do well to restrain ourselves in our efforts to build theoretical Procrustes beds. Any analysis of big structures and large processes must not move beyond geographical and historical recognizability (Tilly 1984:14). The most we can possibly do is to identify what Giddens has called 'time-space edges' (Giddens 1984:184). These may be thought of as critical interfaces of historical and geographical transition. The analysis of transitional periods and regions may teach us more about the structural dynamics of change than the painstaking but static inventory of relatively homogeneous spaces and uneventful times. In a way, the rise of the Nyishangba of Manang as long-distance traders may be interpreted in terms of the coincidence of two such critical interfaces, that of the Tibetan border world as a cultural-ecological and geopolitical frontier area, and that of the clash between a loosely defined ecclesiastical Tibetan state and the growing influence of British-Indian and Chinese imperial power in the 'long' century between 1850 and 1950. As will become clear from the following chapters, these critical interfaces of higher-level geohistorical change have the power of explaining the rise of a set of comparable trading communities all along the Himalayan and Sino-Tibetan border similar to the Nyishangba of Manang.

This brings us to the question whether these larger geohistorical processes of structural change may be conceptualized in such a way as to link structuration at the level of the localized human group to the dynamics of the wider regional setting. To achieve this aim the concept of 'regionality' is introduced here, which stands for the recognizable identity of a particular history of human groups at the intersections of an interlocking whole of locational-physical, political-economic, and socio-cultural universes. This complex concept will be further worked out in chapter 3 in order to set the structural stage for a comparative analysis of Tibetan trade and traders, especially in its borderland forms. The concept of regionality, inspired partly by a Vidalian interpretation of human geography, but also by Annaliste ideas of structural history, rests in the possibility of a descriptive representation which does full justice to the geohistorical boundedness of a process of societal structuration. These high-sounding ideals have been made into the point of departure for this study. I hope they will provide food for thought in the current discussion on regional geography and may prove useful in the context of this study.

Stating the problem

Writing regional geography is not only a matter of the recognition of historicity and regionality, it is also the imaginative description of a theme, a topic, or a particular field of interest within its wider geohistorical setting. There is also the broader disciplinary context, in the sense that certain themes and regions command a higher interest at certain times than others. The thematic focus of this study crystallized around a body of research which has emerged since the late 1950s, having as its main object of inquiry the social anthropology of Tibetan and Tibetanized border populations in the Central Himalaya, especially Nepal. The overriding message brought back from the field by a first generation of students and scholars was that, far from being characterized by static and closed societies, the Himalayan region had always shown considerable mobility of people, commodities and ideas. In the economic sphere this mobility manifested itself through a number of high-mountain communities, whose members were actively engaged in a complex trading system.

Part of this trade was essentially local in character. Home-produced commodities like yaks, mules and dairy products were bartered against domestic products from neighbouring valleys. In addition, a few communities did become involved in the regional exchange of basic products between highly different ecozones. Within this system of exchange, grain from the subtropical middle hills moved northward through the Himalaya, while salt and wool were brought down from the cold and dry plateaus of southern Tibet. Next to this intermediate long-distance exchange of basic goods, there existed a true long-distance trade in luxury goods between the Tibetan and Indian realms, centring on entrepôt markets in the middle Himalayan domain, and dealing in a wide range of low weight for value goods, such as gold, musk, precious stones, coral, pearls, copper and fine cloth. Rising British colonial overlordship in India and the changing geopolitical power structures in the Central Himalaya, i.e. the rise of the Nepalese state in the eighteenth century and the decline of Tibetan power from the nineteenth century onward, affected both the scope and contents of this traditional Himalayan trading network. A partial relocation of trade routes resulted and British and Bengal manufactured goods came to play an increasingly important role.

Until the middle of the twentieth century the high-altitude regions along Nepal's northern border were virtually unknown to Western travellers. The policy of an isolationist Rana regime (1846-1950) had effectively prevented outsiders from visiting these areas, and even the Kathmandu-based government had only nominal control in most of these outlying border areas. It was only after the overthrow of the Ranas in the early 1950s, that Nepal decided to open its frontier to foreigners. In the wake of this watershed development in Nepalese history, geographical and anthropological reconnaissance took place, at first at a rather low profile and focusing by chance on specific communities and localities (e.g. the Sherpa of the Mount Everest region), but later more evenly spread out along its northern border. However, blank spots on the map remained for a long time. Matters were complicated by a tense geopolitical situation, brought about by China's occupation of Tibet in the 1950s, which in turn resulted in a decade-long armed Khampa resistance and an official border closure after 1960. Several strategic areas in Nepal's high north remained 'restricted' for years, to the effect that still in 1975 the British-Austrian anthropologist Von Fürer-Haimendorf, in his encompassing survey of Himalayan trade in northern Nepal, noted the extremely uneven geographic and ethnographic coverage of the resident Bhotia populations (Von Fürer-Haimendorf 1975:132). But after the American 'open door' policy to China, started by Nixon in the early seventies, and a consequent waning of hostilities along the Nepal-Tibet border, bona fide researchers were tentatively allowed to carry out fieldwork in selected border areas. Since then a limited number of Tibetanists, geographers and anthropologists have been involved in completing the jigsaw puzzle of Nepal's Tibetan and Tibetanized border communities.

One of the last virtual blanks on the geographical and anthropological map of Nepal's northern border area was the inner Himalayan high-valley of Nyishang in West Central Nepal close to the Tibetan border. Both Macdonald (1974:33) and Von Fürer-Haimendorf (1975:132) had referred in one sentence to this extraordinary research opportunity and on my first visit to Nepal in 1980 it needed but little persuasion by Dr. Harka Gurung to take up the theme of Nyishangba long-distance trade. It is true, by that time the Nepalese anthropologist Nareshwar Jang Gurung had carried out pioneering fieldwork in Nyishang, but his introductory article in *Kailash* (1976:295-310), as well as his unpublished M.A. thesis for the Institute of Nepal and Asian Studies at Tribhuvan University in Kathmandu (1977a), only summarily covered the topic of long-distance trade. I returned to Nepal in 1981 to carry out a three-month fieldwork among the Nyishangba in their home district of Manang, which ultimately led to my monograph article on the rise of the Nyishangba as long-distance traders (Van Spengen 1987:131-277). While writing up the data, it appeared to me that the Nyishangba case would gain in explanatory power when it could be compared to other trading communities along the Nepal-Tibet border. Thus, next to the question of the particular geohistorical form of the rise of the Nyishangba, the exigencies of comparison with similar communities loomed large on my research agenda for the following years. At about the same time I became interested in the wider geohistorical context of trans-Himalayan trade. With growing knowledge of the Tibetan border world, both in its Himalayan and Sino-Tibetan settings, I realized the need for a conceptual framework capable of relating the single geohistorical group experience to the structural characteristics of a critical time-space edge. To meet the challenge I developed the concept of regionality, which will be elaborated on in chapter 3. Summarizing the above, the following formulation of the research problem has been chosen:

1. What particular geohistorical form did the rise of the Nyishangba of Manang as international long-distance traders take?

2. How does the Nyishangba experience compare to the rise of similar Bhotia groups as conditioned by a shared Tibetan regionality?

Basically, the above formulation of the problem reflects an answer to the recurrent tendency in the social sciences to develop grand theoretical designs. It also reflects a commitment to restore synthetic description to its proper place in regional geography. Such a stance does not necessarily imply an unsophisticated plea for a naïve description. Rather it reflects a conscious effort at informed structural description as an explanatory device. In contrast to formal theories of regional structure which in their application tend to *de-construct* reality, the explanatory power of the concept of regionality rests in its ability to *construct* a creative image of a regional society. This seems important to me, as in the chorological, and even more so the spatial-analytical tradition of mainstream geography over the past four decades, the human propensity to think in images has consistently been ignored.

'Regionality' as the denominator which brings together all those aspects of life which ground human action, ultimately derives its explanatory power from the internal cohesiveness of structures, value orientations, and actions in a concrete geohistorical context. A particular value orientation realizes itself through action, just as action shows the structural interwovenness with the spatial-temporal world. Formulated in this way, we find here the contemporary expression of the Vidalian concept of *genre de vie* supplemented by Sion's emphasis on human mentality. As such it leaves room for the geographical analysis of culture, a sorely neglected theme in most modern geographical studies. But above all, it makes possible a truly human regional geography by not excluding beforehand any pieces of the puzzle, the image of which can only be known after its completion.

The order of things

This study seeks to portray an extended case within a long-term geo-historical perspective. Such an attempt poses several problems of form. First, there is the question of how to relate the case to its wider contextual setting, or in terms of this study, its regionality. Second, there is the recurrent problem of reconciling a structural point of view with a historical perspective in which the unbroken flow of events seemingly dodges structural analysis. Although we may have theoretically solved the latter problem by introducing the concept of 'structuration', it remains extremely difficult to present in one running yet structured narrative the theme or topic one wants to discuss. For it means that an author has to select those traits of a long-term process, which together will yield a certain explanatory power in relation to the problem stated without losing sight of the process as a whole. It requires so to speak a kind of structural imagination which leaves intact the cohesiveness of a particular geohistory, but at the same time employs aggregated conceptions to trace the general in the particular.

The above considerations have played a large part in the basic architecture of this study which by its form attempts to set the stage for answering the two major research questions as formulated in the previous section. The twofold division which has resulted, is that of a structural discussion of the regionality of Tibet in the first part of the book, and a more narrative-like presentation of the Nyishangba case in the second. In between, there is a transitional chapter which tries to identify the geohistorical characteristics of Tibetan trade, in particular with reference to its borderland forms sharing a common regionality.

The regionality of Tibet as set out in chapter 3, begins with a theoretical exploration of the concept of regionality, in particular in relation to the basic ideas of a Braudelian geohistory. After having discussed the latter's merits and shortcomings, the cultural aspect of regionality is worked out and related to the Vidalian concept of *genre de vie*. Ultimately, the monastic imperative is identified as one of the main structural traits of Tibetan regionality, which, together with the dynamics of the wider regional setting, provides a sufficient condition for the explanation of the particular geohistory of Tibetan trade as sketched in chapter 4.

The structural stance as taken up throughout chapter 3 is considerably relaxed in the next chapter, in order to make visible the actual process of historical change from a largely monastery-dominated local and regional trade to a more secular-oriented international trade focusing on newly arisen towns and markets. As such it also sets the stage for comparison with regard to the rise of geohistorically related communities in the border worlds of Tibet.

As the first part of this study is based on an extensive reading of a variety of source materials, we should be careful to weigh the relative truths as presented by their respective authors. The possibilities and pitfalls of these widely disparate modes of inquiry are being probed in appendix 1, just as the fieldwork that was necessary for the second part of this study is scrutinized for its methodological implications in appendix 2.

The Nyishangba case as presented in the chapters 5, 6, and 7, shows the crucial geohistorical interplay of Nyishangba enterprise and the changing external relations of Tibetan regionality through which their commercial 'structuration' was initially realized. The rise of the Nyishangba as international long-distance traders also highlights the importance of geopolitical circumstances at various levels of analysis. Because of the structural importance of these geopolitical conditions, the following chapter will introduce the territorial tug-of-war between the major contenders for power in Central Asia, and its side-effects in terms of state formation over much of the period under investigation, that is the 'long' century between 1850 and 1950.

The conclusion will take up once more the topic of the intrinsical historicity of a multifaceted process of structuration through which a particular regionality gains expression. In doing so, it pays a timely homage to Jules Sion, who made the historical particularity of human life as exemplified in regional life-styles into the touchstone of his geographical endeavour. For, as he himself wrote, 'it is dangerous for a geographer to know the profession of a historian, because one is soon taken for a heretic. But it is more dangerous to ignore history, for the chance of false interpretation and wrong explanation is being multiplied without any reason' (Sion 1925:142, translation WvS).

2

A SHORT GEOPOLITICAL HISTORY OF TIBET

North of the densely settled Indian plains and west of the teeming Chinese lowlands stretch the sparsely inhabited tracts of Inner Asia. And although it is almost a truism to say that some places in this world are less well known than others, it is here that we find some of the least known regions on earth: the desiccated geosynclines of the Tarim and Dzungarian basins, the almost barren Tibetan high-plateau, and the snowbound Himalayan mountains. Tibet in particular has long remained *terra incognita,* though for political rather than physical reasons. Even today, much of Tibet is but sparsely known, the occasional tourist notwithstanding.

Geographically speaking, Tibet consists of a mountain-fringed mosaic of greater and lesser plateaux, gently sloping towards the gorge country of the south-east (see Figure 1). On these high tablelands roam a few hardy nomads, but the major nomad countries, as well as the more densely settled areas of sedentary farming, are all to be found along the less elevated southern and eastern rimlands. Tibet, by all accounts, is a checkered country where people live at altitudes ranging from 1,500 to 5,000 metres and landscapes vary from snow-covered mountains to green pastures beside turquoise-blue lakes. Many of its approximately five million inhabitants live at an average elevation of 3,600 metres and have learned to cope with the thin air and the strong winds that tend to be common in these cold and dry reaches. However, the general perception that Tibet is throughout a cold and inhospitable country must be corrected at once. Tibet is located at the latitude of the Mediterranean, and its lower valleys of settled agriculture in the south-east enjoy a subtropical summer with monsoonal influence creeping up the great lateral river valleys of the Salween, Mekong and Yangtse. But, of course, Tibet is also the land of the great icy wastes, virtually uninhabited save for a wandering herdsman or an occasional trading caravan.

Within the confines of this macroregion a variety of ethnic groups came to be the forebears of a clearly identifiable civilization. From the seventh century A.D. onwards, proto-Tibetan society, politically speaking consisting of the state of Zhangzhung in West-Tibet and a federation of Ch'iang tribes in the east (Henss 1981:24-26), became gradually overlaid with a common cultural veneer, mainly pertaining to language and religion. Nurtured and brought to fruition by a period of political unification following the reign of Tibet's empire-builder Srong-btsan gampo (629-650), the Tibetan language and the Buddhist religion emerged as the hallmarks of a nascent 'Tibetan civilization' (Stein 1987). But full nationhood was never achieved. The contested rise of Buddhism during the Yarlun dynasty may have been a factor here. Politically speaking, however, the rise of the Central Tibetan federation was a great success. Various ethnic groups merged in course of the process, Tibet came out of its relative isolation, and the new political superstructure entered the history of Asia as a military power of the first order. Yet, after this initial spell of imperial bloom, political Tibet greatly fluctuated over the ages, its actual extent being a function of the strength of the Central Tibetan polity at certain key-periods.

The Tibetan empire from the seventh to the ninth century evidently represents such a key-period. The cultural symbolism of state and society, as well as the mythical justification of things political in imperial times, have been explored by Haarh (1969), Stein (1987:28-38), Dargyay (1972), and for the Srong-btsan gampo reign by Macdonald (1971). The ethnic complexity of early Tibet is still in the process of being unravelled. Following Tucci's capital insight that many a noble family from Central Tibet attaches itself to certain tribes in North-East Tibet (Tucci 1949), the French Tibetanist Stein, in a seminal work, traces similitudes in ancestral myths between the Tibetan centre and its north-eastern periphery (Stein 1961). Initially, however, these (Ch'iang) tribes and the Central Tibetans remained unrelated (Thomas 1948:13-36). The most ambitious attempt to date at portraying the early Tibetan empire in its wider political-historical context is the recent study by Beckwith (1987), yet a very useful analysis remains Bogoslovskij (1972), which sketches the social and economic conditions for territorial unification and political overlordship. External relations are also dealt with in the older but still valuable article by Hoffmann (1950).

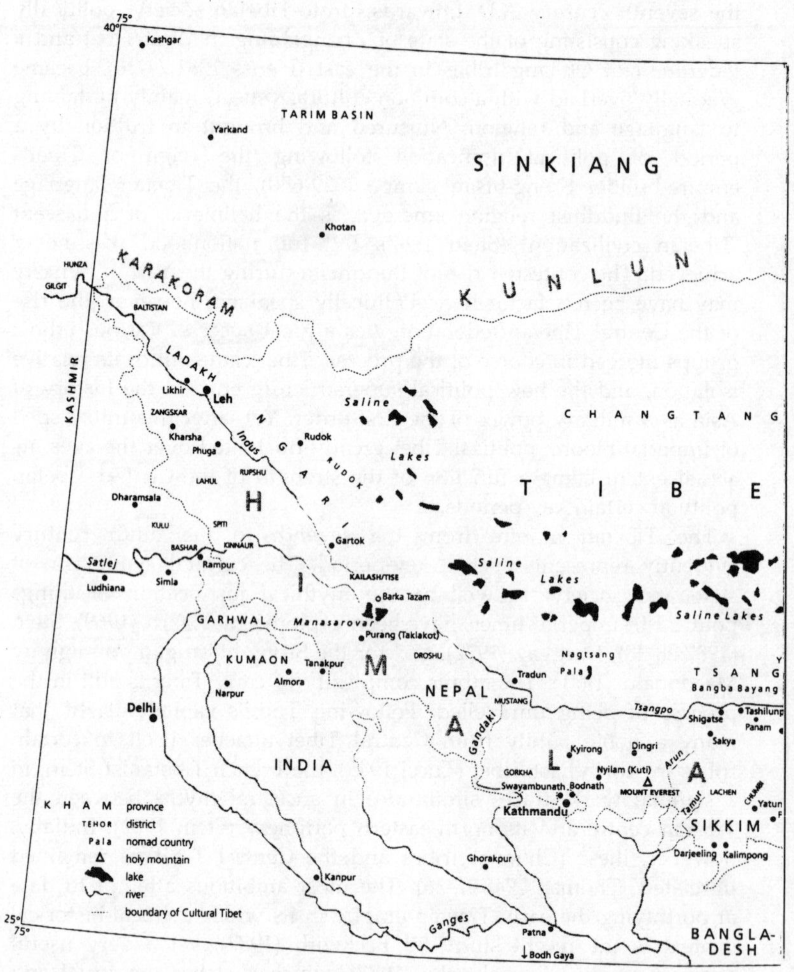

Figure 1 Tibet

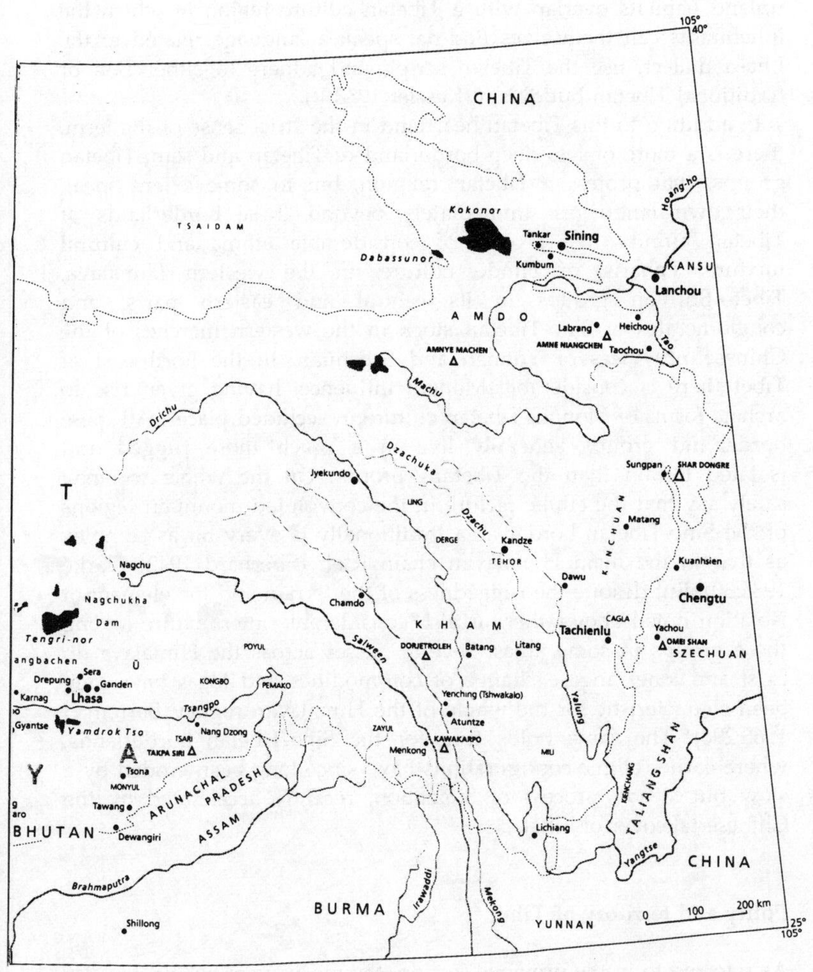
105°
40°
CHINA
TSAIDAM
Kokonor
Tankar
Sining
Dabassunor
Kumbum
Hoang-ho
KANSU
Lanchou
AMDO
Labrang
Heichou
AMNYE MACHEN
AMNE NIANGCHEN
Taochou
Tao
Machu
Drichu
Dzachuka
Jyekundo
LING
Sungpan
SHAR DONGRE
Dzachu
DERGE
Kandze
TEHOR
Matang
KINCHUAN
Kuanhsien
Dawu
T
Nagchu
Nagchukha
Chamdo
Chengtu
Dam
CAGLA
Tachienlu
Tengri-nor
KHAM
Yachou
OMEI SHAN
POYUL
DORJETROLEH
Batang
Litang
SZECHUAN
angbachen
Ü
Salween
Drepung
Sera
Ganden
KONGBO
PEMAKO
Karnag
Lhasa
Tsangpo
Yenching (Tshwakalo)
Yalung
Gyantse
Yamdrok Tso
Nang Dzong
Atuntze
ZAYUL
TSARI
KAWAKARPO
TAKPA SIRI
Menkong
MILI
TALIANGSHAN
Y
Tsona
ARUNACHAL
PRADESH
MONYUL
KENCHANG
Tawang
ASSAM
BHUTAN
Dewangiri
Lichiang
Yangtse
CHINA
Brahmaputra
BURMA
Irawaddi
Mekong
0
100
200 km
Shillong
YUNNAN
25°
105°

'Cultural' Tibet largely coincides with a 'geographic' Tibet, in the sense that the dominant *genres de vie* based on mountain valley and upland habitats overlap with a Tibetan culture region in which the inhabitants call themselves Bod-pa, speak a language related to the Lhasa dialect, use the Tibetan script, and adhere to either Bon or traditional Tibetan Buddhism (Kessler 1983:V).

In addition to this Tibetan heartland in the strict sense of the term, there is a more or less deep borderland of Tibetan and semi-Tibetan groups, that profess a Tibetan religion, but to some extent speak their own languages. Immediately beyond these borderlands of Tibetan affinity live groups of considerable ethnic and cultural mixture: Paharis, of Hindu culture, in the western Himalaya, Tibeto-Burman groups in its central and eastern parts, and conglomerates of Sino-Tibetan stock in the western marches of the Chinese provinces of Yunnan and Szechuan. In the north-east of Tibet there is considerable Mongol influence, having given rise to archaic forms of Mongol-Tibetan culture in secluded places. All these borderland groups generally live in a much more rugged and isolated terrain than the Tibetans proper. On the whole we may safely say that the ethnic picture in the convoluted mountain regions of the Sino-Tibetan border area traditionally is every bit as complex as that in the main Himalayan chain itself (Eberhard 1942, Clarke 1988:30). But despite the ruggedness of the terrain and the element of isolation noted above, there is also considerable intermixture among these groups in some areas. Several passes across the Himalaya do exist and long-range exchange of commodities and ideas have long been characteristic for the whole of the Himalayan region (Berreman 1963:290). The same holds true for the Sino-Tibetan borderlands, where earlier ethnic configurations have since long been eroded by a slow but steady process of Sinization, recently accelerated by the Chinese takeover of Tibet.

Polity and territory of Tibet

As referred to in the previous section, the mechanism behind the rise of the early empire is but dimly understood. Perhaps the introduction of the Tibetan script made a more centralized administration possible. Perhaps too, the official adoption of

Buddhism by Trhisong Detsen (756-797), the king under which the early Tibetan empire attained its greatest territorial extent, generated a semblance of symbolic legitimation of the newly acquired temporal power, although large sections of the still Bon-oriented nobility did fight its initially fragile existence. However, a much more down-to-earth reason for Tibet's military successes at the time may have been the knowledge of forging iron, a secret which was probably passed on to Central Tibet via its south-eastern marches (personal communication Peter Kessler, Wiesendangen, Switzerland). With the death of Trhisong Detsen towards the end of the eighth century, the heyday of the early empire was over. Violent internal struggles during the last days of the Tibetan kings resulted in a general political collapse and a period of religious and cultural stagnation followed. By the beginning of the tenth century the process of fragmentation was complete.

Despite political fragmentation, the spirit of Buddhism lived on in a number of monastic establishments in the far west and east of Tibet. By the beginning of the eleventh century a new religious and philosophic ferment swept the whole of Tibet. Renewed spiritual contacts with India, and possibly a partial transition to a more sedentary way of life, in combination with increasing population, brought a resurgence of monastic life. In course of the process, some of the best organized monasteries entered the political arena. Many of them became wealthy, thanks to pious foundations and donations, and tried to play a role in the ongoing contest for temporal power. Noble families patronized one or another religious order through one of its sacred establishments, and neighbouring princes sought to exploit the newly acquired wealth of the monasteries by securing clan members a place in the spiritual hierarchy. In this way, several monasteries came to form the centres of what could be labelled 'ecclesiastical principalities' (Hoffmann 1961:111-130, Petech 1983: 173-174, Stein 1987:38-46).

From a geographical point of view, the period under consideration is of crucial importance, because it is here that we find the necessary ingredients for a nascent territorial organization of the wider Tibetan realm. This new territorial state of affairs was in essence, though not without modifications, to last right up till the middle of the twentieth century. Monasteries emerged as nodes of political and economic activity. Nomads and sedentary farmers alike were drawn into networks of exchange, more often than not conditioned by the calendar of religious festivals. The monks and lamas created the necessary infrastructure by providing services ranging from the performance of saintly rites to the extension of earthly credit, and the more powerful abbots of the larger monasteries meddled in the higher affairs of state.

Almost without exception the monasteries that stem from this period grew up around charismatic masters, some of whom, like the Tibetan Marpa and the Indian Atisha, had travelled widely in search of learning and quest of teaching. The first new religious school to be founded next to the old Nyingma one, was the Sakya school (1073), based at Sakya on the important Western Tibetan trade route from Shigatse to Nepal. Later, in the thirteenth century, these Sakyas seem to have been instrumental in the coming of Mongol overlordship in Tibet. Yet in time, the waning power of the short-lived Mongol Yuan dynasty (1280-1368) was inevitably accompanied by a loss of Sakya influence (Petech 1983:173-203). Then there followed a period of 'Kagyu ascendancy', either in its Kadampa or Karmapa form. Were Atisha's Kadampas in the great monasteries of Central Tibet first and foremost monks and scholars, the Karma Kagyu masters proved to be skilful temporal incumbents as well. It is during this period that the political history of Tibet did become inseparable from its religious history. As Dowman succinctly writes 'due to the increasing and eventually predominant wealth of the monasteries, temporal power became synonymous with spiritual authority: thus theocracy was born' (Dowman 1988:18).

Any historian dealing with Tibetan events from the ninth to the thirteenth century is bound to draw an unbalanced picture (Petech 1983:174). The tiny scraps of information relating to the years from about 900 to about 1230 are in sharp contrast with the relatively plentiful evidence available for the rest of the thirteenth century. However, the most important secondary source for the 'dark age' of Tibetan history is Petech's concise but highly informed essay itself (Petech 1983:173-203), now supplemented by his monograph on the same period (Petech 1990). The renaissance of Buddhism in the eleventh century and the subsequent rise of the different religious orders is well covered by Hoffmann (1961:111-182), and Tucci (1980:16-46); see also Snellgrove (1987). Brief but useful summaries of the Tibetan 'Middle Ages' are to be found in Tucci (1967:29-38), Stein (1987:38-46), Blondeau (1977:1-22), and Dowman (1988:17-24).

The ultimate boost to Tibetan theocracy was the final victory of the Gelukpas over its rival orders. From the beginning of the fifteenth century, the Tsongkapa 'reformation', on which the Gelukpa rise was based, lured many a former Kadampa disciple into the new 'Virtuous School', stressing monastic and moral discipline. More than any other religious order, the Gelukpas knew how to develop the monastic system. As they grew in power, the Yellow Hats, as the Gelukpas were known to the Chinese, conceived a highly centralized administrative structure, in which every monastery had to acknowledge the Dalai Lama's authority. All this in sharp contrast to the decentralized set-up of the older orders. The newly founded monasteries or *gompas* of Sera and Drepung in Central Tibet, and Tashilunpo in Tsang to the west of Lhasa, quickly developed into political hot-beds attuned to the mood of the times. Patronized by powerful families these monasteries held the key to future political power in Central Tibet. To secure ultimate victory, the Great Fifth Dalai Lama (1617-1682) invited a Mongol army to support the Gelukpa cause, and utterly defeated his Karmapa opponents. In terms of political geography: integrated theocracy gained political control of the country under the authority of the Dalai Lamas. After the establishment of the Yellow Hat sect as the dominant school, the centre of religious vitality and innovation seems to have shifted eastward to the monasteries of Kham and Amdo, where Red Hat activity has always since contested Yellow Hat power (see also Dhondup 1984).

The question that may well arise at this point is whether the newly evolved Tibetan polity can be labelled a true state. In a major article on state formation in Asia, Rudolph cautions us against the use of the 'standard' conception of the state as developed on the basis of European analogues (Rudolph 1987:734). In fact she goes so far as to reject the idea of a monopoly of force so crucial to European definitions of the state. The model of Oriental Despotism too, with its emphasis on the all-empowered state versus a passive, localized, parochial society, cannot find favour in her eyes (ibid.:738). Instead she argues for more attention to the ritual side of state and state formation. Her plea for a concept of 'ritual sovereignty' as a parallel to the European one of 'theocracy', underlines the necessity to combine theoretical notions of a 'demystified, rationalist worldview' with those of a 'historical transmission of a true charismatic substance across generations' (ibid.:740-742). The cornerstone to this ritual house of sovereignty is the cosmological conception of kingship: in terms of things Tibetan, the Dalai Lama as an incarnation of Avalokitesvara, Tibet's patron *bodhisattva* (for the latter concept see chapter 3 and glossary). However, too much emphasis on the cosmological obscures the historical concreteness of state formation in Asia. After all the fifth Dalai Lama did benefit from the presence of a Mongol army to stamp out his opponents. There was clearly 'organized religion' then behind the rise of the Dalai Lamas, no matter how great spiritual authorities some of them may have become afterwards. In that sense, it is perhaps better to speak of Tibet as an ecclesiastical state (Stein 1987:87-92) instead of one based on ritual sovereignty alone. With the development of government after the rise of the Dalai Lamas, this ecclesiastical state assumed a dual character, in which lay officials of the central government, as well as the more independent local states in other parts of Tibet, had monastic counterparts. This administrative set-up ensured a lasting counterbalance of politically minded prelates to an all too aspiring aristocracy. However, the dominance of one religious order over the others, in one way prevented the growth of a real national unity, notwithstanding the fact that by the middle of the seventeenth century the Dalai Lama's regime territorially stretched from the sacred Mount Kailash in the West to the borders of Kham in the East. Beyond the confines of Central Tibet, the political power of the Dalai Lamas was varying. Although the Gelukpas had strongholds in the northeastern province of Amdo, and to a lesser extent in Kham, the local noble houses felt powerful enough to defy administrative interference of the central government. What is more, several nomad tribes did not recognize any political overlordship at all, and the whole of ethnic Tibet may be best described as a spiritual, but politically fragmented federation. Thus, the Tibetan state in the strict 'European' sense of the term, and based on a monopoly of force, did not exist. Though the idea of a measure of ritual sovereignty nowadays facilitates the idea of a 'cultural' Tibet, the political integration of all its parts was never fully realized.

Perhaps it is at a higher level of analysis that ritual sovereignty ultimately destined the historical fate of the Tibetans. In this connection, the relationship between the fifth Dalai Lama and his Qosot Mongol protector Gusri Khan stands out as an example of the concept of Patron and Priest in which 'the temporal support of the lay power is given in return for the spiritual support of the religious power' (Richardson 1984:42). Since the middle of the sixteenth century, most tribes of Mongolia paid spiritual allegiance to the Dalai Lamas, and it was this bond which alarmed the Chinese, as they saw in it a potential rallying point for the consolidation of the Mongol tribes that might eventually threaten their frontiers. In a preemptive move to forestall the possible rise of another great Mongol empire, the Chinese skilfully played upon tribal rivalries within the Mongol camp. After the death of the fifth Dalai Lama (1682), Tibet quickly fell victim to externally induced disorders through their Mongol connection, and eventually had to stand the looting of Lhasa by a rival band of Dzungar Mongols (1717). This gave the Chinese the excuse they needed. Within two years a Manchu Chinese army purged the Tibetan scene, and on the 16th of October 1720, the seventh Dalai Lama in the company of Chinese generals and 'advisers', entered the pillaged and desolated Potala (Petech 1972:73). Once again, historical concreteness overruled ritual sovereignty, the latter now moreover under strain of a Chinese-deepened rift between the Dalai and Panchen Lamas. The Tibet-China road guarded by Chinese soldiers, a Chinese garrison in Lhasa, lay and monastic ministers controlled by a Chinese delegate Tibet seemed deprived of all its autonomy, though the Chinese were careful to surround the Dalai Lama with the highest formal honours as the spiritual head of state. However, the viewpoint that Tibet in the eighteenth century had passed into the status of a Chinese protectorate pure and simple (so eminently represented by Petech 1972), is a Western simplification. Though the Chinese emperor's representatives, the *ambans*, were able to maintain their presence in Lhasa for a long time, Chinese dominance if it ever existed as such, was always contested (cf. Norbu 1990). A series of powerful regents, backed up by a bright counterlight of Buddhist spiritual overlordship, secured Tibet's virtual independence during much of the nineteenth century. The one provision which did have a lasting effect on Tibet was the exclusion of foreigners. Imposed by the

Manchus in 1793, but willingly supported by various conservative factions in the larger Gelukpa monasteries of the Lhasa region, it became the means by which Tibet was subsequently sheltered from rising British and Russian imperialism. But it also meant a further political isolation, which later on made the assessment of international affairs much more difficult for the Tibetans, perhaps to their ultimate detriment.

Major sources covering the period described above are Kolmas (1967), Ahmad (1970), but above all Petech (1972). The Tibetan side of the story is represented by Shakabpa (1967:91-153) and Dhondup (1984). Useful summaries are to be found in Tucci (1967:38-47), Stein (1987:47-53), and Richardson (1984:38-60), the latter approximately stating the 'official' British point of view.

Geopolitics of Tibet: the Himalayan tangle

With growing British influence in India during the eighteenth and nineteenth centuries, a new, epoch-making force made its appearence in Asian history. The sound of the British bugle foreshadowed protracted geopolitical strife in the Himalayan region, resulting in the establishment of British power in a number of frontier districts, and its nominal acceptance in others. Tibet herself too, fired the imagination of the Company rulers of Bengal and soon became the object of considerable speculation with regard to possible trade across the Himalaya. However, British attempts to open Tibet from the south met polite refusal, notwithstanding Hasting's successful missions by Bogle, Turner and Purangir to the third Panchen Lama (1738-1780). In the Central Himalayan region too, British aims at creating handsome spheres of influence for commercial purposes were frustrated, this time by expansionist tendencies among the local rulers. Indigenous state formation in the Central Himalaya focused on the Hindu-tribal encounter so characteristic of the area, in which progressive Hinduization of non-Hindu populations and the alienation of tribal lands, were of paramount importance. Political consolidation of Hindu immigrant groups over lands once controlled by Tibeto-Burman tribes culminated in the rise of a Gorkhali-dominated Nepalese state which by the beginning of the nineteenth century stretched from the Satlej in the west to the Sikkimese border in the east. Overstretching their territorial ambitions, the Gorkhalis were in time reduced to obedience by Chinese and British expeditionary forces. Anglo-Nepalese relations were settled in 1816 by the Treaty of Sagauli, which meant the loss of the Himalayan districts of Kumaon and Garhwal to Britain, and made Nepal retreat into splendid isolation for much of the following century and a half. Later however, friendly recognition of British power in India by the Nepalese did much to improve Anglo-Nepalese relations. Sagauli 1816 also brought a protectorate over Bashahr on the Upper Satlej, as well as other hill states to the west of Kumaon, like Tehri-Garhwal and Kinnaur. In these western marches of the Himalaya, geopolitical rivalry in the first half of the nineteenth century can be basically reduced to three competing powers. Firstly, there were the British, secondly, the Sikh maharaja Ranjit Singh, who had captured large parts of the Panjab and Kashmir, and thirdly, the Dogra chieftain Gulab Singh, who had received Jammu in *jagir* from Ranjit Singh, but in reality was practically independent from the latter (Datta 1970:17). From 1834 to 1841, Zorowar Singh, a general of Gulab Singh, was busy conquering Ladakh and Baltistan, and finally invaded western Tibet, only to be defeated at the hands of a large Tibetan army. The resulting treaty between the Dogras and the Tibetans (1842) confirmed the existing border line between Ladakh and Tibet, but at the same time sealed the fate of an independent kingdom of Ladakh which was extinguished after an existence of almost a thousand years (Datta 1973:150-151). The country merged in the dominions of Gulab Singh, who at the conclusion of the first Anglo-Sikh war in 1846, became maharaja of Kashmir under British protection (Petech 1977:151). The neighbouring districts of Kinnaur, and the formerly Ladakhi-controlled Lahaul and Spiti, were now transferred to direct British rule (Thomson 1852:128). Ladakh itself, as a dependency of Kashmir, came indirectly under British influence.

The rise of British power in the western and central Himalaya, and the inception of Anglo-Tibetan relations in the late eighteenth century, have been the subject of considerable historical investigation. The rise of the Nepalese state too, and the consequent Anglo-Nepalese relations, are now fairly well known through the works of Nepalese, Indian and other historians. Both Bogle and Turner left incisive and generally accurate accounts of their missions to Tibet (Markham 1876:cxxxv-clviii, 1-210; Turner 1800). Cammann

(1951b) gives a handy though China-biased overview of the period. The bare record of Tibetan texts concerning Bogle and Turner has been screened by Petech (1950). Purangir's exploits are recorded by Turner (1800:419-433), Cammann (1951b:69-74, 103-106, 166) and briefly by Petech (1950:345-346). Richardson (1984:68) mentions Purangir's 'clear and circumstantial report', but further references are lacking. Perhaps it is to be equated with Turner (1800:419-433). Early Anglo-Nepalese relations are covered by Sanwal (1965). The ill-fated Kinloch expedition to Nepal (1767) is spelled out in detail by Chaudhuri (1960:13-33). The most thorough and balanced books on the rise of the Nepalese state are those of Stiller (1968,1973), Pradhan (1991) forming a welcome addition. Early British activity in the Western Himalaya becomes visible in Alder's masterly biography of Moorcroft (Alder 1985:107-157, 209-293), and of course in Moorcroft's own version of his journeys (Moorcroft and Trebeck 1841). The political vicissitudes of Ladakh are well treated by Petech (1977:111-152), Datta (1970:16-28), and Warikoo (1988:63-83; 1989). The best study on the Dogra conquest in the Western Himalaya remains Datta (1973). A good overall historical account of the North-Western Indian hill states and their relations with the British has yet to be written.

The Eastern Himalayan world too, increasingly felt the reverberations of growing British power in North India. Here the tiny Buddhist states of Sikkim and Bhutan that had arisen in the seventeenth century, and to a lesser extent the isolated Tibeto-Burman tracts of the Assam Himalaya, became the object of British commercial, and in the end, territorial overtures. After the British had brought the Nepalese to bay in 1815 (Rana 1970), they restored part of the Sikkimese territory to its rightful owners, but in the succeeding decades took whatever opportunity arose to encroach on Sikkimese lands. In 1835 the Darjeeling area was wrested from the maharaja of Sikkim, but not without sharp protests from the Tibetans, who saw their nominal hold over Sikkim lapse. Years of strained relations between Sikkim and the Company followed and in the end led to an expeditionary force into the country to make the pro-Tibetan raja toe the line. March 1861 saw the dictation of a treaty to the Sikkimese, which for the first time officially confirmed the country's political integrity as a 'protectorate' of British India (Mehra 1968b:101-102).

Bhutan experienced similar vicissitudes, starting with the British occupation of Assam in 1826. Even before the British assumed authority in Assam, the Bhutanese had been in the habit of raiding the fertile *duar* lowlands on the Bhutan-Bengal and the Bhutan-Assam border. To prevent further Bhutanese inroads, and in order to reap some of the fruits from the *duars* themselves, the British were anxious to push the Bhutanese back to the line of hills which separate the lowlands from Himalayan Bhutan. However, a mission by Pemberton (1837) had not the desired effect and frontier hostilities continued as before. Later, the Eden mission of 1864 apparently met with more success, but after its departure, the Bhutanese suddenly attacked Dewangiri in the eastern *duars*, and the British had to make a hasty retreat. This led to an outbreak of open hostilities, followed by a short, unequal war over the *duars* in 1864-1865. The conflict ended by the conclusion of a treaty at Sinchula (1865) whereby Bhutan agreed to cede all the *duar* lowlands to the British, while the latter guaranteed 'perpetual peace and friendship' to the Bhutanese (Deb 1973:88, 1976:179-183). In effect, the settling of affairs in this region marked the transition from one phase of colonial policy to another, the first being a period of mercantile interest under Company rule, the second one of commercial agricultural investment under the civil administration of the Raj (English 1985:70).

British territorial influence in the wild and mountainous Himalayan frontier tracts north of the Assam plains was a much more drawn out affair. British relations with the northern frontier began in 1853, when a first agreement was reached with the Monpas, an ethnic group of Tibetan cultural background, controlling the important trans-Himalayan trade route through the Tawang corridor, close to the eastern Bhutanese border (Mills 1950:153, Choudhury 1977:181). But further eastwards the British quest for trade routes and territorial control was thwarted by inaccessible terrain and warlike Tibeto-Burman tribes (Elwin 1958:xvii). The most the newly established colonial administration could do was to safeguard the plains population against the occasional raids of the mountain dwellers. Altogether the nineteenth century was a period in which the British were trying to push the north-eastern frontier back from the plains and up into the mountains just as they had been doing in southern Sikkim and Bhutan. In course of the process, a sort of

'Inner Line' was developed, a more or less strict administrative boundary between the settled agricultural districts of the Assam plains and the tribal hill lands up the Himalaya. Consistent violation of this line by tea planters, who sought to extend their plantations into the foothills of the Himalaya, led to occasionally tense situations, in which tribal raids and punitive expeditions by the British succeeded each other. However, from a geopolitical point of view, the north-eastern frontier area retained its character of a buffer zone between British India and Tibet far into the twentieth century (Barpujari 1981:1-27,113-138).

For one reason or another, Sikkim has not yet found its satisfactory chronicler of events. Nevertheless, a useful overview has been provided by Mehra (1968b:99-111), while a concise political history hails from the hand of Basnet (1974), stressing the Nepalese point of view. British relations with Bhutan are well covered by the contemporary accounts of the political missions to Bhutan, which have been brought together in Eden et al. (1865). The events of the *duar* war are related in Rennie (1866). A thorough and critical historical analysis of the whole period under review (1772-1865) is Deb (1976). A balanced and well-illustrated narrative has now been presented by Aris (1994). Recently, an archival survey of British political contacts with Sikkim, Bhutan, and Tibet, has been attempted by Singh (1988a,1988b). A historical account of the dealings of the British-Indian colonial government with the mountain tribes in the eastern Himalaya is Mackenzie (1884). Elwin (1959) remains indispensable for the nineteenth century North-East frontier area, while a good historical survey of both the Indo-Tibetan and Indo-Burman frontier regions has been provided by Barpujari (1981).

What, then, was the overall geopolitical situation along the southern Tibetan perimeter that had arisen by the beginning of the 1870s? Through the ages, the Himalaya had always served as a refuge for a variety of distinct cultures (Berreman 1960,1963). However, until the unification of a 'greater' Nepal under the raja of Gorkha, political consolidation remained relatively localized. It seems likely that many of the later hill rajas, among whom were the powerful Gorkhalis, derived much of their administrative zeal from the example set by the great Moghul empire in the sixteenth century. Similarly, despite the historical rivalries among the various sects, the monastic institutions of Tibetan Buddhism provided a stable force in the administration of the local Buddhist states like Ladakh, Sikkim and Bhutan. In the course of time, growing British influence from the South came to contain and to a certain extent fossilize this myriad of cultural and political forms. Tiny states were forced into administrative pacts with the British-Indian government, a set-up which tended to emphasize the territorial status quo and made the existing forms of cultural and political organization more rigid. However, in contrast to the western parts of the Himalaya, the British were never able to extend their control into much of the central and eastern Himalayan region. As Richardson succinctly wrote:

> What finally emerged was a Himalayan frontier of India cushioned off from Tibet for almost its entire length by states and tribes in varying degrees of dependency on the Indian colonial government. With most of these states and ethnically affiliated groups the Tibetans too, had their own particular relationships, in general customary and undefined, depending either on the bond of religious allegiance to the Dalai Lama or on the long-established local trade or grazing connections (Richardson 1984:73)

Geopolitics of Tibet: the 'Great Game'

British haggling at the southern borderlands of Tibet, ultimately served the higher purpose of playing the 'Great Game' in Central Asia as well as the rulers of a rising imperial India thought necessary. Throughout the nineteenth and early twentieth century, the geopolitical and territorial tug-of-war between its main contenders, Britain, Russia, and China, shaped many a political action in the frontier lands of Inner Asia (Morgan 1981, Hopkirk 1990). Russia's expansion across the Asian heartland reached its climax towards the closing decades of the nineteenth century, and Britain did not lag behind in pushing her strategic presence in the western Himalayan frontier districts of Chitral, Hunza, Nagar, Yasin and Gilgit (Huttenback 1975, Warikoo 1988:63, 1989).

Moreover, the British meddled in Central Asian affairs by secretly recognizing the newly independent Muslim state in Sinkiang under Yakub Beg in 1864 (Kim 1986), in the hope of containing both Russian and Chinese influence in the area. But by December 1877, the Chinese were back in Kashgar and Yakub Beg was dead (Skrine and Nightingale 1987:11). From the moment the Chinese discovered the secret ploy the British had made with regard to the Muslim rebels, Anglo-Chinese relations showed a further deterioration, which became especially apparent in dealings over Tibet, probably out of fear for British recidivism (Addy 1985:37).

Tibet was the last prize to be won in the Great Game. Its geographical position at the political junction of Asia's three largest land powers, made her into a bone of territorial contention, which came only to be resolved - and then only temporarily so - by blunt imperialist action in the early years of the twentieth century. But well before that ultimate crisis, Tibet had already become the object of secretive as well as open attempts at exploration. Since the early 1860s, clandestine missions of native *pandits*, under the active sponsorship of the Trigonometrical Survey of India, had yielded a wealth of information on the topography of Tibet (Burrard 1915, Waller 1990). Besides the *pandits*, a host of European explorers and adventurers, with or without government support, tried to pilfer away the last secrets of the 'Land of the Lamas'. A glimpse of Lhasa was the much-coveted wish of a generation of late-nineteenth century explorers, who knew the capital of Tibet only by the mind-capturing but not always informative reports of a handful of missionaries and travellers. But despite the determined efforts of Britons and Russians, Frenchmen and Americans, as well as the indefatigable Swede Sven Hedin (Kish 1984), 'Interior Tibet' held out in its struggle against foreign intruders (cf. Petech 1976: 219-252).

It is against this background of persistent and well-sustained attempts at penetration by an active and powerful neighbour, along the entire length of Tibet's southern border, that the Anglo-Tibetan, or rather the Anglo-Chinese relations with regard to Tibet, should be understood. As the Tibetan government refused direct contacts with Britain, China was eager to step in its place, despite the fact that Chinese power in Tibet by the 1870s amounted to a mere fiction. The effects of the humiliating Opium Wars (1839-1842, 1856-1860), and the bitter Taiping Rebellion (1851-1864), which had shaken the Manchu empire to its very foundations, became visible in the reduced status and influence of the imperial *ambans* at Lhasa. However, the overall loss of international prestige, did not prevent China from including a separate article in the Anglo-Chinese Chefoo

Convention of 1876, in which Britain obtained the right for a mission of exploration across Tibet. But as the Tibetans were not consulted about the agreement, they naturally refused entrance to any such mission. The British did not press the matter until almost ten years later, and then suddenly bartered away their Tibetan 'rights' in the Anglo-Chinese Convention on Burma (1886), in which Britain consented to countermand an impending mission (Mehra 1968a:63-73) the personal victim of which was Colman Macaulay, whose preparation and publicity for the first official journey into Tibet now turned upon himself. The collective victim were the Tibetans, who in an effort to forestall Macaulay's armed escort of two hundred men, had crossed the Jelep La into Sikkimese territory and built a fort at Lingtu. The subsequent countermanding of the Macaulay mission was falsely construed by the Tibetans as a sign of weakness on the part of the British, and consequently held on to their Lingtu fortifications, yet were driven out by British troops two years later (Shakabpa 1967:201, Singh 1988a:216-217).

In fear of further territorial pressure on the strategically located Jelep La and the adjacent Chumbi Valley, the Chinese rapidly opened negotiations in India to define the geopolitical status of Sikkim, and in 1890 signed another Anglo-Chinese Convention. In 1893 there followed a further agreement on trade, but no Tibetan representative was party to either convention and 'the farce of Chefoo was re-enacted on a larger scale' (Richardson 1984:77). The Convention of 1890 defined Sikkim's northern boundary as the watershed of the Tista, and gave a joint Anglo-Chinese guarantee of the frontier as laid down. The Tibetan refusal of this boundary rested on the belief that what had originally been Tibetan territory was now marked off as Sikkimese (Li 1956:79-81). Here, in effect, was 'the crux and the starting-point' of the Anglo-Tibetan conflict (cf. Lamb 1986:xi), and in 1895 the Tibetans occupied Gyaogang in the upper Lachen Valley on the Sikkimese side of the border, an area to which they had always had a historical and customary claim. The Tibetans also refused to honour the proposal for a trade mart at Yatung at the lower end of the Chumbi Valley, well into Tibetan territory, and as a matter of fact built walls on their side to prevent anyone from coming down to meet British-Indian traders (Candler 1905:9, 29, Mehra 1968a:78). Both actions served to underline the independent stance of Tibet towards China, and by the end of the nineteenth century, Chinese authority in Tibet can be regarded as nonexistent.

But then fresh clouds started to darken the Tibetan horizon. With the arrival of Curzon as the new Viceroy of India in 1899, a new era of forward policy into Central Asia was ushered. Curzon's ideas about Tibet were a direct offshoot of the fear of Russian expansionist policies in Asia, which in the second half of the nineteenth century had become visible in the progressive occupation of the muslim *khanats* in the area between the Pamirs and the Caspian Sea. Yet Russian influence in Asia had a much longer history than that dating from the Central Asian campaigns alone. Even with a land as remote as Tibet there existed indirect links through the agency of Buddhist tribes of southern Siberia and Mongolia, and that so for centuries already. Bogle, for example, during his mission of 1774-1775, came across large numbers of Kalmuk Mongols in Central Tibet, resorting annually to Lhasa and Tashilunpo for the purpose of trade and pilgrimage (Markham 1876:97-98, 104, 107, 125). Moorcroft too, on his Tibetan journey of 1812, heard rumours about parties of 'Ooroos', Russian subjects, who had come to the annual fair at Gartok in western Tibet (Moorcroft 1818:453). Later in the nineteenth century, Buriat Mongols seem to have visited Lhasa regularly (Tsybikoff 1904:93), bringing products of Western provenance through the intermediacy of small colonies of Russian traders, which had come into existence in Mongolia (Elias 1873:121, 127-128, 138-139, Consten 1919-1920 I: 63-72). Moreover, some two hundred Buriat monks hailing from the Russian pale, were studying in the great Buddhist monasteries of Lhasa (Narzounof 1904:226, 236, 238, Kawaguchi 1909:495-496), and smaller numbers have been reported from eastern Tibet (Futterer 1900:338). Traffic with Tibet by Russian subjects of Asiatic origin, then, appears to have been 'regular and long-established' (Richardson 1984:79-80). One of the 'Russian' Buriat monks studying in Lhasa was Aguan Dorjiev, a brilliant student of Tibetan religion, philosophy and history, who after gaining a title of distinction in scholarship became one of the instructors of the young Dalai Lama. This happened to be the 'Great Thirteenth' Thupten-gyatso (1876-1933), a man of 'considerable shrewdness that grew with age and experience' (Bell 1946). Though it is generally agreed that Dorjiev won the personal confidence of the young Dalai Lama, it remains to be seen whether he was a Russian political agent as has sometimes been alleged. Perhaps the final answer to this question can only be given when the archives in Moscow are opened for public inspection which is now to a certain extent the case (Addy 1985:132, see also Snelling 1993). Nevertheless, Dorjiev's counselling of the Dalai Lama alarmed Curzon very much, especially as it had continued into early adulthood, when Thupten-gyatso had taken the spiritual reins of Tibet firmly in his hands, and aspired to pull at the temporal ones. As Curzon's attempts at direct contacts with the Tibetans had miserably failed, Russian players in the 'Great Game' seemed to be outscoring the British ones (Ghosh 1979:11). Already in 1900, Dorjiev had made his way unobtrusively to Petersburg, but it was his second, and much-publicized mission in 1901, that really stirred up Russophobia among the British, and especially in Curzon's head. In 1902, there were persistent rumours of a secret treaty between Russia and Tibet, which, however, was vehemently denied by the Russian Foreign Office. Nebulous reports about Russian activity greatly stimulated Curzon's anxiety, but studied with a measure of objectivity these rumours lacked confirmation (Mehra 1958:28-42, 1968:140-155, Ghosh 1979:7-16, Addy 1985:59-148).

In this atmosphere of a commonly perceived Russian shadow over Tibet, the idea of an official mission to Lhasa began to take shape. Not that Curzon or anyone else in authority considered a Russian invasion of Tibet very likely, but the idea that a Russian-monitored Tibet was capable of disturbing the peace of India by causing trouble along its Himalayan frontier, made the British dispatch an official but avowedly nonpolitical mission to Lhasa (Richardson 1984:83-84). There is no need to repeat all what has been said about the Younghusband mission, except for the fact that, despite considerable restraint shown by the Home Government in London, it developed into a bloody military affair (Candler 1905:1, Mehra 1968a:224, Richardson 1984:86).

By August 1904, Younghusband had fought his way to Lhasa, only to find that the Dalai Lama and Dorjiev had fled to Urga in Mongolia. A monk-regent, appointed in great haste, obtained the authority from the Tibetan assembly to sign a 'treaty', which was effected without undue delay. This first Anglo-Tibetan Convention sought to enforce the regulations of the Anglo-Chinese agreements of 1890 and 1893, but above all to exclude any foreign power from political influence in Tibet, with the notable exception of the British.

Another clause concerned the opening of trade marts, with British agents at Yatung, Gyantse, and Gartok, through which the British intended to open up Tibet for commercial purposes. The Chinese *amban* at Lhasa was present at the 'negotiations', but for obvious reasons did not sign. Soon after, the expeditionary force, 'to the great surprise and relief' of the Tibetans, began its withdrawal to India two months after its arrival at Lhasa (Richardson 1984:87, 268-271, Lamb 1986:222-255, 263).

The absence of Chinese participation in the Lhasa *Diktat* emphasized Tibet's independent stance towards Peking, but the Anglo-Chinese Convention of 1906 virtually reversed the British and Chinese roles in Tibet by recognizing that China was not a foreign power under the terms of the Anglo-Tibetan Convention of 1904, and consequently had the responsibility for 'preserving the integrity' of Tibet (Singh 1988a:32-39). This diplomatic success for Peking may partly be accounted for by the strong international criticism levelled against the British at the time of the Younghusband mission but is more likely based on the waning Russian threat in Central Asia after Russia's internal troubles in the autumn of 1905 (Skrine and Nightingale 1987:144). These paved the way eventually for the Anglo-Russian Convention of 1907, in which Chinese rights in Tibet were mentioned again. No wonder that Curzon bitterly complained that the Anglo-Russian appeasement had thrown away a century of diplomatic and commercial effort (Richardson 1984:94, Addy 1985:190, Singh 1988a:44). Several outstanding studies have appeared with regard to the imperialist encounter in Central Asia and Tibet. The most complete analysis of relations between British India and Tibet, covering the period of 1766 to 1910, is Lamb (1986). The thorough survey by Singh (1988a:3-162) extends the enquiry up till 1950. Mehra's standard work on the Younghusband expedition (1968a) is already a classic, while Addy (1985) gives an additional perspective on the diplomatic tangle involved. New light on British, Chinese and Russian activities in Sinkiang, in the period 1890-1918, is shed by Skrine and Nightingale (1987), and for the following decades by Nyman (1977) and Forbes (1986). Bell (1946) provides an interesting, contemporary view of the life and times of the thirteenth Dalai Lama. Richardson (1984:73-106), as stated earlier, represents the British point of view, and is useful as an extended summary. Ghosh (1977, 1979:7-16) too, provides a very acceptable overview and synopsis. The official Tibetan version of the period concerned is Shakabpa (1967:192-223).

Geopolitics of Tibet: China resurgent

The wanderings of the thirteenth Dalai Lama in Mongolia, northeast Tibet, and finally China, in the years immediately after the Younghusband expedition, had the beneficial effect of making Tibet's supreme head of state more aware of the complicated game of international politics. In due time, he acquired a reasonably balanced insight into the vulnerable position of Tibet among the great powers. China in particular showed her true face by thrusting a subordinate position upon the Dalai Lama during his visit to Peking in 1908. His complaints at the imperial court about the atrocities of a Chinese general by the name of Chao Erh-feng in the eastern Tibetan province of Kham were simply ignored, and his plea for an autonomous Tibet rejected. Tired by the noncommittal attitude of Russia's representatives he had met in Urga, and worse, the humiliation received at the hands of the Chinese while in Peking, the Dalai Lama turned towards the British, perhaps not fully appreciating that Britain had deliberately weakened her position in Tibet by signing the Anglo-Chinese Convention of 1906, in exchange for matters of higher political concern elsewhere (Bell 1946:65-89, Stoddard 1985:47-56).

It has been argued that the Chinese venture in Kham during the period 1904 to 1911 was a direct response to the threat posed by the Younghusband expedition (Sperling 1976:13). This may well be near the truth, as the original purpose of Chinese forward policy in that area seems to have been the creation of a Chinese-administered frontier province by the name of Sikang in order to prevent the British from progressing further eastwards (Stoddard 1985:23). To that end, plans for Chinese settlement schemes in Kham were quickly set up, a first specimen of which was implemented near the eastern Tibetan town of Batang in 1904 (Hosie 1905:45, Sperling 1976:12). In spring 1905 open rebellion against Chinese presence in the area broke out, as a result of which a high Chinese official was ambushed and killed. Chinese reaction was prompt, and the arrival of Chinese troops in Batang and Litang - another place of rebellious incidence - quelled for the moment any resistance (Teichman 1922:20-21). From this time on, the conscious effort to bring Tibetan Kham into the Chinese political and cultural mould, is largely a record of the work of Chao Erh-feng, the Chinese frontier commissioner-cum-army commander, who had only one objective to guide him, being 'to sinicize K'am as far as possible, and to secure the province as a source of profit for China' (Sperling 1976:20). Chao's exploits have been differently judged, but for the Tibetans he was a 'butcher', intent on destroying their precious religion and imposing a harsh Chinese rule on their lands (Teichman 1922:36-37, Sperling 1976:30-32).

From a geopolitical point of view, Chao's rigid, not to say murderous strategy, was a complete success. By the end of 1909, the Chinese commander had brought the whole of eastern Tibet under a degree of control such as had never existed before. And when, as a logical sequence to Chao Erh-feng's campaigns, Lhasa eventually fell into Chinese hands in February 1910. The British, though perturbed and lodging a formal protest with the Chinese (Teichman 1922:29) simply stood by and watched the things to develop (cf. Stoddard 1985:57).

The Dalai Lama, having returned to Lhasa only two months before from Peking after an absence of more than five years, just managed to escape the vanguard of Chao's Chinese army and fled Tibet for a second time. Ironically enough, his flight ended up in British India, the land of his onetime enemy. The British, bound by the 1906 convention, chose to adopt a neutral stand, giving shelter to their high Tibetan refugee at Darjeeling, but ignoring his plea for help. The future looked bleak for the Tibetans but history was to decide otherwise.

The eclipse of the Manchu empire, which had already become visible in the nineteenth century, precipitated a full-blown revolution in the Chinese heartland in 1911. Chinese authority in Tibet soon collapsed and by June 1912 the Dalai Lama was back in Lhasa. However, the newly arisen Republican government of Yuan Shih-kai, reasserted its rights in Tibet by promulgating a decree, stating that 'Tibet, Mongolia, and Sinkiang were to be treated on the same basis as provinces of China and were to be considered as integral parts of the republic' (Richardson 1984:103).

The Tibetan reaction was a formal declaration of independence in February 1913 (Shakabpa 1967:246-248) in fact preceded one month earlier already by the signing of a treaty with Mongolia, although the latter allegedly lacks official status (Bell 1924a:304-305, Mehra 1969). Nevertheless, in Tibetan eyes it was an 'effective affirmation' of the country's *de facto* independence (Addy 1985:273). At this point the British thought it opportune to convene a tripartite conference between Tibet, China, and Britain, which they managed to host in Simla 1914 (Van Walt van Praag 1985). The background to the British offer to act as an 'honest' broker in the negotiations was the overriding geopolitical concern for a stable buffer state north of the Himalaya, as a barrier against Russian expansionism. At the same time the British were keen on solving their Himalayan boundary problems with China, as Chinese troops had violated British-Indian territory in 1910 and again during the Poyul and Zayul campaigns in 1911 under Chao's successor Fu Sung-mu (Teichman 1922:31, Sperling 1976:29, Barpujari 1981:167-168, Singh 1988a:58-59, Lamb 1989).

From the very beginning British manipulation at the Simla conference seems to have been rife. According to a seminal article by Nyman (1976) there existed two parallel levels of negotiation:

> On the official level Sir Henry McMahon dealt solely with the rectification of the Himalayan frontiers, while on the unofficial level Sir Charles Bell drew up an oral *quid pro quo* agreement about incorporation of the Tawang area into British India in exchange for a secure Sino-Tibetan boundary in Kham and certain minor British undertakings (Nyman 1976:169)

The importance of the Tawang region as referred to above, lay in its potential as a commercial entrepôt, but more so in its strategic location on the threshold of Assam. Despite the fact that Tawang, as a part of the Mon-yul corridor, had been under Tibetan administration for centuries (Aris 1980:9), it was bartered away by the Tibetan delegation at Bell's oral promise of British military support in the form of arms and ammunition to keep the Chinese in Kham at bay (Kingdon Ward 1938:614, Cutting 1940:227, Singh 1988a:84). Therefore, an agreement over the McMahon line, as a definite Indo-Tibetan frontier in the eastern Himalaya, was not the primary object of the Simla conference. That proved to be the hidden

Tawang-Kham deal, which would influence Anglo-Tibetan relations for many years to come (Nyman 1976:160-161).

However, at the official Simla level, it was decided that Tibet and China would both recognize the newly demarcated Indo-Tibetan boundary, as well as assent to a plan for the creation of an Inner and an Outer Tibet (see Figure 2). The latter proposal was an attempt to bridge the gap between rival claims over eastern Tibet, and implied a truce along the historic Sino-Tibetan boundary of 1727, running roughly along the upper course of the Yangtse. But in the end, the Chinese Foreign Office in Peking refused to ratify the agreement initialled by her representative at Simla, I-fan Chen.

The Simla Convention of 1914, then, failed to produce the tripartite solution to the Tibetan problem the British had sought for, and sowed the germs of a legacy that for a long time afterwards continued to plague relations between India and China (Greenhut II 1982:42).

The Tibetans too, had second thoughts about the inconclusive agreement. Still in 1921, when Sir Charles Bell visited Lhasa on an official mission, the Dalai Lama, in a private moment, suddenly turned to the former and said: Lön-chen, why was Tibet divided into two, Inner and Outer Tibet, at the Simla conference? (Bell 1946:206). There was reason to ask so, for the British stand in the Sino-Tibetan border question had not always been unequivocal. Stoddard (1985:59) even goes so far as to accuse the British of complicity with the Chinese for intervening in the 1918 Sino-Tibetan hostilities, at the very moment the Tibetans were busy capturing large parts of eastern Tibetan territory, which they had always regarded as theirs. But as things stand in terms of the bare historical event, the British consular agent for western China, Erich Teichman, effected peace negotiations between the various Chinese and Tibetan frontier authorities resulting in a provisional boundary between Szechwan and Tibet, which happened to coincide to a considerable extent with the old eighteenth century line of the Manchus (Teichman 1922:58). Yet, Khampas and Andowas, the Tibetan inhabitants of Kham and the north-eastern province of Amdo, continued to fight against Chinese intrusions during much of the first half of the twentieth century (Shakabpa 1967:268, Goldstein 1989:221-224).

Tibetan geopolitical history until the beginning of the twentieth century may be interpreted as an ongoing process of self-

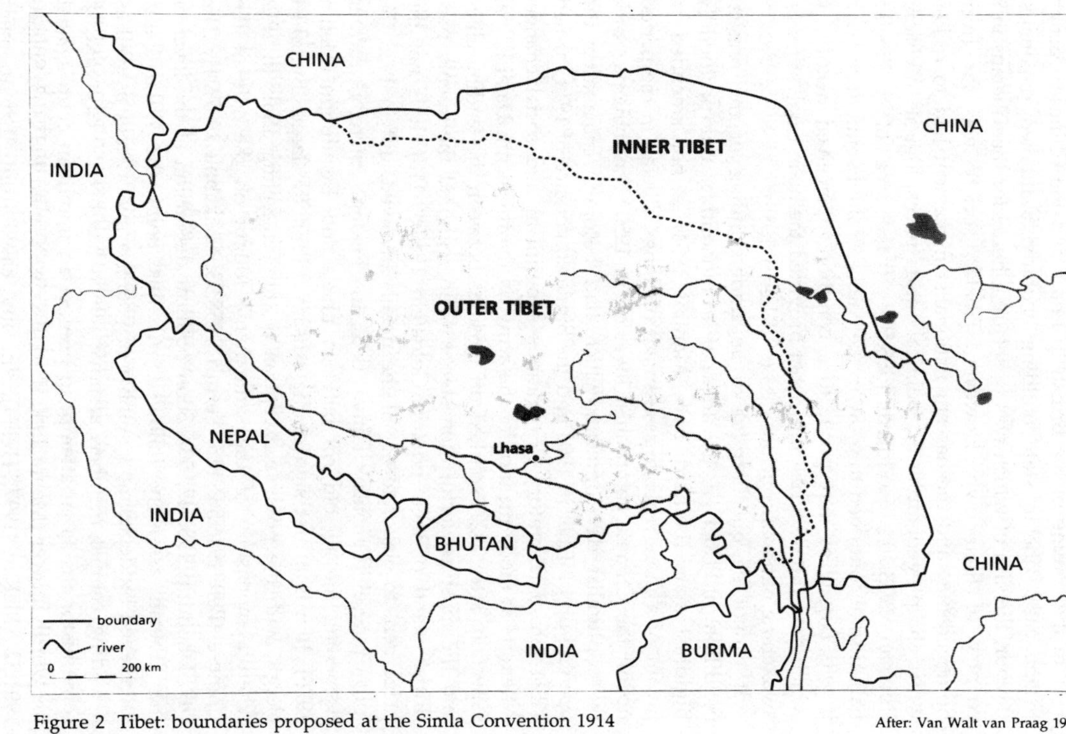

Figure 2 Tibet: boundaries proposed at the Simla Convention 1914

After: Van Walt van Praag 1987

identification, in which Tibetans sought to create a state which would guarantee the survival of their civilization.

With the coming of the British to Lhasa and the Chinese reaction in the east, Tibetan state building acquired a marked nationalist flavour, the aim of which was to secure a home for the Tibetans in a country of their own. However, Tibetan society was far from homogeneous, and the nascent nationalist movement had to reckon with sharp geographical, political and psychological divisions (Nyman 1983:104, Stoddard 1985:50). If the idea of a Tibetan nation-state continued to grow in the course of the twentieth century, it was largely as a response to a commonly perceived history, in which the Chinese thrust into Tibet provided the main catalyst for an awakening national conciousness (cf. Klieger 1989).

It cannot be but harmful to an understanding of the present condition of Tibet, if the idea of a monolithic and profoundly Buddhist state (Bernard 1939, Maraini 1954) is not amended in favour of a more realistic assessment of things Tibetan in the period up till the Chinese communist invasion in 1950. The dynamics of a more pluralist development, which had become visible after the opening up of Tibet in 1904 and the Simla conference of 1914, turned Tibet into a laboratory for cautious experiment and social change. Attempts at modernization of the army by the thirteenth Dalai Lama, especially after 1921, sparked off tensions between the leading elites and the most powerful monasteries, who regretted the openly pro-British stand of their pontiff (Goldstein 1989:89-110). It is not the place here to elaborate on all the details involved, but in 1923 the 'pro-Chinese' Panchen Lama fled to Peking, thereby further deepening the age-old rift between Lhasa and Tashilunpo (Mehra 1976). It was a first sign of the tension within the larger Buddhist clergy, with the possible exception of the Tengyeling affair in 1912 when a monastery of the same name fought on the side of the Chinese (Bell 1946:56, 125, Ferrari 1958:93, Shakabpa 1967:241, 245, 249, Dhondup 1986:47, 50). Soon political dissension at the level of the Tibetan assembly followed. At this point the Dalai Lama intervened by deposing a number of young army officers, as well as a leading cabinet member, a move which has been interpreted by some historians as an attempt to prevent an imminent coup against his wordly power (Mehra 1980 II: xxiii-xxiv, Nyman 1983:103, Spence 1991:52, McKay 1997:111-114). In any case, from that moment onwards, the Dalai Lama chose to steer a clearer course of conservative Buddhist politics in order to keep up Tibetan territorial integrity against two powerful neighbours (Stoddard 1985:62-65). The course of events also showed the existence of a 'nationalist' undercurrent in Tibetan society, which, by definition, was neither pro-British nor pro-Chinese. What it did not show was a deeper and more hidden rift between progressives and conservatives, a rift which ran right across traditional lines of cleavage.

When the thirteenth Dalai Lama died in 1933, the international political situation of Tibet entered a new period of turmoil. In 1934, an attempt to establish a Tibetan republic along modern lines failed, and the reformist faction in the national assembly was duly silenced (Goldstein 1989:186-212). This course of events speaks for the continued importance of conservative power in Lhasa during a period of weak regency following the Dalai Lama's death. Khampa secessionism in the east too, and its progressive and partly pro-Chinese undercurrent, failed to achieve its aims, its main propagators ending up in exile in Chinese-controlled Batang or British-administered Kalimpong (Shakabpa 1967:274-278, Stoddard 1985:77-80, Patterson 1990:23, 25-26, 55). But as time wore on, modernist influences kept creeping up into Tibet. The more enlightened section of the aristocratic Tibetan élite began sending their children to India in order to obtain a Western education for them. Likewise in the 1930s, a number of young Tibetans from Kham and Amdo studied in China, some of them at Nanking, the Kuo-mintang headquarters.

However, from the beginning of the 1940s onwards, relations between the young Tibetans from the east on the one hand and Republican China on the other underwent a radical transformation (Stoddard 1985:88). This change was largely the result of Chiang Kaishek's highly chauvinist policies, in which all ideals of racial equality were sacrificed on the Han altar of cultural and political assimilation. This ideological crusade against neighbouring races was accompanied by increasing pressure on their territories, eastern Tibet being again the victim of Chinese aggression from 1943 onwards. Many progressive Tibetans from Kham and Amdo now moved to Kalimpong in order to join the exile community of mostly progressive aristocrats from Central Tibet. In due time, a Progressive Party of Tibet was founded, but its development was frustrated by

British intelligence activity (Stoddard 1985:94-103, Goldstein 1989:454-458).

World War II brought new pressure on the territorial integrity of a politically neutral Tibet. Attempts to persuade the Tibetan government of the necessity to build a road from India to China through Tibet, in view of a concerted war effort, failed. The Tibetans feared that the Chinese were more interested in using the road as a means of Chinese penetration into Tibet and consequently refused cooperation. In the end they agreed to have nonmilitary goods transported through existing routes to China, mainly to placate the United States that had entered the Tibetan diplomatic field by hinting at the importance of a free and independent Tibet. However, once a new Yunnan-Burma road was opened in 1944, the pressure on Tibet was eased (Richardson 1984:159-164, Van Walt van Praag 1987:70-73).

With the war over, and communist victory near in China, the Tibetans of Kham started to prepare themselves against Chinese invasion which by 1948 seemed imminent. Already in 1935-1936, the passage of bands of communists through eastern Tibet had wrought havoc (Kaulback 1937:560, Schäfer 1938:268-269, Hanson-Lowe 1940:366, Fürholzer 1942:347-348, Duncan 1952:221, 236, 238-239, Loup 1953:97, Thomas 1959:72-73), and reminiscences of their atheist stance made the Tibetans fear the worst. In the autumn of 1950 the People's Liberation Army overran the eastern Tibetan borderlands. Lhasa reacted by proclaiming the fourteenth Dalai Lama head of state, and subsequently sent a peace delegation to China in late December 1950, convinced of the futility of any further resistance. A Seventeen Point Agreement was signed between the two nations, bringing to a close Tibetan independence which had survived unimpaired since 1912. The treaty provided for ostensible self-government under the rule of the Dalai Lama but gave China military control of the country and the exclusive right to conduct foreign relations (Karan 1976:15-18, Grunfeld 1987:104-110, Van Walt van Praag 1987:142-149). One cannot but agree with Kvaerne's observation that:

> the consistency of Chinese policy towards Tibet throughout the twentieth century and the Tibetan resistance against the Chinese in Kham and Amdo, particularly after 1950, was the direct culmination of the conflict which had

> started not with the communist takeover but fifty years earlier with the campaign of Zhao Erh-feng (Kvaerne 1987:70)

Taking the argument one step further, one could perhaps blame Curzon and Younghusband who, after all, provoked the Chinese reaction in the east. But such monocausal reasoning obscures later British policy towards Tibet, which in the final analysis was guided by the idea of a Chinese-guarded bastion against a perceived Soviet-Russian threat in Central Asia. Only with the Chinese defection towards the communist camp, did it suddenly become clear that the whole geopolitical and strategic set-up had failed, landing Tibet in a less than enviable position after 1950.

It is not the place here to analyse extensively the course of events in Tibet after the Chinese took over. Suffice it to say that the Sino-Tibetan 'honeymoon' did not bring the peaceful modernization of Tibetan society the Chinese had hoped for. In fact, dissension in eastern Tibet, from where rebellious activity has been reported as early as 1952, developed into open revolt, culminating in the siege and destruction of the Litang monastery in 1956 (Andrugtsang 1973). From that time on, there was open and considerable rebellion in Kham, probably compounded by KMT and CIA intrigue (Mullin 1975, Grunfeld 1987:127-128, 147-160). 1959 saw the long expected outburst of violence in the Lhasa area of Central Tibet, and in the confusion that followed, the Dalai Lama managed to escape to India. His flight, and that of many Tibetan refugees after him, heralded a scaling-up of Tibetan resistance, which was put down ruthlessly by the Chinese. After the revolt of 1959 China launched an all-out campaign to integrate Tibet fully in the Peoples Republic (Karan 1976:36-51) a process physically made worse by the Red Guards' rampage through Tibet after 1966. All but a handful of the thousands of monasteries and temples were destroyed 'many taken down brick by brick until not a trace was left' (Grunfeld 1987:181). The material but more so the psychological scars of the Cultural Revolution in Tibet have seriously contributed to the seemingly unbridgeable gap between the Tibetans and the Chinese. However, an independent Tibet seems an unlikely option for the future, if only for the uncompromising stand the Chinese communists have taken against any form of political liberalization. Perhaps, under changed circumstances, a Tibet with a greater degree of autonomy could be possible (Thurston 1988:72) but it would still be a country very much within the Chinese perception of a geopolitical world order.

The historical literature about twentieth-century Tibet has of late been enriched by a number of substantial books and articles. Besides the 'detached' point of view represented by the former British diplomat Richardson (1984) an even more detached and independent analysis of the rise of progressive forces in Tibet during the first half of the twentieth century, is the excellent book by Stoddard (1985). This is a rich and original study deserving close scrutiny (cf. Kvaerne 1987). Another conspicuous contribution to the recent history of Tibet is Grunfeld (1987), though his occasionally uncritical use of sources detracts from its value. Nevertheless it brings up much hitherto neglected information, generally strengthening the Chinese interpretation of events in Tibet after 1950. An equally thorough analysis of the historical and legal status of Tibet is Van Walt van Praag (1987). Valuable specialist contributions to the period under review are: Teichman (1922), Sperling (1976), Nyman (1976, 1983), and Mehra (1974, 1976). The well-known book by Avedon (1984) is controversial and the author's throughout pro-Tibetan point of view (see also Avedon 1987) has met with a fair amount of criticism (Clarke 1988). Goldstein's substantial book on the political history of Tibet, 1913-1951 (Goldstein 1989), is a mine of written and oral sources for the period concerned. And always Singh (1988a,1988b) should be consulted.

From frontier to boundary

For a long time in history Tibet can be regarded as to have fallen outside the effective territorial control of China though not outside the Chinese perception of a geopolitical world order (Ginsburg 1969:335). In fact, Tibet did not enter clearly into Chinese territorial policy until Ch'ing times, and it is only from the early eighteenth century onwards that Chinese pressure in the Sino-Tibetan borderlands made itself more strongly felt. The Chinese *ambans* in Lhasa, however, did not amount to more than a token presence.

A useful conceptual distinction in the discussion of the geopolitics of Tibet is that between frontier and boundary. According to Kristof, elaborating on ideas put forward by Sir Henry McMahon in 1935 (Lamb 1964:14) and in outline already by Curzon (1908), a frontier is an outward-oriented march land, a border area in which the effective territorial control of the central state is limited. It is also an area of potential expansion, that of a forward-moving culture, bent on occupying the whole belt in front (Kristof 1959: 270-271). A boundary, by contrast, is an inward-looking 'bound', a sharp dividing line, incorporating territories under the exclusive jurisdiction of a modern state. With the changing territorial nature of the state, in the sense of a fully exercised national sovereignty within sharply defined limits, it comes as no surprise that a regular trait of former frontier areas has been their transformation into fixed boundaries. However, the historical purpose of Chinese geopolitical policy was to control the frontier rather than to obliterate it (Lattimore 1951:240).

This frontier-boundary transformation is clearly demonstrated by the events following Indian independence in 1947, and especially the communist takeover in China in 1949. Until that time, the specific nature of the Tibetan administration, as well as the inaccessibility of the mountainous terrain, had produced not a few anomalies and ambiguities in the Himalayan region, unsuspected at earlier times but acquiring substance with the Chinese occupation of Tibet in 1950 (Lamb 1964, Woodman 1969). Chinese road building in southern Tibet in the late fifties and the concomitant military buildup left India no other choice than fundamentally reassessing its northern frontier policies (Van Eekelen 1964). This meant doing away with earlier British policy in the Himalayan borderlands,which had produced a fossilizing effect, reducing the force of direct contact and the necessity of boundary-making (Kirk 1962:164). Already in 1950 the anachronistic Rana regime in Nepal had been removed, and in due time Sikkim and Bhutan were forced into closer defensive pacts with India, the former being eventually forced to merge with India in 1975 (Gupta 1975, Shukla 1976, Singh 1985). However, major zones of direct Sino-Indian confrontation remained, ultimately leading to short border wars in Ladakh, and along the McMahon line in the eastern Himalaya in 1962 (Bhargava 1964, Woodman 1969:278-301, Barpujari 1981:296-334). The open hostilities that were involved, remain a perfect illustration of the bid for power in a shrinking frontier area (cf. Ganguly 1989).

However, the wish to establish a clear boundary line in the Himalaya, though understandable from a Chinese and Indian point of view, overlooked the fact that the Himalayan region has functioned in the past not merely as a barrier but as a geographical region in its own right (Macdonald (ed.) 1982, Macdonald 1987:3). What the Chinese and Indian politicians and cartographers, intent on fixing an unambiguous line on the map in an area of difficult terrain failed to appreciate, was that in fact neither China nor India could claim 'exclusive parentage' of Himalayan societies. The single boundary line was therefore a typical lowlander's concept neglecting economic and cultural realities in the wider frontier region (Kirk 1962:156). Notwithstanding the above, the Himalayan border area, having always been characterized by patterns of functional economic integration, and for that purpose an undivisible region, was transformed into an almost impenetrable boundary after 1962. Centuries-old patterns of trade and communication across high mountain passes ceased to exist overnight and it was not until the early 1980s that the first traders and pilgrims were tentatively allowed to set foot on Tibetan soil again. Yet the frontier-boundary transformation is too real to expect a return to earlier conditions.

The Sino-Tibetan border area provides us with an altogether different story. As earlier referred to, the Sino-Tibetan encounter in the eastern part of Tibet during much of the opening decades of the twentieth century, followed by full-blown occupation in the 1950s, literally erased a sensitive frontier area between China and Tibet. Already in 1904, the Chinese had moved forward in the eastern Tibetan states of Chala, Litang and Ba, causing the inhabitants to rise, often at the price of the total destruction of their monasteries and the extermination of its monk populations. The recapturing of some of these Chinese-held lands after the fall of the Manchu empire in 1911 and the following Sino-Tibetan peace treaty as negotiated by Teichman in 1918, established a provisional border line which ran from the Upper Salween near Menkong via Batang to the Upper Yangtse valley (Teichman 1922:47, map 4; see also Figure 2). This line held out to about 1929. After that date, desultory fighting caused minor alterations in the effective boundary to occur but the real territorial shake-up occurred only after the Chinese frontal attack in 1950.

We know very little of what really happened in large parts of the Sino-Tibetan border area, especially for the period after 1950. But in terms of geopolitical status, it is obvious that a formerly real but shifting boundary in a frontier area under strain, has now been replaced by full Chinese sovereignty in the area. The need for a fixed line on the map has disappeared under these circumstances. All this in sharp contrast to the, in places, still contested Himalayan boundary. It is the differential nature of these frontier transformations and its inevitable political-economic consequences for regional organization, that will provide us with an analytical focus in the chapters to come.

3

THE REGIONALITY OF TIBET

The Tibetan geopolitical experience as described in the previous chapter has basically been presented as a low-profile theoretical affair. History by its contingent nature, does not lend itself easily to hard-and-fast views on the rise and demise of states, whether rooted in models of coercive force or cosmological symbolism. Moreover, it would be a mistake to conceive of geopolitical processes as a set of reified reins, sufficient in itself to guide the course of a particular regional history. The message seems clear enough. No premature massaging of facts, no manipulation by exclusion, but the informed ordering of lived realities as conditioned by a variety of societal and geohistorical universes.

The term universe is used here as an analytical tool to indicate a set of related elements relevant to the discussion of a particular problem. Our problem is to lay bare the geostructural characteristics of a particular regional history. Notwithstanding the indivisible nature of human lived reality and the general interwoven nature of universes, a single-aspect universe can be put under the microscope for analytical purposes, as has been done in chapter 2. However, we should not ignore its relations to other universes. Thus, when we speak of the geopolitical history of Tibet, we necessarily imply questions about its economy, its society, and its culture. From a regional geographic point of view this means that the character of a particular region, or the 'regionality' of a place, is seldom if ever defined by the course of its geopolitical history alone. In fact, the concept of regionality stands for the recognizable identity of a particular history of human groups at the intersection of an interlocking whole of locational-physical, political-economic, and socio-cultural universes. It is therefore much more than a single-universe regionality. The idea of a regional identity as defined above, supersedes older, chorologically-oriented ideas about the region as an a-historical container of place-bound facts and tends in its application to discard regional inventories in favour of narrative-like representations of evolving regional life. Yet, regionality, by the very locational-physical quality of human life, necessarily gains shape around a number of 'earth-bound' characteristics that change only slowly through time. The physical expression of this 'boundedness' is precipitated in a set of nodes and routes, which gives a particular regionality a 'geographicity' of its own (De Bruijne 1976:40). Tibetan regionality too, is grounded in a set of establishments and movements, which for want of a better term, may be conventionally labelled 'regional structure'. But it is a regional structure in motion, the outcome of an ongoing interplay between geographical context and human historical life, between structure and social agency.

The concept of structure stands for something arranged in a definite pattern of organization, while social agency is the force of human action through which socially ordered regularities are brought about. Thus, the question of regionality becomes one of finding out the way in which a specific regional structure in interaction with social agency gives pattern to an unbroken flow of localized events. The concept of social agency as the historical evolvement of human groups also allows us to see these localized events as the manifestation of value-oriented action (see chapter 1). The real problem here is the differential realization of value-oriented action by human beings in interaction with their regional structure. Human history is therefore not a loose succession of 'wild cards', but a contingent sequence of events, that is, conditioned but not determined by the structural characteristics of the universes upon which they draw. As human life is first and foremost social agency in interaction with regional structure, there is necessarily a sort of 'structuration' an intrinsically historical process which gives structural form to a particular regionality. Thus the above call for narrative-like representations of evolving regional life is also a call for a structural representation, one in which the essential 'boundedness' of human life has been taken into account (Van Paassen 1976, 1981, Baker 1984, Pred 1984, Driver 1988).

Regionality and Braudelian geohistory

In a way, the emphasis on the regionality of human life is related to the structural history as put forward by the French school of Annaliste historians, which rose to prominence after World War II (Iggers 1975:43-79, Bourdé et Martin 1983:171-200, Burke 1990). Having their roots in the geographical *tradition vidalienne* (Berdoulay 1981), the Annalistes rejected the idea of history as a loose sequence of political events, and argued for the structured nature of human reality as conditioned by its geographic and socio-economic settings. The conception of history as fully contingent process was suspect, and individual action was necessarily embedded in durable structures.

Braudel, as one of the main propagators of this 'new' geohistorical faith, explicitly tried to incorporate the dynamics of the material world into his work. Introducing a conceptual triad of *durées*, three kinds of time that link the temporal to the geographical and socio-economic world, he laid the analytical foundation for his two-volume *La Méditerranée et le monde méditerranéen à l'époque de Philippe II* (first edition 1949, second revised edition 1966). Two decades later, he used this tripartite division again in his *Civilisation matérielle, économie et capitalisme, XVe - XVIIIe siècle* (three volumes 1979), though cast in a slightly different mould. First came the *courte durée*, the history of short, rapid oscillations and events, which Braudel largely equated with political life. He did not really appreciate the latter, doubting the lasting imprint of such an *histoire événementielle*. History, according to Braudel, was primarily made at two other levels, that of the *moyenne durée*, the slowly changing patterns of social and economic development and the *longue durée* which sought to grasp an almost immobile history of man's relations with the milieu surrounding him. The idea of a *moyenne durée* was closely associated with the notion of *conjoncture*, a complex of waves of intermediate length like price curves, interest rates and demographic progressions. But beneath the waves of *conjoncture* lay the history of deep-seated structures: geographical, biological, as well as mental (Braudel 1958:731). Braudel definitely favoured the *longue durée*, the long-term secular trend of societal development, with the partly cyclical and 'conjonctural' changes as a good second (Braudel 1958, Hexter 1972:503-505, Kinser 1981:70-72, Kirby 1986). It must be said in fairness, that most critics doubted the feasibility of such a project, and many of them came to the conclusion that the plan of superimposing *durées* did not always or often work, because the wholesale configuration of all elements involved lay beyond the grasp of a single individual (Hexter 1972: 532, Kinser 1981:77-78). In defence of Braudel it may however be argued that his emphasis on the *longue durée* has made historians more aware of the 'geographicity', the locational-physical boundedness of human life which changes only slowly through time.

As Braudel's emphasis is generally on the material aspects of human life, culture does not loom large in his analyses. Although lip service is paid to the *ordre culturel* in the third volume of his *Civilisation matérielle* (Braudel 1979 III:51-55), the binding power of religious and political structures are under-exposed in his work (cf. Hexter 1972:519-520). This has certainly to do with the personal predilections of Braudel. His conception of history is starkly coloured by his 'exchangist' view of human life (Tilly 1984:69), and in a way by his preoccupation with long-distance trade, which makes him first and foremost an economic historian. At the same time, he recognized the importance of culture (Braudel 1966 II:95-163), but left it to others to trace the intricacies of it.

One of the most interesting attempts to give culture a structural place in the analysis of 'le phénomène humain total' at the level of a civilization is to be found in the work of the French culture historian Paul Mus. In his 'Projet d'un ouvrage sur les civilisations de l'Asie du Sud-Est' (Mus 1977:109-121), he presents a way of looking at the Southeast Asian world, in which an ethno-geographical base ('le *socle* qui n'est pas exclusivement économique') gains substance by its historical interaction with a kind of cultural superstructure ('le *rajout*'), which makes the base essentially into a culturally moulded substrate.

The process of cultural moulding at the level of a civilization takes the form of political centralization supported by elaborate ritual in order to ensure the historical continuity of a *noyau-pilote,* a kind of ceremonial centre where the holders of power renew their cosmic-political energy (cf. Geertz 1980:123-124, and his concept of the 'theatre state'; see also Wheatley 1971). However, earlier in this chapter, I have already expressed my doubts about the explanatory power of single-aspect phenomena hailing from only one analytical universe. Precisely because the survival of the *noyau-pilote* can only be understood by looking at the regional structure in which it is embedded, the question of geostructural form forces itself on our discussion. Mus recognizes this problem by admitting that at the socio-political level of a kingdom, centralization, next to civilizational influence, is also a function of urban development, of rural-urban differentiation, and of material support for the centre in exchange for protection, both in terms of mental-religious satisfaction and physical protection (Mus 1977:112). At the supraregional level, the historical viability and continuity of the *noyau-pilote* can only be guaranteed by its integration into long-distance trade networks, facilitating movements of luxury products (ibid.:118). The latter turn in Mus's argument reminds us very much of Braudel's 'exchangist' view of human life as earlier referred to.

Because of Braudel's almost exclusive focus on commercial exchange in both *La Méditerranée* and *Civilisation matérielle*, he moved, naturally enough, to affirm the primary historical importance, if not the decisive role of towns and routes (Braudel 1966 I:253-254, 1979 I:421ff., Kinser 1981:75, Claval 1988:402). As geographicity in terms of towns and routes is closely related to the generation of movement and vice versa, he also introduced the blanket concept of an *espace-mouvement*, an area, in which the spatial and historical coherence of its movements makes it into a whole (Braudel 1966 I:253-254). Actually, the concept of an *espace-mouvement* should be seen as a prelude to Braudel's later idea of an *économie-monde*, as introduced by him in the third volume of his *Civilisation matérielle* (Braudel 1979 III:12). An *économie-monde*, according to Braudel, is an economically autonomous part of the world, essentially capable of being self-sufficient. Its spatial structure is subject to several general rules, the most important being those that have to do with the changing geographical extent of an *économie-monde* through time, the dominance patterns of its major urban centres, and the hierarchical nature of its composite zones (ibid.:12-33).

In an Asian setting and application, Braudel, somewhat surprisingly, distinguished only one *économie-monde*. Actually, he calls it a *super-économie-monde*, which marches under the rather illogical name of *Extrême-Orient* (Far East), because it comprises the subregional economies, or rather the *économies-mondes*, of both India and China, the Malayan world acting as a pivot of exchange (ibid.:451). Tibet in this view is thought to have been linked to the long-standing *économie-monde* of China, as were Korea, Indo-China, Yunnan and Mongolia (ibid.:14). India, although a great national market, is thought of as less integrated than the Chinese one, and only appeared more clearly on the international scene with the rise of British India. According to Braudel, Tibet may be seen as part of a diffuse frontier zone enveloping, or at least bordering, the Chinese core area. Such theorizing highlights once more the 'march' character of Tibet, and by implication the existence of *zones neutres* - areas, districts, or *pays*, outside the regular network of exchanges (ibid.:30-31). Thus Tibet, in addition to being a geopolitical frontier zone, as outlined in chapter 2, also was an economic-geographic periphery in Braudelian terms, linked up with the fortunes of its neighbouring *économies-mondes*.

The idea of fluctuating prosperity of an *économie-monde* in response to a long-term secular trend, although in itself insufficiently understood (ibid.:61-63), is an attractive complementary feature of Braudel's theorizing, as it allows for the historical dynamics of regional organization to be incorporated in our analysis. The prosperity, for example, of Tibeto-Himalayan economy and society in the seventeenth century, was undoubtedly linked to the flourishing of the adjacent Indian and Chinese *économies-mondes* (ibid.:420-452). When by the beginning of the nineteenth century, an overall decline had set in, especially in China, Tibet too, gradually lost in economic importance, only to be drawn slowly into the orbit of a rising British-Indian *économie-monde*.

Next to the relative neglect of culture, the second dimension where Braudel's analysis does not fully succeed is that of the incorporation of short-term political upheaval, and, to a lesser extent, that of medium-term geopolitical change. I deliberately use the word 'perhaps' here, because the relevance and repercussions of political change at the level of analysis of an *économie-monde* may be regarded as less to the point. Yet it is precisely because of the fact that the level of analysis of this study lies well below that of an *économie-monde*, I think it necessary to incorporate the geopolitical dimension in our analysis. Not in terms of empire, as may be relevant at the level of an *économie-monde*, but rather in relation to the state as a political-administrative structure with enough organizational power to wage war over a variety of internal and external conflicts. It is indeed the state with its accepted or rejected monopoly of power, which continues to shape, or to plague for that matter, human life at national, as well as regional levels.

In this section we have discussed the major structural characteristics of Braudelian geohistory as to be found in his two major works. Moving freely between his *Méditerranée* and his *Civilisation matérielle*, we have selected those concepts which contribute to a better understanding of the long-term structural changes in the regionality of a particular society. We have seen how a given set of towns and routes may be viewed as a spatially bounded whole, which, by the coherence and continuity of its movements, acquires an identity of its own. Finally, we have introduced Braudel's concept of an *économie-monde* as an historically traceable economic macroregion, which governs the long-term changes of its subordinated regions.

Braudel's emphasis on the historical character of various *économies-mondes*, makes him sceptical about the explanatory power of an all-embracing and all-penetrating capitalist world-system, as for example developed by Wallerstein (1974a, 1974b). His objection to Wallerstein's vision is that it tends to explain away, in a top-down direction, much of the geographical diversity and historical contingency which Braudel, despite his attempts at a structural approach, takes for granted. Braudel in a bottom-up direction, discovers as it were various and very distinct *économies-mondes*, the historical dynamism of which answers to a large extent the coherence and autonomy of its internal relations. Thus, he avoids the Eurocentrism of Wallerstein, who tries to impress on his readers the omnipresence of a Europe-centred world-capitalist development, in which the people outside Europe are denied a geography and a history of their own (Asad 1987, Kearns 1988). Braudel, a professional historian steeped in the *tradition vidalienne*, refuses to fall in that trap. He therefore only reluctantly admits to the existence of an *économie-mondiale* (Braudel 1979 III:12), some sort of 'economy of the world' which however he considers conceptually less important than his historical *économies-mondes* (Braudel 1977:80-81).

The problem of culture has been briefly discussed too, and we have seen that Braudel's economism does not generally allow for sufficient attention to the binding power of culture. The present author hopes not to fall in *that* trap. The role of geopolitics too, seems underexposed, and at the level of analysis of the Tibetan polity deserves fuller discussion. This happened to be the substance of chapter 2 of this study. Thus, the basic ordering principles in this survey of Tibetan regionality are firstly, its relative cultural-historical homogeneity in terms of language, religion, and way of life, secondly, its geographicity as precipitated in its network of monasteries, towns and routes, and thirdly, its wider regional setting in terms of adjacent *économies-mondes* and their specific geohistorical structures.

Tibet as a culture region

In a regional geographic sense, Tibet is not only defined by a shared geopolitical experience within some vaguely defined Central Asian boundaries, neither is it only a sort of appendix to the great historical *économies-mondes* of Asia, it is also a culture region in its own right. The nature of a particular regionality as defined by the cultural universe from which it springs, deserves fuller elaboration than is generally believed. Even Braudel, though not fascinated by the problem of culture (Burke 1990:38-39) recognized the importance of mental-cultural structures of *longue durée* (Braudel 1958:732).

The physical expression of Tibetan regionality in terms of culture, its cultural 'geographicity' so to speak, can be approached from two different angles. Firstly, there is the spatial extent of the culture region as defined by a number of cultural markers. Secondly, there is the way in which Tibetan culture expresses itself through its principal establishments and movements. The first implies basically an inquiry into the zonal extent of dominant patterns of communication and ways of life. The second requires a closer look at the mechanism through which Tibetan culture, in particular in its religious aspect, came to yield the monastic 'geographicity' for which Tibet has become so renowned.

In terms of a particular way of life, the importance of culture has obviously to do with the long-term development of a set of shared ideas, concepts, and values in relation to the material world in which they took shape. In fact, the classical Vidalian concept of *genre de vie*, as a cultural-ecologically determined life-style, rested in the permanence of its material relations, notwithstanding later conceptual problems in view of an industrializing and urbanizing world (Vidal de la Blache 1911a, 1911b, 1913, Sorre 1948). But it was above all a permanence of techniques (Gourou 1973:17-52) and less an overarching structure of ideational values and coextensive communication.

The two basic *genres de vie* in Tibet are sedentary agriculture on the one hand, and full pastoralism on the other. Although nobody knows exactly the proportion of herdsmen to sedentary farmers in historical Tibet, not to mention all shades of mixed activity in between, there is no question of minimizing the importance of nomadic pastoralism. Nomads are to be found everywhere and contribute an essential part to Tibet's diet and clothing. The English botanist and professional Tibet traveller Kingdon Ward even maintains that Tibet should primarily be looked upon as a grazing country (Kingdon Ward 1948:60) and indeed, many scientific reports and travel accounts have impressively given evidence of the existence of a nomad 'empire', in particular along the inner rim of the Changtang plateau, the grassland flats of the Tsaidam basin and the rolling valleys of Amdo. Yet, for all that, a certain predominance of sedentary agricultural areas seems evident, at least near the larger cultural centres (Stein 1987:67).

Thus, underlying the wider Tibetan culture region is an ecological complex of yak-dominated pastoralism in association with a barley and buckwheat-based sedentary agriculture. These respective *genres de vie* also canalize social life. Social organization on the basis of a shared fund of socio-cultural knowledge, provides a set of systematic rules for contacts in daily-life situations between farmers and herdsmen. They recognize each other as Tibetans because they share a set of common social institutions like polyandry, clan exogamy and the indivisible nature of family property. They respect the same taboos, enjoy the same games and swear the same oaths. Theirs is a shared culture, dominated by the basic values and concepts of Tibetan civilization. For both, Tibetan Buddhism is the existential focus of human life, and although the grassland nomads have only a perfunctory interest in the stationary monasteries of their sedentary neigbours, they swear by their movable religious structures, generally large tents with ceremonial equipment, which follow the wanderings of the tribe (Duncan 1952:82-83). Itinerant lamas are held in high veneration and journeys of pilgrimage too, loom large in their religious imagination.

In terms of zonal homogeneity, the geographic grouping of culture has led geographers to the development of the culture region concept. A culture region may be defined as a relatively homogeneous area in which culture finds symbolic expression through a set of shared ideas, concepts, and values, which assume the form of historically communicated experience across smaller or larger areas and within more or less sharply defined boundaries (Wagner and Mikesell 1962, Wagner 1972, Mikesell 1978, Ellen 1988). In a way, the geographical interpretation of a culture region relates to the culture area concept put forward as a heuristic device by ethnographers of diffusionist persuasion earlier this century. They did so in order to map and classify American Indian groups on the basis of their ecological background (Wissler 1917). The weakness of an ecologically defined culture area is its liability to deterministic interpretation and may therefore be better delineated in terms of a shared cultural symbolism. In this way, a culturally defined field of communication and interaction may be constructed, which by its historical-particularist nature overrides ecological differences (Forde 1934:464-465). Historically transmitted culture can usually be traced over a clearly defined area for a longer period of time. It is only in that sense that culture can be correlated with the ecology of a particular area. Not with the naïve intention of reconstructing a history of unilineal adaptation to a given environment but to identify culturally related *genres de vie*, which, despite possible differences in environment, fit together in a wider culture region (cf. the ethno-geographic *socle* of Paul Mus (1977:118).

In the previous chapter the Tibetan culture region has been defined as one in which the inhabitants call themselves Bod-pa, speak a language related to the Lhasa dialect, use the Tibetan script, and adhere to either Bon or traditional Tibetan Buddhism (see Figure 3). The historical communication of this cultural fund may be thought of as a twofold process. Redfield in his *Peasant society and culture*, distinguishes between the 'Great' and 'Little' Tradition as two different ways in which 'civilization' is handed down (Redfield 1956: 70-71). The Great Tradition is cultivated in schools and monasteries, the Little Tradition has more to do with the power of the spoken word and keeps itself going in the lives of ordinary people, and perhaps, behind the screen, of not so ordinary ones. Although the original Redfield-Singer version of GT and LT very much hinges upon the idea of the city and the court as the location of the Great Tradition, and, therefore, is perhaps less applicable outside the great monastic cult centres of Tibet, I feel the concept is useful as a heuristic device.

The Great Tradition in Tibet was basically transmitted via the omnipresent monasteries, where the doctrines of the most important schools of thought in Tibetan Buddhism were being taught. In spite of all their differences, these schools were entirely in agreement on many points, the basic assumption common to all of them being 'the existence of suffering, and man's consequent desire to overcome this suffering and to reach the state referred to as 'liberation' (Tucci 1980:47). All these schools had their own fund of doctrinal histories, hagiographies and ritual practices but except for the popularized forms of the life histories of the greater saints and incarnations, like Atisa, Milarepa, and a few Dalai Lamas, the intricacies of the highly formalized systems of thought escaped the ordinary nomad or farmer. In addition, there were remnants of Bon, representing the oldest, partly pre-Buddhist tradition in Tibet.

The Great Tradition of Tibetan Buddhism reproduced itself in terms of a culture region by the numerous links and lines of communication that existed between the various monasteries, its monks and its learned lamas. The exchange and codification of ideas was made possible by a relatively high degree of mobility. Novices to the monasteries, or successful students, as well as artists, could be sent to parent houses or great centres of learning and education, like Sera near Lhasa or Labrang in Amdo. As the Tibetanist Michael Aris wrote:

> Lamas could escape the confines of the immense power of localism and the little polities in which they were living, by their travels, thus extending the reach of their own schools and of the whole cultural empire of which they formed a part (Aris 1988:9)

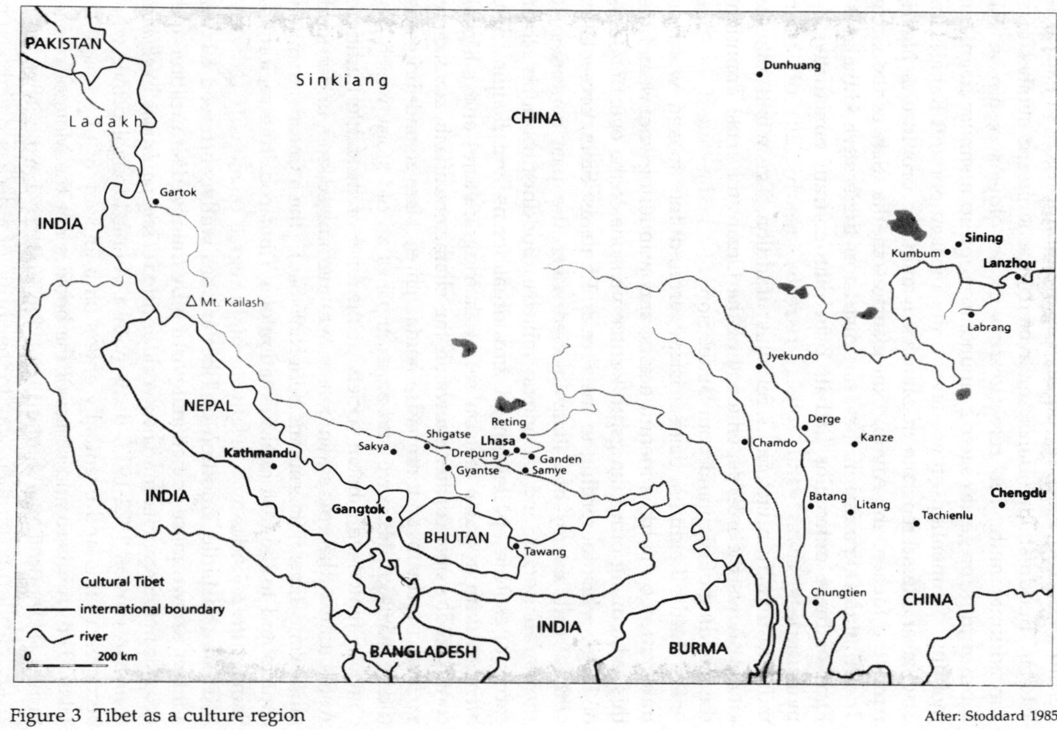

Figure 3 Tibet as a culture region

After: Stoddard 1985

Pilgrimage too, and not only so for the lamas, provided an opportunity for cultural communication over greater distances (cf. Ferrari 1958:xxi). Lhasa, of course, was the ultimate goal of each true Tibetan Buddhist, the Dalai Lama being the supreme symbol of a supraordinal faith. Yet, reminiscences of an older worship in the form of pilgrimages to sacred mountains kept up a similar degree of mobility. To mention only a few of the most important: Kailash (or Tise) near the sacred lake of Manasarovar in the province of Ngari, Amnye Machen in Amdo, Kawakarpo on the Salween-Mekong divide, and Takpa Siri in the Tsari district of the eastern Himalayas. Each of these mountains had its own pilgrim trail, punctuated by monasteries, caves and other retreats, nearly all of them monopolized by a victorious Buddhist tradition. The whole state of affairs shows the interdependency of the Great and Little Tradition, the blending of high and popular religion.

The Little Tradition gained shape around the spoken word as transmitted by bards, itinerant actors, and wandering yogins. In time this led, among other things, to written versions of the epic of 'Gesar of Ling', which according to the French Tibetanist Stein, presents us with a true mirror of Tibetan society over the past centuries. It shows all social and religious milieus: Buddhist ones in their exoteric, esoteric, philosophical and ritual forms and Bonpo ones, blended with popular religion set in their agricultural and pastoral contexts. The epic further shows all the characters of Tibetan society at large: farmers and nomads, feudal chiefs, lamas and brigands (Stein 1959:459). Here we find an example of an old story, which has come to symbolize Tibetan society at the level of the Little tradition. And because the epic's symbolism was recognized and understood all over Tibet (Hermanns 1965:295-346) the Gesar tradition contributed to the historical formation of a Tibetan culture region (cf. Samuel 1992, 1994).

Great and Little Tradition of Tibet are brilliantly portrayed too, in a lesser known piece of fictional writing by the Swedish explorer and geographer Sven Hedin. The work entitled *Tsangpo Lamas Wallfahrt* (German edition 1922-1923) deals with a young Mongol prince who becomes a lama and eventually enters on a journey of pilgrimage to Tibet. The true hero and object of the book is not the Mongol prince turned Tsangpo Lama himself, but the collective experience of a group of pilgrims on their way to the shrine of a deceased eighteenth century Panchen Lama in Central Tibet. The story is pervaded by the spirit of land and life in Inner Asia, and although fictional, shows a better understanding of daily life in Tibet than some of the learned treatises on Tibetan society and culture, if only for the consequent mole's eye view chosen by the author (cf. Kish 1984:106).

The Great Tradition as historically communicated high culture, rested in the case of Tibet in the transmission and elaboration of a particular form of Mahayana Buddhism via an omnipresent system of monasteries. Though Braudel showed a general unwillingness to allow for the autonomy of culture (Burke 1990:51) the question remains to what extent culture as an independent variable of societal organization can be isolated. Thus, in a Tibetan application, we may take up once again the problem which Max Weber formulated already in 1917, about the improbability of a flourishing civilization capable of creating an ever more increasing religious literature and art in a cold desert some 5,000 metres above sea level (Weber 1978:316). If he made the hierarchic, rigidly organized monastic Buddhism of Tibet with its boundless power over the laity into the cornerstone of his argument, he did so because he believed that Tibetan Buddhism as a commonly accepted overarching structure of ideational values and symbols, showed sufficient autonomous power to create in essence a prebendal monastic system. The related but more worldly phrased question as to why the productive surplus went comparatively easy into supporting artistic and scholarly work in the monasteries and into maintaining a relatively opulent life-style for some of the high lamas, remains an intriguing one, and cannot be avoided in any discussion of the mechanism through which Tibetan religion came to yield its particular monastic 'geographicity'.

The above statement of the problem suggests that there existed a sort of 'traditional' Tibetan society, but this is of course social science fiction. Despite the popular image of Tibet as static, its societal set-up showed definite changes over time and can only be understood when these changes are taken into account. In terms of a discussion of Tibetan Buddhism, we have to look then for changes in its philosophical and theological convictions, as well as its ritual procedures, insofar as they shed light on the development of the monastic system in Tibet. The first question to answer is whether Tibetan Buddhism as a particular form of Mahayana Buddhism, can be seen as fundamentally different from other Mahayana traditions, and if so, whether these differences can in one way or another account for the dominant role of the monastery in Tibetan society.

Mahayana Buddhism is that particular form of Buddhism in which the stern struggle for personal Enlightenment, or Buddhahood, is exchanged for the ideal of becoming a *bodhisattva,* a being that has attained the highest levels of purity but compassionately refrains from entering *nirvana* in order to save others. Thus, the normative aim of Mahayana Buddhism is not the personal escape from the suffering of the world, as in Theravada Buddhism, but the ability to free others from their suffering. To become a *bodhisattva* was the supreme ideal of Mahayana Buddhism, especially in its Tibetan form (Snellgrove 1987:60-61). In addition, a strong emphasis on ritual practice developed, in particular in its tantric form. The *tantras* were a body of later Hindu and Buddhist scriptures strongly marked by mysticism and magic. Through tantric ritual, its teachings, procedures and techniques, the layman could cross the liminal threshold of Buddhahood (ibid.:117-294 for the tantric side of Indo-Tibetan Buddhism).

Tantric practice provided a method to an end, and as such needed an instrument for its performance. This was to be found in the person of the tantric teacher, whose rites centred on particular tantric deities. Insofar as the tantric teacher carried out the ritual performance successfully, he could use the released powers of the deity invoked to the benefit of his disciples. In its Tibetan form, access to these superhuman powers was usually mediated through the lamas, masters of religious knowledge and ritual practice. Lamas were distinguished from ordinary monks by their special qualities, be they religious learning, ritual effectiveness, or attainment of Buddhahood. In fact, there were far fewer lamas than monks (Tucci 1980:44).

The literal Sanskrit equivalent of 'lama' is 'guru', a religious teacher in the traditional Indian sense, but Tibetan lamas are also a number of other things. Samuel (1978:52-56) distinguishes four aspects of the lama's role, starting with the lama as guru, i.e. someone who can act as a religious teacher of tantric practice. Next comes the lama as performer of tantric ritual. Indeed, it is the lama's role as ritual performer *par excellence* for the benefit of the lay population, that may be regarded as a specific Tibetan development within the wider framework of Mahayana Buddhism. Lamas of proven sanctity and tantric ability might well attract disciples, and eventually become the head of a monastic establishment. Thus, a third role aspect is the lama as the abbot of a monastery, or in the case of large ones, a high monastic official. The status of abbot paved the way for more worldly power as well, and many abbots became important persons in the Tibetan political system. Finally, there are the so-called 'incarnate lamas', or *tulku*, persons believed to be the reincarnation of dead office-holders. In the sense that the 'incarnate lama' is physically present in Tibetan eyes, and as such presents a 'physical manifestation of Buddhahood', it is impossible to view the devotional aspects of Buddhism in Tibet independently of the cult of the lamas (Samuel 1978:56). All *tulkus*, as mentioned above, are to be considered as Buddhas, in particular as manifestations of specific *bodhisattvas*. They are a kind of 'Living Buddhas', the cult of which became widespread.

In time, acceptance of the doctrine of the reincarnation of lamas became pervasive in Tibetan Buddhism. As such, the highly innovative and unorthodox concept of the 'Living Buddha' may be singled out as one of its main distinguishing features. The first recorded Tibetan *tulku* was probably identified in 1284 (Wylie 1978:580) but the system only gained importance with the rise of the Gelukpas in the fifteenth century (see chapter 2). Over time, the number of 'Living Buddhas' steadily increased, and may at one time have been over a thousand (Samuel 1978:55). Not all 'Living Buddhas' were of equal status. Generally, the older the line of incarnation, the higher the status. Frequently, lineages were traced back to the founder of a particular monastery, and in the case of the Dalai Lamas even came to include four of the early kings who are associated with the introduction of Buddhism in Tibet. In a political sense, the Dalai Lama's claim to rule Tibet was strengthened by the assertion that 'the Dalai Lamas *were* in fact the greatest of the early Tibetan kings returned to life' (ibid.:55).

Having arrived at this point of the argument, the mechanism by which Tibetan religion came to yield its monastic geographicity should become clear. Tibetan Buddhism has a number of characteristics which sets it apart from other Buddhist societies. In particular the all-important role of the lamas as religious teachers, performers of ritual, and incarnated *bodhisattvas*, may provide a sufficient explanation for the rise of monastic power in Tibet. Only the lamas could act significantly to work salvation from the earthly 'wheel of existence'. The supreme mediating function, in particular of 'Living Buddhas', made the layman into a willing contributor of the material infrastructure needed to support 'lamaism'. The communities of monks attached to these charismatic lamas may be explained by the wish to live in close proximity to these sources of salvational power. Quite a few are the stories of a run away youngster in search for his spiritual teacher (cf. Wallace's edition of lama Geshe Rabten autobiography, Wallace 1980:7-11). The Search for the Guru is certainly a Tibetan theme (e.g. Milarepa) and although Geshe Rabten seemed more concerned with practising *dharma* than finding the teacher as such, his 'root lama' was obviously very important to him (personal communication G. Samuel). Aziz has some nice comments on the root lama in her *Tibetan frontier families* (Aziz 1978:223ff.). Also, many children were given by their parents to the monasteries, in order to gain a more direct access to the fountain of salvation (for a European parallel see De Jong 1995:640-644). In turn, communities of monks made it possible for the layman to make donations, and to obtain religious merit in return.

The place of the monastery in Tibetan society as sketched above, is false insofar as it conceals long-term changes in the position of the lamas and the vitality of monastic life. The rise of the Gelukpas since the fifteenth century and the heyday of their influence in the 'long' seventeenth, undoubtedly fostered the development of a vigorous monastic system. But the following centuries showed that even the strict ethical code of the Gelukpas could not prevent a softening of the monastic ideal. The growing wealth of the monasteries, their increasing involvement in worldly affairs and the loss of hierarchical organization, all worked towards a decline which had become particularly noticeable by the second half of the nineteenth century. By then, their hold over the lay population had occasionally degenerated into heavy-handedness, yet their general function as dispensers of salvational power stood still upright.

Thus, Tibet as a culture region, for a long time generated a semblance of territorial binding power through the shared symbolism of its religion. But the independent role of the monasteries probably also worked against further centralization of political authority. It is even possible that Tibetan Buddhism, through its emphasis on the mediating role of the lama, provided the ideological basis for decentralized forms of religious power, which ultimately proved detrimental for a nascent national unity (cf. Samuel 1982:221). It is another indication why culture cannot be left out of any analysis of Tibetan regionality. The work of Samuel has now culminated in a major study on the role of Buddhism in Tibetan societies (Samuel 1993) which, though not going undebated, has the great virtue of placing Tibetan religion in an anthropological and geohistorical perspective.

The regional structure of Tibet

Tibet may be divided into several large, vaguely bounded areas, whose outlines by and large reflect some sort of regional-economic coherence in terms of nodal organization and related systems of movement. Thus they also reflect a certain historical continuity in terms of Braudel's *espace-mouvement* as earlier referred to, though at a much smaller scale-level. Major areas in this sense are Ladakh, Ngari, Ü-Tsang, Kham and Amdo, all situated, as a kind of meso-regional clusters, on the edge of the Changtang Plateau (see Figure 1). Some of these, like Ladakh and Kham, differ vastly in geographical background, are located as far apart as two thousand kilometres, and have looked for centuries to lands as different as India and China. The relative importance of these areas depended on the extent to which they managed to become local core regions, centres of regional exchange and political power. This partly depended on the productive capacity of the land, and partly on its location in respect of other core regions. If both of these were favourable, and backed up by political and ritual genius, circulation increased, commerce flourished, and market-places multiplied. Together with the absence of war and conflict, these factors decided on the historical continuity of regional clusters of habitation and exchange. In addition, there were regions where Tibetan culture had once taken root, but for reasons of changing relative location increasingly fell outside the regular networks of communication, or perhaps were drawn into competing ones. Regional exchange in these places tended to be of a more extensive nature, religion of a less institutionalized kind, and political overlordship vacillating.

Within these larger clusters of regional habitation and transitional peripheries, a secondary division into smaller localities was the rule. Many a minor plateau area, as well as fertile sections of river valleys and ethnic derelict lands, bore their own names, sometimes overlaid with the broader supraregional labels of live or defunct principalities, major monasteries, or tribal chiefdoms. Each of these *pays* had its own characteristics, depending on the lie of the land and the community that lived in it. 'To every district its own dialect, to every lama his own doctrine' as Kaulback (1939:231) quoted a current Tibetan proverb, a saying which expresses in itself the idea of a distinct place in a world of limited circulation.

One could argue that in a regional-organizational sense, Tibet never developed beyond a cell-like structure, dominated by a hierarchy of greater and lesser monasteries. On these monasteries focused nomad networks, pilgrim itineraries, and regional trade routes, making the average monastic establishment into the basic building block of Tibetan regional organization (Tucci 1980:8-12, 158-162). At the local level, the key position of the monks manifested itself in their hold over the organization of production, the distribution and exchange of labour and occasionally the ownership of extensive lands and herds. At the regional level, monasteries acted often as market-places, the seasonal rhythm of their fairs attuned to the calendar of religious festivals. The largest and most favourably located monasteries were masters in accumulating wealth through the skilful manipulation of pious donors and the organization of long-distance trade ventures. Generally, trade on behalf of the monasteries yielded a substantial revenue and trade monopolies were jealously guarded by the monks. By and large, the monasteries, and certainly the larger ones in their appearance as fully fledged monastic towns, were the major structural components around which Tibetan regionality gained shape.

The ritual authority which formed the basis of this micro-regionality was necessarily supplemented by the mobility of the nomads and the servility of the farmers, the latter more deeply steeped in a tradition of creed and credulity than the former. As a result, the sedentary farmers appear to have been more completely under the domination of the monks than the nomads, yet in some places monasteries had been able to extend their power over entire nomad tribes, ultimately superseding their chiefs or reducing them to a very subordinate position. On the other hand, many tribes and chiefs successfully resisted such ecclesiastical domination (Ekvall 1939:69). Nomads and sedentary farmers were distinguished by location, the nomads occupying the grazing country of the plateaux and the farmers living in the valleys. A 'vertical' trade existed between the two, resting on the local exchange of complementary products. The nomads bartered their salt and animal products for the farmers's grain, but in the fringe lands of Tibet farming and herding were sometimes combined to produce the required livelihood. The really mobile nomads shifted their flocks over considerable distances and, depending on the season, engaged in intermediate forms of long-distance trade. Also, nomads easily and rapidly turned into robbers in times of bad winters or political troubles. Some segments of tribes developed into bands of professional highwaymen, as was for instance the case among the Golok of northeastern Tibet (Roerich 1967:55).

The servility of the sedentary farmers as referred to above, should not be understood in the 'pejorative sense of exploitation always and everywhere'. If Tibetan landed society of the pre-1950s can be labelled 'feudal' in one way or another, it is because in a technical sense the idea of a contract between lord and vassal, in the form of legitimate and accepted surplus appropriation (Bloch 1978:145ff., 450-451) did hold for Tibet. As in medieval Europe the contract took the form of access to land in return for certain services, mostly in terms of labour and a share of the harvest. Both the aristocracy and the clergy acted as landlords, the omnipresence of monastic power in Tibet giving a distinct 'ecclesiastical' flavour to Tibetan feudality (Carrasco 1959:84-120). However, to hint at the technical correctness of an analytical category called feudalism, should not obscure the fact that real exploitation to the detriment of the farmers did occasionally occur. Although feudal-like institutions were counter-balanced by tribal and communal forms of organization (Stein 1987:207), a number of monastic establishments developed into a real 'pest' for the common people - the phrasing is Filchner's (1906:1-2) - and estates of the landed aristocracy too, were not always reminiscent of Arcadia. Yet Chinese allegations current in the 1950s and 60s, that the majority of the Tibetan population was 'downtrodden, oppressed and exploited', a view more or less shared by Grunfeld (1987:11-14) are in need of further substantiation, as indeed is the whole debate on the nature of 'class' in traditional Tibetan society (cf. Goldstein 1989:56-60).

The mobility of the nomad was generally matched by the mobility of the pilgrim. Pilgrimage as a devotional exercise had always been an aspect of Tibetan regionality, based on a restless search for merit. Many were the places where natural energy and magical powers were thought to enrich the pilgrim's *karma*, and mountains, monasteries and caves were the object of many a protracted journey (Blondeau 1960, Dowman 1988, McKay (ed.) (1997b). Near these power-places sprang up a brisk trade in sacred medicinal plants and religious artifacts, carried on by a host of mendicant monks and itinerant traders. Punctuated by the religious calendar of a particular place or establishment, the fair or *mela* attached could well develop into an important seasonal marketplace, characterized by the harmonious blend of commercial enterprise and spiritual devotion. Major festivals could draw numerous pilgrims, and traders of all sorts flocked to the accompanying fairs. Periodicity of the more secularly oriented markets was naturally influenced by population density and aggregate demand. It was also subject to the seasonal going of trails, winter being the preferred time of trade and travel. Some of the more important markets specialized in a limited number of goods and products like tea, wool, and horses. Favourably located break-of-bulk points between major ecozones sometimes developed into small trading towns, which acted as entrepôts and control centres of caravan traffic. Sometimes too, a hierarchy of seasonal *melas* at different altitudes existed in certain transitional areas.

Of a different order were the long-distance trade operations carried out by specialized merchants in luxury goods. Already at the time of what has been labelled 'the early medieval *florissance* in Eurasia' from about 600 to 840 A.D. (Beckwith 1977:89), an increase of international trade in products of low weight but high value had become noticeable in Tibet too, and the following centuries saw the continued importance of long-distance exchange. Gold, musk, and gemstones took first place and were exported to Central Asia, China and India. Besides, many other products found their way to or through Tibet in return. This long-distance trade in luxury goods generated collective and distributive trade patterns focusing on the trading towns and larger monasteries of Tibet. Lhasa, as a major node of exchange, was at the centre of a network of routes leading to the frontier markets of Leh, Kathmandu, Kalimpong, Tachienlu, and Sining. Transit trade via Lhasa emerged as one of the main pillars of Tibetan prosperity, though its importance fluctuated over the ages. The multinational origin of its merchants gave a cosmopolitan flavour to its bazaar area, and the tens of thousands of pilgrims from faraway lands made the population swell considerably at the time of a major festival.

The structural characteristics of Tibetan regionality reported on above should not make us believe that the regional organization of Tibet was either static or homogeneous. On the contrary, far from being frozen groups in an icy and immovable landscape, monks and nobles, farmers and nomads, pilgrims as well as traders, were the main articulating groups between individual activity and the regional stage on which their drama constantly unfolded. Where nodes of group activity gained shape in geographically traceable establishments and movements, something became visible of a particular regional structure bound by its own dynamic parameters. In that sense, Tibet emerged as a multifaceted milieu of human encounters, profoundly historical in its nature, and ultimately dependent on its unique regionality.

The monastic imperative

Historical Tibet and its culturally related border areas cannot be understood in some depth without referring to the monastic background of Tibetan society. From the earliest travel reports onward, it had become clear that monasticism as a way of life held sway in large parts of the Tibetan highlands. The more pressing is the question to what extent and in which way monks and monasteries helped to shape the regionality of Tibet.

An inquiry into the significance of Tibetan monasticism for everyday social and economic life, as well as the regional organization that sprouts from it, requires us to look beyond the received wisdom of travelogues and expedition reports, because the time-specific conventions inherent to that genre may further distort an act of reconstruction and interpretation already difficult enough in itself. Generally the high lamas were out of favour with the writers on Tibet at the turn of the nineteenth century, as indeed was the religious system of 'Lamaism' itself (Bishop 1989:57). In fact, we witness here the head-on collision between two utterly incompatible mental worlds, that of 'medieval' monks in a Tibetan setting on the one hand, and that of 'rationalist' European travellers on the other. The latter, in a way, had the same problems in understanding Tibetan society as confront the modern historian or geographer in interpreting the European medieval world, because their imagination falls short of grasping medieval mentality *tout court*. The idea of a Living Buddha is as alien to the modern mind as the Immaculate Conception. The result is an unnecessarily harsh judgement on the role of monks and monasteries in Tibetan society, which may not have differed much, except in scale, from their European counterparts in medieval Europe. In both settings, the unifying force of their respective cultural symbolisms yielded order and stability in times of weak political overlordship, despite the inevitable excesses inherent to any administrative system of some scale.

The mental world which made Tibetan monasticism flourish was much akin to its European image, in the sense that the search for salvation from the 'wheel of existence' through monastic ritual (Tucci 1980:161) was matched by the Christian monk's incumbent prayer for the repentant sinner, in order to obtain satisfaction (Lawrence 1989:70-71). This basic feature of the medieval religio-penitential system in part explains the eagerness of chiefs and princes to found and endow monasteries in both Tibet and Europe (cf. Southern 1993:95). Moreover, the ideal of renunciation and voluntary poverty appealed primarily to the rich, which emphasized the aristocratic touch in the population of many of the larger monasteries (ibid.:71,156, Carrasco 1959:157, Snellgrove 1987:41). However, and especially in Tibet, there were large sections of ordinary monks performing lesser tasks, comparable to the services rendered by lay brothers to fully ordained and cloistered monks in the European tradition.

The history of monasticism is the history of monastic life between eremitical ideal and cenobitical compromise, between dilution and reform, between extremely secluded localism and free-roving mendicant mobility (see the excellent book by Lawrence, 1989). Although the eremitical tradition always had its followers, it was the cenobitical tradition, or monastery-based collectivity of monks - and occasionally nuns (see Havnevik, n.d., 1990) - which came to be the most common form of monastic life. As Tucci rightly observed:

> The stable residence in monasteries, the obligation to participate in the divine services with their fixed timetable, the strict regulation of all external aspects of life, the memorization of the basic rules and their mastery in conformity with the study precepts - all these tend to force the life of the community into a fixed structure, which preserves the supremacy of the community as a collectivity over its individual members (Tucci 1980:113)

Here Redfield's Great Tradition was guarded, but, as in Europe with the Benedictines, the Cluniacs and the Cistercians, the continual growth of secular power of the Sakyapa, Kagyupa, and in particular Gelukpa monasteries, necessarily led to a considerable softening of the originally strict monastic observance. Monasteries developed into centres of political and economic power, and the combination of the two gave birth to a system of monastic feudalism, which proved to be long-lasting, especially in Tibet. Yet, as in Europe, the monastic community, through its liturgy and ritual, continued first and foremost to assure spiritual assistence to the laity (Lawrence 1989:70ff., Tucci 1980:161). Indeed the structural parallels between Tibetan and medieval European society are such that the French Tibetanist Stein made them into a focal point of discussion in the epilogue to his well-known book on the civilization of Tibet (Stein 1987:206-208). This does not mean that there is a complete institutional similarity between the two societies, but that a related structural order we are used to see in its European guise, has a counterpart in a distinctive Tibetan form.

The one big difference between European and Tibetan monasticism seems to me its scale and its general hold over society. More than in Europe, monasteries in Tibet were an omnipresent feature of regional organization and political-economic dominance. Also, a larger share of the population entered the monastery. Stein (1987:87-88) even gives an estimate as high as one-fifth of the total population. The three great monasteries in the neighbourhood of Lhasa, Drepung, Sera and Ganden, may, at the end of the nineteenth century, have been the home of some 20,000 monks (ibid.:87). When Tucci visited these places in 1948, they were thought to harbour 7,700, 6,600 and 3,300 monks respectively (Tucci 1956:102). In addition, there was a whole score of smaller monasteries (Ferrari 1958:41-48, Henss 1981:171-198, Dowman 1988:38-146). In contrast, the ordinary resident population of Lhasa at the beginning of the twentieth century, numbered probably not more than ten to fifteen thousand (Tsybikoff 1904:735), a figure which may have doubled during the following decades (Tucci 1967:23). The monastery of Tashilunpo near Shigatse is thought to have given shelter to 3,000 monks (Narzounof 1904:239, cf. Kawaguchi 1909:250 - 3,300), the actual number being another indication of the town-like character of the larger Tibetan monasteries (see for their general physical layout and architecture: Mortari Vergara et Béguin 1987). The great monastery of Labrang in Amdo, according to Li An-che (1982:5), could boast of some 3,600 inmates in 1938, while the nearby located Kumbum contained close to 4,000 resident monks and an additional 3,000 lay brothers and travelling monks (Tafel 1914 I:213-214, cf. Filchner 1906:5-6, 20). Several other regionally important monasteries like Litang, Batang, Chamdo and Kandze, each had thousands of monks.

If we compare the above figures with those of the main abbeys of medieval Europe, we have to conclude to a significant difference in scale, in particular at the level of the individual monastery. Cluny, at the height of its power around A.D. 1100, only harboured some three hundred monks. Rievaulx, the Cistercian stronghold in Yorkshire counted hundred and forty choir monks as against five hundred lay brothers at the death of one of its major abbots in 1167 (Lawrence 1989:125,178). Other monastic establishments had generally well under a hundred inmates. And that at a time of widespread religious fervour and general economic and demographic growth in Western Europe. The above figures stand in sharp contrast with those for the larger Tibetan monasteries with their thousands of monks. Also, the share of the monks in the total population was probably much lower. However, a comparison with the Byzantine monastic complex of Athos in Greece should be interesting, but falls outside the scope of this study.

To understand the social and economic role of monasteries, and to explain the almost universal economic success of Buddhist monasticism, it is necessary to hint once more at the mental world in which these institutions took shape. Far from being 'corrupt' and 'degenerate' as some writers with regard to Tibet have tried to make us believe, the monasteries by their function of 'translating' gifts into religious merit for the donors, developed into a kind of storehouses for local goods (R.J. Miller 1961:427-428). These common property funds of individual monasteries were basically drawn from four sources: landed property, herds of large and small livestock, trading goods and interest on loans (Tucci 1980:158). Though this may sound quite worldly, and abuse can certainly not be ruled out, the basic effect of the monastic movement was positive. As Murphy in his 'Comment' on Robert Miller (1961) states:

> The monastery brought some social order and peace to Inner Asia and provided sanctuary for persons and for goods. They concentrated capital and acted as primitive banks. They facilitated travel and trade by their better protected caravans which cheapened transport costs, and by offering hospitality to travellers (R.J. Miller 1961:441)

An important source of income for the monastery was land. Landed property in the form of estates or village land resulted in part from repeated endowments, in part from the incorporation of lands of other monasteries, and in part from colonization efforts in frontier areas (Carrasco 1959:123, R.J. Miller 1961:442, Tucci 1980:158, cf. Lawrence 1989:128-129 for Western European parallels). The feudalism of monastic estates enters the picture where it concerns the necessary labour to work these lands. Generally, as in medieval Europe, these properties were managed in much the same way as the great estates belonging to secular lords. The pioneering survey of Carrasco (1959), makes it clear that peasants stood in various degrees of dependence to monasteries, but generally lived under better conditions than the tax-paying peasants and farm-servants under a secular chief (Carrasco 1959:149). The majority of them, however, were unable to rise above subsistence level. Pastoralists largely escaped monastic domination, but for the sale of their produce still depended on their relations with the monks. The small nomad country of Bangba Bayang, for example, annually bartered its yak, sheep, and dried meat for wheat and barley at the monastery of Toling Tsurpu, as did the nomads from neighbouring Yangbachen (Combe 1926:112-113; for a visual impression of 'Hyang-pa-chen' see Hayden and Cosson 1927:92-93).

In addition to the barter with the local herdsmen, monasteries derived a variable but not inconsiderable income from trade, which consisted primarily of the buying and selling of goods from China and India. As the Japanese monk Ekai Kawaguchi put it 'priests are not too proud to deal with secular dollars and cents, and monasteries often trade on a large scale' (Kawaguchi 1909:458). This occasionally amounted to greed, but in general, trade was just another means to make the monastic establishment into a viable economic unit. The involvement of Tibetan monasteries in trade will further be dealt with in the following chapter.

In principle, each monastery formed a self-existent and if possible self-sufficient entity. Yet further examination of the monastic system reveals an intricate network of parent houses and dependent convents which came into being as a result of the way in which about a dozen mother monasteries branched out in the course of Tibetan history (B.D. Miller 1961:201, Tucci 1980:160). But, as Beatrice Miller rightly points out, this is of course a somewhat simplified picture. In fact, in many instances major subsidiary monasteries had dependent branches in their own right, so that a daughter monastery served locally or regionally as a mother monastery (B.D. Miller 1961:201). There is a kind of functional hierarchy, then, which despite its obscurity in the older monastic orders, very much constituted a web of doctrinal and partly economic control in the reformed ones, linking the local monastery to the big monastic complexes in Central and East Tibet.

An illustration of the social and economic role of Tibetan monasteries in their traditional-feudal and functional-hierarchical setting, although now under great strain, is still to be found in the North-Indian district of Ladakh. As in neighbouring Tibet, the population of Ladakh is predominantly Buddhist in its Tibetan form and as such the *gompa* or monastery plays a pivotal role in everyday district life. Monasteries are the vital structural components of a regional organization based on a mixture of sedentary agriculture and livestock farming, as well as some full pastoralism (Carrasco 1959:4-10, 159-180, Dollfus 1989:19-33). As there is a clear three-tier hierarchy of *gompas* (Singh 1977:355), ranging from the village monastery via a few intermediate establishments to the major monastic complexes in Central Ladakh, the Buddhist clergy controls, to a considerable extent, the economy of the district through ownership of land and through exploitation of its resources (Carrasco 1959:175-178, Grimshaw 1983:124-126, Tsarong 1987). Thus, groups of villages are tied to a medium-sized *gompa*, which in turn is functionally linked to one of the main *gompas* located in or near the Indus Valley. Karsha *gompa*, for example, the most important monastery of Zangskar, and harbouring some 150 monks, is upwards related to the monastic complex of Likhir in Central Ladakh, but downwards in the hierarchy controls a domain equalling 1983 km^2, of which 97 ha of arable land. Within this domain, thirty villages are economically tied to Karsha (Neyroud 1985:279, cf. Singh 1977: 359-360, 368-369, table 1, who gives 18 villages which control 107 ha of arable land). The linkage systems involved (ibid.:365-366) imply an intraregional system of movements, not conditioned by external circumstances, and wholly dependent on local and regional exchanges. The example of Ladakh is interesting, because it shows a regional organization along traditional lines, which stands now under great pressure in Tibet proper.

In summary, monasteries constituted the basic building blocks of traditional Tibetan society. Their economic success and their social acceptance rested in their functional ability to translate economic gain into religious merit. Their feudal hold over a basically land-based society differed in essence not substantially from medieval Western European examples, except in scale. Only very slowly their position was being eroded by the rise of other forms of regional economic life, in which towns and international trade came to play an increasingly prominent role. It is to the latter issues that we turn now.

Of towns and routes

Although speculation must play an important part in any interpretation of urban origins, the case of Tibet is sufficiently well known to allow for an outline of how things actually evolved. In one way, it may be argued that the monastic movement and the founding of monasteries throughout the Tibetan highlands precluded a genuine urban development. In another, it may equally well be argued that the monasteries formed a substitute for urban life, and in fact were the particular expression of urban form in Tibet.

Towns, in the sense of free places, not dominated by ecclesiastic rules and discipline, more open to economic enterprise, and located at accessible places, were few in Tibet (Macdonald 1929:248). What towns existed had grown up around a celebrated monastery, or near a feudal *dzong*, the fortified residence of a local military aristocrat (for an interesting example see Rawling 1905a, 1905b, plate facing page 198: Lhatse fort and monastery; see also Hähnert 1925:151-153). Commerce consisted in supplying these towns and monasteries with agricultural products in exchange for articles of local manufacture and, to a certain extent, foreign luxury goods. The latter low weight for value commodities occasionally trickled down to monasteries and feudal strongholds in the form of gifts by pilgrims, or the merchandise of itinerant traders. Only when increased circulation, in itself a sign of greater political stability, made possible real long-distance trade ventures, the secular town gained in importance. Initially, the markets had been held in the locational shadow of the monastery or the *dzong*, which provided the necessary protection for its traders (Mumford 1961:251, cf. Tafel 1914 II:312-313, who mentions the *Klosterfriede* of Labrang). With growing security, and perhaps as a result of the sheer size of the transactions involved too, separate trade villages developed at a certain distance from the monastery as was for example the case with Sangtawa near Labrang (Fletcher 1979:29, Henss 1981:238), and Lusar near Kumbum (Rockhill 1891b:58-62, Rijnhart 1901:9, Filchner 1906:21-24, Maillart 1937:65). Near the *dzongs*, or feudal strongholds, town-like settlements appeared, and at junctions of great trade routes, godowns, caravanserais, and customs houses began to form the nucleus of many a town in genesis. If conditions were stable, some well-placed trade villages gradually acquired urban functions, and the subsequent history of many a town was largely concerned with the emancipatory struggle of its merchants to obtain the rights and privileges of a free town dweller. By virtue of their cosmopolitanism, and perhaps their wealth, this was easier for foreign traders than for Tibetan ones. Thus, foreign traders came for a long time to dominate the Tibetan long-distance trade scene. It is here that we find a first indication of the distinction between regional exchange focusing on lesser monasteries and local strongholds, and a long-distance trade in luxury goods, which largely bypassed the traditional places of exchange, concentrating on the larger fairs and towns newly arisen (cf. Mumford 1961:255-256 and Pirenne 1969:35-38 for European parallels).

Lhasa as the focus of absolute political and religious power was one such place (cf. Paul Mus's concept of *noyau-pilote*; Mus 1977:118). Its relative size, its cosmopolitanism, its trade, its wealth, and above all its sacredness, reflected its status as the *primus inter pares* among Tibetan towns. Economically speaking, Lhasa was essentially a city of transit trade (cf. Kozlow 1925:262, Chakrabarti 1990:16). As direct communication between India and China, though not altogether impossible (see Pelliot 1904, Kingdon Ward 1927, Kuo 1941), was hampered by the inaccessibility of the jungle-clad mountain terrain of the Burma-Tibet-Yunnan triangle, the preferred route was through Lhasa and its subsidiary towns: not an easy journey either, but a comparatively safe one for goods and traders. Commercial interaction across these vast distances was basically a stepwise middlemen trade, with fixed trading communities in the larger entrepôt places. In this way, groups of Ladakhi, Kashmiri, Newari and Chinese traders had virtually come to monopolize the entire long-distance trade in Tibet, each community occupying its own niche in Lhasa society, and in a few places elsewhere.

Thus, Lhasa's cosmopolitanism was basically a function of its location as a long-distance trade centre connecting the Indian and Chinese 'wings' of the *super-économie-monde* as earlier referred to. But it also stemmed from Lhasa's position as the Rome of Buddhist Central Asia, which brought pilgrims from the entire Himalayan region, the Sino-Tibetan borderlands, Mongolia, and even Russia, to the sacred capital of Tibet. This pivotal role was already recognized by Bogle towards the end of the eighteenth century when he described Lhasa as 'the centre of communication between distant parts of the world' (Markham 1876:125). In a complementary way, Sir Charles Bell, the British representative in Tibet during the early 1920s, commented on the extraordinary concentration of power in Lhasa, noting that 'more than in most countries, the social, political, and religious activities of Tibet centre in their capital' (Bell 1924b:89-90).

The supreme position of Lhasa as the hub of the Tibetan world is graphically presented in Figure 4, showing a network of towns and routes, spatially centred on the Tibetan capital. Lhasa occupies the proverbial place of the spider in a web spanning the Tibetan highlands from Leh in Ladakh to Tachienlu on the Sino-Tibetan border, and from Sining in Northeast Amdo to Kathmandu and Kalimpong in the Himalayan states of Nepal and Sikkim (cf. Grenard 1904:289-292). Yet, in a sense, this bare outline of towns and routes is misleading, because it reduces clusters of varied types of settlements to single points, and sinuous roads across high mountain passes to straight and simple lines. It leaves out the lesser towns and routes, and it also ignores the fact that much trade in locally produced goods, even if transported over greater distances, was of a periodical nature. Therefore, the towns shown only partly reflect the location of periodic markets and fairs, which have a network and a hierarchy of their own. Reconstruction of these market systems awaits further elaboration, but in the following chapter a preliminary sketch will be attempted.

If we draw an outline of towns and routes for eighteenth century Tibet, two characteristics stand out. First, its openness to the outside world, bringing Kashmiri, Armenian, Muscovite, Chinese, and Newari traders to Tibet. Second, its basic orientation toward China, with Nepal as its backdoor for trans-Himalayan trade (Boulnois 1983:123 ff.). This openness lasted in the first instance to the Dzungar troubles at the beginning of that century (1717-1720), after which Muscovites and Armenians seem to have pulled out, and in the second instance to the end of the century, when the Chinese position in Tibet had temporarily been fortified by their campaign against the Nepalese in 1791-1792, but which brought in its wake a further isolation of Tibet as a whole (see chapter 2). The trade emporia to suffer most from these developments were Sining on the Sino-Tibetan border in Kansu, and Kuti along the highroad to Kathmandu. A similar process involving a locational shift in trade as a result of changing geopolitical circumstances, took place in Western Tibet and Ladakh, where the shawl-wool trade via Leh to Kashmir came under pressure from rival trade channels through Kinnaur, Bashahr, and Kumaon, after the Anglo-Nepalese War of 1814-1816 had placed these territories in the hands of the British (Datta 1970:20).

Complementary to the decline of Sining in Northeast Tibet was the rise of Tachienlu on the eastern border of Kham in the course of the

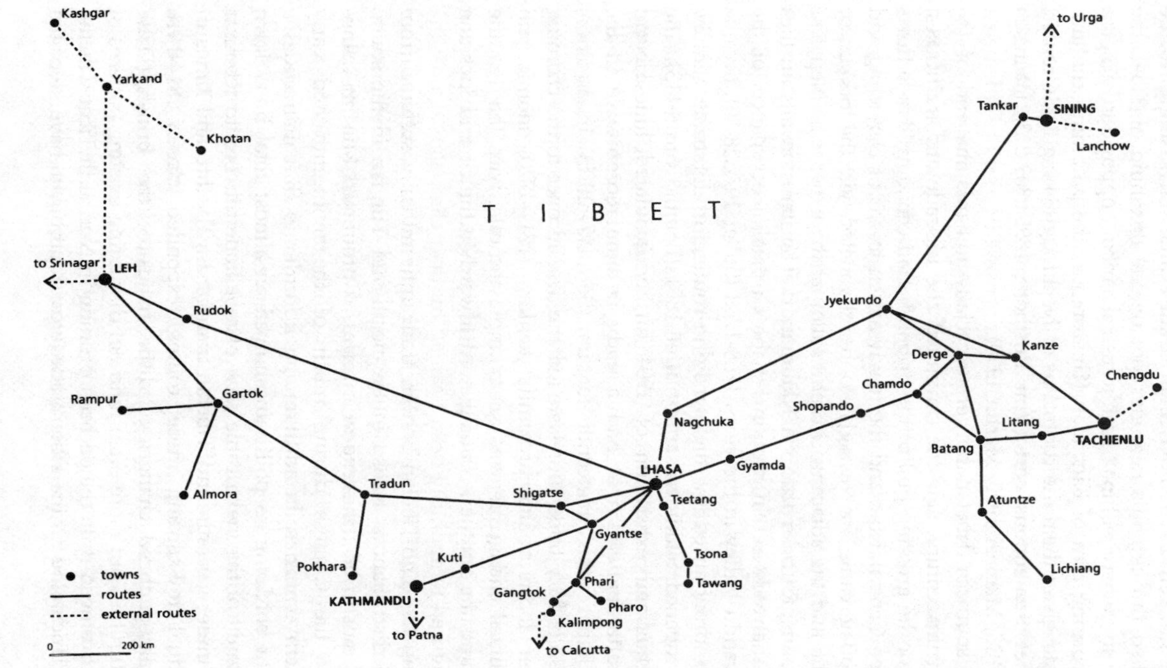

Figure 4 The Tibetan trade network before 1959

nineteenth century. Sino-Tibetan trade came increasingly to be funnelled through this new entrepôt on the threshold of Tibet, the more so where China had crushed tribal opposition in the neighbouring area of Kinchuan (Gyarong) in the preceding century. This had given them the control over the through-going trade routes, albeit at tremendous cost (Von Rosthorn 1895a:309-313, Haenisch 1934-1935, Mansier 1990, Martin 1990).

The southern Tibetan border, especially towards the end of the nineteenth century, saw the continued rise of trade and traffic as a result of the growing pull of the British-Indian economy. Trade flows between Central Tibet and the newly arisen towns of Darjeeling and Kalimpong came increasingly to be channeled via the Sikkimese Jelep La and the adjacent Chumbi Valley at the expense of Nepalese routes, in particular that via Kathmandu. The isolation of Nepal, a process already set in motion by the Gorkhali's occupation of the Kathmandu Valley in the years 1765-1768 (Stiller 1972:28-30), became further pronounced by the partly re-routing of its trade via the newly opened Sikkimese artery after 1861 (Lamb 1986:88-113). The Younghusband expedition of 1904 further facilitated Indo-Tibetan trade after patterns that had already become recognizable in the latter half of the nineteenth century (Sen 1971:23ff.). In addition, some secondary trade routes waxed and waned over time, according to their location and proximity to key areas of economic and geopolitical change, as was for example the case with the Tawang route and the southern Batang road towards Atuntze and Lichiang (see Figure 4).

Along the Sino-Tibetan border, trade intermittently suffered from severe disturbances. Kansu in the north and Yunnan in the south, turned out to be the scene of a series of protracted Muslim risings against the Chinese during much of the nineteenth and early twentieth centuries. In addition, public order in Szechuan and the adjacent border areas of Kham showed an almost total breakdown on account of the inextricable clew of rebellion and counter-rebellion by Chinese warlords and Tibetan insurgents. The life and times of individual towns and trade routes responded closely to these externally induced changes or disorders, sometimes bringing new opportunities, but more often than not disrupting existing patterns of trade. But even if there had been profound peace in the Sino-Tibetan borderlands, the China-Tibet trade would probably have declined anyway, because of the tendency for commerce to pass over sea via Calcutta (cf. Prejevalsky 1876 I:35, Bell 1928:130), after freight rates had consistently fallen since the middle of the nineteenth century.

The wider regional setting

Regionality as the historical genesis and identity of place and people is as much a product of internal conditions as of external relations. The geographically relevant external relations of the wider regional setting of Tibet have necessarily to do with the locational-physical, political-economic, and socio-cultural universes of its neighbours. In terms of locational-physical characteristics, we might think for example of trade relations made possible by the complementarity of ecozones, which through their proximity to each other, may generate a demand for products that can not be grown or bred in their respective physical settings. Further, political stability enhances the wealth of places and the economic viability of exchanges involved. The intensity of these exchanges may be influenced in turn by a degree of social and cultural affinity between places, an affinity which may grow or decline in the course of history. Finally, population dynamics and geopolitical change may drastically alter the wider regional setting, and by implication, the regionality of a place. A particular regionality, and its concomitant geographicity, is thus much more than the historical course of an *économie-monde* and its associated areas. And although we would do grave injustice to Braudel's masterly effort to infuse history with a material substrate, or a geostructural base for that matter, the fact remains that there is a streak of 'economism' in his work, which detracts attention from equally important life spheres and contexts. Therefore, a true regional geographic analysis, as I have pointed out before, should go beyond the single-universe investigation of a place, and have an eye for the *multifaceted* character of human encounters, which ultimately shapes its unique regionality.

Tibet, by virtue of its location, necessarily touches upon its Chinese and Indian neighbours. Its northwestern border is formed by the mighty Kunlun barrier with its subsidiary mountain ranges, which separates the cold and high desert of the Changtang Plateau from the warm and low-lying Taklamakan desert. Both Changtang and Taklamakan are sparsely populated, the former even more so than the latter. In fact, the Changtang is almost devoid of human settlement, while the Taklamakan in Sinkiang allows for scattered patches of oasis cultivation near the desert entry points of a few rivers. Sinkiang down the centuries was the main thoroughfare for the silk trade between China and the West. It nurtured the southern branches of the old Silk Road by providing food and water at critical points along an otherwise waterless desert track. The bulk of the silk trade was first and foremost in the hands of Central Asian transit traders whose emporia studded the string of oases between Northwest China and Bactria (Klimberg 1982:24-37). The prosperity of the caravan towns seems to have lasted until the end of the eighth century A.D., after which the decline of Chinese T'ang rule in the Tarim basin coincided with problems of increasing desiccation (Hoyanagi 1975:86).

The wealth of these caravan towns lured many a prospective empire builder to Central Asia and shortly after the middle of the seventh century the oases of Kashgar and Khotan passed out of the Chinese sphere of influence into the hands of the Tibetans (Beckwith 1987:39). Although the degree of Tibetan domination in the Tarim basin has been the subject of some debate (ibid.:197-202), it seems unquestionable that the Tibetans for a time held sway over its western part (cf. Stein 1907, Emmerick 1967), an overlordship which must have been more than superficial in view of the number of Tibetan cognates in Khotan Saka, a basically Iranian language (Bailey 1971, 1979:vii-ix).

Waning Tibetan influence to the north of the Kunlun brought a disruption of communication with the oases of the Tarim basin. The introduction of Islam and the concomitant disturbances in large tracts of Central Asia after the tenth century further slackened the pace of intercontinental long-distance trade across Turkestan. But it was the crisis in the overland caravan trade in the seventeenth century (Steensgaard 1973), which made the Tarim Basin into the commercial backwater it had become by the beginning of the eighteenth century. Yet, native Andijan merchants from across the Pamirs kept up an intermediate long-distance trade in luxury goods, which intensified with the rise of the Khoquand *khanat* in Ferghana and the establishment of Ching power in Eastern Turkestan during the second half of the eighteenth century (Saguchi 1965:66-67). The nineteenth century saw a further breakdown of order in Turkestan. Yakub Beg's exploits have been briefly mentioned in chapter 2, but it was the muslim rebellions in Kansu from the middle of the century onwards that completed the isolation of an already downward transitional area. However, Kashgar and Yarkand, in the western Tarim Basin, were able to ward off the worst effects of these macroregional changes by intensifying their trade with Russian Turkestan and India (Deasy 1901:285, 295, Skrine 1926:xi, 81, 106, 108, Bosshard 1929:444-446).

To cut a long story short, external relations of Tibet with Chinese Turkestan were virtually nonexistent over the ages. The direction of movements was basically east-west and vice versa, the cultural affinity between the two regions after the tenth century almost nil, and population density throughout low, causing demand to stagnate at insignificant levels. Moreover, the complementarity of ecozones was nullified by the remoteness of population concentrations, and, last but not least, by the barrier character of the Kunlun which has been described as the 'most absolute of frontiers' (Grenard 1904:39).

Of a different order were Tibet's external contacts with Mongolia. Apart from the early Mongol overlordship in the thirteenth century, and the Mongol support for the Gelukpas in the seventeenth (see chapter 2), Mongol interest in Tibet was primarily of a religious nature. Monastic missions bringing the strict ethical code of the Gelukpas to Mongolia from the sixteenth century onward, laid the foundations for a socio-religious order after the Tibetan Buddhist model. In 1578, the Tibet-Mongol connection was given symbolic expression by an exchange of honorific titles between Altan Khan, the most powerful chief among the southern Mongolian tribes, and Sonam Gyatso, a Gelukpa abbot with an outstanding reputation. Here the dignity of the future Dalai Lamas was born, the term 'Ta-le', 'Ocean (of Wisdom)', being of Mongolian extraction, and a promising mission field in the Mongolian steppes opened up (Bell 1931:110-118, Snellgrove and Richardson 1980:183-184).

Mongols, in the following centuries, proved to be the staunchest supporters of Tibetan Buddhism. Mongol pilgrims visited Lhasa, and Tibetans ventured north to Urga, the modern Ulan Bator, where the grand *Hutuktu*, the incarnate Buddha of Mongolia, came to occupy the third place in the Tibetan patriarchate, after the Dalai and Panchen Lama. The Mongolian dignitary was invariably a Tibetan, and Mongolian monks in Tibet, of which at the beginning of the twentieth century there were an estimated one thousand (Tsybikoff 1904:731), often were among the most learned and devout lamas. Two yearly caravans plied between Lhasa and Urga, bringing gold, silver, and luxury goods from northern provenance to the monasteries of Tibet (Tsybikoff 1904:746, Kawaguchi 1909:456), in exchange for good quality woollen goods, Buddhist images and books, as well as other religious paraphernalia. In addition, private pilgrims and traders from all over Mongolia found their way to the holy city of Lhasa, seeking to combine spiritual quest with worldly gain. The pilgrimage for Tibetans to Urga was less common.

Urga, the Mongolian Lhasa, by the time of Prejevalsky's visit in 1870, was the home of an estimated 10,000 monks next to another 20,000 odd inhabitants (Prejevalsky 1876 I:11). Its habitus reflected the strange blend of culturally disparate societies and geopolitically contentious powers. Actually, the town was divided into two halves, a Mongolian and a Chinese one, the former being called Bogdo-kuren, i.e. 'sacred encampment', while the latter, at some five kilometres distance, went by the Chinese name of Mai-mai-cheng, i.e. 'place of trade' (ibid.:8, cf. Ossendowski 1922:232-233, 235-236). In between, well situated on rising ground near the bank of the river Tola, was the two-storied house of the Russian consul, with its wings and outbuildings (Prejevalsky 1876 I:8). It protected the interests of Russian trade and traders between the entrepôt of Kiakhta on the Russo-Mongol border and Kalgan, the Chinese caravan town just across the Gobi desert.

Economically speaking, Mongolia's external relations were first and foremost with China, Russia trying to enter this commercial network from the 1870s onwards (Elias 1873:110 note, 121, 127-128, 133-136, Consten 1919-1920 I:22-33, 63-72). Growing Russian influence in Mongolia made it possible for Kalmuk and Buriat pilgrims from southern Siberia to cross Mongolia by way of Urga, and indeed, between 1870 and 1904, many of them succeeded in making the trip to Lhasa (Grünwedel 1900: X, Tsybikoff 1904:727-729). It brought a trickle of trade from these northern lands to Tibet (Macaulay 1885:92-93, 95, 97) but in essence, relations with Mongolia, and even Russia, had a cultural background. Moreover, the cultural communication that existed was at times badly interrupted by Muslim rebellions in Kansu, the Chinese province bordering on southern Mongolia and northeastern Tibet. The Dungan insurrection, for example, which plagued Kansu between 1862 and 1873, put an eleven year's stop to the annual pilgrim caravans bound for Lhasa (Prejevalsky 1876 I:78, II:257, cf. Lattimore 1928:56). Nevertheless, Tibet-Mongol relations withstood the wear and tear of time, and it should come as no surprise that the 13th Dalai Lama sought shelter in Urga at the time of the Younghusband expedition (1904). A temporary lapse in the protracted geopolitical tug of war between Russia and China over Mongolia even allowed the latter country to proclaim its independence in 1911, which was short-lived, however (Onon and Pritchatt 1989). After the rise of the Russian-monitored People's Republic of Mongolia in 1922, the Tibet-Mongol connection slowly withered away, and for all practical purposes may be considered as extinct by 1950 (Bosshard 1950:262-269).

In terms of a discussion of the wider regional setting of Tibet, the Mongolian connection, after the beginning of the eighteenth century, though culturally important, was never an essential marker of Tibetan regionality. Its religious character, its economic insignificance, and its political irrelevance, all testify to a geographically minor external relation squarely placed across the dominant patterns of spatial organization relative to China. It is therefore to the latter country that we must turn now.

China is the one overriding factor in any discussion of Tibetan regionality in terms of its external relations. If Braudel made Tibet into a subsidiary area of the Chinese *économie-monde* (Braudel 1979 III:14) he did so with good reason. Notwithstanding the age-old but intermittent economic relations between India and Tibet, dating back to at least the seventh century A.D. (Slusser 1982:5, Petech 1984:24-30) the bulk of Tibet's trade till deep in the nineteenth century was with China (Bogoslovskij 1972:42, Yoshinobu 1983, Boulnois 1983:123). Already at the times of the Chinese T'ang dynasty (7th-9th centuries), the road between Lhasa and the Kokonor region in Northeast Tibet was the life-line of Sino-Tibetan contacts (Sato 1975, see also Schafer 1963) and remained so until the decline of Sining in the eighteenth century. After that time, Chinese political and economic presence also made itself felt in the Kham-Szechuan border area. In particular the Tachienlu-Lhasa road via Batang and Chamdo, or alternatively via Jyekundo, came to play the role of a vital trade artery between Tibet and China, making possible the exchange of gold, musk, rhubarb, and wool for Chinese luxury goods like silk, porcelain, and especially tea, for which the Tibetans had developed an extreme liking since the eleventh century (Petech 1983:177). However, the bulk of the wool and rhubarb trade continued to be transacted via Sining, possibly because of cheap transport possibilities down the Huang-ho and by camel across the Ordos desert (cf. Köhler 1952).

The pull of the Chinese economy lies in its vast market opportunities. Though the ordinary peasant was perhaps a poverty-stricken creature in a disintegrating nineteenth-century China, the sheer number of people made up for whatever prosperity was lacking at large. Moreover, population figures for the Red Basin of Szechuan and the frontier regions of Yunnan were on the increase from the eighteenth century onwards, mainly as a result of immigration from the drought and rebellion-plagued Northern provinces and the overpopulated coastal regions in the East and the South (Ho 1959:287). The proximity of these relatively well-populated border provinces, especially Szechuan, to the main clusters of population in the Eastern Tibetan province of Kham, provided the background against which a long-distance trade in luxury goods could develop. Together with the complementarity of the respective ecozones, this explains the endless strings of caravans and tea carriers struggling along winding roads and across abysmal mountain passes between Yachow and Tachienlu, so vividly portrayed by many a traveller or resident in the area (cf. Duncan 1952:49-65, and Figures 16, 17 and 18 on pp.66-67 of the same book). Tachienlu emerged as the main entrepôt between Szechuan and Kham, but lesser-known frontier markets like Sungpan to the north and Lichiang in Yunnan had their own share in Sino-Tibetan transfrontier commerce.

The geopolitical background to this intensification of Sino-Tibetan relations has already been dealt with in chapter 2 and need not be repeated here. Suffice to say that the border area as a whole, increasingly saw the rise of Chinese imperial, if not imperialist power, materially backed up by a steady flow of Chinese colonists into the lower-lying valleys of the mountainous Chinese westlands.

A good example here is the Kienchang Valley in the Lolo-dominated Taliang Shan of South Szechuan (Legendre 1910, Feng Han-yi and Shryock 1938). In a way this pattern was repeated in the Chinese-dominated but genuinely Tibetan territories west of Tachienlu, where Chinese garrisons guarded the main roads, but had only a minimal say in the affairs of the pastoral hinterlands higher up in the mountains (Teichman 1922:77, Hanson-Lowe 1940:362-363). In the less densely populated Kansu-Tibetan border area, slow and relatively peaceful displacement of sedentary Tibetans by Chinese settlers has been reported from the Upper Tao river (Combe 1926:143, Ekvall 1939:29-47). The Tibetans in northern Yunnan shared a similar fate (Fitzgerald 1943:55). However, Chinese political-military moves with the objective of controlling more extended parts of Tibet, in particular as from 1905 onwards, were bloody and caused great resentment among the Tibetan population, especially when their local chiefs were beheaded or their monasteries sacked.

Thus the pattern of external relations arising from this brief survey of circumstances and events in the Sino-Tibetan borderlands, in combination with geopolitical and demographic changes affecting the area, points in the direction of an intensified Sino-Tibetan encounter, both in a political and economic sense. Eastern Tibet, through its main economic relations, may be thought of as increasingly tied to the Chinese *économie-monde*, though civil war in Szechuan in the 1920s, as well as continuing Chinese-Tibetan border clashes, intermittently caused a disruption of transfrontier commerce (Combe 1926:143). However, World War II gave an unexpected boost to trade and transport from Central to Eastern Tibet, in view of the necessary overland supply lines from India to a Japanese-besieged China (Goullart 1957:102-105). The communist victory in China during the years following the war, and the subsequent annexation of Tibet by the Chinese in 1950, further emphasized the importance of the China connection, especially in Kham and Amdo, both of which were silently incorporated into the existing Chinese provinces of Szechuan and Chinghai. The position of Central and Southern Tibet turned out to be more complicated, not only because the major strongholds of Tibetan Buddhism were to be found there, but also because the dominant patterns of external relations were with India and the Himalayan world rather than with China.

Tibet by virtue of its location was the natural thoroughfare for the trade in light and valuable goods between India and China. As earlier referred to, Lhasa was essentially a city of transit-trade, an entrepôt for the long-distance exchange of luxury goods by foreign traders. However, and in addition to this grand network of long-distance commerce, there was a highly fragmented local and regional trade across high mountain passes all along the vast Himalayan frontier. Basically it was a trade in salt and wool from the high nomad lands on the rim of the Changtang in exchange for the grain of the sedentary farmers of the Himalayan middle hills. Via a series of seasonal frontier fairs these salt and wool flows were channelled across a limited number of mountain passes by local middlemen, who had come up with grain from the southern side of the Himalaya. The nature and extent of the activities of these middlemen, generally members of Buddhist communities living in the high Himalaya at the fringe of the Tibetan culture region, depended partly on their control over through-going routes, and partly on privileges granted to them by local principalities or states. Of course, this is an extremely simplified picture, which, as it stands, is more applicable to the Western and Central Himalaya than to its eastern reaches.

In the course of the nineteenth century, Himalayan state formation increasingly started to condition these regional trade flows. State formation also had a powerful effect on the long-distance commerce in luxury products between India and Tibet. In fact, it brought about locational shifts of the region's major trade routes as they became integrated with a succession of ever more centralized Hindu and Buddhist polities. These processes were compounded by the expansion of British political influence throughout the Himalaya as described in chapter 2. In particular the rise of the Gorkhali kingdom of Nepal in the Central Himalaya from the middle of the eighteenth century onwards, and its collision with British colonial power spreading out from its power-base in Bengal at about the same time, were formative factors in complex intertwining processes of economic development and geopolitical change. As Richard English, an American geographer and anthropologist wrote succinctly:

> British and Gorkhali rivalries in the Himalaya came to a head chiefly over the desire to control the major trans-Himalayan trade routes through the Kathmandu Valley and eastern Nepal. For the British, these routes promised

> access to untapped markets for their own manufactured goods in Tibet and China. The rulers of Gorkha, on the other hand, looked to this trade as a source of revenue with which to finance further expansion along the Himalayan perimeter. British forces eventually succeeded in containing Gorkhali ambitions early in the nineteenth century but not without conceding to their broad demands for territorial sovereignty - guarantees which led to Nepal's virtual isolation from the world for more than a century (English 1985:62)

Complementary to Nepal's fossilization as a traditional Hindu state, was the conservation of the Buddhist monastic principalities of Sikkim and Bhutan, which guarded the important trade route via the Jelep La and through the Chumbi Valley into Central Tibet. They also controlled a number of passes which were used in regional trade, just as the semi-independent petty Buddhist state of Mustang in northcentral Nepal held the key to a secondary trade route along the Gandaki river. More westwards, British colonial power stretched right up to the Tibetan border, and the British even built a direct road from the Ganga Plain to Tibet by way of Bashahr and Kinnaur. This Hindustan-Tibet road was ill-conceived, however, as the main concentrations of population in Tibet were located much more to the east along the Central Tsangpo Valley and its tributaries. Still further eastwards, the jungle-clad Himalayan ranges in what is now the Indian state of Arunachal Pradesh, and along the northern Burma frontier, formed an almost impenetrable natural barrier. The one exception was the Tawang corridor as referred to in chapter 2, which benefited from a slightly drier climate combined with easy access to the central region of Tibet.

Thus there arises a highly diversified picture of Indo-Tibetan frontier relations. As far as the economic side of the coin is concerned, there were no serious obstacles to trans-Himalayan commerce, which indeed flourished in the seventeenth century, when northern India under the Moghuls, Kashmir, the Kathmandu Valley, and Central Tibet formed ever so many centres of economic and cultural exchange. As such, it may be argued that Central Tibet, not only for its physical proximity to India but also for its factual economic relations, was at least partly tied to the Indian *économie-monde*. But it is the political side of the coin which contradicts this natural state of affairs. With growing geopolitical isolation of Tibet and Nepal during the nineteenth century, Indo-Tibetan trade relations became more and more strained, a process encouraged by the Chinese, and applauded by conservative Tibetans, who tried to keep British-colonial interests at bay on the cis-Himalayan side of the mountains. However, the Younghusband expedition of 1904 temporarily reversed this trend, and in the following decades, Central Tibet in particular, greatly increased the volume of its trade with Bengal. It showed once more that the geostructural characteristics of Central Tibet made it a more suitable trading partner for India than for China. The disturbances in the Sino-Tibetan frontier area in the 1920s as earlier referred to, further emphasized the primacy of the Indian connection, even to the point that a Tibetan observer in the mid-1920s could contend that 'Lhasa trades almost entirely with India' (Combe 1926:143). But the post-1950 annexation of Tibet by the Chinese communists brought a return to the former geopolitical isolation of Tibet. In particular after 1959, the Himalayan frontier was turned into an almost impenetrable barrier, the effects of which were felt all along its course for many years to come.

This chapter has provided a broad outline of the regionality of Tibet. It discussed some of the geostructural characteristics which inevitably 'bound' the social agency of human groups, and give structure to their actual historical experience. The picture that arises is one of a fragmented, inward-looking Tibet, enjoying a homogeneity in cultural-regional terms. Historically, Tibet gained shape as a kind of culturally defined *espace-mouvement*, in which Great and Little Traditions were transmitted via hierarchies of monastic settlements, extended journeys of pilgrimage, and itinerant performances by bards and actors. Its links of cultural communication provided a nascent ecclesiastical polity with a measure of territorial binding power.

If Tibetan state formation failed, it was largely due to the fragmented nature of its internal economic relations. The basically self-sufficient nature of monasteries within their local settings, prevented the rise of a coherent *espace-mouvement* in economic terms. Though a semblance of political, economic and cultural unity was perhaps achieved in the seventeenth century, mainly on the basis of a long-distance trade in luxury goods, Tibet's major clusters of population were generally too small and too far apart to allow for meaningful economic exchange at the level of daily necessities. Moreover, ecological complementarity of products in a horizontal sense was lacking. A compounding factor was the spatially disparate orientation of Tibet's major regional clusters, which by virtue of their location *vis-à-vis* their respective *économies-mondes*, had always worked against Tibetan economic integration. Together with the adverse geopolitical winds blowing at critical moments in Tibet's history, cultural Tibet failed to achieve full metamorphosis into an independent economic and political unit (cf. Nyman 1983:104, note 5). It is against this background of a multifaceted Tibetan regionality, in particular with regard to its external relations, that a fuller discussion of the geohistory of Tibetan trade will be attempted.

4

THE GEOHISTORY OF TIBETAN TRADE

If in the previous chapters we have chosen to analyse Tibetan regionality in terms of geopolitical and geohistorical categories, it is because they set the structural stage and provide the analytical means for a discussion of the main theme of this inquiry, that is the role of trade in Tibet and its culturally related border worlds. But as trade is also an activity which gains shape by the social agency of its traders, and the culture from which their 'professional' action springs, there is a need to qualify our analysis of trade and traders in terms of its social and cultural context as well. Was it not already the regretted Van Leur, the young Dutch historian, who defended more than fifty years ago that form of economic history which is more adjusted to the nature and structure of other ages and civilizations (Van Leur 1955:40)?

If this observation still holds true today, we may wonder whether the mere analysis of trade in terms of supply and demand graphs and the construction of 'economic man' is the best way to tackle the problem of trade in a basically non-commercialized historical Tibet. Not that the latter survived unimpaired to our day, but we would be well advised to realize that there is more under the analytical umbrella than a 'scarcity-of-means' dominated world with fully rational actors as the fountain from which all economic wisdom springs (Polanyi 1957). Actually, 'scarcity' is as much a culturally determined as a historically articulated concept regarding 'economic' needs. This implies that any discussion of trade in relation to societies characterized by a low degree of commercialization must take into account non-economic factors and show an awareness of the time-specific context through which particular needs gain form. What is considered scarce in one culture or period may not necessarily be so in others.

To give but one example, 'economic' needs may be defined in terms of the pursuance of much leisure time in order to satisfy culturally specific ends. Sahlins' 'original affluent society' comes to mind here as one in which the ends of economic efficiency and resource maximation have been made subordinate to ends of psychological well-being and communal welfare (Sahlins 1974:1-39). Though a rather Utopian view because it neglects the productive strength of a society's resource base, the 'economic' mechanisms involved, such as mutual reciprocity and communal redistribution, clearly show alternatives to individual profit maximation, alternatives which may be helpful in discussing certain less common forms of economic exchange in a not yet fully commercialized Tibetan setting.

In itself, the rise of supraregional and cross-cultural trade relations, and its concomitant trade diasporas of long-distance merchant communities (Curtin 1984:1-14), is not a sufficient condition to make non-market exchanges through reciprocity and redistribution fully obsolete. But the coming of Western industrialism and the large-scale manufacture of goods for sale, was. It undermined the position of the long-distance trader as a cultural broker and a dealer in specific luxuries. It created a new kind of trader. To sell arms, to traffic slaves, to deal in opium, were the almost 'natural' consequences of a changing value system in which the communal good was exchanged for the individual profit. The ceremonial function of tribute-paying missions to divine rulers soon became a thing of the past. The 'culture of trade', as a set of rituals necessary to guarantee the safe return of the trader from a potentially risky journey, came to be regarded as superfluous. The verbal agreements between trusted trading partners were replaced by written statements of indifferent agents. Price-setting in sectoral and regional markets began to dominate the trading scene at the cost of individual barter arrangements. Money increasingly made the trader's world go round.

The geohistorical context which facilitated this change was the era of colonialism, with its subtle if crooked forms of commercial penetration. One of them was the rise of a sort of 'informal empire' in the nineteenth century (Curtin 1984:240ff.). The quintessence of informal empire was its indirect way of exercising influence in an area without territorial expansion. Such an arrangement protected interests that were really vital, without the cost of ruling over an alien society. In an Asian setting and application, the British treaty ports in China may be considered as cases in point. The British-established trade marts in southern Tibet after the Younghusband expedition of 1904, fall in the same category. The office of the Chinese *ambans* in Lhasa too, from the eighteenth century onward, may be regarded as an early form of consular representation for the safeguard of imperial and commercial interests.

Indeed, it is this geohistorically transitional period, stretching roughly from 1850 to 1950, which forms the background to our discussion of trade relations in the Tibetan world. The choice for the period concerned is justified because it covers the final days of disintegration of Central Tibet as an ecclesiastical state based on a long-distance trade in luxury goods. In addition, it shows the decline of foreign merchant communities, but also the corresponding rise of Tibetan trade initiatives as a response to the changing geohistorical parameters of adjacent *économies-mondes*. The period chosen is also crucial in terms of geopolitical change. The 'frontier' character of Tibet as described in chapter 2, gave way to contending imperialist spheres of interest, ultimately leading to a Chinese-dictated Indo-Tibetan boundary in the Himalayan region. In fact, this frontier character, in combination with Anglo-Chinese imperialist rivalry forms the structural geohistorical background against which any discussion of a changing Tibetan trading region must be set. Even so, change has not been uniform for a variety of geographical and historical reasons. It is the stated purpose of this study not to overlook those differences.

The traditional barter complex

'The chief economic wealth of Tibet lies in its nomad cattle-breeding districts. Deprive Tibet of its cattle-breeding regions and the country would starve' (Roerich 1967:42). This shrewd observation by a Russian Tibetanist, who crossed the Changtang in 1925, highlights the vulnerability of Tibet's valley economies in terms of grain self-sufficiency. And indeed, the sedentary agricultural areas, especially in the west, but also in the densely populated valleys of eastern Tibet, did not always produce enough food to provide the nomads with the necessary grain. Fortunately, the nomads were generally able to produce a surplus of animal products, especially wool, which could be bartered against the grain of the valleys, or perhaps exchanged for larger consignments of foodgrains from outside Tibet. In addition, there was the salt, for which there was ample demand in the cis-Himalayan region and in eastern Tibet. Thus, the traditional Tibetan trade complex rested, with considerable regional variations, in the exchange of wool and salt for foodgrains and tea, the latter of which may be regarded as a daily necessity within a Tibetan context. At a higher level of analysis, the export of wool made possible the accumulation of some wealth in the hands of monasteries and traders, a wealth that was generally used to import a few luxuries from abroad.

Contrary perhaps to popular wisdom, an economy founded on pastoralism is not infrequently an economy of relatively high involvement in the market (Khazanov 1984:202). According to this author, a distinction must be made between the two different types of trade between nomads and the outside world. Firstly, direct exchange and trade, basically with agricultural and urban societies, secondly, mediation or participation in the trade between different sedentary societies, and the services and other contacts linked to these (ibid.:202).

The first form is mainly an example of the 'vertical trade' as mentioned in the previous chapter, that is the local exchange of animal products of the plateau-dwelling nomads for the grain of the valley-resident farmers. It is this trade to which a Tibetan nomad still referred when the American anthropologists Goldstein and Beall conducted research in the Pala nomad country of western Tibet in 1987: 'You see,' he said, 'we live off the products of our animals. Every year our sheep provide wool, skins, meat, milk and butter which we use for food and clothes as well as for bartering with villagers to obtain barley, tea and so forth' (Goldstein and Beall 1989:49). The inclusion of tea in an otherwise home-produced set of trading articles as referred to in the above citation, shows once more the important position of tea in the barter complex under discussion.

The second form of nomad trade is less dependent on the productive capacity of nomadism *per se*, but more on the power of transportation offered by its yaks, *dzos* (a cross-bred), goats and sheep. The control over pack-animals in combination with a favourable location astride distinct ecozones, as well as a thorough knowledge of routes in difficult terrain, made the nomads or semi-nomads of Tibet's border areas often into middlemen-transporters in a trans-regional and cross-cultural trade. If the right combination of animal control, favourable location, ecosystematic complementarity and sufficient demand existed, long-distance caravan trading and the supplying of caravan traders were sometimes more profitable for the nomads than was the direct exchange of pastoral for agricultural products. In addition, a specialized animal trade developed in some border areas, which provided a sort of mixture between the two forms mentioned above. Examples of the latter were the large-scale trade in Amdo-bred cavalry horses for the Chinese army at the Kansu horse fairs (Ekvall 1939:56, cf. Serruys 1975:86), as well as the annual sale of tens of thousands of sheep to Nepal at the time of a major Hindu festival (Harrer 1952:56, Brauen 1983:38,44).

Nomads in Tibet are mainly to be found in the broad band of grasslands which runs along the rim of the Changtang from Amdo in the Northeast via Central Tibet to the Indian border in the Southwest. But in many of the higher areas elsewhere in Tibet and the Himalaya, pastoralism both in its full-blown and its mixed forms are part and parcel of the local economies. Nomadism and related activities in Tibet are still insufficiently documented, although we do have a number of written reports and monographs of varying quality at our disposal (Tafel 1914, Combe 1926:100-117, Roerich 1967, Ekvall 1939:48-82, Kingdon Ward 1948, Hermanns 1949, Norbu 1983, Clarke 1987, Goldstein and Beall 1989, and Jones 1996). From these, as well as from a number of erratic references across a disparate set of complementary sources, we have to distil the meaning and importance of trade in Tibetan nomad life.

The nomad way of life is one of inherent mobility. The necessary shifts of nomad camps to assure continuous and good grazing feature prominently in daily and seasonal routines. But as pasture-grounds, in particular around the fixed winter encampments, had the character of non-alienable land owned by specific clans or tribes (Ekvall 1954:46-47), movements tended to be restricted in space. Moreover, groups of herders that were living nearer to the settled agricultural areas stood in varying degrees of dependency to monasteries and feudal chiefs, the liens involved being ever so many restrictions to the free movement of nomad subjects (Goldstein

1988:15-17). Even the independent Golok nomads of the upper Hoang-ho or Machu basin in eastern Tibet were subject to the supreme moral authority of the lamas and depended for the barter of their animal products on the regional monasteries in the neighbouring valley-areas (Guibaut 1947:219, Chakrabarty 1982:19). In a wider sense then, their movements too, were necessarily structured, not to say restricted.

Beyond this world of local exchanges lay the regional networks of nomad and related middlemen trade. Especially in the drier parts of western Tibet, insufficient grain could be grown, even under irrigation, to feed the nomad populations outside the valleys. Consequently, a whole system of grain imports had developed over the centuries, which were paid for by wool and salt. The salt trade had its productive origin in the lake-lands of Central Tibet and the Tsaidam basin. Latter-day research has discovered forty-six kinds of salt minerals in the saline lakes, among which fourteen are borates (Shi-yang and Bing-xiao 1981:1724-1725).

The borates, in the form of raw borax or tincal, commanded a good sale in Europe, in particular during the first half of the nineteenth century. The demand by the European porcelain industry was met almost exclusively by the Tibetan trade, but the discovery of borax in the Italian province of Tuscany, as well as its chemical production later on in the century, brought to an end this lucrative trade (Brown 1984:117-119). As some of the nomads must have been involved in the first stages of this long-distance trade, it may have brought a certain wealth to their communities, which however declined at the eclipse of their monopoly. The borax-digging at Phuga in Ladakh, for example, was already past its heyday in 1847 (Thomson 1852:66). The export of borax from Tibet to China however, continued unabated (Hosie 1905:27).

What was left was the export of non-borate salts for daily use in the Himalayan border lands, insofar as they could compete with imported sea salt from the south. Salt from the Tsaidam basin in Northeastern Tibet was brought to the eastern Tibetan province of Kham, where it formed one of the staple trades. The salt was brought down by the nomads from Amdo and exchanged for the barley of the densely-settled agricultural valleys along the Yangtse (Drichu) and Yalung (Dzachu) (Teichman 1922:175). Southeastern Tibet obtained its supplies of salt from the brine wells on the banks of the Mekong at Yenching or Tshwakhalo (Desgodins 1885:343-344) but its sphere of influence being small, it had to compete with salt coming down from the Tsaidam basin and the Nagchuka area, which harboured at Nagchu a kind of transit market for the products of many Central Tibetan nomad countries. Salt, then, was an important trade product for the nomads, as they alone possessed the transport capacity and the mobility making possible the exploitation of salt at its places of production.

The best outline of the salt trade in western Tibet has been given by the Austrian engineer Peter Aufschnaiter, who lived and travelled extensively in the area during and shortly after World War II. According to him, salt was produced at a number of saline lakes, the most important of which were Drabye Tshaka (cf. Combe 1926:164), two hundred kilometres north of Tradun, and Andar Tshaka, ten days north of Namru Dzong; further Bilog Tshaka and Tsondzong Tshaka in the same area (Brauen 1983:31,152). Except for Tengri-nor, the big lake Northwest of Lhasa, other salt lakes, as reported on by several pandits, like Chak Tshaka (Burrard 1915 I:111-112) and Kai Tshaka (ibid.:1915 I:164) are difficult to locate, but may be found more to the west in the Rudok area, another reputed area of salt production (cf. Hedin 1910-1913 I:66). Chak Tshaka is perhaps identical with the lake shown near the town of Qagcaka as marked on the Royal Geographical Society Map of Central Asia (32.6N 81.8E); London: Macmillan 1987. These saline lake areas were connected by a number of nomad routes to a series of salt depots in villages generally situated just north or south of the Tsangpo river, like Karnag in Uyug (Brauen 1983:152,132 (map), Panam in the Gyantse area (ibid.1983: 147), and Drandong near Sakya (ibid.1983: 169). However, the precise location of the latter remains uncertain. As mentioned before, salt from the central saline lake region may also have found its way eastwards via Nagchu to the district of Kongbo. The British political agent Bailey, on his 1913 journey in Southeast Tibet, came across the village of Kapu along the lower Tsangpo, the inhabitants of which were trading Kongbo salt for Abor (Adi) cotton from the south (Bailey 1957:75) But at Pari Chote near Nang Dzong (ibid.1957:169 (map), slightly to the west, Golok nomad traders annually bartered salt hailing from Northeast Tibet (Burrard 1915 II:30, cf. Guibaut 1947:83), indicating an interference of salt of western and northern provenance in Southeast Tibet. The same kind of nomad trade in salt existed in Northeast Tibet, where the German medical practitioner Dr. Tafel, on his journey in the Kokonor region in 1906, met a number of Chamri Tibetans plying a salt line between Dabassu Nor in the Tsaidam basin and Tankar, the main outlet for Tibetan goods in the Amdo-Kansu border area (Tafel 1914 I:297).

So much for the details. The general picture that arises is one of a number of salt-producing regions where nomads fetched the salt and brought it down to seasonal markets, monasteries and villages. From there it was transported onwards to a series of frontier fairs along the Sino-Tibetan and Himalayan borders. As the inhabitants of the western Himalaya, Nepal, Sikkim, Bhutan, and Upper Assam almost totally depended on salt from outside, either Tibetan or Indian in origin, they had to engage in the trade for this absolute necessity. In terms of an *espace-mouvement*, it is interesting to see to where the salt from Tibet reached. In the Himalayan region this was generally down to the middle hills. This rather vague term for the reader unfamiliar with things Himalayan, stands for the extensive spur landscape on the southern side of the main Himalayan chain, in which it was difficult to penetrate from the south due to its jungle-clad nature, but in which several inroads of trade existed from the north across high passes (see the illustrative map for Nepal in Hagen (1972:123, here reproduced as Figure 5). The trade across these passes was in the hands of locally dominant Bhotia populations, who visited the seasonal frontier fairs in southern Tibet and transported the salt to the lower-lying regions on the cis-Himalayan side. There is much to say about the term 'Bhotia', which refers to the Tibetan or Tibetanized border populations along the Indo-Tibetan frontier, but their status generally boils down to a historically arisen class of cross-cultural traders in response to ecosystematic complementarity, as well as a rising British-Indian *économie-monde vis-à-vis* Tibet (the crucial reference is: Brown 1984; see also Prasad 1989).

In exchange for the salt, several grains found their way into Tibet, in particular its western parts where the climate showed less clemency than in its eastern reaches. Rice, for the higher classes, was imported from Zayul and Pemakö, low-lying regions in southeastern Tibetan territory. But as these were far away from the main centres of population, additional rice of a superior quality was brought in from

Assam, Bhutan and Nepal (Markham 1876:119, Rockhill 1891a:237, note 2, Burrard 1915 I:18, Wessels 1924:249, Bell 1928:118, Aziz 1978:96-97). Because of its upper-class background, the rice trade was a government monopoly (Burrard 1915 I:177), the trade being controlled by officials at its major points of entrance. In Tsona Dzong, at the northern end of the Tawang corridor for example, there was a so-called 'rice-official' which saw to it that the salt brought in from Yamdrok Tso, was exchanged at favourable rates for rice under his very eyes (Bailey 1957:255). A very prosperous nomad country like lower Droshü in the borderlands of Tsang and Ngari, could also afford to buy Nepalese rice in exchange for salt (Combe 1926:115).

The main food imports in western Tibet, however, consisted of barley and to a far lesser extent wheat. As Lee Shuttleworth, a British-Indian civil servant observed, a constant stream of grain comes up from Lahul and Kulu to Rupshu and beyond as these countries produce insufficient crops for the support of their inhabitants (Shuttleworth 1922:261, see also Pant 1935:220). Incidentally, the deficiency was already noticed by Moorcroft a hundred years earlier (Moorcroft 1818:447). George William Traill too, the commissioner for Kumaon in the early years of British administration in the area noticed that the staple trade of the Bhotia import was grain in order to make up for the shortages in western Tibet (Traill 1832:37). According to the latter observer, the grain-salt trade complex extended in the winter months down to the middle hills of Kumaon, where wheat, rice and coarse grains were purchased, loads of which were transported in springtime on sheepback to the Bhotia villages close to the passes. When the snow on the high passes had melted, trading forays into the Tibetan highlands were only a matter of days (ibid.1832:37-38).

Anyone interested in this trans-Himalayan Bhotia trade, which lasted in essence to the Chinese border closure in the early 1960s, can do no better than to turn to the extensive structural descriptions by Brown (1984:42-68) and Chandola (1987:68-105). However, the colour of everyday life in the area is better conveyed by the older, but still very useful study by Pant (1935:17-224), as well as the short but informative article by Tyson (1953). The latter author reports that border trade in 1952 was still chiefly by barter. As to the articles of

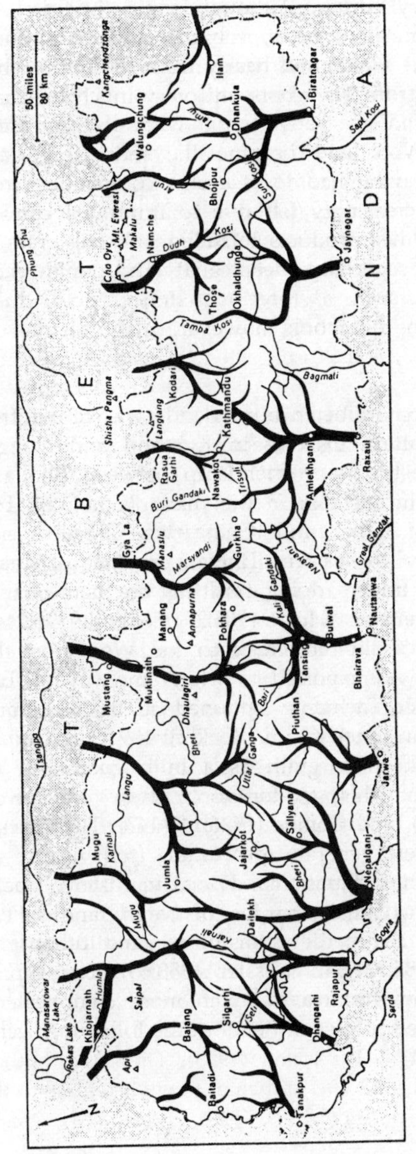

Figure 5 Principal trade routes in Nepal before 1959

commerce, little had changed in comparison with Traill's times more than a century earlier. Although some 'luxuries' such as sugar, Indian tea, metal utensils, tobacco and matches had come to supplement the wheat and barley from the middle hills, the articles brought back from Tibet bore still very much the mark of a nomad society engaged in petty trade with its sedentary agricultural neighbours. Wool had become the most important export, the Tibetan salt having had to face stiff competition from Indian salt, which was increasingly felt due to improved communications (cf. Field 1959). Other products included yak tails, furs, hides, carpets, and livestock, especially sheep, goats and ponies, supplemented by little luxuries such as precious stones, gold dust and filigree silverware. On the whole however, trade seemed on the decline (Tyson 1953:143,146).

Trade in the Sino-Tibetan borderlands was of a different character. Unlike the pattern existing in Kumaon and along the Nepalese border, where bonds of friendship between Bhotias and Tibetans played a significant role in the marts (Chandola 1987:89-105), the trade between Tibet and China was largely monopolized by merchants from the eastern Tibetan province of Kham. These were either private traders doing business on their own account or on behalf of monasteries (Hosie 1905:29, Coales 1919b:244). Trade goods were partly of a different character too. Wool from the northeastern nomad areas was exported to China by way of Tankar (Rockhill 1891b:111) while Tachienlu siphoned off the wool produced on the high plateaus in inner Kham (Rockhill 1894:370, Guibaut 1947:29). In return did not come grain as a bulk good, but tea. Interesting descriptions of this tea-for-wool trade are given by Coales (1919b:244-245), and Combe (1926:140-147). The necessary grains for the nomads were generally procurable from nearby valley areas, as the slightly better climatic conditions in eastern Tibet permitted the production of a small surplus of barley and wheat, which was bartered with the herders for butter and other animal products (Desgodins 1885:339,342, Kessler 1983:65). The supralocal tea and wool trade however, was a much more complicated affair, which will be described in greater detail in the following section.

The tea and wool trade of Tibet

The tea from China may first have reached Tibet towards the end of the seventh century A.D. (Bogoslovskij 1972:42). About 1040 there was a brisk trade in horses from Sining in exchange for tea from Szechuan (Petech 1983:177), and the following centuries saw the rise of tea as the national beverage of Tibet. By the second half of the nineteenth century, the self-styled 'Pioneer of Commerce' T.T. Cooper could write, 'the whole business in life of the Tibetans seems to be to procure a sufficiency of tea' (Cooper 1871:225). Tea is usually prepared with butter and salt, and an average Tibetan can consume forty or fifty cups a day (Macdonald 1929:38), making Tibetans a race of 'enormous tea drinkers' (Bird 1899:332). Consequently, tea was in great demand, and towards the end of the nineteenth century ten to fifteen million pounds were imported annually into Tibet by way of the frontier markets of Tachienlu, Sungpan and Atuntze (Rockhill 1891b:277,281n, cf. Hosie 1905:79).

Tea for the Tibetan market was almost exclusively grown in the Chinese province of Szechuan, where the prefecture of Yachow was the collecting centre of a number of tea-growing districts (Baber 1882:193, Hosie 1890:93). The trade at Yachow was controlled by Chinese tea firms (Cooper 1871:171, Rockhill 1891b:277, Bailey 1945:33), which prepared the tea for export to Tibet by packing quantities into coarse rectangular 'bricks' (Baber 1882:194, Bailey 1912:334). From Yachow the tea was carried to the Sino-Tibetan frontier town of Tachienlu by way of human porterage, as the terrain to be crossed was too mountainous to allow for the use of pack-animals. The porterage was performed by 'a very nationality of porters', the so-called Giama Rongbas (from Gyalmorong?) who inhabit the cultural fringe land between the two towns (Burrard 1915 II:233, cf. Cooper 1871:187). From Yachow, the tea carriers saw their loads over a distance of some two hundred kilometres to Tachienlu, where the tea generally changed hands from Chinese to Tibetan traders. With old-established firms, business was put through without a written contract, but the use of paper, being introduced from China, gained in importance in the early decades of the twentieth century (Combe 1926:142-143).

Tachienlu, familiarly known as the Shanghai of Tibet (Stevenson 1932:616), yet harbouring a mere five thousand inhabitants (Graham 1924-1925:34), was a veritable node of trade routes (Edgar 1930-1931: 5-8). Although Chinese-ruled since the beginning of the eighteenth century, the town had been able to retain its Tibetan atmosphere, as it really lay well within the Tibetan culture region which was thought to extend right up to the Tung river a few kilometres to the east of the town. Tachienlu was the major break-of-bulk point for a variety of goods leaving and entering the eastern Tibetan province of Kham, human porterage as a mode of transport at this point being replaced by pack-animals and vice versa (Baber 1882:196, Von Rosthorn 1895b, Burrard 1915 II:233, Limpricht 1922:143, Migot, n.d.:89ff.).

Tea too, was subject to this operation. Thus the Tibetan purchaser removed the less durable Yachow wickerwork and repacked the tea in relatively small brick-like loads, a number of which were tightly sewn together in a yak-skin cover, especially the better quality teas destined for the Lhasa market (Rockhill 1891b:278, Burrard 1915 II:233, Combe 1926:143). In addition, Chinese and Tibetan duties had to be paid at Tachienlu for fixed quantities and qualities of tea entering and leaving the town (Baber 1882:195, Rockhill 1891b: 277,280). After that the tea was ready for its onward journey into the highlands of Tibet (see Duncan 1952:67, figure 18).

The distribution of tea over Tibet after it had left Tachienlu proceeded in two ways. The better quality teas bound for Lhasa went by the so-called Janglam road, a northern route via Dawu, Kandze and Jyekundo (Burrard 1915 II:234, Combe 1926:144, Edgar 1930-1931:6-7; see also Figure 4). Along this road most of the pack-animals were yak. The Canadian-Dutch missionary Dr. Susie Rijnhart, who tried to reach Lhasa with her husband in 1897, met immense caravans of yak with loads of tea from Jyekundo, the number of yak in each caravan amounting from 1,500 to 2,000, with the merchants well-dressed and well-mounted (Rijnhart 1901:280). However, brigandage was rife, and a few days later they heard of fifty robbers having killed several men and driven off their yak with loads (ibid.:286). The lesser quality teas, meant for consumption in eastern Tibet, went by the Junglam or government road, a more southerly located route which ran through Litang, Batang and Chamdo (Bonin 1911:243-244, Burrard 1915 II:234-235, Weigold

1935:238-239). Along this road, tea was sold to resident merchants in the towns, who further distributed packages of tea in their hinterlands (cf. Duncan 1952:96). Unfortunately, the southern road, in particular beyond Litang in the 1920s, was even more rife with brigands than the northern one (Combe 1926:146, Shelton 1923:128).

Tea was distributed 'throughout the length and breadth of Tibet' (Bell 1928:121). Firms from Lhasa bought large quantities from eastern Tibetan traders and retailed them in western Tibet, for example at Barka Tazam, a centre for the distribution of China tea not far from the Kailash-Manasarovar pilgrimage area (Combe 1926:116). At lower levels of distribution the retail trade of the tea was in the hands of monasteries and their lamas (Baber 1882:199-200, Hosie 1905:78, Tafel 1914 I:220) and tea was so widely used as a commodity of trade that quantities were sometimes used as currency which even the most lawless nomad-brigands would accept (Rockhill 1891b:279-280, Burrard 1915 II:234). Most of the first quality tea went to the larger monasteries, but also to the aristocrats in Lhasa and a few places elsewhere (Hosie 1905:78). Tea eventually found its way to Bhutan (Burrard 1915 II:235), to northeast Tibet (Tafel 1914 I:304), and also to Ladakh (Moorcroft and Trebeck 1841 II:350, Aitchison 1874:32). Prices that had to be paid for consignments of tea increased with distance from Tachienlu, those in the west of Tibet generally fetching the highest prices, but difficulty of terrain too, had a price-raising effect (Rockhill 1891b:279, Combe 1926:145).

Although the greater part of the tea imports from China into Tibet was channelled via Tachienlu, smaller amounts were taken in by way of Atuntze into southeastern Tibet and via Sungpan into Amdo (see Figure 4). Rockhill (1891b:281) gives an estimate of a million pounds by either way. Cooper (1871:301) had noticed a very fine black tea from Yunnan being exchanged for musk at Atuntze, but according to the prince-explorer Henri d'Orleans, who visited the town some twenty-five years later, the tea imports of the place were few (d'Orleans 1898:218). The frontier market of Sungpan, however, to the north of Tachienlu, may have carried a more voluminous tea trade. A legitimate amount of tea was exported from Szechuan via Kuan hsien to Sungpan (Rockhill 1891b:112, Bird 1899:332, Hosie 1905:75-76, Fergusson 1911:84,163). Here the traders, mainly Sharbas from the Sungpan area itself (Tafel 1914 II:75), had to face several tax-barriers on the Szechuan-Chinghai border that were evaded with the collaboration of the southern Amdo frontier monasteries (Filchner 1906:6). Their tea eventually reached Tankar and Sining (d'Ollone 1911:292; see also Rock 1930:181, showing the photo of a tea caravan west of Labrang), but the amount carried was relatively small as the road beyond Sungpan was dangerous on account of brigands and difficult terrain (Futterer 1903:7-8, Tafel 1914 I:304, Duncan 1952:62). However, the Sharbas also exchanged tea with the nomads in their homelands (Tafel 1914 I:309).

The Chinese tea monopoly in Tibet was a thorn in the flesh of the British administration in India. From the second half of the nineteenth century onwards, speculation about Indian tea flooding the Tibetan market was rife (cf. Macaulay 1885:86-91), but the Tibetans, with a little help from the Chinese, sedulously guarded their trade, and prevented any Indian tea from penetrating Tibet (Desgodins 1885:348). Strangely enough, the Younghusband expedition of 1904, and the subsequent opening of British-controlled trade marts in southern Tibet, did not bring the expected influx of Indian tea (Bell 1928:121-122). Problems of taste (Hackmann 1907:81-82, Burrard 1915 II:237) proved to be a powerful cultural factor of *longue durée* in the refusal of teas hailing from Assam and Kashmir. Thus the projected tea trade into Tibet via Sikkim and the Chumbi valley came to nothing (Macdonald 1929:125).

The tea trade of Tibet was in the main an inward-looking affair. Tea steadily came to pervade even the most remote districts, though not always by the choicest means (Burrard 1915 II:388). In contrast, the wool trade was largely an outwardly directed phenomenon, based on an externally generated demand and involving relations far beyond the grasp of the ordinary nomad farmer. In particular after 1890, wool increasingly found its way to Europe and America, where the coarse Tibetan sheep wool was used in the carpet-making industry. But before this international 'boom' trade gained full shape in the early decades of the twentieth century, the fame of the Tibetan wool rested in another supraregional circuit, that of the shawl-wool or *pashm* of western Tibet.

Pashm is the fine wool of a particular type of goat, whose main habitat is to be found in the region between Lake Pangong on the Ladakhi border and Lake Manasarovar near the sacred peak of Kailash (Ryall 1879:446). Together with musk, a natural perfume, it was one of the two products for which Tibet was known to the outside world since the Middle Ages. One source even notes that the word 'Tibet' derives from the Persian 'Tibbat', which means 'fine wool' (Raverty 1895:82). Be that as it may, by the fifteenth century, this fine Tibetan wool commanded a regular sale in Kashmir, where it was manufactured into wollen products of high quality, in particular shawls. The most important shawl-wool producing area was the western Changtang, with its districts of Rudok and Gartok bordering on the neighbouring kingdom of Ladakh. After the Tibeto-Ladakh-Mughal War of 1681-1683, Ladakh had to accept a trade monopoly under which the Tibetan authorities undertook to supply the entire wool of western Tibet to Ladakh, while the Mughals agreed to buy all this wool for her Kashmir-based weavers. As it was a profitable arrangement for the Ladakhis, they eagerly accepted this monopoly, and any attempt to export the shawl-wool to areas other than Ladakh was severely punished by the Ladakhi and Tibetan authorities (Datta 1970:18).

With the coming of the British in India, the traditional framework of trans-Himalayan trade came under pressure from the south. In 1812, the intrepid traveller William Moorcroft reached Gartok in disguise, and after a few days succeeded in procuring eight loads of the passionately desired shawl-wool in a neighbouring village. As he later on reported, 'I consider this day (the 30th of July, 1812) as the epoch at which may be fixed the origin of a traffic which is likely to be extremely beneficial to the Honourable Company' (Moorcroft 1818:459). And so it proved to be. As time went by, the reorientation of the shawl-wool trade to the south, in combination with an influx of skilled Kashmirian weavers, worked wonders for a nascent shawl-wool industry in the plains centres of Amritsar, Narpur and Ludhiana (Datta 1970:19-20). To break the Ladakhi monopoly on Tibetan wool, the import of *pashm* along the newly established Satlej route through the British-protected state of Bashahr was silently encouraged. After 1815, Rampur, the capital of Bashahr, began to develop into a real transit-trading centre of shawl-wool, while Kinnaur, towards the Tibetan border, emerged as a smuggler's nest of *pashm* wool (Gerard 1841:116).

It is not the place here to dwell at length on all the geopolitical intricacies and territorial adaptations which went together with a reorientation of trans-Himalayan trade towards the south. Moreover, these have been aptly and succinctly analysed by Lamb (1986:43-67) and Datta (1970), the latter in particular focusing on the dynamics of the shawl-wool trade. Suffice it to say that further locational shifts in the wool trade occurred towards the end of the nineteenth century. The rise of the Kanpur wool mills is an important explanatory factor here (Brown 1984:115-116), but as to the volume of trade, it should be remembered that the Anglo-Chinese Convention of 1886 too, indirectly promoted the wool trade from Tibet, as it encouraged the Chinese government to take a more lenient stance towards the vexed question of Indo-Tibetan trade (Richardson 1984:284-285). In particular in the 1890s, the Taklakot-Tanakpur route through Kumaon, which almost directly tapped the wool trade of the Manasarovar region (Sherring 1906:262, cf. Pranavananda 1950: 117-120), came to dominate the Tibetan trade to India at the cost of the Rampur route through Bashahr (Brown 1984:116). The trade itself, however, remained firmly in the hands of indigenous traders like Lahuli, Bashahri, and the Bhotia from Kumaon. Apart from this trade in good quality *pashm*, the coarser sheep wool from western Tibet also used to be an important export product, though its range was more limited than that of the *pashm*. The supply was almost wholly obtained from the salt-laden flocks visiting the seasonal frontier marts along the the Tibetan border, where the sheep were shorn by Bhotia buyers resident on the cis-Himalayan side of the passes. Only after being shorn they returned, if they did, to Tibet, laden with the much sought-after grain. A good example of such a seasonal wool mart was Patseo, in northern Lahul, so well described and photographed by Shuttleworth (1923); see also Prince Peter (1963:310-311). The opening of British-controlled trade marts in South-Central Tibet (McKay 1992), and the growing importance of the Sikkim-Chumbi route in the wake of the Younghusband expedition of 1904, brought further changes in the spatial organization of the wool trade. These may, however, be better interpreted in relation to developments in the wool trade along the Sino-Tibetan frontier. But before doing so, a few observations are due with regard to the nomad countries that produce the wool.

As pointed out before, nomad countries in Tibet are mainly to be found along the southern and eastern rim of the Changtang wastelands. These pastoral *pays* are not of equal prosperity, due to a variety of reasons. Combe, who edited the observations of 'a Tibetan on Tibet' (viz. Paul Sherap, or Dorje Zodba), gives a brief overview of the nomad countries Dorje was personally acquainted with, and though impressionistic, the few pages convey the image of a number of widely disparate nomad societies (Combe 1926:103-115, endmap). First of all, there are differences in resource base, the eastern and northeastern nomad countries generally enjoying higher precipitation, and consequently having better grazing grounds than their counterparts in western Tibet (Kingdon Ward 1948, Vaurie 1972:11,19). But whether a nomad country made a more prosperous impression or not also depended on its external relations, and the differences in wealth noted by Dorje Zodba in the 1910s and 1920s must have been at least partly related to their location *vis-à-vis* potential buyers of nomad products, or to their capacity to control crucial transport routes. The prosperous nomad country of Dzachuka, for example, almost certainly benefited from its location near the old 'kingdoms' of Ling and Derge on the Upper Yangtse (Drichu), and Tehor on the Upper Yalung (Dzachu). Dzachuka was also favourably located near the crossroads of trade routes at Jyekundo, from where wool and hides could be transported to almost every direction. The relative prosperity of other nomad countries like Dam, Nagchuka and Nagtsang was possibly related to their location near the great cult centres of Central Tibet. Nagchuka and Dam, for instance, sent yak, sheep, dried beef, butter and cheese to Lhasa, and brought back wheat, rice and cloth (Combe 1926:111). In addition, Roerich mentions wool finding its way to Lhasa, where it was sold to government agents or private establishments, who in turn had it sent to India (Roerich 1967:41).

The wool trade of northeastern Tibet, which tapped the nomad countries that were to be found in the Tsaidam basin, the Kokonor Lake region, and the Upper Hoang ho or Machu reaches, only seems to have become important and of sufficient scale to be noticed by outsiders by the 1890s (Rockhill 1891b:111). During the eighteenth and the greater part of the nineteenth century, most of the wool from this area was traded with the non-Chinese residents of the Sining region, wool never having been popular with the Han Chinese. But with the growing Chinese hold over Sinkiang after the defeat of Yakub Beg (in 1877, see chapter 2), and the reluctant opening up of China to Western interests in the second half of the nineteenth century, a reorientation of the northeastern wool trade of Tibet took place in an eastward direction (Fletcher 1979:38). As the Kansu borderlands were predominantly inhabited by Chinese muslims (or Hui), the growing number of Sino-Tibetan contacts in this area meant first and foremost a Tibetan-Hui encounter, in time creating a multi-faceted Tibetan-Hui economic and cultural interface (Lipman 1981:117-119). Through these Hui intermediaries, the Tibetan wool eventually reached Tientsin on the northeast China coast, from where it was shipped to Europe and America (Learner 1933:80, Scott 1934:24). By 1895, the wool had already assumed some importance in the economy of northeastern Tibet (cf. Rockhill 1894:90), and by the 1920s, World War I and its post-war economic boom had provided a tremendous stimulus to all participants in the wool trade. The heyday of Chinese wool exports fell in the mid-1920s (Lipman 1981: 116) but afterwards the trade declined, firstly as a result of the disturbed nature of the Ninghsia and Kansu states in the late 1920s, and secondly by growing Japanese influence in Manchuria in the 1930s, which discouraged foreign capital. The Japanese invasion of China in 1937 gave the *coup de grâce* to the Tibet-Tientsin wool trade, eliminating the eastern half of the trade route up to Paotou on the Middle Hoang ho (cf. Cammann 1951b:43ff.)

What we are interested in here, is the way in which the Tibetans of the northeastern grasslands became involved in this internationally oriented wool trade, as well as the particular structural form this process assumed through its Hui intermediaries and their contacts with the Tibetans. Traditionally, the wool trade of the nomads focused on a few frontier towns and monasteries. The nomads stayed as long as a month near the market towns, taking part in temple festivals, doing business, and making pilgrimages to nearby sacred places (Bird 1899:379, Tafel 1914 II:277-278, Ekvall 1939:53, Li An-che 1948:45).

With the increased demand for wool in the second half of the nineteenth century, two developments in the wool trade of northeastern Tibet took place. Firstly, the growing importance of a few wool collecting market towns and monasteries along Amdo's Kansu frontier, and secondly, the growing number of Hui (Chinese muslims) venturing into the Tibetan nomad lands to buy the wool on the spot for the lowest price. The first development became visible in the rise of Tankar, a Tibetan frontier town to the west of Sining, as a wool collecting centre (Rijnhart 1901:134,230, Tafel 1914 I:181, Coales 1919a:242, Fletcher 1979:30). The great monastic towns of Kumbum and Labrang too, through the development of their neighbouring trade villages, provided the necessary infrastructure for the growing trade of wool (for Kumbum, see Rockhill 1894:90, Carey 1902:155, Li An-che 1948: photo and caption following page 40; for Labrang, see Futterer 1900:326, Tafel 1914 II:313, Fürholzer 1942:199 (photo), Fletcher 1979:28). In addition, Jyekundo, near the southern border of Amdo, emerged as a great wool collecting centre (Teichman 1922:92). But as the distance from Jyekundo to Tankar (and Sining) was considerable, and the intervening stretch of country subject to Golok robbery (Tafel 1914 II:152), the wool from Jyekundo also found its way out of Tibet via the Szechuan frontier markets of Sungpan and Tachienlu. From there it was transported to the wool mills of Shanghai (Teichman 1922:97), that is to say until about 1918, after which renewed hostilities in the Sino-Tibetan borderland disrupted this very lucrative trade (Combe 1926:141). Tankar, however, remained by far the biggest wool exporting market of northeastern Tibet, because of the transport advantages it enjoyed (Coales 1919a:242).

The Tibet-Tientsin wool trade rested, at least partly so, in the possibility of cheap river transport down the Hoang-ho to Paotou, a burgeoning break-of-bulk point on the northern loop of the Middle Hoang-ho near the Ordos desert. Here the wool was repacked and subsequently transported by camel to Tientsin, and after 1923 by rail to Peking (Köhler 1952, Lipman 1981:120-123). The river transport between Lanchou and Paotou was a monopoly of the Hui, but it is the Tibetan side of their trade which deserves closer scrutiny in the context of this study.

There is an extremely interesting chapter in Ekvall's *Cultural relations on the Kansu-Tibetan border* (1939:48-62), describing the economic and cultural interaction between the Chinese muslims of West Kansu and the nomadic Tibetans of Amdo. The Hui venturing into Tibetan territory were mostly muslims from Sining, Heichou, and especially Taochou (Tafel 1914 II:248, Rock 1956:65, Lipman 1981:117). In fact, the Hui came to occupy the supreme role of economic middlemen and cultural brokers between the widely disparate Tibetan and Chinese societies involved. In this respect they resemble the Sharba of Sungpan (Tafel 1914 II:309), and also their

Bhotia confrères of Kumaon along the Indo-Tibetan border. Their success as middlemen can be partly explained by their location on the Sino-Tibetan border, and partly by their knowledge of Tibetan, which gave them a tremendous advantage in borderland commerce (Ekvall 1939:51,61). Having access to both Chinese manufactures and Tibetan nomad products, they could work an exchange, which greatly enriched themselves, and at the same time guaranteed a further strengthening of Hui-Tibetan trade contacts. It is worth citing Ekvall, as his facility with the Chinese language, his smattering of Tibetan, and his long-term residence in the area, have made possible a unique insight in the intricacies of border society.

> The Moslem trader goes into the Tibetan country for periods of time from three months to two years. Though he travels in a company which oftentimes represents a rather large caravan, nevertheless he will stay, with at best one or two companions, for a long time in very intimate association with a Tibetan community...When a caravan reaches a tribe it breaks up, each group going to its particular host...The traders have no particular rights except as guests of their hosts in the tribe. This 'guest-host' relationship is of varying degrees of cordiality, ranging all the way from a life-long warm and intimate friendship to a very casual and mercenary association... During their rather extended periods of residence in the Tibetan country, many of the Moslem traders take temporary Tibetan wives, and those who do not have numerous sexual affairs with the free and easy Tibetans (Ekvall 1939:53-54, 62)

The wool brought back from these trading ventures into Tibetan territory, was either sold to Chinese representatives of foreign export firms resident in Tankar or the big monasteries of Kumbum and Labrang (Tafel 1914 I:181,347n, II:313), or brought down to Lanchou, or even Paotou by the Hui themselves, in the hope of maximizing their profit margin. This could well be done, as the river transport on the Hoang ho was largely a muslim monopoly and fruitful schemes of collaboration existed between the buyers and transporters of wool (Lipman 1981:120).

The collapse of the Tibet-Tientsin wool trade at the end of the 1930s, due to geopolitical strife and outright war, had only limited repercussions on the Tibetan nomads. Their wool exports could be partly re-channelled via Sungpan and Tachienlu, and even when the latter route had become impracticable because of civil war in Szechuan, as well as renewed Sino-Tibetan frontier fighting, part of the wool produced in the northern nomad countries found its way to foreign markets via Lhasa and Kalimpong (Radhu 1981:167-168). Until 1930, some of the wool also reached Russia by way of a relatively undisturbed Sinkiang (Bosshard 1929:447-448).

The Indo-Tibetan trade through the central Himalayas deserves a small section of its own, because it fruitfully extends our earlier discussion of locational shifts in trade in the western Himalayas, and because it had major consequences for the export of wool from Tibet. Traditionally, trade across the central Himalaya went by Nepal, especially via the Kathmandu valley, where the Newar had come to occupy a supreme position as economic middlemen and cultural brokers between India and Tibet (cf. Lewis 1984). In a sense, they played a role similar to that of the Bhotia of Kumaon, but on a much grander scale, and in a vastly different geohistorical setting. With the stifling of their trade under the Gorkhali government after 1768, and the isolationist policies of the Rana in the nineteenth century, Bhotia populations along Nepal's northern border came to supplement, and partly replace, the trade of the Newar. The Arun valley, for example, or more precisely its Tamur tributary, in eastern Nepal, developed into an important trade route (Sen 1971:31, Von Fürer-Haimendorf 1975:121, cf. Morris 1923:165-166), but this could not prevent a further decline of Indo-Tibetan trade via Nepal. With the growing hold of Britain over Sikkim after 1861, and Bhutan after 1865, but in particular after the Anglo-Chinese Trade Convention of 1890 (see chapter 2), trade again shifted eastwards, and within two decades the Chumbi valley route succeeded in capturing Nepal's leading position in the trade with Tibet. By the turn of the twentieth century, Kalimpong had definitively replaced Kathmandu as the entrepôt of trans-Himalayan trade, even to the extent that Newar merchants from Kathmandu shifted their locus of activity to Kalimpong (Uprety 1980:166-167). The growing trade via Chumbi also had a remarkable effect on the Tromowa, the local inhabitants of the Chumbi valley. Just like the Kumaon Bhotia, who were favoured by their location as trans-Himalayan transporters, the Tromowa grew rich in a few decades towards the end of the nineteenth century. Their success was the result of the combined effects of their transport monopoly and the rise of British power in the central Himalayas (Campbell 1875:137, Ryder 1905:370-371, Walsh 1906, Bell 1928:113-114, 120-121, 130-131). But after the Younghusband expedition of 1904, they had to face competition from big Marwari and Tibetan traders, especially where it concerned the wholesale trade of wool, which rose to great prominence in the first four decades of the twentieth century.

By 1944 wool comprised over 90 per cent of Tibet's annual exports, some destined for the American east coast (Brown 1984:115). The international wool trade had come to dominate the Tibetan economy to the extent that the Tibetans were greatly at a loss when World War II cut the export to foreign markets. In the decade before the war, the southward-bound wool trade via Kalimpong had become an arena of competition for the Marwari from India and a class of newly arisen traders from central and eastern Tibet. One of the most powerful among the latter was Yarpel Pangda Tsang from Kham, who had become the Tibetan government's major trade agent (Stoddard 1985:77-78). The fortunes of Pangda Tsang rested in particular in the wool trade, though Marwari competition had by no means been broken. Already in January 1932, the thirteenth Dalai Lama had written a letter to the American journalist Suydam Cutting, strange to say, one of the few contacts of Tibet with America, in which he pointed out the importance of passing by Marwari middlemen trade at Kalimpong:

> From now onward if Pangda Tsang could deliver the wool at a fixed price to the buying agents of the big American wool merchants at Kalimpong (trade town of northern Bengal) without having to pass through the hands of the Malwaris (woollen merchants of Kalimpong) and thereby doing away with the middlemen's profit, it would be of great advantage to the government (Cutting 1940:177-178)

Cutting succeeded in establishing a few trade contacts and for a couple of years some of the wool from Tibet found its way directly to the American market. But the war cut off the export and the Tibetans were temporarily without this source of revenue. Thus it should come as no surprise, that when the Americans Ilia Tolstoy and Brooke Dolan visited Tibet in the autumn of 1942, they were approached by Pangda Tsang, asking them when the United States would again buy Tibetan wool (Tolstoy 1946:178).

Almost imperceptibly we have moved in our analysis from the traditional barter trade in salt and grain to the growing importance of a long-distance commerce in tea and wool, the latter in particular being subject to the vagaries of the world-market and the geopolitical predicament of its transport lines. Growing trade in the wake of the Younghusband expedition tended to emphasize the British-Indian connection, a process being reinforced by the internal chaos in China in the 1920s and 30s, when the overland trade bound for Tibet, except that for tea, was diverted via Calcutta and other Indian centres (Macdonald 1929:125). The locational shift of the Tibetan wool trade is but one example of this process of spatial reorientation. This largely externally induced process also brought changes in the long-distance trade of luxury goods, a one-time important pillar of Tibetan prosperity. It is to this trade and to the versatility of its fairs and markets that we turn now.

The long-distance trade in luxury goods

Behind the above, almost self-evident caption of this section lie hidden two conceptual problems. To put it bluntly, what is long-distance trade and what do we understand by luxury goods? These questions are important, because in a Tibetan context, trade beyond the local exchange of daily necessities has, in variable degrees, always formed an important pillar of the Tibetan economy. Von Fürer-Haimendorf, for example, in his well-known book about the role of trade in Nepal's northern border communities, stated with regard to the Sherpas of Khumbu that 'one may venture the estimate that up to 1959, external trade, i.e. trade with areas outside Khumbu, accounted for between one-third and one-fourth of the Sherpa's total income from all branches of their economy' (Von Fürer-Haimendorf 1975:73). A similar estimate for Tibet as a whole seems a near impossibility, in view of the lack of adequate statistics for traditional Tibet, and, after the Chinese takeover in 1950 the almost wholesale destruction of monastic records and private papers - where these existed. However, it seems likely that many areas in Tibet would not have been viable without extensive involvement in long-distance trade.

But when may this trade be called long-distance, and who were actually involved in it? Within the context of this study, long-distance trade has been defined as that form of commercial activity which involves the crossing of international boundaries, or the penetration into a non-familiar culture or society, or both. Schrader (1988:6-10) gives a useful descriptive categorization of all shades of long-distance trade ranging from subsistence-oriented small-scale trade to large-scale profit-oriented commerce. His finely-tuned typology makes it possible to see the different stages through which aspiring traders may pass before they end up as fully-fledged long-distance traders - or not. But he makes it also clear that many of these stages overlap and that single households or even whole ethnic groups may be engaged in different forms of trade at the same time (ibid.:10).

Basically, his typology boils down to a continuum ranging from small to large traders and their trade. This distinction does not necessarily imply that small traders did not venture over greater distance. In fact, they did, but their journeys, for the majority of them involved, seldom penetrated deep into foreign territory and usually did not extend the one-month time limit. It was again Von Fürer-Haimendorf who recognized the primordial distinction between small and big traders in a Tibeto-Himalayan setting. According to him, small traders were generally farmers who engaged only occasionally in trade, combining the sale of locally or regionally produced goods with the purchase of daily necessities not procurable in their home area. On quite a different level lay the trading operations of the bigger merchants, who had practically left farming and derived most or all of their income from commerce (Von Fürer-Haimendorf 1975:68). The latter stage is characteristic for those traders who wanted to embark upon a career as a full-time trader.

This study focuses in particular on the flexibility of traders along the large-scale and genuine long-distance extremity of the continuum mentioned above. The trade on this end was usually in non-essential, luxury products, generally low weight for value, easily transportable, and high in price. To this category belonged traditionally much sought-after commodities like amber and musk, but also coral and turquoise, supplemented by silk from China and indigenous cotton from Nepal. With the rising importance of the British-Indian *économie-monde*, these were partly replaced by cheap Indian-made textiles, as well as a whole array of modern European goods for the use and entertainment of the richer classes in Tibet. The almost chronic disturbances in a fading imperial China and the birth pangs of the new republic, reduced Tibetan contact with the Chinese *économie-monde* considerably, but of course the proximity of eastern Tibet to China could and can never be nullified or neglected in terms of potential economic integration. However, the historically specific trade situation that arose from these circumstances with regard to Tibet in the first half of the twentieth century, was one of an increased orientation towards the south, i.e. India, where the *Pax Britannica* guaranteed a safety of roads and the unrestricted movement of goods, except for salt. In particular after the Younghusband expedition of 1904, trade steadily increased and became of a more intentionally organized and large-scale nature.

Historically speaking, the career of a full-time long-distance trader often implied a change of residence, perhaps even to another country with a foreign culture, producing the outline of what might eventually develop into a trading minority. Such trading minorities were generally patronized by local power holders, who saw in the presence of long-distance traders the possiblity of fortifying their position by means of active involvement and protection of their trade. In such a situation, the economic surplus necessary for the maintenance of a state structure and bureaucracy might be critically dependent on fluctuations in trade, themselves caused by external political factors, or even outright geopolitical change. In a Tibetan application, this theorizing may at least partly explain the formation of the Dalai Lama's realm in Central Tibet in the seventeenth century, in combination with the rise of Lhasa-based trading communities like the Nepalese Newari and the Indian Kashmiri. It may also explain the steady decline of these communities in the second half of the nineteenth century, as the long-distance trade on which their prosperity rested, was critically injured by the shrinking 'frontier' nature of the Tibetan territory as outlined in chapter 2. The growing Chinese pressure in the eighteenth century, the mounting Russian-British-Chinese stalemate in Central Asia in the nineteenth, and the Anglo-Chinese encounter in Tibet in the twentieth, may all be interpreted as ever so many external drawbacks to the development of trade in the Tibetan culture region. However, the second half of the nineteenth century and the first half of the twentieth also saw a relatively independent Tibet, whose boundaries were successfully defended against the Chinese in the east (except for the brief period 1910-1912), and sufficiently guaranteed by the

British, to allow for the temporary rise of Sino and Indo-Tibetan border communities as trans-frontier and cross-cultural traders. It is this spectrum of historically specific trade contexts for small and big traders from different Tibetan regions, that will be analysed in the remainder of this chapter.

Pilgrimage, fairs, and trade

In discussing the regionality of Tibet in the previous chapter, the prominent place of pilgrimage has been briefly mentioned. Pilgrims were many, as were the power places where the pilgrim's *karma* could be restored or enriched. The essential element of pilgrimage in its Tibetan form (after ancient Indian models) was the circum-ambulation of cult objects, whether mountains, lakes, temples, monasteries or caves (Blondeau 1960:205). What makes pilgrimage relevant in the context of this study is its close relation to economic activity, in particular trade. Though it is impossible to tell whether pilgrimage created trade or vice versa, it seems undeniable that the large flows of pilgrims generated by Lhasa and a few other centres contributed to the growth of a network of international exchange, spanning the length and breadth of Central Asia (ibid.:212). But regional centres of pilgrimage too, drew numerous worshippers.

Lhasa as the supreme focus of pilgrimage in the Tibetan Buddhist world, harbouring its highest incarnation, the Dalai Lama, attracted pilgrims from all over Tibet and even beyond. Particularly at the times of a major festival, such as the great Monlam Prayer following the Losar or New Year celebrations, the population of Lhasa, which was ordinarily perhaps fifteen to twenty thousand, swelled to four or five times this number (Bell 1924b:95-96, cf. the eighteenth-century Capuchin missionary figure of 80,000 inhabitants as quoted by Snellgrove and Richardson 1980:224). Tashilunpo too, the seat of the Panchen Lama near Shigatse, drew tens of thousands of pilgrims, single audiences at major celebrations bringing together six thousand pilgrims and lookers-on before the great Living Buddha (Hedin 1910-1913 I:304, see also plates 111 and 112). Numbers of pilgrims to other famous places of pilgrimage, such as the sacred mountains of Kailash, Kawakarpo, and Takpa Siri also ran into the thousands, especially during the years of 'High Pilgrimage', which occurred in twelve-year cycles (Sherring 1906:283, Duncan 1952:132, Blondeau 1960:210).

Pilgrimage was such an institutionalized feature of Tibetan regionality that several pilgrim guides to shrines great and small came to be written (see for example Ferrari 1958, Blondeau 1960:213-217, cf. Dowman 1988). Pilgrim itineraries around sacred mountains and lakes were spelled out step by step, whole pilgrim rounds to a variety of sacred places annotated, while later versions even catered for the need of pilgrims going to Bodh Gaya and related places in India (Blondeau 1960:216-217). The range of the great power places of Central Tibet was considerable. Pilgrims flocking to Lhasa and surrounding places came from Ladakh, Ngari, the Himalayan border districts of India, the kingdoms of Nepal, Sikkim and Bhutan, faraway districts in Southeast Tibet like Pome and Zayul, petty semi-independent states like Mili and Chala, nomad countries all over Tibet, the provinces of Kham and Amdo, further from Mongolia, and even Southern Siberia, the homeland of the Buddhist Kalmuks and Buriats. In its range, the above pilgrim network resembles the network of towns and routes as shown in Figure 4, though more routes from all over Tibet should be spaced in to obtain a picture nearer to reality (cf. Hedin 1910-1913 II:203). It is possible, and even probable, that the importance of regional centres of pilgrimage has always been underestimated, in particular of those outside the confines of Central Tibet. Besides Kailash, which is relatively well known (Pranavananda 1950, Stoll 1966, Snelling 1983, Tucci 1989:97-172), as well as the big Gelukpa monasteries of Kumbum and Labrang in Amdo (Filchner 1906, 1933, Li An-che 1982), there were many places of pilgrimage never or only seldom visited by outsiders, and consequently we are only erratically informed about them. What to say for example about the holy mountainside of Lapchi Kang on the Nepal-Tibet border and one-time abode of Milarepa (cf. Macdonald 1990:199, Huber 1997; for Halase in eastern Nepal, see Macdonald 1985), which was visited annually by thousands of pilgrims according to the Cambridge botanist Wollaston (1922:10). Or the but dimly known Takpa Siri in the district of Tsari, where various villages are said to have subsisted on the money they could earn by providing transport for the numerous pilgrims (Dunbar 1915:2-6, Kingdon Ward 1936:390,

Ludlow 1938:9, Fletcher 1975:94; see also De Rossi Filibeck 1990 and Huber 1994). Or again the holy mountains of Shar Dungri, Norththeast of Sungpan (Tafel 1914 II:277-278), Amne Niangchen East of Labrang (Li An-che 1948), the twin-peaks of Dorjetroleh, Northeast of Gartok in Kham (Duncan 1929:116-117, 1952:132) and last but not least Kawakarpo, the 'mountain of silver snow' on the Salween-Mekong divide (Bacot 1908, 1909:93-142, Kingdon Ward 1913: plates XXI and XXIX facing pages 98 and 150, Gregory and Gregory 1923: plates XI and XII, facing pages 216 and 232, Handel-Mazzetti 1927:186-190, Duncan 1929:51). All these must have generated considerable flows of pilgrims, creating a culturally defined *espace-mouvement*, which however was also characterized by concomitant forms of commercial activity, ranging from the pedlar's hawking to the prince's caravan trade (for further aspects of Tibetan pilgrimage see now: Macdonald (ed.) 1997, McKay (ed.) 1998).

The high mobility of people in the context of pilgrimage, the scale at which it took place, as well as the vast distances covered by the pilgrims, all contributed to the likelihood of trade. Pilgrims were sometimes away for over two years (cf. Tafel 1914 II:253) and had to barter their way to Lhasa and other places. The pilgrimage of farmers and herders was often combined with petty trade (Carrasco 1959:213) their cattle being used as walking merchandise. In addition, they might have saved some of their agricultural surpluses while still at home, which were now carried in the form of bundles of tea, parcels of gold dust, and silver talents (Markham 1876:83). Devotees generally managed to combine religion with a little business and the shops of Lhasa and the fairs of Kailash definitely felt their presence (Sherring 1906:159, 283-284).

At times of great religious festivals, supraregional fairs under the protection of the monasteries saw the gathering of numerous trading pilgrims. The demand generated by the seasonal clustering of large numbers of pilgrims also brought together regular traders from all over Central Asia and adjoining countries. In addition, fakirs, mendicants, and charlatans tried their luck, performing their tricks and selling their magical medicines. Perhaps we can do no better than to cite at some length the eye-witness report by Susie Rijnhart, who assisted in the celebration of the yearly 'Butter God Festival' at the monastery of Kumbum in 1897.

> For some days previous to it the roads leading to the lamasery are literally covered with travellers arriving from China, Mongolia, and all Tibetan territories. Some are mounted on horses, driving before them their heavily-burdened yaks; others, of higher rank, are borne on stately camels, with long retinues of pedestrian pilgrims following behind. There are priests with closely shaven heads and wooden knapsacks thrown over their shoulders, and laymen with long, tattered sheepskin gowns and short wild-looking hair. As the pilgrims arrive, the rooms of the lamasery are first occupied, then the black tents of the Tibetans begin to rise until the entire valley and hillside become as one vast encampment resounding with the shouts and laughter of men, women and children, the whining of camels, the neighing of horses and mules, the barking of dogs, the clattering of gongs and cymbals, the blowing of horns and the ringing of bells. On the main road to the temple are scores of white tents of Mongol and Chinese merchants who come not only to pay their respects to the Buddha, but to dispose of their wares, consisting chiefly of cutlery, needles, cloth boots, tea, charm-boxes, idols and other articles (Rijnhart 1901:115)

Of course, not all of these fairs were of the same importance. In fact, there was a whole hierarchy of greater and lesser sacred places with their corresponding fairs, structurally perhaps not unlike the geographer's Central Place system. Sacred places of different levels had corresponding pilgrim fields, creating a kind of nested hierarchy ultimately encompassing the entire population of Tibet and its culturally related border worlds (cf. Bhardwaj 1973:6-7, for an example from the Indian Himalayas). In practice, such a set-up meant that some fairs were held less often than others, were of longer duration, and offered a greater variety of goods, in addition to a high or even temporarily increased degree of sacredness of the locality involved. The twelve-year 'High Pilgrimage' and corresponding Khumb mela near Kailash is a good example of the latter (Sherring 1906:28, Hedin 1910-1913 I:191). Let us briefly cast a glance now at two very specific Tibetan items of luxury trade, that were often to be seen at places of pilgrimage: medicinal herbs and precious stones.

Temporary and chronic illness has always been part and parcel of the *condition humaine*, and pilgrims too, did not escape that predicament. Weakened perhaps by insufficient food on their long journey across high passes, quite a few of them were afflicted by strange ailments that needed to be cured. As the mountainous areas of the Himalayas and eastern Tibet yield many an officinal herb of proven effect, herb collectors and medicine sellers plied their trade successfully at the crowded fairs. Monasteries too, were sometimes centres of herbal medicine preparation (cf. Harrer 1952:162). At the fairs, herbs also changed hands from collectors to wholesalers, who transported greater quantities to the lowland markets of India and China (Heim 1933:65, and Figure 45 facing page 56). This trade had already a long history and may be traced back to the seventeenth century (Finch 1611, as quoted by Stein 1918:173, Tavernier 1692, as quoted by Lévi 1905-1908 I:94, Hamilton 1819:86). Especially the rhubarb trade developed into a long-distance commerce of stable profit and great range. We shall briefly return to this trade in a following section.

The step from herbal medicines to precious stones such as traded at the fairs of Tibet, is less than one might think at first sight. In a world full of symbolism as traditional Tibet undoubtedly was, gemstones had their own meaning attuned to the need of the hour. One of them was the healing power stones were thought to possess, and consequently their appreciation as medicine ranked next to their valuation as ornaments. Turquoise, for example, the widely appreciated gemstone of Tibet, was in high demand in both qualities (Walker-Watson 1983:17, cf. Filchner 1933:413). In addition, coral, pearls, amber, rubies and jade found their way into Tibet, the low weight for value quality making them a preferred item for the itinerant traders plying the fairs. Precious stones came from Afghanistan, India, Burma, and Turkestan (Ryall 1879:450, Kawaguchi 1909:453-454, Calhoun 1929:708ff., Deasy 1901:156; for amber, see Jest 1987:228-230), but less so from the Himalayas (Heron 1930:21). If they could afford it, Tibetans spent fortunes on ornamentation. The Tibet explorer William Gill, in his *River of Golden Sand*, left us the following significant passage:

> The Tibetans, both men and women, are possessed of a taste also amounting to frenzy for coral and turquoises; and the immense quantity of these that are used is surprising. The scabbards of their swords, the covers of their charm-boxes, their earrings or bracelets, all are ornamented with coral and turquoises (Gill 1880 II:107)

Consequently, precious stones commanded a glorious sale, and not only in pilgrim centres. Tibetan pilgrimage came to extend beyond its immediate cultural domain from the beginning of the nineteenth century onwards. The one exception to this general statement was the Kathmandu valley in Nepal, which had already been visited for centuries by Tibetans, especially in wintertime (Hamilton 1819:212-213, Oldfield 1880 I:11, Snellgrove and Richardson 1980:202). Since the era of the seventeenth-century Malla kings, when free circulation across the Himalaya was still the rule, Tibetans increasingly had come to create their own niche in valley society, a position best visible near the stupas of Bodnath and Swayambunath (Wright 1877:27, Lévi 1905-1908 II:319, 332, 336). The German scholar Kurt Boeck, in his well-illustrated book on his journey to India and Nepal in 1898, gives an interesting impression of what he calls the Tibetan village of Bodnath (Boeck 1903:293-301; see also the frontispiece of the same book). According to him, Tibetans visited the Kathmandu valley in wintertime to exchange salt, yak tails, and woollen blankets for grain, and in addition were dealing in gold dust, turquoise, agate, rubies, and other precious stones, together with medicinal herbs (ibid.:294). They still did so recently at the time of the Tibetan New Year (personal communication A.W. Macdonald).

Apart from these pilgrimages and trading ventures into the Kathmandu valley, journeys to places well outside the Tibetan cultural sphere of influence, in particular India, did become fashionable in the course of the nineteenth century (Blondeau 1960:218-219). The holiest place to visit for the Tibetans was Bodh Gaya, where Buddha attained enlightenment under a *pipal* tree. As the Indian plains are scorching hot in summertime, these journeys of pilgrimage too, took place during the winter season, over time accelerated in pace and volume by the beginnings of railway transport in the Ganga Plain, and the increasing orientation of Central Tibet towards a rising British-Indian *économie-monde*. These journeys of pilgrimage, especially in its extended form throughout the northern plains and the Indian Himalayas, were instigated by the rich who gained merit by paying poor people to go on pilgrimage for them. From the beginning of the twentieth century onwards, they came to regard Kalimpong in the Sikkim Himalaya as their main point of departure. However, it also became the refuge of stranded pilgrims, who, venturing into the plains, had lost all their money and now tried to make ends meet by selling off their personal belongings (ibid.:219). The more successful traders and pilgrims on their way to Bodh Gaya, often passed through Calcutta, satisfying both their natural curiosity for things beyond the Tibetan ken and their passion for trade (Richardus 1989:41).

To avoid a one-sided picture, it should be mentioned here that similar developments took place in eastern Tibet, though on a smaller scale. With the rise of Tachienlu on the Sino-Tibetan border, quite a few Tibetans, ventured into China, especially to the great pilgrim mountain of Omei Shan in southern Szechuan (Cooper 1871:176, Baber 1882:42, Hosie 1905:9, Hackmann 1907:9). Urga in Mongolia too, as the seat of a primary Living Buddha, became the object of pilgrimage and trade for Tibetans from Amdo, as well as for monastic trade missions from all over Tibet (Tsybikoff 1904:96, Ossendowski 1922:235, cf. Tsybikoff 1992). The two-year stay of the Dalai Lama in Urga (1904-1906; see chapter 2) may temporarily have emphasized its renown as a centre of pilgrimage.

Thus, pilgrimage to sacred places, whether by private pilgrims or monastic missions, had a definite economic effect becoming visible in the commercial activities accompanying major religious festivals. In fact, these fairs as they were commonly called, have been defined as 'annual gatherings of buyers and sellers at a particular place and time for the purpose of trade, often following a religious function, and accompanied by forms of amusement and entertainment' (Longman Dictionary 1988) a description which well fits the Tibetan situation. However, when the scale of the trade increased, fairs often assumed a more secular character, in which the exchange of goods came to dominate the religious celebrations.

From the sacred to the profane

In the period under investigation, the 'long' century between 1850 and 1950, fairs gradually shed their aura of being predominantly religious festivals. The larger the fair, the greater the attraction for full-time traders, who in the course of the nineteenth century came to consider monetary profit to be the leading motive for their attendance. For them the fairs were not places of karmic restoration, but arenas for economic competition. In order to maximize profits they sought to realize optimal locational conditions by turning footloose, visiting theatres of commercial exchange, even when these were not, strictly speaking, the product of a religious festival. Specialized itinerant traders became a regular feature of fairs that were more a response to the changing geohistorical conditions of long-distance trade than the slavish following of the pilgrim crowds near Living Buddhas or sacred mountains. In particular the Himalayan border regions became the scene of a whole series of frontier fairs that reflected the growing orientation of southern Tibet on a rising British-Indian *économie-monde*.

The distinguishing feature of fairs as commercial gatherings was their theoretical openness to all trade and traders, irrespective of their provenance. As such they could flourish in times of limited political interference and in areas outside effective governmental control, 'frontier' conditions that were satisfied in the 'long' century of Tibet and its borderlands. But if we look at the geographical distribution of fairs, it is also clear that they were commonly held in fringe zones of different ecozones and culturally disparate *économies-mondes*. Though Tibet cannot properly be called an *économie-monde*, both the ecozonal and the cultural fringe argument hold in regard to the location of its fairs. The European parallel, in particular with regard to the great medieval fairs of France and Germany, is interesting, but cannot be given any space here (but see Allix 1922:532-569, Pirenne 1969:83-89, Braudel 1966 I:347-350, 1979 II:63-75).

The above theorizing fits well in with Braudel's characterization of India and China in terms of the development of their fairs (Braudel 1979 II:104-109). India, according to Braudel, is the land of fairs *par excellence* (ibid.:106-107). Perhaps this may be explained by the decentralized nature of its political organization over much of its history, in contrast to China, where fairs only seem to have flourished in times of desintegration of the Chinese central polity. From the moment onwards that fresh political unity was achieved, and the Chinese bureaucracy restored to its former efficiency, fairs in the interior of China declined, but remained intact in a few frontier zones (hypothesis put forward by Etienne Balazs, quoted by Braudel 1979 II:109). This distinction between India and China may well explain the relative preponderance of fairs along the Himalayan border of Tibet, and their paucity along the Sino-Tibetan one. Consequently, the presence of itinerant traders and pedlars, on which the fair as a commercial phenomenon rested, was far more pronounced in Tibet's southern reaches than in its eastern ones (see Figure 6).

Though not exhaustive, the map shows the main fairs of the Tibetan culture region, as well as the 'counterfairs' on the cis-Himalayan side in the late nineteenth/early twentieth century. Basically, the distribution of fairs reflects the major collecting and distribution centres along trade routes breaking through the main Himalayan chain. What the map does not show, is the seasonal as well as the long-term dynamics of their occurrence. The fair at Gartok (Rawling 1905a, 1905b:272), for example, was followed by the one at Kanam in Kinnaur near the Tibetan border, and finally moved on to Rampur, the capital of the former state of Bashahr (Cable et al. 1929:99, Pallis 1949:68, Singh 1990:246). Or, alternatively, the wool collected at Rudok moved down to Patseo in Upper Lahul, from where the fair shifted in turn to Sultanpur, the wool being sold to down-country purchasers during the Kulu Dussehra festival (Harcourt 1871:69, Shuttleworth 1923:558, Den Doolaard 1962:33, Prince Peter 1963:310-311). This sequence of seasonal *melas* or fairs at different altitudes facilitated the trade along the major commercial circuits, which, with the growing importance of the wool trade towards the end of the nineteenth century, served to emphasize Western Tibet's integration with the British-Indian *économie-monde* (cf. Tucci and Ghersi 1935:4-6). Figure 6 also fails to convey the long-term dynamics of the fairs mentioned. For example, the then Deputy Commissioner of Almora, Sherring, stated that 'Taklakot (or Purang) is undoubtedly a rising centre' (Sherring 1906:205), which undoubtedly is true, as it came to funnel the wool trade from all over the Kailash region in the direction of the Kumaon Bhotia villages and the counterfairs on the Indian side of the border. The Gyanima fair was another essential link in this chain (ibid.:159-160, 206). Still further eastwards lay the Gandaki valley, a major Himalayan breakthrough in West-Central Nepal, harbouring an age-old trade route between Tibet and India. However, the centralized nature of the Gorkhali state in the nineteenth and twentieth century, probably prevented the full flowering of fairs in the area. In addition, the Rana regime in Nepal (1846-1950), with its isolationist policies, further stifled trade by overcontrol, though smuggling along this route may have received a boost by these restrictive policies, based as they were on the sale of trade monopolies to a few big traders (cf. the rise of the Thakali, for which see Manzardo 1978:14-48). Long-distance transit-trade via the Kathmandu valley and the border towns of Kyirong and Nilam

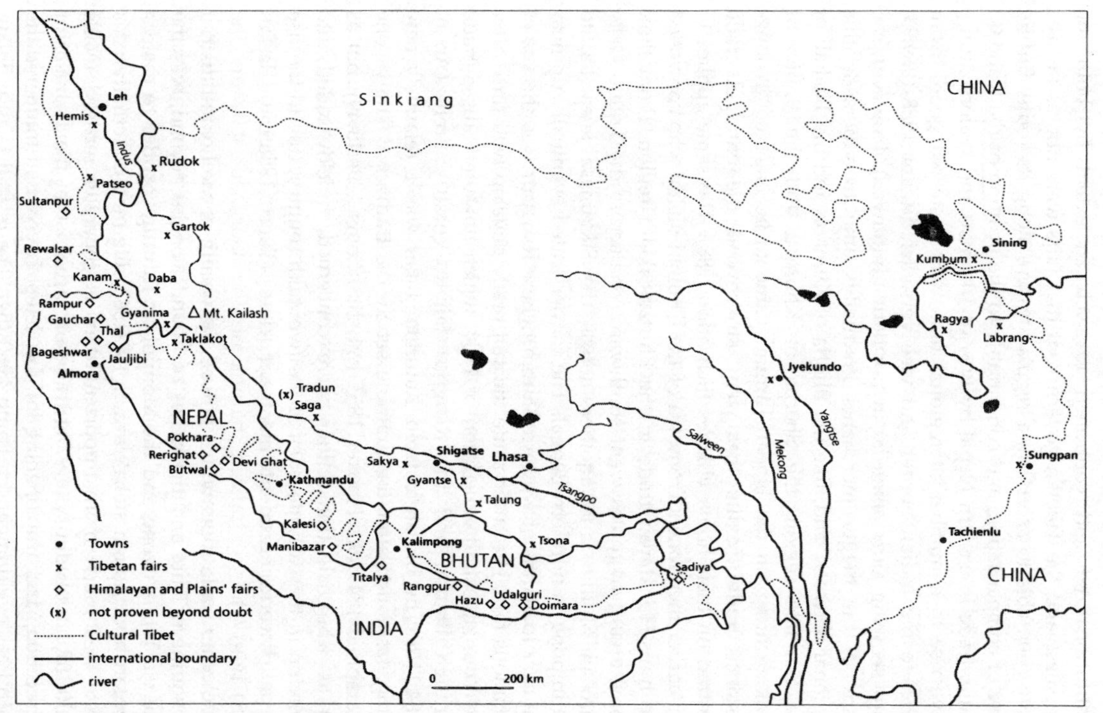

Figure 6 Main fairs 19th-20th centuries

(Kuti) to the great monastic cities of Central Tibet, had been institutionalized and controlled to such an extent by both the Nepalese and the Tibetan government that fairs were not, as far as I have been able to ascertain, a regular feature along its route. But by way of compensation, and comparable to the position of the Gandaki route, trade in eastern Nepal by way of Khumbu and Walongchung, gave rise to a number of regional fairs, which steered goods from Tibet to the Indian border and vice versa (cf. Sagant 1968-1969:93, map showing *foires annuelles* in northern Limbuwan). However, the trade of the bigger merchants gradually came to supersede this regional network, and, like the Bhotia of Kumaon and the Thakali of the Gandaki region, the Sherpa of Khumbu and the Bhotia of Walongchung on the Upper Tamur came to be engaged in long-distance trade circuits that went far beyond the entrepôt trade centred on their home villages (Schrader 1988). The same applies to the earlier mentioned Tromowa of the Chumbi valley who controlled the trans-Himalayan trade in the Bhutan-Sikkim region. From their home area, two routes went southward, one across the Tremo La to Paro in Bhutan, and another, across the Sikkimese Jelep La, to Kalimpong in northern Bengal. The former ended eventually up near the *duar* lowlands of western Bhutan, where Rangpur was the site of a famous fair. The latter route did not really develop well until after the Younghusband expedition of 1904, which however caused trade through Bhutan and the Rangpur fair to cease entirely (Anon. 1984:116). The British-fostered Kalimpong fair was a relatively new thing, fashioned after the example set by the traditional Titalya one (Campbell 1849:490, Hooker 1855 I:91, II:8, Louis 1894:48-49), but as far as wholesale transactions were concerned, quickly faded into oblivion in the early decades of the twentieth century, due to the rise of a powerful resident merchant class (Tucci 1956:159, Radhu 1981:163-171).

Another trade route which tapped the wealth of the Lobrak district of southern Tibet and the riches of Ü and Kongbo beyond, was the one via Tsöna dzong and the Monyul or Tawang corridor to eastern Bhutan and Assam (Chakravarti 1976:365, Figure 2). Actually, this route was much more important than is generally realized (Mills 1950:157, Choudhury 1977:181), but again the Younghusband expedition, and the opening of the Jelep La route, smothered its potential development (cf. Lamb 1960:354). The related fairs at Tsöna

(Bailey 1914:358, Burrard 1915 I:177-178), Doimera, Udalguri, and Hazu (Markham 1875:312, Elwin 1959:10-11, 1958:XIX) in all probability suffered accordingly.

Fairs along the Sino-Tibetan border were far less common than in the Himalayan region. This does not mean that commercial exchange was unimportant. In fact, the volume of Tibet's China trade had always been greater than its trade with India, and on top of that, more institutionalized. Since the beginning of the eighteenth century already, Tachienlu and Sining had grown as the major break-of-bulk points between China and Tibet. Trade was in the hands of Chinese merchants, though with the crumbling of Chinese power in the second half of the nineteenth century, Tibetan traders were able to make successful inroads into this monopoly (Desgodins 1885:337, Bower 1894:282). Fairs comparable to those in the Himalayan border world, were only to be found near places of supraregional exchange like Kumbum, mentioned earlier in this chapter, Jyekundo (see the lively description of the annual fair at Tashi gompa by Grenard 1904:128-130), or Ragya (Rock 1930:162, photo on page 157), the latter being but a relatively tiny affair. Although annual tribal fairs did exist on the Sino-Tibetan border (Duncan 1952:100), large ones seem to have been the exception rather than the rule. Gill mentions an annual fair at Sungpan, where Si-fan, the Mongols of Kokonor, and the Mantzu brought skins of all kinds, musk, deer horns, rhubarb, and medicines, which they exchanged for crockery, cotton goods, and little trifles (Gill 1880 I:379, cf. Bird 1899:379). But as the bigger trade of the place lay in reality in the hands of the locally dominant Muslim Chinese, trade with the Tibetan and Tibetanized border populations had progressed beyond the 'equal exchange' of goods at a relatively open fair. In fact, these borderlands had developed into a smuggler's paradise for tea, musk, opium, and modern weapons, a sort of Sino-Tibetan 'Wild West', in which Sungpan, and in particular the neighbouring hamlet of Matang, occupied a prominent place (Bird 1899:333,424, Tafel 1914 II:248). The latter author is worth quoting.

> A remote market-place like Matang is nowhere in the world a centre of civilization. In Matang daily life stands under the sign of the brutal. Orgies of all kinds, savage drinking-bouts, and trade in children, women and grown-up slaves are rife...No day passes without a wrong. There is thrusting and

> stabbing, there is smart money being paid as an act of reconciliation at the sound of horns and trumpets and if not, the fighting goes on and on (Tafel 1914 II:248, author's translation)

The atmosphere described, resembles that of the Tibetan border town of Dingri Gang-gar as portrayed by Aziz (1978:37,101), or the one I still personally witnessed one evening in the early 1980s in a Nyishangba-frequented inn at the village of Chame in the Manang district of north-central Nepal. It seems an unavoidable concomitant of fortunes lost and won in one evening and the general stress which accompanies the more oblique side of cross-cultural border trade.

The slow extinction of fairs in the Himalayan region and their virtual disappearance along the Sino-Tibetan border in the period under review, had everything to do with the rise of a more professionalized trade circuit, focusing on urban markets and a few through-going transport routes, like the one across the Jelep La to Kalimpong, or the main Tibet-China road via Tachienlu. Fairs dwindled insofar as they were meant to provide a wholesale market for specialized traders. The latter increasingly shifted their activity to the towns, where the grander scale of the business precipitated new forms of a capitalist-oriented trade in the hands of a few trading families or firms. Wholesale trade became of age, and developed quite independently from the traditional trade circuits centring on the fairs and local markets. The bigger itinerant traders established themselves as resident merchants, who through their commercial agents tried to develop direct lines of exchange with a few merchants or institutions on the other side of the border. The Marwari of Kalimpong and the case of Tibetan government traders like Pangda Tsang have been mentioned, and others too, sought to join this more formalized trade.

To make the picture of Tibet as a trading region complete, we still have to focus on the transformation of traditional, long-distance trade in luxury goods by foreign traders to a more open, yet increasingly government-controlled trade. And as the government of Tibet had close links to the bigger monasteries, it should come as no surprise that these are relevant again to our discussion.

The ecclesiastical state and trade

Earlier in this chapter we have hinted at the relevance of long-distance trade for local power holders. It is quite likely, though not proven beyond any doubt, that the rise of the Gelukpa order in Central Tibet, and its consolidation into a kind of ecclesiastical state in the seventeenth century, was at least partly related to the wealth generated by long-distance trade (cf. Gaborieau 1973:17-18). In fact, the whole issue deserves a separate investigation, which goes beyond the limits set for this study. According to Snellgrove and Richardson (1980:156), the great monasteries of central and eastern Tibet, from the fourteenth century onwards already, grew rich on their China trade, which, disguised as 'tribute missions' to the Emperor's court, served no other purpose than the trade in luxury goods (cf. Fairbank and Têng 1941). These 'government'-controlled trade missions were really large caravans equipped by the leading monasteries of Tibet, who in doing so succeeded in amassing more wealth than was probably good for them. In addition, the heyday of the seventeenth century Gelukpa administration, saw the flocking of hundreds of foreign traders to Lhasa, of whom Kashmiri, Newari, and Chinese were the most important (Gaborieau 1973:14-36, Lewis 1984, Markham 1876:258-291). Lhasa, as the centre of the Tibetan Buddhist world, also received a kind of tribute missions, for example the Lapchak from Ladakh (Petech 1977:161-162, Radhu 1981, Bray 1990), which connected central Tibet to the Afghan and Kashmir-Yarkand trade circuits. As outlined in chapter 3, trade was partly of a transit nature, which explains perhaps the 197 Kashmiri trading houses in Lhasa in the eighteenth century (Boulnois 1983:129, after Chinese sources). The location of Central Tibet between major civilizations and ecozones, made it into an ideal transit-corridor at a time when railways and cheap transport by sea had not yet arisen. Moreover, the highlands of Tibet were a distinct ecozone in themselves, from which many a special product could be procured. Trade was of a luxury nature, goods of low weight for value like musk, rhubarb, gold and precious stones, dominating the scene.

Musk, a natural perfume derived from the indigenous musk-deer, from times immemorial had served to put Tibet on the mental map of Asian and even European long-distance traders. Medieval Arab sources mentioned it in connection with Tibet (Hedin 1917-1922 I:50-52). Marco Polo too, knew of it (1982:104, 173, 176), and William Finch, an early seventeenth-century merchant drew attention to it in his 1611 report (Stein 1918:173). The French traveller Tavernier tells us of musk from Tibet being sold at Patna as early as 1692 (Lévi 1905-1908 I:93), and Bogle refers to it as one of the principal commodities, together with gold dust, with which the Tibetans paid for their imports from Bengal (Markham 1876:6, 115, 183). Musk over the centuries, remained a very lucrative business, even attracting agents from European firms to the Tibetan borderlands. In the second half of the nineteenth century, markets for musk developed in Sining, Tachienlu, Lichiang and Darjeeling, part of the commodity offered being in transit from Lhasa (Rockhill 1894:71, Weiss 1912:41, Burrard 1915 I:22, II:330, Gregory and Gregory 1923:205, Sagant 1978: 112; see also Jest 1987:230-237).

Rhubarb, valued as a drug, also played an important role in long-distance trade, especially towards China, where the Chinese held a virtual monopoly over its export to Europe in the eighteenth century (Cammann 1951a:32n). But in Tavernier's time, a century earlier, rhubarb was also brought to Gorakhpur and Patna in northern India (Lévi 1905-1908 I:94, cf. Jacquemont 1843 I:172). In the nineteenth century, Muslim traders from Sining exported quantities of rhubarb to Kiakhta on the Russo-Mongolian border (Prejevalsky 1876 II:70n), Sining being the chief depot for the rhubarb trade in northeastern Tibet (ibid. II:83, Kreitner 1881:727-728). Tachienlu was another major centre of the rhubarb export in the Sino-Tibetan borderlands (Rockhill 1891b:283-284).

Gold too, was an important item in keeping the balance of Tibetan trade upright. Over the centuries, the gold of Tibet had acquired a mythical reputation, but a Tibetan El Dorado did not exist, and quantities mined were relatively small (Boulnois 1983:71-85). Gold digging and washing took place at several localities in northwest and eastern Tibet (Lindegger 1982:183, map, 44-45n, Boulnois 1983, endmap), the gold being transported to Lhasa and Shigatse (Burrard 1915 I:22), and a few of the larger monasteries along the major trade route with China, like Litang (Gill 1880 II:93, Rockhill 1894:357), and Batang (Cooper 1871:417). Actually, very little of the Tibetan gold found its way to India (Ryall 1879:449, Shuttleworth 1923:557), rather, Indian silver rupees were coming in, in order to pay for the wool exported to Ladakh and Kashmir. However, gold did flow out of Tibet into China, Tibet's major trading partner until the early twentieth century. According to Shuttleworth (1923:557), 30,625 pound sterling in Tibetan gold entered Tachienlu alone for the year 1913 (cf. Hosie 1905:80).

The precise extent to which monasteries were involved in trade will probably always remain a relative mystery. Where Tibetans chose to write down their life experiences, these had not, with few exceptions, to do with economic affairs. Moreover records which may have existed at one time, were largely destroyed after the Chinese takeover. Which leaves us with the writings of outsiders, mainly travellers and a few scientist-explorers. It is to one of the former that we owe the following immortal observation, which, as a mirror of the time in which it was written, i.e. the late 1930s, succinctly summarizes the relation of the sacred to the profane: 'the monks of Tibet, though cloistered from the vulgar world, have a nice sense of business' (Hanbury-Tracy 1938:58).

This situation was the outcome of a long historical process, in which the conditions and demands of everyday life, as well as the continual growth in power of the monasteries, had necessarily led to a considerable softening of the originally strict monastic observance (Tucci 1980:110-111). This in turn created the ideological basis for a further involvement in trade, even to such an extent that it became institutionalized within the monastic organization (cf. Tsarong 1987; I have not been able to consult this reference personally). Incarnations turned secular insofar as they could make big money (Prejevalsky 1876 II:46-47, Tsybikoff 1904:746, Rock 1930:161), but perhaps there is some stereotyping involved in painting the monasteries and the Living Buddhas as the greatest traders of Tibet (Carrasco 1959:213). After all, there were big and small monasteries, rich and poor *gompas* (Cutting 1940:195), and among the monks 'all the graduated shades of poverty and wealth that you see in mundane cities' (Huc and Gabet 1987 II:59, cf. David-Néel as quoted by Middleton 1989:121, Patterson 1990:52). Nevertheless, it is true that monasteries were important economic centres (Tucci 1980:130), some of which had deteriorated into dens of exploitation for local villagers and visiting pilgrims (Huc and Gabet 1987 I:89,92, Gill 1878:93, Carey 1887:743, Hosie 1905:45, Filchner 1906:12). It is quite likely, however, that reform measures under the stern rule of the thirteenth Dalai Lama

(1895-1933), counteracted the worst excesses (Bell 1946:54-55). Anyway, monasteries had grown rich by their legitimate functions, and sometimes by their illegitimate actions. Their pivotal position in Tibetan society made them into 'immense reservoirs, into which flowed, by a thousand channels, all the wealth of these vast regions' (Huc and Gabet 1987 II:180). Their strong financial position made them engage in money-lending (Rockhill 1894:357, Futterer 1900:326, Hosie 1905:45, Carrasco 1959:213), as well as trade (Desgodins 1885:334-335, Bower 1894:282, Kawaguchi 1909:458, Bell 1928:125, Filchner 1933:218), and there was a tendency for the bigger monasteries to monopolize certain products and trade flows, which led to occasional clashes with private traders and among themselves (Stein 1987:92, cf. Macaulay 1885:16,44).

In the big trade caravans from Lhasa and Shigatse to Sining and Tachienlu (Rockhill 1894:255, Das 1902:193, Bonin 1911:247), business interests of monasteries and loosely organized government offices intertwined. As government officials were drawn from two parallel groups, one lay, consisting of a number of noble families, and another religious, formed by a special group of monks trained for government service (Carrasco 1959:80, cf. Richardson 1984:18-27, Goldstein 1989:6-20), it is not surprising that the great caravans were the combined effort of monks and nobles. The British naturalist Pratt, who happened to be in Tachienlu on the 19th of June, 1890, witnessed the arrival of the Shigatse/Tashilunpo caravan, which had been on its way for five months (Pratt 1892:196-197, the photo in between these pages; cf. Grenard 1904:97). It consisted of horses and cross-bred *dzos* and brought principally narrow-striped woollen cloth, and finely coloured, very thick woollen rugs, which were exchanged for Yachow brick tea. Yet, the higher lay officials in the government also traded on their own account (Bower 1894:282, Burrard 1915 I:69). References to monasteries engaged in trade are numerous in the Tibet literature. Monastic trading institutions had agents and stewards in all Tibetan border towns, and relied on the 'free' transport services (*ula*) forced on populations living near the through-going trade routes (Kawaguchi 1909:458, Burrard 1915 II:243, Hanbury-Tracy 1938:228-229, Bailey 1945:51-52). The bigger caravans were escorted by hundreds of soldiers, as mounted bands of nomad robbers, in particular in the east and the northeast of Tibet, were prone to attack the heavily-laden yak and *dzo*-trains (Das 1902:193, Duncan 1952:129).

The monasteries most heavily involved in international trade were undoubtedly Sera, Drepung and Ganden. At the time of the riot of March 1883 between Nepalese shopkeepers and Tibetans in the Lhasa bazaar (Uprety 1980:96-98), many monks of the monasteries mentioned above, joined in the disturbances, because the Nepalese were powerful rival traders (Macaulay 1885:45). The Lhasa government was powerless, as they feared the potentially destructive fits of a generally conservative clergy. Many monasteries outside the Lhasa area too, in particular those situated near major transport routes (Goullart 1957:157), were engaged in trade. Tashilunpo (Brauen 1983:158), Sakya (Cassinelli and Ekvall 1969:311-312), Chamdo (Das 1902:156), Litang (Bonvalot 1891:234, Hosie 1905:47), Kandze (Coales 1919a:236-237), and Kumbum (Rijnhart 1901:9,30, Tafel 1914 I:219-220), were all major centres of commercial activity, having monk-agents or lay representatives of noble birth in all the major towns of Tibet, and in a few larger cities beyond (Hosie 1905:29, Bell 1928:126). The most important staple trade of the monasteries was tea (Tafel 1914 I:220, Coales 1919a:237, Filchner 1933:218), which was sometimes sold on a compulsory basis to dependent convents, neighbouring villages, and nomad tribes, the tea being smuggled in on occasion (Tafel 1914 II:75).

From the 1880s onward, there was a definite tendency among the higher classes to grow more and more luxurious in their style of living (Kawaguchi 1909:456). This was inevitably brought about by the foreign trade of Tibet and the arrival of goods of foreign origin. The latter were increasingly brought to Tibet by the Tibetans themselves. Actually, the rise of a British-Indian *économie-monde* in the course of the nineteenth century, tempted Tibetan traders to try their luck beyond the immediate Tibetan pale. Campbell (1849:490) came across a party of Tibetans en route to Darjeeling in December 1848, Rennie (1866:308-309) too, noticed Tibetans in the Darjeeling bazaar, and Samuel Bourne photographed four Tibetan traders in the streets of Simla during the winter of 1868 (Bar and Desmond 1978:66). Simla, the hill-station and summer residence of colonial India remained the object of an occasional trip 'abroad' by a handful of

Tibetans for many decades to come (cf. Rankin 1930:7). By the turn of the century, Tibetan trade ventures into India had become quite frequent, and it was Kawaguchi who met a Tibetan by the name of Lha Tsering who had lived for a long time in Darjeeling (Kawaguchi 1909:447-448). A related development took place at Tachienlu on the Sino-Tibetan border where the British soldier-explorer Hamilton Bower bumped into a Tibetan trader who had been twice to Calcutta via Lhasa, and had made a lot of money, particularly on musk (Bower 1894:243). Tankar and Sining in Northeast Tibet too, attracted traders from Central Tibet (Prejevalsky 1876 II:185, Rijnhart 1901:144, Filchner 1929:117), and in 1890, Rockhill came across an old Tibetan trader from Shigatse, who had made the journey between Lhasa and Tankar four times and had moreover been to Peking, Tientsin, Urga and Manchuria (Rockhill 1891b:112). Tafel too, met another specimen of this widely travelled class of traders, this particular one having visited both Calcutta and Peking (Tafel 1914 II:167).

During the period of Bell's direct diplomatic involvement with Tibet (1910-1921), a growing number of Tibetans went abroad (Bell 1928:109). This was definitely facilitated by the outcome of the Younghusband expedition (1904). Political obstacles for commerce across the Himalaya were removed, and a few British-controlled trade marts established inside Tibetan territory (Lamb 1986:256ff., McKay 1992). In the course of the process, the Indo-Tibetan trade via Darjeeling shifted to the newly arisen town of Kalimpong, which was more suitably located for the caravans coming down from the Jelep La and the Natu La (Bell 1928:113, Tucci 1956:10). The most important items of trade were in the hands of a few families, whose agents resided in Kalimpong and elsewhere. Although there were some wealthy private traders in Lhasa, most of the trading families served in one way or another the interests of the Tibetan government and the monasteries on which its power rested (Carrasco 1959:213, cf. Brauen 1983:158).

A good example is the Pangda Tsang family 'consortium', which had branches in Calcutta, Shanghai, and Peking (Bell 1928: 130). Its origin dated back to the privileges received from the thirteenth Dalai Lama after the Chinese occupation of Lhasa in 1912. In a few years, Pangda Tsang created a trading imperium that extended across the length and breadth of Tibet. In due time, he had his elder son, Yarpel, sent to Peking with the intention of setting up a commercial agency, while two others went to eastern Tibet, in order to tap the Southwest China trade (cf. Gregory and Gregory 1923:112). In India the network included Kalimpong and Calcutta (Radhu 1981:168, Stoddard 1985:77). In fact, the Pangda Tsangs belonged to those traders who controlled large sections of the Tibet-China trade as earlier referred to. Other trading families from Kham were Sadu Tsang, 'the all-embracing merchant' (Winnington 1957:185-189), Gyanag Tsang, and Andru Tsang, the later resistance-leader against the Chinese in the 1950s (Andrugtsang 1973:9-10). With the rising tide of disturbances along the Sino-Tibetan border in the 1930s, most of these corporate trading families settled in Kalimpong (Radhu 1981:168). Yarpel Pangda Tsang, after the death of his father, quickly developed into the most important trader of Tibet, effectively being for years the government's commercial agent in the British-controlled trade mart at Yatung (Patterson 1990:38), and later in Kalimpong (Prince Peter 1963:474). Basically, the fortunes of Pangda Tsang rested on the wool trade as described earlier in this chapter. It was Yarpel Pangda Tsang, who asked Brooke Dolan and Ilia Tolstoy on their visit to Tibet in 1942 when the United States would buy wool again (Tolstoy 1946:172,178).

The 1930s and 40s saw a proliferation of the Lhasa-Calcutta trade via Kalimpong (Tucci 1956:12). Apart from the big shots in the Tibet trade mentioned above, many a smaller trader succeeded in earning a decent livelihood. And if the regular trade failed, there were always the many sidelines by which he could try to make ends meet. Gambling and smuggling were among the most common strategies to overcome temporary misfortune (Bell 1928:117, Tucci 1956:33). The sale of imitation stones or adulterated musk provided yet another (Hanbury-Tracy 1938:181, David-Néel 1953:293). And then there was of course the opium, and not a newcomer for that matter (Edgar 1874:45-47, Lewin 1879:681, Hosie 1905:28, Stötzner 1924:107, Harrer 1952:141, Goswami 1982, Norbu 1986:71). The Tibetans did a brisk trade during World War II, especially when the Burma road to China had been cut, and a transit trade developed to Lichiang in northern Yunnan by way of Kalimpong, Gyantse, Lhasa and Chamdo (Goullart 1957:102-105). After the war, trade and commerce continued to flourish, and as such may be regarded as the most dynamic aspect of the Tibetan economy in the years just prior to the Chinese takeover (Wiley 1986:10, cf. Shakya 1990:98).

The geohistory of Tibetan border trade

Though the descriptive material offered in this chapter may at times have seemed a little tedious, it served a purpose. If we look close enough, we see a geohistorical structure of Tibetan trade unfold before our eyes, with the help of which it is possible to explain the rise, and, to a certain extent, the demise of the cross-cultural and trans-border Bhotia traders, in particular along its Himalayan fringe. After all, the first part of this study was meant to provide the context for the second part, not in the sense that everything that has been written in the latter can solely be understood by referring to the former, but at least the wider geohistorical context has been cleared, and the origin of the rise of one of these communities, viz. the Nyishangba of Manang, made plausible.

Let us briefly recapitulate. Traditional trade in Tibet and its borderworlds rested on the local and regional exchange of salt, wool, and grain. In addition to this barter complex, there was a long-distance trade in luxury goods like musk, medicinal herbs, and precious stones, which initially focused on monastic fairs and supraregional places of pilgrimage. On top of that, and perhaps increasingly so with monastic and government control over its mining operations, gold too, by virtue of its low weight for value, served as a long-distance bridging trade commodity, in particular in its quality as payment for the numerous tea imports from China into Tibet.

With the growing impact of the British-Indian *économie-monde* in the nineteenth century, the long-distance trade in wool acquired new dimensions, locationally shifting as it did from Ladakh to the Indo-Tibetan borderlands further eastwards, and institutionally being organized on an ever grander scale, as well as monopolized by rising groups of Bhotia traders. The resulting trade networks centred in particular on the Bhotia villages of Garhwal and Kumaon. The partly self-imposed geopolitical isolation of Nepal, to the detriment of its one-time supreme trade route via Kathmandu, equally expressed itself in the rise of a number of Bhotia communities as long-distance traders along Nepal's northern border. The trade of these Bhotia communities flourished in particular during the second half of the nineteenth century, but suffered from the opening of British-controlled trade marts in Tibet after the Younghusband expedition and the opening of the Chumbi valley route to Central Tibet via the Sikkimese Jelep La.

In addition to this locational funnelling via a few routes, trade became increasingly controlled, not to say monopolized, by a few big merchants, who had settled in the newly arisen towns of Darjeeling, and especially Kalimpong. These merchants were not only members of the age-old trading communities, like Kashmiri or Newari, who had patronized Lhasa and its monastic government since the seventeenth century. In fact, it also concerned a class of newly arisen Tibetan traders hailing from Kham, who had managed, with the support of privileges received from the Tibetan government, to monopolize the wool trade across the Central Himalayas. They had left their eastern Tibetan trading fields, not because the Chinese *économie-monde* had suddenly ceased to exist, but because political disturbances and geopolitical strife made for very unsettled conditions all along the Sino-Tibetan frontier.

The intensification of commercial activity along the Himalayan border during the transitional 'long' century between 1850 and 1950 made possible, firstly, the rise of the Bhotia middlemen, and secondly their decline following locational reshuffling and institutional reorganization. Therefore it is patently false to blame solely the Chinese occupation of Tibet for the demise of Bhotia trade along the Indo-Tibetan border. Rather it is the compounded effect of the growing pull of the British-Indian *économie-monde* with its greatly improved transport networks, railways as well as roads. However, the Chinese border closure of Tibet after 1960 certainly speeded up the process of a southward reorientation of the Bhotia communities, not to mention the complete disruption of Indo-Tibetan trade circuits as fostered by a professional class of long-distance merchants. The latter were the real victims, but the flexibility of their capital made them easily participate in a new upsurge of international trade, i.e. the one related to the post-1960 boom of the economy in Southeast Asia.

Thus, our conclusion must be, that the temporary rise of Bhotia trading communities along certain sections of the Himalayan border, with its concomitant forms of itinerant trade, were in the end conditioned by the particular geohistorical setting and dynamics of its neighbouring *économie-monde*. This geohistorical context made Bashahri, Kumaon Bhotias, Thakali, Sherpa, Walongchung Bhotia, Tromowa and Monpa into thriving trading communities, and that so within a few generations. As such they structurally resemble certain communities along the Sino-Tibetan border, like the Hui of western Kansu and the Sharba of the Sungpan area. This overall resemblance should not blind us to the wide variety of forms which came to characterize this Bhotia trade under very different geopolitical conditions. The second part of this study will show that a particular location, a specific geopolitical context, or an early orientation on a neighbouring *économie-monde*, may produce unsuspected forms of trade, and go a long way to explain the extraordinary rise of the Nyishangba of Manang as international long-distancence traders. Hence Macdonald's exhortation: 'the long-range business ventures outside Nepal in South East Asian countries of groups such as the Manangba provide exciting subjects for research' (Macdonald 1974:33). The Nyishangba then: to them the floor.

5

THE NYISHANGBA OF MANANG

When Pierre Gourou published his voluminous regional geography on Asia in 1953, he referred in one sentence to the inhabitants of 'Manangbhot' as a rather atypical but significant example of a Himalayan community engaged in embryonal forms of international trade (Gourou 1953:408). Apparently he had read Tilman's contribution to the *Geographical Journal* of 1951, where the author allows us a glimpse of what he calls 'an unusual kind of Himalayan community' (Tilman 1951:265). The latter observation is of less importance than the fact that a gifted geographer like Gourou gave it a place, however restricted, in an interesting, synoptic study of Asia. For it shows that a perceptive mind like Gourou's was able to select a seemingly trivial piece of information, the subject matter of which was to become a major feature of Nepal's economic landscape within thirty years time.

The rise of the Nyishangba as long-distance traders in South and Southeast Asia, deserves fuller elaboration than the one sentence Gourou spent on it. By now, the existing reports on Nyishang and the Nyishangba, most of them based on several months of fieldwork or residence in the area (N.J. Gurung 1976, 1977a, 1977b, H.B. Gurung 1980, Koirala 1981, Cooke 1985a, 1985b, 1986, Van Spengen 1987, Schrader 1988, Pohle 1986, 1990, Sagant 1990, and now Watkins 1996), enable us to sketch the regional context and outline of circumstances that gave rise to increased participation of a Himalayan trading community in the wider, and perhaps rising *économie-monde* of the Southeast Asian world. In fact, the following three chapters contain the essence of my contribution to *Kailash* (1987, no.3-4, 131-277), which highlighted the rise of the Nyishangba as international long-distance traders (cf. Schrader 1988:182, Sagant 1990:152). The present chapter seeks to provide a brief overview of local district life and the changes that have occurred in the wake of growing involvement in trade. Two further chapters deal *in extenso* with the historical interplay of Nyishangba enterprise and the geostructural context through which their trading successes were realized.

Historical background

Nicely tucked away beyond Annapurna Himal and with no direct exit towards Tibet, lies Nyishang - or Manangbhot - the most western part of the present-day Manang District in North-Central Nepal (Figure 7). Nyishang, being the head-valley of the Marsyangdi river extends some twenty kilometres in an east-west direction. It lies at an average altitude of 3,500 metres and is the homeland of a seasonally fluctuating population between some two and four thousand inhabitants. Nyishang forms part of the Tibetan culture area, although strictly speaking the present-day language of the area is not considered to be a Tibetan dialect (Mazaudon 1978:158, Glover and Landon 1980:31). But in many other respects, mainly referring to material culture and religion, the strong Tibetan influence is undeniable. Moreover, several male inhabitants of the valley are able to speak Tibetan as a second language, in particular the elder ones, and some of them know how to write it.

The dawn of civilization in Nyishang may be traced back to at least the times of later Se-rib (12th century), then a political entity encompassing many villages in the neighbouring Gandaki valley south of Lo (Mustang). References to Nyishang as a tributary area to Se-rib were recently found in two local histories pertaining to Ga-rab Dzong of Thini (Jackson 1978:209-210). According to an early eighteenth century chronicle describing the political situation during the heyday of the Gungthang royal dynasty, Nyishang possibly fell under the jurisdiction of this southern Tibetan state in the 13th and 14th century (Jackson 1976:45). However, by the end of the 15th century Gungthang's power had declined so much that a Mustangi author could describe Nyishang as a tribute-paying area to the newly established principality of Lo (Jackson 1984:9-10, note 19).

There were, quite certainly, periods of relative independence for the Nyishangba and the references contained in the documents mentioned above, should not be taken as a definitive proof of

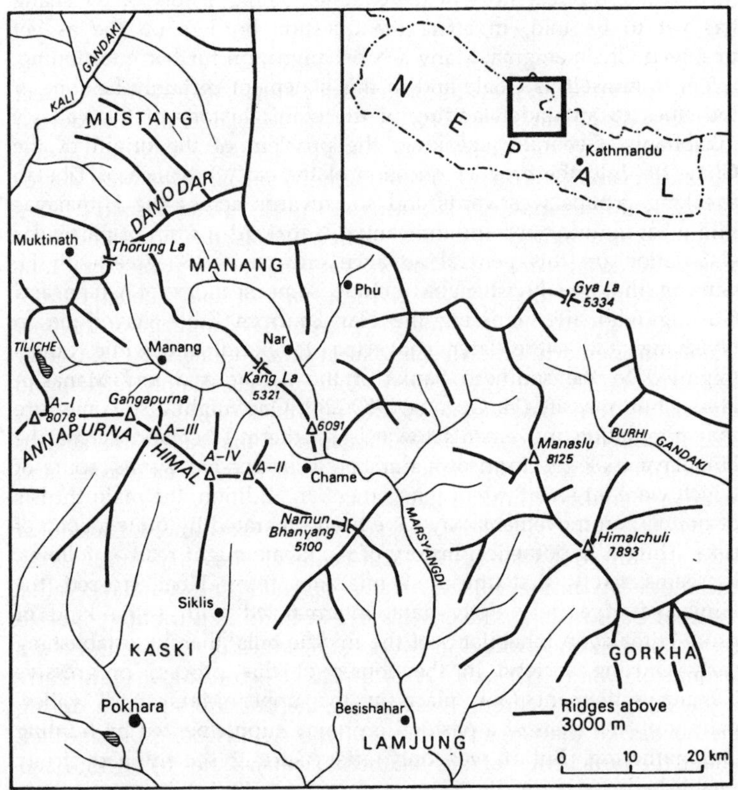

Figure 7 Manang in Northwest-Central Nepal

permanent subjugation of the isolated Nyishangba community. Now we may ask, who were these early inhabitants of Nyishang? If you question a Nyishangba nowadays about his ethnic identity, he will claim to be Gurung, or at least refer to his recently adopted Gurung surname, as do the people of Baragaon in neighbouring Mustang. Meanwhile, the real story of the complex ethnic history of Nyishang has yet to be told. In effect the question borders on the as yet unsolved Ghale enigma. Many a Nyishangba, on further questioning, refers to himself as Ghale and in this statement certainly lies one of the clues to an understanding of the ethnic history of the valley's inhabitants. Generally speaking, the problem of the origin of the Ghale fits into the broader question of the early advance of Tibetan speaking groups westwards and southwards across the Himalayas into what is now northern and central Nepal. As a form of particular elaboration on this general advance one tends to agree with H. Gurung that the Nyishangba include some sections of Ghale and Gurung who after crossing the Nar La from Tibet stayed on in Nyishang and were later converted to Buddhism while others migrated to the southern flanks of the Annapurna and Manaslu-Himalchuli massifs (H. Gurung 1980:226). One might also conjecture that population movements towards southern Tibet and across the Himalaya took the form of a number of successive waves, some of which were larger in extent than others. In addition, the main thrusts of population movement may have been separated by quite a span of time. Thus, a hypothetical history of the Ghale might read as follows. It seems likely that the first migrants from Tibet crossed the Himalaya at a very early date, intermarried with some kind of proto-Himalayan inhabitants of the middle hills, thereby establishing early Gurung society. In the course of this process progressive Gurung settlement took place in the upper Marsyangdi valley, mainly on the basis of a pastoral economy supplemented by hunting and gathering. But it was only after Gurung society had firmly established itself in its new environment that Ghale rule was established from the North (cf. Sagant 1990:163-164).

Until now the origin of the Ghale has remained obscure. Their incursion into the northern parts of present-day Nepal has possibly something to do with the political vicissitudes of the Gungthang dynasty in the southern Tibetan region of Tsang during the 13th and 14th century (cf. Jackson 1976:44-49). The background to their ethnic identity may yet be further unravelled through linguistic research in the two main Ghale clusters presently to be found in north-central Nepal, that is in Nyishang and may be Nar-Phu (a northern side-valley of the upper Marsyangdi) and in the villages of Barpak and Uiya in north-east Gorkha, where, according to Glover and Landon, people have 'a radically more different form of speach than either Tamang or Thakali' (Glover and Landon 1980:30). Further linguistic research has recently confirmed the latter statement (Nishi 1982:159, 192n). The Ghale clans of northern Kaski and Lamjung, such as those of Siklis, Ghandrung and Ghalegaon, to which Pignède refers (1966: 34, 135, 166-169, 197-198), as well as those found in some upper Ankhu Khola villages (Toffin 1976:37) or in Langtang (Hall 1978:56-57, Frank 1982:263), should be considered either as descendants of the Ghale who crossed the main Himalayan range into the middle hills, and were largely assimilated by the local Gurung or Tamang, or as recent offshoots of the Barpak and Uiya clusters, as may be the case in the Langtang area. In both cases the original migrant groups were probably small, a fact that could account for the loss of their Ghale language proper.

Local oral histories as found in Ngawal and Braga sustain this tentative outline of Ghale history. The first king of Ngawal is said to have been Syamrang Ghale. When he and his kinsmen ventured into territory occupied by Gurung shepherds, friction between the two groups arose. According to one informant from Braga, most land of Nyishang had been settled by Gurung clansmen, when the Ghale started spilling over from their Nar-Phu stronghold into Gurung territory. The former were neatly outplayed by the latter (this is the central theme of many oral traditions in the area) and in time Nyishang became Ghale-dominated.

The Buddhist renaissance that took place in Tibet from the 11th century onwards, introduced among others the Kagyudpa order into a mainly Bonpo and Nyingmapa milieu (Snellgrove 1981:214, Snellgrove and Richardson 1980:170-171). Through the Ghale connection with Tibet, Buddhism in its Kagyudpa form, found its way to Nyishang. The Tashi Lakhang temple of Phu emerged as the main Kagyudpa establishment in the area (N.J. Gurung 1976:307), but through the Ngawal line of Ghale kings, Braga too, obtained an important Kagyudpa *gomba*. Founded by the second lama son of the fifth Ghale king of Ngawal, the Braga monastery dating from the

15th century (Snellgrove 1981:214), is possibly contemporary with Bodzo *gomba* near Manang, which, as the story goes, was founded by a great lama of Tibet. Around this nucleus of three main *gombas*, Ghale life pivoted spiritually, supporting quite substantial communities of monks.

Ghale rule in Nyishang did not only bring changes in the religious and political sphere, but also effectively changed the dominant *genre de vie* of the valley. Where the Gurung were mainly high-altitude pastoralists and shifting cultivators at lower altitudes (Macfarlane 1976:25) the Ghale showed it was possible to establish a sedentary agriculture on the alluvial river terraces along the Marsyangdi. On the basis of an elaborate irrigation system, and within the wider framework of a mixed stock-breeding and cereal-growing economy, it proved possible to cultivate certain strains of barley and buckwheat in an area which receives less than 350 millimetres of precipitation. This agricultural practice guaranteed food in a high-altitude environment for about seven to eight months out of twelve, depending on the weather circumstances and the amount of labour available.

From the very beginning of Ghale settlement in Nyishang it seems unlikely that a full year's livelihood could be procured on the basis of local resources alone. It is therefore plausible to suggest an extra-local component in the subsistence strategy as followed by the early Ghale. Of course one could argue that in absence of a land question in early Nyishang, it should have proved possible to grow enough food in summertime to provide for a full year's demand. But as is often the case in traditional farming systems, it is not physical resources that are the restrictive factors in the realization of a balanced subsistence strategy, but the availability of sufficient labour. It follows then, that, even in a situation where there is no pressure regarding the availability of land, it proves impossible to grow enough food within the short span of time of a particular growing season and within the technological limits set by the organizational capabilities of the population involved.

Though the above reasoning may provide an explanation for the origin of extra-local activities, especially in wintertime, it does not explain why the Nyishangba as a group came increasingly to play the role of traders, and that so at a very early date. N.J. Gurung made the poor agricultural conditions of Nyishang the cornerstone of his argument in explaining the excellence of the Nyishangba as traders (N.J. Gurung 1976:301-302), but one tends to agree with H.B. Gurung that their special position in trade is more likely to have a 'historical' basis, as the poor agricultural productivity of Nyishang is in no way different or more acute than in other Himalayan valleys of similar physical background (H.B. Gurung 1980:227). The latter author heard a legend in Gaon Shahar that the Nyishangba were granted privileges by the Lamjung raja as a reward for their fine workmanship in the construction of the Lamjung fort at Gaon Shahar (ibid.:226). This legend was largely confirmed by two older Braga informants, that is to say, they knew the story of the Ghale who built a fort in Lamjung, but did not mention any privileges in return. What seems important in these traditions is not so much the actual historical event to which they refer, but that they assume one or another relationship between the upper Marsyangdi valley and the middle hills of Lamjung. Apart from occasional war, one may speculate on the existence of barter trade between the two different ecozones, as they had to offer each other products for exchange, which could not be obtained in their respective home areas. As far as the Nyishangba were concerned, this arrangement meant the import of rice from the middle hills to overcome their seasonal food deficit.

On the whole, we should avoid the idea that trading activities of the Nyishangba emerged suddenly somewhere at a point in history. It seems far more likely that trade always played a certain role in their subsistence strategy and that so from early days onwards. However, their excellence in trade, compared to other but similar communities, must have to do with other than ecological factors alone, a problem which we shall again refer to in the concluding section of this study. For the moment it suffices to say that by the end of the eighteenth century, the Nyishangba had established themselves as a trading community, that was able to secure written evidence of their privileged position in trade from the newly established Shah dynasty at the Kathmandu court.

It is said that the first royal order granting trade privileges to the Nyishangba dates back to 1784 (1841 V.S.) (N.J. Gurung 1976:299, Koirala 1981:121). This date falls within the reign of Rana Bahadur Shah when Lamjung had already been incorporated into the fastly growing Gorkhali state with its capital in the Kathmandu valley. It may be doubted, however, whether this gesture reflects more than nominal power of the Gorkhali kings in Nyishang. Although useful from a Nyishangba point of view, in the sense that free trade was guaranteed to them throughout Gorkhali-controlled territory, the actual political power seems to have been intimately tied up with the local chieftainships of the upper Kali Gandaki valley. Especially Baragaon seems to have had considerable political and economic influence in Nyishang, at least so just before the rise of the Thakali in the middle of the 19th century (N.J. Gurung 1976:302, Pant and Pierce (eds.) 1989:21). This state of affairs is corroborated by a *lalmohar* given to the Nyishangba by king Rajendra in 1825 (1881 V.S.), in which he asks the *dhaapa* councils of the Nyishang villages to comply with the traditional rules concerning dealings with Baragaon. The document further suggests a growing independence of the Nyishangba by stating that neither group was allowed to suppress the other. At the same time their trade privileges were being reconfirmed:

> No custom and other kinds of taxes will be imposed on the goods of the Nyishangba by custom-offices, government authorities and individuals as long as the Nyishangba pay *harsala* and *nirkhi* taxes once a year to the government (N.J. Gurung 1976:308)

The Mustang raja, although entitled by the Gorkhali government to a customary due from Nyishang since 1790 (1847 V.S.) (Regmi 1975:330), should not be considered an effective power factor in the area. The chiefs of Baragaon and Nyishang held their own, and it was only after the rise of the Thakali *subbas*, that the effects of the latter's economic growth on neighbouring groups began to be felt (Von Fürer-Haimendorf 1975:150, Manzardo 1978:50). Especially during the tender of the *subba*-ship by Harkaman (1860-1903) the position of the Baragaunli quickly eroded into one of debt (Messerschmidt and N.J. Gurung 1974:207, Manzardo 1978:29). The period referred to roughly coincides with the arrival in Manang of some leading families from Jarkot in the Gandaki valley some five generations ago, who did probably so to escape Thakali pressure and indebtedness (N.J. Gurung 1976:301). The eclipse of the Baragaunli competitors left more room for the Nyishangba, who again succeeded in getting their privileged position recognized by the Kathmandu court through a series of successive documents. A *khadganisana* of 1857 (1914 V.S.) confirms the decline of Baragaon by asking the Nyishangba to re-direct their former tax obligations from the Bist of Jarkot to the Thapatali Darbar in Kathmandu through the Lamjung regional tax collecting office (ibid.:308).

Already some years earlier - in 1846 (1903 V.S.) the Nyishangba free trade position had been guaranteed again by a royal order, whose promulgation was incited by the complaint of a Lamjung *mukhiya* about harassment by Nyishangba parties (Koirala 1981:122). In 1883 (1940 V.S.) Rana Uddip Simha issued a reminder document stating that 'you - the Nyishangba - will reap the same benefits from trade as you did before, as long as you pay your annual taxes to the Darbar' (ibid.:122).

We may wonder whether these documents (for a full overview see Cooke 1985a:303-310, Pant and Pierce (eds.) (1989) were genuinely meant to sustain the Nyishangba trading activities or rather acted as a sign from the Kathmandu-based government to underline its political influence in an area where it had only nominal control. In any case, Nyishangba trade seems to have flourished, by now even beyond the Nepalese border, where trading parties could occasionally be seen on their way to the urban centres and regional fairs of Bihar and the United Provinces. Towards the close of the nineteenth century, custom officers started to charge import duties, but in due time the Nyishangba felt so ill-treated that they appealed to the Kathmandu court. As a result, a government regulation against the levying of duties at the Thori customs point (Chitwan) was issued in 1905 (1962 V.S. (H.B. Gurung 1980:227). In the first week of April 1933 (1990 V.S.) Juddha Shamser lent again an ear to Nyishangba complaints and, while restating their duty-free trade across the Nepal border, he slightly increased at the same time their relatively limited tax obligations (Koirala 1981:112), a not uncommon policy action, reported upon as early as 1904 (1961 V.S.) (Regmi (ed.) 1983c:139). The documents referred to above, indicate a rather sophisticated agreement between the central administration and a specific peripheral group. Although the parties involved viewed the arrangement from a different angle, the net-result was the same: government support in the delicate field of long-distance trade.

The district setting

The political border between Nepal and Tibet does not coincide exactly with the main Himalayan chain or with the watershed between the Ganga and the Tsangpo (Brahmaputra). As a result we find in the very north of Nepal a number of trans-Himalayan high valleys that are inhabited by groups that have retained their Tibetan language and culture. Most of the larger valleys are to be found west of Manaslu, in an area where altogether some 25,000 square kilometres of semi-arid land is situated at an average altitude of 4,000 metres. Access to these high valleys from the north is most of the time difficult and communication depends largely on crossing high passes which more often than not exceed the 5,000 metre limit. Access from the south into these valleys is, or rather was, even more difficult, and only along major river trenches and passes across the main chain of the Himalaya some intercourse with the Nepalese middle hills existed. Generally, these corridors of communication show considerable cultural fusion, but the more isolated valleys display a genuine Tibetan background. Dobremez and Jest distinguish the following territories from west to east, mainly on the basis of language, geographically limited endogamy and territorial isolation: Byans, Humla, Mugu, Dolpo (Chharkabhot), Lo (Mustang), Nyishang (Manangbhot), Nar, Nub-ri, Tsum, Langtang, Yolmo (Helambu), Solu-khumbu and Walung (Walongchung) (Dobremez and Jest 1976:34). To this list Rolwaling, west of Khumbu should be added (see Figure 8). The ethnic groups involved live at an average altitude of some 3,200 metres and at a latitude ranging from 28 to 30 degrees north. They share an exceptional physical and ecological milieu characterized by high altitude, slight rainfall (250-400 mm), severe winters and a steppe-like vegetation.

Nyishang forms a part of the present-day Manang District, a newly created administrative unit north of Kaski and Lamjung (H.B. Gurung 1980:223-240). The area is surrounded by high Himalayan mountains and covers in effect the headwaters of the Marsyangdi river and its tributaries. Depending on altitude, amount of precipitation, and to a certain extent cultural identity, three micro-ecological zones may be distinguished within the district:

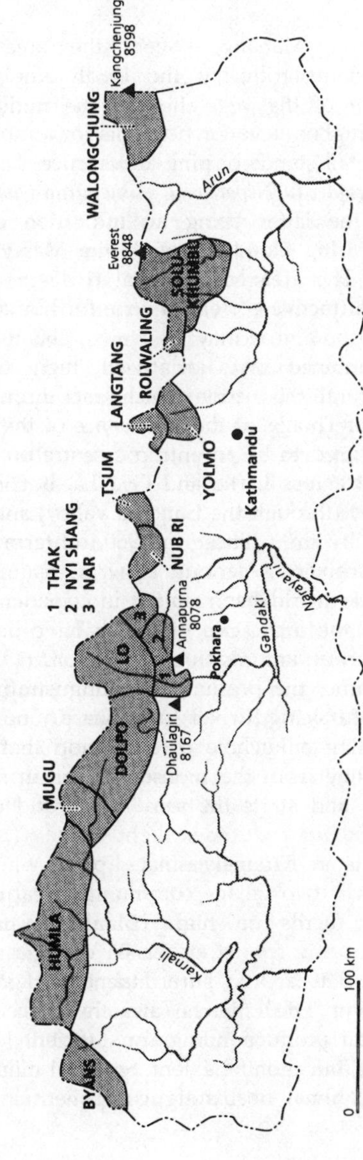

Figure 8 Tibetan and Tibetanized border communities in Northern Nepal

Gyasumdo (Tingaon), Nar Phu and Nyishang (Pohle 1986, 1990:3-8; see also Figure 9).

Gyasumdo, or lower Manang, covers the area along the Marsyangdi river and its tributary the Dudh Khola. Here the subtropical appearance of the vegetation of the middle hills has almost vanished. The higher elevation accounts for a more temperate climate, giving rise to tall stands of pine and spruce (Dobremez and Jest (1969), *Carte écologique du Népal, no.l, Annapurna-Dhaulagiri)* with dense undergrowth, the latter being an indication of the deep penetration of rain-bearing clouds through the Marsyangdi gorge during the monsoon. The area between Tal (1645 m) and Chame (2,651 m) is the most attractive ecological zone for human settlement in the district. Two crops a year may be grown, and the amount of rainfall received, combined with relatively high temperatures, guarantees an agricultural production which lasts through the year. Formerly, the village of Thonje, at the confluence of the Marsyangdi and the Dudh Khola, used to be an entrepôt centre on a secondary trade route with Tibet across Larke and Gya La, but with a major rival trade route nearby (through the Gandaki valley) and the closure of the Tibetan border by the Chinese in 1960, off-farm activities in the form of trade received a serious blow. Gyasumdo's former openness to the outside world has resulted in considerable cultural mixture and layering, the intricacies of which have been masterly unravelled by the American anthropologist Mumford (1989).

To the west of Chame, the present-day administrative centre of Manang District, the Marsyangdi river turns sharply northward and again westward, creating a keyhole configuration that shields the upper Marsyangdi valley from the monsoon rains in summertime. Here ends Gyasumdo and starts the semi-arid world of Nyishang and Nar Phu.

The Nar Phu valley is an extremely isolated place, where some 800 inhabitants, divided over two village communities, earn a living by raising extensive yak herds on high Himalayan pastures and growing some barley on a few stretches of riverine terrace (N.J. Gurung 1977b, Chorlton 1982, Von Fürer-Haimendorf 1983). Due to the high elevation (over 3,800 metres) and the perceived lack of arable land, agricultural production is only sufficient to meet food requirements for about four months a year. Seasonal migration to the middle hills and the animal husbandry component in the village

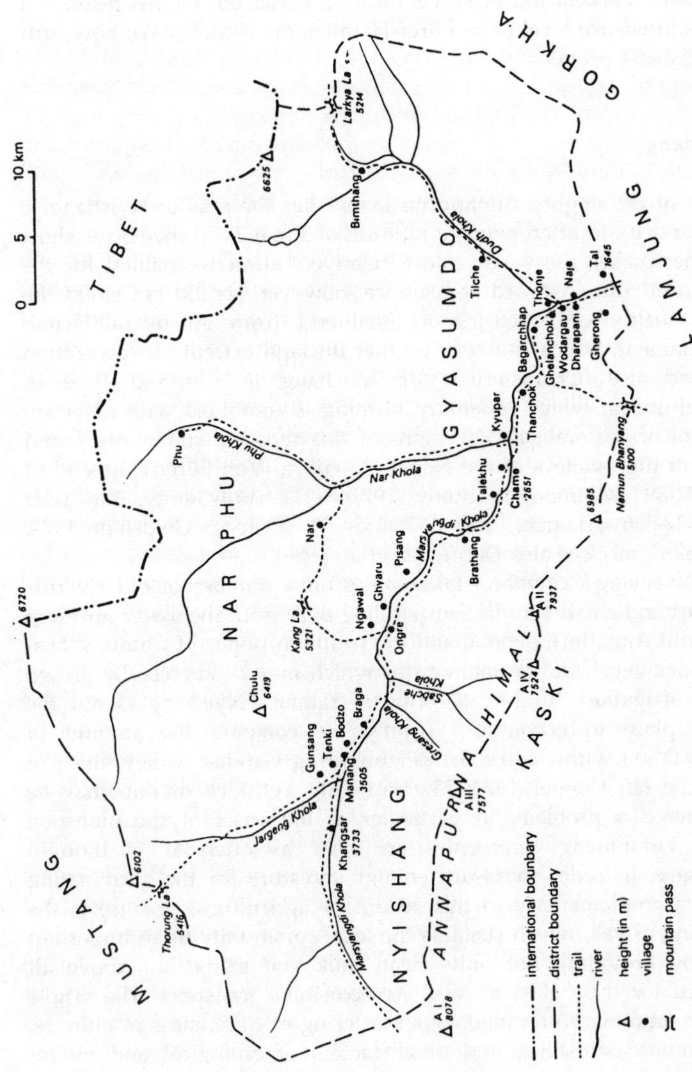

Figure 9 Manang District

economy save the enterprise from collapsing by providing the necessary markets and products for local barter but the net result is a bare subsistence level (Von Fürer-Haimendorf 1983:75). We now turn to Nyishang proper.

Nyishang

North of the mighty Annapurna massif lies the *pays* of Nyishang, a semi-arid basin at an average altitude of some 3,500 metres. A short summer makes the valley into a relatively attractive habitat for the local residents. Outward appearance, however, should not cloud the bleak reality of procuring a livelihood from an overall harsh environment, which can only be met through extreme specialization in land use. Characteristic of Nyishang is a mixed type of agriculture, in which sedentary farming is combined with a certain amount of pastoralism. Variations of this type are commonly found in other high valleys of the Nepal Himalaya (Von Fürer-Haimendorf 1975:42-59 (Khumbu), Sacherer 1977:99-111 (Rolwaling), Kawakita 1957:327-336 (Tsumje), Jest 1975:135-153 (Dolpo), Goldstein 1974: 259-267 (Limi); see also Dobremez et al. 1986).

In Nyishang cultivation takes place on a number of old riverine terraces and small alluvial fans spilling over from the lower northern slopes of Annapurna Himal and the southern slopes of Chulu. Wheat and buckwheat are the main crops which may be succesfully grown under irrigation. In overall terms of rainfall, Nyishang is not the worst place to encounter, if only we compare the amount of precipitation with that of the neighbouring Gandaki valley north of Tukuche (cf. Donner 1972:473, map 120). Yet, lack of rain may be considered a problem, in particular at the onset of the monsoon when rainmaking ceremonies are held as often as is thought necessary, in order to assure enough moisture for the germinating crops. Complementary to this sedentary agricultural practice is the breeding of yak, which sustains the local community in an important way by providing not only meat, milk and skins, but above all manure for the fields, as well as occasional transport. The whole system amounts to an ingenious mastering of differences in altitude, exposure to sunshine, and other factors of ecological and micro-climatological nature, which altogether makes for a living for about seven to eight months a year under average circumstances (see for a more extended discussion of Nyishangba agriculture Cooke 1985a:50-72, Van Spengen 1987:155-168).

Contrary to Cooke (1985a:65), the present author holds the view that differences in landownership exist and that at least some landless households are 'in the game'. A cadastral survey was non-existent in 1981, and earlier land-tax records, as for example available for most Gurung villages (Macfarlane 1976:50), could not be traced for Nyishang, and probably do not exist, for the Nyishangba never paid any land taxes to the Kathmandu government. According to some informants there is a standard measure of land, an amount which should ideally be within reach of an average household, that is to say, one of real Nyishangba descent. The few Tibetan and Baragaunli households in the village, however, do not possess any land, while other families own just a quarter of what is considered 'normal' and necessary to feed an average family. On the other hand, a few households are reported to have as much as eight times the standard measure of land, an indication of intra-village economic stratification in terms of landownership. Differences in respect to the latter seem to have been less pronounced before 1930, but were never absent according to local informants. The same applies to stratification in terms of pastoral assets.

Pastoralism is a significant component in the subsistence strategy as practised by the Nyishangba. The pastoral pattern of Nyishang resembles that of the village of Til in Limi, to which Goldstein (1974:262) refers as an intermediate 'third' pattern next to large-scale pastoralism on the one hand and minor pastoral activity for domestic use on the other. It is characterized by a period of winter pasturing at protected valley sites, interrupted by intervals of stable-based foddering during spells of bad weather. This system requires less manpower than an all-year pastoralism, thereby creating spare time, while retaining the economic and cultural benefits of animal-herding.

Spare time used to be invested in forms of subsistence trade in the middle hills during the winter months. Especially in times of bad weather or crop failure, small parties of Nyishangba visited neighbouring Lamjung and Gorkha, bringing with them local products like herbs, musk and woollen fabrics, which they bartered for food. But as these seasonal movements went unrecorded it is very difficult to gain a clear picture of their earlier substance and range.

Population and settlement

Although the present-day inhabitants of Nyishang mostly refer to themselves as Gurung, many of them admit to having Ghale ancestors. Alongside this majority of 'pure' Nyishangba, we find an early strand of Tibetan immigrants woven into the fabric of some of the older villages like Ngawal and Braga. The Tibetans concerned moved in some generations ago and are hardly distinguishable nowadays from the real Nyishangba. Over the years they acquired the same rights as their fellow villagers through original wealth and progressive intermarriage. After the occupation of Tibet by the Chinese in 1959, some ten refugee households settled in Braga, but were removed from the village in 1966 (N.J. Gurung 1977b:234). Pockets of Tibetan resistance fighters were removed from the wider region in 1975 (Mullin 1975:34, Avedon 1984:122-129). Only a few younger descendants were left behind, who are now working as labourers for the Nyishangba but have seldom acquired any capital in the form of land. After the refugee Tibetans had been removed, seven Baragaunli households from the neighbouring Gandaki valley were admitted to take their place, probably to solve the labour question. In addition a *kami* or blacksmith household is found in some villages.

The Nyishangba still act as an endogamous ethnic group, but much of the earlier status hierarchy (N.J. Gurung 1976:301-305) has disappeared. As one informant put it 'money is more important nowadays than descent'. Yet the idea of a larger endogamous group is still very much alive, and anyone who breaks the rules in this respect meets with considerable objection.

Nowadays seven main villages may be distinguished, differing from each other with respect to age and number of households, but less so in outward appearance, which clearly shows their common fund of Tibetan cultural identity. The three older villages are undoubtedly Ngawal, Braga and Manang, the latter being an enlarged reincarnation of an earlier site (Bodzo) on a nearby hill-top north of the present-day location. These sites have developed around

Buddhist monasteries, the founding legends of which are still locally known. The legends focus on the Gurung-Ghale encounter, highlighting the prevalence of the latter over the former, and possibly refer to events in the fifteenth century.

Khangsar, to the west of Manang, originated as a religious community too, but is certainly of later date than either the old Bodzo site near Manang or the Braga and Ngawal *gombas*. Pisang too is of later origin, and probably dates back to the seventeenth century. Tenki is a relatively recent off-shoot of Manang, not older than three or four generations, according to local informants. The same applies to Ghyaru that used to be a subsidiary settlement to Ngawal, but gained an independent status somewhere in the middle of the nineteenth century.

According to the Population Census of 1971 (National Planning Commission, Central Bureau of Statistics 1975) - earlier data are not available - the total population of Manang District was 7,436 in the early seventies (Population Census 1971, Vol.I, table 1) and 7,021 at the beginning of the 1980s (Population Census 1981 as referred to in Statistical Pocketbook Nepal 1988:10). 'Manang', probably covering here Nyishang and Nar Phu, is reported to have had 5,810 inhabitants (Population Census 1971, Vol.I, table 5). If we subtract the 850 inhabitants said to have been living in the Nar Phu valley in 1971 (N.J. Gurung 1977b:230), we come to an estimate for Nyishang proper of close to 5,000 in 1971. A survey of 1979 (S.B. Gurung and Prodypto Roy 1980, table 1) gives an estimate of 672 households (Manang:196, Tenki:60, Braga:120, Ghyaru:82, Khangsar:64, Ngawal:80, Pisang:80, Bodzo:10). Multiplying this number by 5.5 (the observed average number of persons per household in Braga), an estimate for the 1979 population might be given as close to 3,700. The latter figure fits well in with the 1982 one of 3,736 as given by Pohle (1986:123, table 2). Two observations should be made here. Firstly, the figures mentioned refer to resident and non-resident population alike, but we should be aware of the fact that the larger part of the village population migrates to Pokhara, Kathmandu and elsewhere in wintertime, where small but close-knit communities have become a regular feature of urban life. In other words, numbers given are maximum numbers and the actually resident village population is highly fluctuating between twenty and eighty per cent of the figures mentioned, depending on the season and the village chosen. Secondly, the enormous drop in total population within ten years is striking. Even if we assume estimates to be rather crude, the sharp decline in population, which continues unabated, remains evident.

These population dynamics are a direct result of the growing involvement of the Nyishangba in international trade. In fact, trade over the years has developed into the single-most important determinant of village life. Generally, trade precipitated an overall decay of valley life, in particular with regard to traditional agriculture and community organization. Processes of out-migration and permanent settlement in towns like Pokhara and Kathmandu have been discussed elsewhere (Van Spengen 1987:232-244), and it will suffice here to present a brief overview of recent change in the conditions of local valley life.

The decay of traditional valley life

When anthropologists - or geographers for that matter - have travelled thousands of kilometres to write the definitive monograph on their chosen village, town or region, they expect contrary to their better knowledge and judgement a relatively unspoilt world to unfold before their eyes. That is why, when Tilman visited Nyishang in 1950 he was more than a bit dismayed when one of the local inhabitants reacted to his unannounced appearance by pulling out a camera to immortalize the intruder (Tilman 1952:140). A few years later, Kawakita and his party had to make a hurried exit to escape the flying bullets of modern rifles (Kawakita 1957:67). And when in 1977, after years of total closure to outsiders, the first tourists were tentatively allowed to gaze at Annapurna's north face, they discovered a near-cosmopolitan population, well-versed in the intricacies of modern trade and travel: another paradise lost for the romantic researcher.

The changes have come fast, even in this remote upper valley. At least from the early 1970s onwards, the total population showed a sharp decline, which has brought the figure down from a reported 5,000 (Population Census 1971) to an estimated 3,700 in 1979. Demographically speaking, the age-group of 15 to 45 is conspicuously absent from the ranks, even in summertime, with the exception of many women within the (biologically) reproductive age-brackets. In particular, the less well-to-do among the latter are hard hit by the long absence of the men. Being responsible for tilling the land and looking after the livestock, the women work long hours and there is a tendency towards using children's labour in the poorer families. Aged persons from both sexes too, are mobilized to keep the traditional village economy going. To solve the labour question, many of the richer households have been hiring labour for many years already. Manzardo for instance, came across several men from Thak Sat Sae in the neighbouring Gandaki valley who had worked in Nyishang during their youth (Manzardo 1978:52), and in 1953, a Japanese scientific party met a number of hired Mustangi labourers on their way home from Manang (Kawakita 1957:316 and 327). The practice of hiring labour possibly dates from the late twenties when international trade ventures acquired an all-season character, thereby excluding participation of the male Nyishangba in agricultural activities. Labourers for the western part of Nyishang were mainly drawn from the neighbouring Gandaki valley across Thorong La, in particular the Muktinath area but labour contracts with places as far as Baglung, right in the middle hills, have been reported as well. Ngawal and the more easternly situated Nyishangba villages seem to have relied more on labour from Nar Phu, Larke and Nub-ri.

Since the 1960s, alternative and often more lucrative opportunities have arisen as a result of the ever-growing number of tourists in the hills. This applies in particular to the Gandaki valley, which has become one of the major trekking routes in recent years. It caused a decline in labour supply from across Thorong La, which has partly been made up for by an increasing number of Gorkha labourers coming into Nyishang since 1974. This halting supply, together with the amelioration of the trail along the Marsyangdi and increasing population pressure in the middle hills, seem to be the sufficient conditions for an explanation of the recent influx from Gorkha. Perhaps these labourers are willing to work for lower wages too than their Gandaki counterparts, ten rupees, two meals and some alcohol being considered an acceptable reward for a days toil and moil in 1981. The preference for a particular category of Gorkha labourers rather than those of Lamjung, may perhaps be explained by a common culture but this assumption rests only on one labourer from Laprak (a village in the Ghale cluster in northern Gorkha). Women labourers too from the same area, have been seen working in the fields. An occasional servant from the Terai, a Tibetan tailor or carpenter, and a *kami* or blacksmith household complement this labour picture. In fact the whole issue deserves further investigation.

The labour question, however, is but one aspect of a changing traditional agriculture as described earlier in this chapter. With growing long-term absence of the men, rising family incomes and in the end permanent out-migration, several other changes have been effected as well. Today abandoned fields are a common sight in Nyishang, and herd sizes are said to be declining. Irrigation systems are in need of repair and traditional local trade is breaking down.

Abandoned fields in the northern border areas of Nepal have been reported upon by several authors, but we need to distinguish between old-time fallows of debated origin (Hagen 1972:83 (deterioration of climate), Dobremez and Jest 1976:78 (fatal epidemics), cf. Heuberger 1956:25), and the more recently abandoned fields as a result of permanent out-migration, for example those in Thakali territory in the neighbouring Gandaki valley or those in Nyishang.

In the 1950s, however, land was far from being abandoned. Under the influence of rising family incomes, the earlier land transactions of the 1930s and 40s - involving a couple of hundred of rupees - were dwarfed by the sums of money invested in landed property after Singapore and Bangkok had been really 'discovered' by the Nyishangba. Good quality land occasionally changed hands for thousands of rupees. The more traditionally-minded traders spent their excess money in the acquisition of prestige-rich yaks which were even being imported from areas as far away as Solu-Khumbu (cf. the beginnings of Sherpa prosperity - see Von Fürer-Haimendorf 1964:11). But this stir of speculation lasted only for a short while. With the rise of Pokhara and Kathmandu as places of future speculation, most traders lost interest in their home district. On the balance, then, it produced a temporary rise in land values, the trend being reversed in the 1960s as a result of investment opportunities elsewhere.

Indeed, since the mid-sixties, the land market in the district has lapsed, not to say collapsed. For the richer families this fact was without significance, but for the less well-to-do households it meant easier access to a formerly scarce resource. In 1981, land could easily be obtained on a one-third/two-third sharecropping basis, the larger share going to the tiller. Up till now, however, the Nyishangba have refrained from selling their land to outsiders. The most recently abandoned fields are easily recognizable, especially in summertime, when a fairly homogeneous layer of parasitic plants has taken hold of them. Plots that have been abandoned for a longer time already, are generally identifiable by their tumbled-down enclosures. On the whole, abandoned fields are located farthest from the villages.

The average amount of abandoned land as encountered in Nyishang in 1981 may be tentatively set at 15 to 20 per cent. With regard to the situation in Tenki, for example, it was reported that an amount of 150 *muri* (yield figure) had been given over to fallow. As one *muri* equals 20 *pathi*, and an average household sows 6 *pathi*, giving a maximum yield of 300 *pathi*, then the stated amount of abandoned land is (150·20) equals 3,000 *pathi* : 300, which is the equivalent of some ten households, which is 15 to 20 per cent out of a total of sixty households. This percentage fits reasonably well in with the number of fifteen households reported to be permanently absent from the village, the discrepancy probably be explained by the fact that some absentee households have their land still worked by others.

Another crucial field which is suffering from the present labour shortage, is the maintenance of irrigation channels. The system (see Van Spengen 1987:163-164) is slowly losing its fine regulating qualities, due to a neglect of the vital sluicing sections. Presently the five days of free labour a year per household for the common purpose of channel maintenance are frequently dodged by the absentee landowners. The system shows signs of exhaustion, which will eventually lead to the exclusion of land farthest from the main channels, regardless the quality of the land. To fight these unsolicited developments, fines of rupees 200 per household have been imposed by the village councils in case of neglect, a negligible amount for the successful trader. Yet the arrangement netted a lumpsum of 13,500 rupees in 1980, a sufficient amount to hire enough labour to counteract the worst consequences of absentee labour.

Pastoralism is on the decline as well. With the current shortage of labour, the care for the animals has inevitably decreased. Children and older persons guard the pasture-grounds, the herding cycle is breaking down, and the gathering of winter fodder is yet another burden to the women in a daily time-budget already filled to the brim. For quite some time, the decline of pastoralism could be slowed down by employing Tibetan refugees as herdsmen, in particular after 1960. But the removal of most Tibetans from the district in 1966, meant a severe blow to a high-altitude pastoralism already under strain. The result has been a steady decline in herd-size, especially where it concerns the yak, notwithstanding its cultural valuation.

The most conspicuous signs of decay in material district life are the many vacant houses, many of which have fallen into serious disrepair. Locked doors are a common sight, some of them having already been closed for more than ten years. As Pohle observed in 1983 'In the Mano quarter of Manang (...) 63 houses are abandoned of a total number of 168' (Pohle 1988:87). But this is Manang, the main village, where most of the trading households come from. Because many houses have been built in the speculative period 1950-1965 but have never been occupied, the villages seem even more deserted than is actually the case. Especially on a summer day when women and children are working in the fields and the older men are guarding the high pastures, the villages convey the impression of a ghost-town, resembling wintertime.

Altogether, the people themselves are well aware of the decay of district life and the loss of social cohesion. They recalled how pretty the villages looked thirty years ago, and despite the archetypal longing for something that was not there either thirty years ago, the overall feeling is one of decreased social responsibility. This feeling is shared by young and old alike, men as well as women, though for different reasons. The young rejoice in their relative freedom but lack the security of traditional village life. The older men complain about their loss of ascribed status and the relative neglect of traditional religion by the young. Most women suffer from an overload of daily work. The worst is considered to be the inflation of social and communal duties, nowadays more often than not translated into ever-increasing sums of money. Several fines have been imposed by the village councils for the most common forms of neglect and the money raised in that way was said to have accrued to a fund of 2.1 million rupees in 1981. These 'savings' are used for the maintenance of roads and the repair of bridges. Recently, 3 *lakh* of rupees have been invested in an apple-plantation near Brathang, just outside the upper valley. In addition, some 13 *lakh* of rupees have been set aside for a small hydroelectric project near the Ongre plain.

Another sign of inflation is the rise in the amounts of indemnification that have to be paid in the private sphere. Breaking off an engagement asks for a compensation of 5,000 rupees, a swift divorce after formal marriage will cost up to 10,000, while a straight break-down of a long-standing marriage may give rise to claims as high as 20,000 rupees (1981). Building a house for the newly-weds will average a good 9,000 rupees, an affair that could be organized for less than a thousand rupees ten years earlier. Goods and money to a total amount of 7,000 rupees may be distributed in one burial ceremony and considerable but varying sums are spent in the many summer *pujas*. The money thus collected is used for the maintenance of religious artifacts, the subsistence cost of the *gomba* community, or the wider village celebrations on the occasion of a visiting *thulo* lama. Pisang and Braga, for example, were each in the course of building a huge prayer-wheel in 1981, while a large amount of money was spent on celebrating the visit of Kanchen Ruemberse, a one-time refugee-lama from Tibet, who enjoyed hospitality for many years in Nyishang before proceeding to Buddh Gaya (India) in 1968. Indeed, it is in the religious sphere that the decline of traditional district life seems least pronounced (cf. Pohle 1988:88).

If you ask the Nyishangba how their valley will look like in the not too distant future, the more realistic among them admit that most of the inhabitants will probably have settled elsewhere. But at the same time they foresee the further development of what is now a nascent tourist-industry. Since the district has been opened up to foreigners in 1977, growing numbers of tourists have come to visit the magnificent upper valley and many of them stay on for one or two days before attempting to cross Thorung La to Muktinath on the Gandaki side or vice versa. In response to this influx, some households have taken to the habit of providing meals to passers-by, and the more enterprising among them have started real country hotels, especially in Manang. Inhabitants from Manang, too, have taken over the most accessible and flat pieces of land in the Ongre plain on the southern bank of the Marsyangdi. A STOL-airstrip has been built there, and a few of the bigger traders from Manang have taken to the hotel business as a kind of safety-valve in times of old-age or financial disaster. Yet one wonders how viable the recent rise is. The upper valley remains a remote destination, the crossing of Thorung La tricky, even in summertime, and the weather unpredictable, which makes regular flight schedules as yet uncertain. Moreover, winter comes early at 3,500 metres.

Only the future can tell how far the above reflections are off the mark. One thing is sure, however: the complex process of permanent out-migration that has been set in motion, is irreversible. The Nyishangba know it and time will do the rest.

Comparative perspectives

As it is the stated purpose of this study to put the Nyishangba case in a wider comparative perspective (see chapter 1) we may well, having arrived at this point, briefly review the geohistorical experience of structurally related groups. After all, it is only by careful comparison that we might gain more insight in the general processes of structuration at work.

From a comparative point of view it is a fortunate circumstance that the formerly scarce information about the Walongchung area in Northeast Nepal (Hooker 1855:196-221, Von Fürer-Haimendorf 1975: 121-131, Bista 1980:174-176; see also Figure 8) has recently been supplemented by additional materials and field reports. Firstly we have the historical anthropological study by Steinmann (1988) which focuses on the relationship between Walongchung society and their local henchmen in the face of growing interference by the Nepalese state. Secondly, there is the much more mundane study by Schrader, devoting a small chapter to recent changes in Walongchung (1988: 264-291). Together these sources point in the direction of a once well-established but highly fluid trading network. The inhabitants of Walongchung seem to have risen as long-distance traders by virtue of their location at a break-of-bulk point in the upper Tamur region, where the goods brought by yak caravans from Tibet were transferred on to the backs of porters for the onward journey to the south. This entrepôt position, sanctioned by the Nepalese government from the late eighteenth century onwards for reasons of control of the strategically important Tipta La, produced a relatively sophisticated trading community, the richest traders of which dealt in luxury goods and ventured abroad to places as far as Shigatse and Lhasa on the one hand, and Kathmandu, Darjeeling, and Calcutta on the other (Steinmann 1988:83, Schrader 1988:288). Walongchung was once a small town with more than two thousand inhabitants at the beginning of the twentieth century. Its community was adversely affected by the political upheaval in Tibet in the 1950s and 60s and the restrictions in trade resulting from it. Natural disaster and Khamba refugee problems too, caused a further decline in the entrepôt function of Walongchung (Von Fürer-Haimendorf 1975:130). Nowadays, only a small village remains consisting mostly of locked and empty houses, and inhabited by no more than one-tenth of its former population (Steinmann 1988:181-183, Schrader 1988:289, 291). Tourism has been unable to counterbalance the general decline of the area, as it is still restricted and therefore inaccessible to foreigners.

Thakali economy and society in the Gandaki corridor in between the Dhaulagiri and Annapurna massifs is relatively well known (Jest 1964-1965:26-49, Bista 1971:52-61, Von Fürer-Haimendorf 1975: 132-222, Iijima 1977:69-92, 1982:21-39, Manzardo 1978, 1982:45-60, Parker 1985, 1988:181-194, Vinding 1984:51-105, Vinding and Bhattachan 1985:1-23, W.F. Fisher 1987, Von der Heide 1988). The rise of the Thakali to economic power and regional overlordship dates from the mid-nineteenth century when Nepal was at war with Tibet (1857-1858). Services of political brokerage rendered by a leading Thakali, impressed the Kathmandu Darbar, which conferred on the person in question the title and privilege of *subba*. In addition, he received a monopoly for the salt trade emanating from Tibet. In this way the Thakali headman acquired the necessary prerequisites for economic and political power, a title with influence and the apparent support of the central government (Iijima 1977:75). The Thakali were, of course, favoured by situational factors. The bottleneck gorge of the Kali Gandaki Valley helped to funnel the entire trade through their hands but the near collapse of the state of Mustang and its raja in the last quarter of the nineteenth century seems to have provided the overall geopolitical impetus (Bista 1971:57, 60). The salt monopoly brought considerable wealth to a number of Thakali families. Despite rival bids for *subba*-ship from neighbouring Tingaun by Gurung clansmen they held their own, even to such an extent that the Ranas declared an end to their monopoly in 1928 (Manzardo 1978:37). From that time onwards, traders started to travel to the south in increasing numbers. The subsequent formation of a new trade network in the period 1928-1962, brought massive changes to the Thakali community. In the course of the process, Tukuche became the major trading centre in Thakali territory, where, up till 1959 at least, merchants imported sheep, goats, yak, *dzo*, horses, mules, woollen pelts, hides, fur, butter and cheese, as well as rock salt from the northern high plateaus in exchange for Nepalese and Indian commodities such as rice, wheat, barley, pulses, buckwheat, oil, chilis, paper, cotton, cotton cloth, metal utensils, guns and gun-powder (Iijima 1977:80). The Tibetan affair of 1959-1962, however, reduced this trade to insignificance, as a result of which a good number of Thakali in Tukuche accepted the advice of a leading Thakali headman to migrate *en masse* to such southern cities as Pokhara, Kathmandu, Bhairawa, Butwal and Tansing (ibid.:87). The southward shift of the Thakali has been the object of some research. Depending on their measure of success in business, they have settled in the bigger trade centres where they now act as middlemen in a growing wholesale business. Moneylending too, features occasionally in their dealings and a few have transformed themselves into incipient industrial capitalists (Iijima 1982:28,30, Vinding 1984:78-83, Von der Heide 1988:22-28).

Several explanations have been offered for the rise of the Thakali: locational, economic and political, as well as cultural. None of these seems a sufficient condition in isolation. Even Parker, whose analysis of the culture of Thakali entrepreneurship is a useful complement to earlier, economic anthropological studies, has to admit that Thakali wealth is the result of a 'fortuitous interaction between culture and circumstance' (Parker 1988:193). My view as to the nature of that 'circumstance' will be presented in the epilogue of this study.

To the west of the Gandaki Valley, easy passes across the main chain of the Himalaya become fewer and long-distance trade, though not unimportant in the local economies, is less well developed than in either the Walongchung or Thakali cases mentioned above. Trade is in the hands of a few Bhotia communities like those of Tarangpur in Tichurong on the southern edge of Dolpo district (Jest 1975:159-169, J.F. Fisher 1986), Mugu and Karan on the upper Mugu Karnali (Von Fürer-Haimendorf 1975:227-237, Clarke 1977:299-305, H.B. Gurung

1980:52-66, B.C. Bishop 1990:301-303) and the Nyinba villages in the district of Humla in the northwestern corner of Nepal (Goldstein 1974:265-267, 1975:95-98, Von Fürer-Haimendorf 1975:250-267, H.B. Gurung 1980:93-120, Rauber 1987a:65-87, 1987b:200-228, Levine 1988:215-226, B.C. Bishop 1990:303-310; see also Bancaud and Macdonald 1982). What these communities have in common is their winter exodus to the Nepalese middle hills and its concomitant long-distance trade ventures, which brings them to the Nepalese border bazaars (B.C. Bishop 1990:312, 321-322). In a way, this exodus resembles the winter migration of their Bhotia confrères in the neighbouring Indian Himalaya of Kumaon on which Pant already reported in the 1930s (Pant 1935:175-186). Recent developments have shown a number of Mugu and Humla traders to venture as far as Kalimpong and Dharamsala, thereby greatly extending their commercial range. Similar developments have been reported from Tsum on the upper Buri Gandaki (Kawakita 1957:338-339), Baragaon in the Gandaki Valley (Schuler 1983:30-31,55), and Helambu in North-central Nepal (Clarke 1980:96-97).

A likewise development has taken place among the Byanshi of far western Nepal. First noticed and described in some detail by Jest (1974:252-255), and subsequently taken up by Manzardo, Dahal and Rai (1976:95, 110-111), these changes, at a certain level of abstraction, very much resemble those experienced by other Himalayan high-altitude dwellers. According to Jest, the Byanshi practice long-distance forms of trade, in the course of which they buy textiles and other manufactured goods in Almora and even Calcutta, and sell them in the middle hills of Kumaon. The early control of the musk trade in the region has probably allowed for their original capital formation, which facilitated a smooth transition to the retailing of modern goods. The border closure of the 1960s accelerated the pace of change, which ultimately led to permanent out-migration of Byanshi to the Terai and even Kathmandu, where a few families are now engaged in wholesaling operations and the development of cottage industry (ibid.:109).

Best known of all indigenous Tibetan communities in Nepal are the Sherpa of the Solu-Khumbu region (Von Fürer-Haimendorf 1964, 1975:7-105, 1984, Oppitz 1968, Ortner 1978:10-32, 1989, especially 19-23, Limberg 1982, J.F. Fisher 1990, Brower 1991, Stevens 1993).

Traditional Sherpa trade with the Dingri area of Tibet (Aziz 1978:95-116) as well as their forays into the middle hills (Von Fürer-Haimendorf 1975:60-73) has undergone considerable change. In Solu-Khumbu too, the restrictions on cross-border trade imposed by the Chinese from 1960 onwards, greatly affected long-distance trade. Fortunately, by this time, mountaineering and tourism had brought new economic opportunites to the Solu and especially the Khumbu villages. These new ventures turned out to be less prone to monopolization than traditional long-distance trade had been. Tenancy and debt, which had increased during the pre-1960 years (Miller 1965, but see Ortner 1989:118) became less outspoken through secondary sources of income in principle available to every member of the community. As a result, few of the younger men remained to work the land of the wealthier landowners, who in consequence lost one of their lines of control over the less favoured population. Soon a decline in agricultural organization became noticeable. By the early 1980s Khumbu's traditional subsistence agriculture had come under great strain, mainly due to an omnipresent labour shortage and a beginning out-migration of the wealthier households (Bjønness 1980, 1983). In summary, the ability to earn high wages has facilitated the accumulation of capital, which the older generation invested in land and cattle but which modern Sherpa are prepared to invest in tourist facilities both at home and in Kathmandu. A few speculative-minded among the latter have now taken to the habit of international trade (Von Fürer-Haimendorf 1984, Fisher 1990).

From a comparative point of view, it is clear that the rise of the Nyishangba as long-distance traders to the south was not an isolated development. The above survey of Tibetan communities living in Nepal's northern border areas points in the direction of a growing economic pull from the south in the wake of a rising British-Indian *économie-monde*, accelerated by geopolitical changes in the Himalayan region at large. However, what needs further exploration and explanation in the context of this study is the peculiarity of the Nyishangba, who, from a relatively early date onwards, developed a southward-bound trading network on a scale quite unknown to other Nepalese communities, with the possible exception of the Newar of the Kathmandu Valley. It is therefore to the complexities and intricacies of the geohistorical rise of the Nyishangba as long-distance traders that the following two chapters are devoted.

6

THE EMERGENCE OF LONG-DISTANCE TRADE VENTURES

Trade, as it developed over the years, brought increased mobility for a majority of the Nyishangba. Nowadays, one hardly finds a grown-up member of their community that has not been outside Nepal and many of them are acquainted with Singapore, Bangkok and Hong Kong. Of course, the rise of the Nyishangba as long-distance traders did not take place overnight. In effect, it took several decades for them to translate their initial gains into the relative - and for some of them - absolute wealth that is so characteristic of their Kathmandu-based community today. The whole process of increased mobility boils down to a progressive integration into the wider Southeast Asian economy, in particular with regard to its urban centres of capitalist advancement. Content and context of this process provide us with the subject matter for the present chapter.

The Indian connection

As earlier referred to, we should avoid the idea of Nyishangba trading activities suddenly emerging at some point in time. Rather we should imagine a slowly growing trade sector, in which regional barter and exchange of locally produced goods increasingly made room for supraregional forms of trade. This extension beyond regional boundaries in the course of the nineteenth century and the opening up of alternative trans-Himalayan trade routes caused occasional friction between neighbouring groups but the quarrels involved do not seem to have affected the Nyishangba very much.

The late nineteenth and early twentieth century saw increasing competition between the Thakali and Gurung *subbas* over trade privileges in the north-central region of Nepal. For a time, the Marsyangdi route to Tibet through Tingaun proved to be a viable alternative to the Gandaki one, as a result of skilful manoeuvring by Man Lal Lamichane, a Gurung clansman (Messerschmidt and Gurung 1974:203). The latter became the chief tax functionary of Larkya, which gave him considerable influence in the area. In due time, he extended his local administrative jurisdiction by arranging his two sons to become, jointly, *jimuwals* of Nar Khola. There was no provision for such an agent in Nyishang, which makes one believe in the continued relative autonomy of the upper valley, although its inhabitants seem to have appreciated Man Lal as a broker between them and the Kathmandu court (ibid.: 205).

In the meantime, Nyishangba trading parties, as earlier referred to, continued to come down in wintertime from their snowy habitat, in order to escape the cold and engage in profitable trade ventures. Their main destination up till the beginning of the twentieth century seems to have been the middle Ganga plain with its crowding urban centres and in particular so the trade fairs (*mela*) near Benares, Patna and Gorakhpur (cf. Blunt 1912:94,68). Here they may have met with Kashmiris and Gosains, who acquainted them, verbally at least, with their Indian-wide trading network, extending from Rajasthan to the Coromandel coast, and from Kashmir to the Bay of Bengal (cf. Uprety 1980:50-51n).

Was it a coincidence, then, that Kawaguchi, a Japanese agent on his way to Tibet, came across a Nyishangba party of more than fifty people in Arughat on the Buri Gandaki, or should this fact be interpreted as the firm entrenchment of a well-organized extra-local component in the subsistence economy of the Nyishangba by 1899 (Kawaguchi 1909:41)? Probably the truth lies somewhere in between. Trade, on the part of the Nyishangba, was an important activity in the winter season but purposively organized trading parties venturing beyond the middle Ganga plain do not yet seem to have fallen within the limits of their trade horizon. Nevertheless, Kawaguchi's observation confirms earlier legal documentary evidence on the Nyishangba as a Himalayan trading community of more than local importance. But this importance should not be overrated, at least not for the turn of the century. In my opinion, wider trade ventures to for example Delhi or burgeoning Calcutta may have taken place sporadically at this time but they were confined to small kinship-based groups, in contrast to the larger territorially defined trading parties. Only after the smaller groups had safely returned home with unmistakable evidence of market opportunities elsewhere, larger groups of Nyishangba began to find their way to the emerging centres of urban colonial activity in British India.

Early trade ventures, that is, before the attraction of Calcutta was fully felt, were based on an exchange of products derived from different but complementary ecozones. Foodgrains, in particular rice, were imported from the middle hills into the trans-Himalayan high valleys, while specialties from the alpine zone found their way into the Ganga plain. Major high altitude products, besides the Tibetan rock salt, were musk and officinal herbs, both of which were an established trade item from the earliest days of Nyishangba mobility. The low weight for value characteristic of these products made them excellent long-distance bridgers, while their specific qualities (i.e. fragrance and healing) guaranteed unbroken demand in the Indian urban markets.

Musk was obtained at home, as the musk deer (*Moschus moschiferus*) primarily inhabits rhododendron-juniper and birch forest at higher altitudes between 3,600 and 4,200 metres (Bhatt 1977:96), a habitat description which fits well in with the general ecological background of Nyishang and neighbouring areas. Officinal herbs too, were locally collected and dried for trading purposes, the most common species being *Nardostachys grandiflora* from the valerian family, marketed as *jatamansi*, *Picrorhyza scrophularaeflora*, a gentian species, and *Aconitum violaceum*, the latter being used to combat fevers (Manandhar l980: 47,61,55,20, Dobremez and Jest 1976:182-184, Pohle 1990:23-26). These 'luxury' items were occasionally supplemented by young Tibetan mastiffs, goat skins and yak tails, as well as home-made mufflers and blankets. Thus, trade at the turn of the century had a definite territorial base, the monopoly of which was only broken in the early 1920s. The first cracks in this home-based trading system appeared when individual members of families from Manang and Braga started to procure musk and herbs from Himalayan areas other than Nyishang. Between 1900 and 1925 a number of small nuclear groups, usually consisting of a few close relatives, started to find their way into Himachal Pradesh and Kashmir, where alternative sources of herbs and especially musk could be tapped. One older informant referred to the progressive nature of these new trade ventures.

Having travelled with his father to Delhi for two subsequent seasons in order to sell herbs and musk from Nyishang (around 1915) they found their way into Jammu the next year, tramped for eleven days through the Pir Panjal and ended up in Delhi again via Rawalpindi and Lahore in the present-day Pakistan.

For a short period before 1920, Delhi was considered a suitable place for buying trips into the western Himalaya, where Simla, Kulu, Dharmsala, Jammu and Srinagar provided the rallying points for local hunters, poachers and herb collectors to sell their products. In a sense we find here the first true specimen of Nyishangba long-distance trading, because trade had become fully detached from the place of origin of its intermediaries. Products were no longer collected by the Nyishangba themselves but purchased on a restricted wholesale basis with the aim of selling them in the larger urban markets of northern India. Occasionally, the price of musk fell below what was considered to generate an acceptable profit. One or two Nyishangba reacted by going to Bombay but this was quite exceptional before 1920 and most of the others fell back into the less speculative trade of the middle Ganga plain. A typical example of these early Delhi/Kashmir ventures is to be found in the story as told by a 76-year old Braga informant:

At the age of twelve (about 1917) he was asked to become a porter in a small group of relatives preparing for their annual trip to India. Having stumbled down the difficult Marsyangdi route, the group reached the Thori customs-post in about a fortnight. Crossing the border to Narkatiaganj (Bihar), the trip proceeded by train to Amritsar via Gorakhpur and Delhi. In the latter places most of the home-collected herbs were sold and with the money raised, musk wholesaling in the lower Kashmir ranges took place. This newly acquired musk was then hawked about in Amritsar and Delhi. On their way back the group bought cotton cloth and dyes in Kanpur as well as a small amount of domestic goods, the former being resold in Bandipur and the Lamjung hills. The net profit per person per trip tended to range between 500 and 600 rupees, a considerable amount for that time, and it is probably here that we find the first signs of capital accumulation on a limited scale.

Railway construction in the northern Ganga plain in the period 1875-1910 (Sen 1977:72-74; Regmi (ed.) 1983b:72-75), may have played a catalysing role in the formation of these early assets.

In particular the construction of feeder lines up to the Nepalese border provided the Nyishangba parties with better accessibility to the towns of the Ganga plain, and through them to more distant places. Two additional factors regarding the ultimate choice for a particular market-place may be added, language and religion. In the case of the Buddhist and 'Nepali-speaking' Nyishangba, the general requirement of sufficient potential customers for any merchant, may be refined by pointing at the cultural background of the buying public involved. It is quite certain that the Gurkha cantonments at Dharmsala, Dehra Dun and Almora (cf. Vansittart 1890:97) offered specific chances for the Nyishangba, not in the least so because many Nepali immigrants had settled near these places (Sagant 1978:110). At the same time certain Buddhist religious fairs, as for example those at Rewalsar (cf. Cantwell 1995) and Buddh Gaya (cf. Bhardwaj 1973:141-142, 145n) provided them with additional market opportunities. It is significant in this respect that Hindu religious fairs and places of Hindu pilgrimage were less popular as potential markets. The golden Sikh temple of Amritsar, however, as well as Sikh *gurdvaras* in other places, enjoyed considerable popularity with the Nyishangba. For one thing this may have had to do with stiff competition from Hindu merchant castes, for another with a common minority status as shared with the Sikhs in a Hindu-dominated society, though not in the Panjab itself. Yet, free boarding near the Sikh temples may have been a much more down-to-earth reason for this popularity.

Calcutta and the Assamese 'frontier'

If the Delhi decade featured as a prelude to early Nyishangba ventures, the Calcutta connection, from the 1920s onwards, resounded a solid fugue, the themes of which set the stage for a basic long-distance trade pattern in the years to come. At the same time, however, the free stance taken towards the *Leitmotiv*, permitted improvisation along individual lines. As hinted before, too strict an interpretation of what was happening when and where should be avoided. Although the structural characteristics of the basic pattern have been plainly identified, no clear-cut stages stand out in the development of Nyishangba trade and considerable overlap is the rule rather than the exception.

From the 1920s onwards, the single-most important focus for Nyishangba trading activities became Calcutta, which emerged during the nineteenth century from the Bengal delta as the British imperial capital in India. Its functional importance as a colonial service-hatch attracted a large population and in terms of the sheer size of the market, Calcutta and its hinterland offered opportunities to the Nyishangba they had never dreamt of. Yet, the question arises why they entered the Calcutta scene so late, that is long after the hub of Bengal achieved its position as a commercial metropolis. In my opinion, the distances involved do not offer a sufficient explantion, as the accessibility by rail to Calcutta was no worse than to the lower Himalayan ranges of the United Provinces. Rather we need to look at the nature and origin of the trade products involved and the progressive extension of regional trade links into Assam. In essence, the shift from the United Provinces to Bengal and Assam may have had to do with the ease of procuring natural products from the Himalayan middle hills, combined with culturally-derived market opportunities in the Calcutta region.

The former remains recognizable in the continued search for musk and herbs in Sikkim, Bhutan and the North-East Frontier Agency up till the 1940s, the latter gained importance with increasing numbers of Nepali immigrants into the eastern foothills of the Himalaya and the Assamese lowlands in the period 1911-1931 (Morris 1935:202-210; Sagant 1978:110). To point at culturally derived market opportunities is to obscure, however, the general geohistorical situation, which gave rise to the increased numbers of migrants. The preconditions for such an immigration were set by the British colonial advancement into the lower Himalaya in Bengal and Assam. The establishment of tea plantations, the wild caoutchouc boom and the rise of hill stations turned the traditional seasonal migrations of the middle hill-dwellers into more permanent movements of labourers, settlers and petty traders. Colonial needs gave rise to new trade networks which groups like the Nyishangba helped to give distinctive form. They played their little role in the 'scramble for Assam' with ardour, taking advantage of the eruption of alien enterprise as a welcome addition to their more traditional trade ventures (see Figure 10).

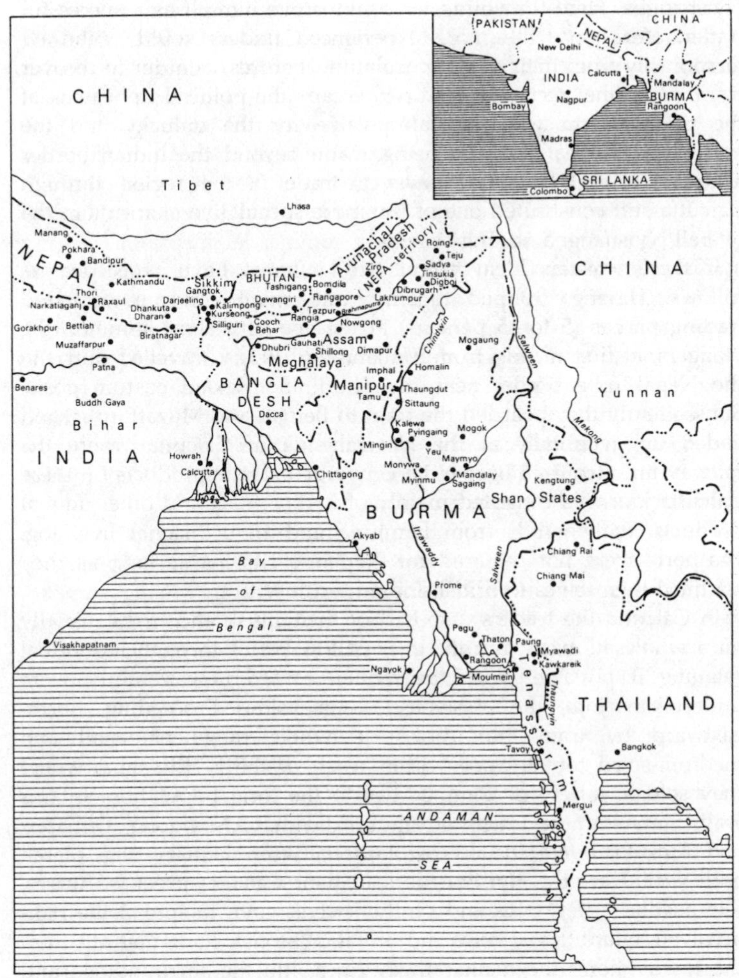

Figure 10 Places visited by Nyishangba traders in the period 1930-1950

At the outset it must be stated that the Assam region from the 1920s well into the fifties remained an essential trading field for the Nyishangba. Here the youngster could prove himself as a successful trader. Here, too, the more experienced traders could withdraw temporarily from their more speculative ventures, in order to recover from some unexpected losses or to escape the political upheavals of the time. Assam was the safety-valve for the unlucky and the incapable, the real fortunes being made beyond the Indian border after 1930. In the 1920s, however, trade in the region through Calcutta still constituted one of the more speculative elements in the overall Nyishangba trading system.

If there was an ideal-typical trip, it must have proceeded as follows. Having grouped together into small and medium-sized trading parties (5 to 15 persons) at the end of a short summer, the villagers, at first mainly from Manang and Braga, travelled down to the Nepal-India border near the Thori and Raxaul custom posts. Subsequently they boarded the train to Bettiah and Muzaffarpur, and ended up eventually at the Howrah-side of Calcutta where the railway lines from all over India converged. Trade products on these Calcutta journeys consisted mainly of herbs, musk and other animal products, daily goods from Lamjung and an occasional live dog. Passports were not required for Nepalese citizens as long as they confined themselves to British-Indian territory.

In Calcutta the traders disposed of their musk and herbs, usually on a wholesale basis, but in times of low prices through individual retailing if possible. With the money earned new ventures were undertaken into the Assamese countryside. Proceeding north-eastward by train into Assam, a whole range of small and medium-sized towns came within reach of the Nyishangba, where they sold a variety of commodities to the local population. In this way, the Assamese towns of Dhubri, Gauhati, Nowgong, Dimapur and Tinsukia were visited regularly between January and March each year. Here the Nyishangba sold their Calcutta procured wares, like needles, safety-pins and synthetic dyes, and, to spread the risks involved, quantities of coral and imitation stones. Radiating out from the towns along the main railway lines into the surrounding rural areas, clusters of Nepali settlement were visited, and chains, caps, belts and ribbons from Nepali origin found their way into the countryside.

But the Nepali immigrants were not the only target of the Nyishangba. Rural Assam had long been renowned for its weaving and home-made cloth, the emphasis being on special fabrics like *anday* (Varadarajan 1988). In addition, some cottage silk industry existed (cf. Spate et al. 1972:605). These home-producers now became the object of new trade opportunities by selling them needles and dyes, while purchasing the finished *anday* and some silk from them. The dyes were sought after up to the Bhutanese border, where the better *anday* was produced. Here, Tibetan Dukpa visited the Bhutan *mela* along the Indian border, selling herbs and musk to the occasional Nyishangba trader. After completion of a full four to five month cycle, the trading parties returned home again via Calcutta where they sold most of the *anday* and bought manufactured goods for personal use and status, like porcelain wares and cotton dress after European fashion. The remaining assets were used to buy rice in the Lamjung hills.

The ideal-typical trip, as sketched above, was prone to develop variation, extension and, through time, change in content. Some traders would specialize in one or two products, while others, according to their particular measure of success, were bound to generate a wide spectre of markets and products. The whole business displayed a definitive speculative element: small fortunes were won, but heavy losses occurred from time to time.

Two variations in the main pattern may be distinguished. Firstly, there was a tendency for the richer and more successful traders to show a greater mobility and to operate more along individual lines. Secondly, from the mid-thirties onwards, and especially so during the Second World War, Assam and adjacent areas proved to be a viable trade field in its own right. The former variation may be illustrated through the story as told by a Braga Nestor, one of the four 'strong' men, who dominated the affairs politically and economically in the upper valley during the 1940s and 50s.

Trade ventures in this period were of highly fragmented and diversified nature. While the men would visit the more distant places like Kohima (Nagaland) and Imphal (Manipur), the women from Shillong searched the Bhutan *mela* for wool, which they converted into mufflers and blankets. The Godam *mela* near Cooch Behar, too, was a much frequented place for this purpose. In addition, large numbers of *kukhris*, manufactured by a Nepali immigrant in Kurseong (near Kalimpong) found their way into Assam as far east as the Digboi oilfields, where quite a few Nepali were employed as watchmen and labourers. Calcutta remained important for some time as a market for leopard and tiger skins. These were purchased from Tamang and Limbu hunters in the Dhankuta area of East Nepal, brought down by foot to Dharan and by bus to Biratnagar on the Nepal-India border, where they were passed on into Indian territory under somewhat mysterious circumstances.

Generally speaking, Nyishangba trading activities in Assam reached their zenith in the late 1940s. By this time, specialization in certain trade items had become quite common. Some traders stuck to the traditional herb and musk trade, but others emerged as specialized dealers in rings and semi-precious stones. The latter development came increasingly to the fore after the Nyishangba had discovered Burma as a major source of stones in the 1930s. The more speculative-minded traders felt immediately attracted and gave Nyishangba enterprise an extra dimension in the next twenty years or so, an episode which remains to be discussed in a later section. As a rule, however, small groups of traders would pursue whatever opportunities arose, the actual choice for a particular product or locality being dependent on the subtle interplay between demand and supply in a highly fragmented market. In the course of this process, traders started to move beyond the Bhutan *mela* near the Indian border, in order to tap cheap sources of herbs and musk themselves.

Traders tramped through the eastern Himalaya, taking the towns along the Assam railway line on the northern bank of the Brahmaputra as their points of departure. In this way, Rangia, Rangapore, Lakhumpur and Sadiya became key localities through which traders found their way to Dewangiri and Tashigang in Bhutan, as well as the Frontier Division towns of Bomdila, Ziro, Roing and Teju in the present-day Arunachal Pradesh (see Figure 10). The Lohit Frontier Division proved to be a major source of cheap herb stocks, in particular *mishmi-tigta* (*Swertia chirayita*). Large quantities of the latter were supplied by members of the locally dominant Mishmis, but after 1952, the Nyishangba were largely pushed out of this wholesale market by stiff competition from Bengali and Burmese traders.

If these ventures into the eastern Himalaya seem to be romantic versions of extra-local trade opportunities, every-day reality was more like a double-edged sword. Poaching for musk deer and the subsequent smuggling of the musk past mountain check points and border posts involved the risk of large fines or even temporary imprisonment when caught in the act. On the other hand, small fortunes could be made if successful in bringing down a few *tola* of musk or quantities of restricted herbs to the Indian markets. There was a definite illegal aspect, then, in some of the dealings of the Nyishangba, a characteristic for which they are still known. In fact, the rise of Burma as a source of semi-precious stones (Calhoun 1929: 708-712), renewed the temptation of crossing borders illegally in view of possible windfall profits. Some of the Nyishangba were indeed prepared to take great risks, but others sought to establish less remunerative yet safer lines of trade through more permanent contacts with Nepali immigrants near the Gurkha cantonment of Maymyo in central Burma.

Burmese days

> Everything in Mogok was arranged in terms of precious stones (J. Kessel in *La vallée des rubis*, Paris: Gallimard 1955, ch.11)

From the early 1930s onwards, the Nyishangba discovered the Mogok 'stone tract' in Burma as the original source of the gems they had come to know already from the great Calcutta metropolitan bazaar. Increasing knowledge of the Mogok area was precipitated by rising numbers of Nepali immigrants in central Burma, attracted as they were by the Gurkha cantonment of Maymyo. Through these Nepali settler contacts, the ruby mart at Mandalay and the native gem bazaar in Mogok lost much of their relative obscurity and became well known to the Nyishangba (see Figure 10). Having been a source of precious stones for centuries, the Mogok area fell from 1887 onwards under the provisions of the Upper Burma Ruby Regulation as promulgated by the British (Turrell 1988). It empowered the government to notify the boundaries of the stone tracts and to make rules regarding the mining, cutting, possession, buying, selling and carrying of precious stones (Coggin Brown 1933:513 ff.). In 1889 the Burma Ruby Mines Ltd. was floated, while being entrusted the first lease, but it was not until 1895 that profits were made. The heyday of European ruby mining fell between 1898 and 1907 after which a decline set in due to technical set-backs and a wavering demand. The situation never recovered and in 1925 the company went into voluntary liquidation. A skeleton organization continued to work, however, until the lease terminated. Operations finally ceased at the end of June 1931.

From the commencement of the British era, registration of the mines was adopted to prevent illicit working. After termination of the Burma Ruby Mines lease, native mining slowly recovered the lost terrain, but a stricter system of licence fees was introduced in 1932. Only Burmese citizens were considered as potential lessees, a rule which, in theory at least, confined activities of foreign nationals to the field of trade.

The smaller stones which formed the bulk of the output were sold in Calcutta, Madras or Bombay or auctioned at the mines in parcels to brokers and dealers from various parts of the East. These in their turn passed the stones on to others or to the local cutters and middlemen, whence they reached the jewellers of the bazaars or the travelling pedlars, who distributed them in all directions. In the latter quality we already encountered the Nyishangba in Calcutta and Assam, but only after 1932 - a date explicitly mentioned by a Ngawal informant - Burma became attractive as a source area of stones. Apparently, control on illicit mining and related operations had lapsed after termination of the Company lease in 1931 and the result was a host of Marwari, Tibetan and Chinese traders gathering in the Mogok area in the view of possible windfall profits. It is here, that the first Nyishangba entered the scene as professional gem dealers, not hindered by the aura of illegality that surrounded the business.

The journey to Burma proceeded initially by sea through a liner from Calcutta to Rangoon at the cost of 15 rupees. Imitation stones and rings purchased in Calcutta were sold on the pavements of the Burmese capital, while some traders travelled two days westwards to Ngayok bay, a cheap source of coral stone and cowry shells. Leaving Rangoon after one or two weeks, the traders occasionally visited the towns along the Mandalay railway line but their major destination was the central Burma region, where they frequented the main clusters of Nepali settlement.

The more prudent minds engaged in selling a mixture of daily goods, partly of Nepalese origin, partly from Rangoon. In addition, a few capitalist-oriented traders started to lend money to the new rice cultivators of the Irrawady delta. As Trager writes:

> The opening of the Delta to rice cultivators found them (the Burmese) as willing in-migrants and cultivators working at what they knew. They began in traditional Burmese fashion as peasant proprietors, 'holding' or 'owning' the land while they 'used' it. But the demand for rice transformed subsistence into commercial agriculture and required capital for the exploitation of one cash crop. The capital, loans to tide the cultivators over the seven months' growing season and for other purposes, came mainly from the *chettyars* (Trager 1966:146-147)

Within the Burmese context, the bulk of this type of money lending was indeed in the hands of Indians. But a former strongman from Braga was engaged in exactly the same business and, according to him, a few more Nyishangba were involved as well, especially those who had settled down in Burma more permanently and in a few cases had even married Burmese wives.

A second - and popular - way of entering Burmese territory was the illegal crossing of the border through the jungle-clad areas of Nagaland and the Manipur state. This route offered a fair chance of passing the border unnoticed, where identity cards or passports were lacking and illicit trade in musk and gems shaped quite a few ventures. The gains involved must have been worth the trouble for the passage was a difficult one:

> Mosquitos, sandflies, leeches, and other pests make life extremely irksome for the greater part of the year. The only means of communication is by Naga paths, steep and narrow (...) transport is difficult (...) and there is no food obtainable to feed a large party in the more inaccessible areas (Lambert 1937:309-310)

A lively illustration of an early Burma career reflecting the common blend of illegal border crossing, money lending and gem smuggling in the years before the Second World War, is the story of a 68-year-old Braga informant:

In 1932, Tshiring (a pseudonym), accompanied by a couple of close friends, travelled to Imphal in the usual way. Hence they proceeded on foot straight eastward and found their way to the Chindwin river town of Homalin on the Burmese side of the border. Sailing down the Chindwin via Thaungdut, Sittaung, Kalewa and Mingin, the party ended up in Monywa, where the members parted temporarily, in order to sell their mixed stock of herbs, daily goods and rings separately. From Monywa our informant took the train to Myinmu and Sagaing in the Mandalay region, a reputed area of Nepali immigrant settlement. Through these and other contacts Tshiring grew familiar with the idea of buying stones himself in the Mandalay gem market, and eventually discovered the Mogok bazaar as the cheapest source of the best stones. Returning to Burma the following years for increasingly longer periods at a stretch, he eventually settled down in Myinmu, where he owned a small general store from 1938 onwards. The Myinmu store became the nexus of a medium-sized trade network, stretching across parts of central and lower Burma, covering such diverse activities as rice trading, money lending and gem smuggling.

To keep the train going, the more permanent sales and supply lines were manned by fellow Nyishangba, foreshadowing the elaborate forms of corporate trade, in which they were to excel after the Second World War. All in all, the above case provides us with an example of expanding capitalist enterprise in Burma during the thirties. But then disaster struck.

At the end of 1941, the Japanese invaded Burma from the south. Rangoon fell in early March 1942 and by the end of May they had cut the Burma road. The British evacuated Mandalay, precipitating an exodus from Burma in the direction of the Indian border, which has only recently been described in some detail (Tinker 1975). Between 400,000 and 500,000 refugees fled by land to Indian territory over the Taungup pass to Chittagong and by the Tamu border road to Dimapur. Estimates of dead range between 10,000 and 50,000 (ibid.:2-4) and the whole episode has been described as a 'monument to human endurance'.

The Nyishangba too, fell victim to the general upheaval following the Japanese attack on Burma and many of them made a hurried exit. Especially the more successful traders were hard hit, losing important sums of fixed capital and outstanding credit. On the other hand, the poorer itinerant Nyishangba quietly left Burma in the way they had come: illegally and unnoticed through the jungle of the West Burma ranges. Materially speaking, the latter category largely survived the blow but in terms of future gains they lost access to a highly profitable Burmese market. Thus, the Nyishangba fell back into established patterns of itinerant trading in Northern India and especially Assam. At the same time, however, they seized upon opportunities provided by the general war situation in the area, guided by the password that applies to all times of conflict, rebellion and war: scarcity. Large numbers of refugees, the omnipresent movement of soldiers and the unexpected disturbance of supply lines offered fresh chances for traders who were wont to act in circumstances beyond their immediate control. The aura of semi-legality surrounding at least part of the Nyishangba community, fitted well in with the exigencies of the time, and quite a few Nyishangba moved along new paths of speculative trade. Besides stones and musk, rice and dried fish found their way to the garrison towns along the Burma front, and, for a time, Kurseong and Kalimpong manufactured *kukhris* were a much sought after item by British and American soldiers. In return quantities of army goods, including some arms, trickled down into the remotest corners of Assam through mutually profitable black market arrangements.

The war in Burma dragged on well into 1945, but the ultimate allied victory did not simply mean a return to the old colonial order. Burmese nationalism had grown tremendously during the war and the rising demand for dominion status or even outright independence evoked a state of socio-political flux under the inspiring leadership of *bogyoke* Aung San. The postwar years saw a tense political struggle, in which Aung San triumphed as supreme leader, who managed to put Burma on the road toward ethnic unity and federal union. Full independence was achieved in January 1948, but not before Aung San had been murdered in a factional attempt at coup. Deprived of its major stabilizing force, Burmese independence proved to be a fragile structure, the political and ethnic cleavages of which produced major insurrections and eventually a full-scale civil war (Trager 1966:95ff.).

Within the above painted historical parameters, the Nyishangba tried to recover their lost terrain in the Burma region from 1946 onwards. Some of them took up the old stone trade, emanating from Mogok, but gradually a number of them became involved in food wholesale operations, especially rice. This proved to be a lucrative business in a war-devastated area, now moreover facing the inextricable clew of rebellion and counter-rebellion, so characteristic of the time.

The stone trade received a fresh impetus after the war through private concessional mining. A few Nyishangba managed to obtain Burmese citizenship, which put them on a par with Burmese nationals regarding the acquisition of concessions. Some Nyishangba settled permanently in Mogok and Mogaung as professional gem and jade dealers, but others engaged in a nationwide itinerant trade, covering such diverse items as semiprecious stones, pearls, rings, rice and dried fish. On the legal side of the business, the Nyishangba acted as tiny middlemen and hawkers, in order to secure a decent livelihood. The more opaque side of Nyishangba enterprise, however, comprised of moneylending - including the occasional harassment of defaulting debtors - and the smuggling of stones across the Thai border, either through Thai middlemen or the Nyishangba themselves.

For some time, rice-trading in the Tenasserim, peninsular Thailand and northern Malaya became a blurred field of legal and illegal activity in which a number of Nyishangba, possessing Indian passports or Burmese identity cards, prospered. In the years during and especially after World War II, the smuggling of rice became a common practice. The introduction of a rice export tax by the Thai government, the so-called rice-premium, further encouraged traders to make easy profits in external markets without passing through customs (Silcock 1967:231-257).

The thriving mixture of encashable opportunities as seized upon by the Nyishangba is reflected in the details of some of their life histories. A 53-year-old Braga informant recalled, not without pleasure, how he purchased stones in Mogok and rings in Paung (north of Moulmein) and tried to get them across the Thai border as quietly as possible.

The journey from Mogok down to Lower Burma proved more than once to be a difficult one, in which highway robbers and armed insurgents formed a major threat to Nyishangba merchandise, not to say Nyishangba life. Intermediate urban markets like Pegu (where they usually changed trains), Thaton and Moulmein provided intervening opportunities, but the bulk of the stones was meant to be smuggled across the Thai border. To that purpose, the town of Kawkareik had developed into a dealer market for whatever things might be profitably passed on into Siamese territory, including stones, which were paramount for the Nyishangba. The most courageous traders moved on to the small Thaungyin river town of Myawadi, where under cover of the night Thai middlemen crossed the river to inspect the batches of stones offered, and, if interesting, carried them off to Bangkok. Occasionally, traders took the risk of placing the stones in the hands of befriended border dwellers, who were expected to share their profits with traders on their return from the Thai capital. The two or three Nyishangba possessing full Burmese citizenship were able to avoid these risks and made the trip to Bangkok themselves as early as 1947.

From 1948 onwards, the Burmese situation steadily deteriorated. Communist insurrection, combined with factional and ethnic rebellion, notably Karen, brought the country again on the verge of a total breakdown. Given the circumstances, the Nyishangba were more or less forced to stick together as much as possible, and they now moved around the country in bands of five to ten men. Activities centred on the Burma-Thai border facing the Andaman Sea ports of Mergui and Tavoy. Here, unspecified quantities of rice were passed on into Burmese territory and found their way to the towns of central Burma. The latter ventures in particular were not without risk, and in late 1948, eight Nyisbangba - mistakenly taken for spies - were shot in Paung. A few weeks later, three villagers from Khangsar were killed on a river boat near Prome, a major centre of rebellious incidence. From then on, Burma became less popular as a trading field, especially so among the more prudent minds. Yet, a number of die-hards remained active, seizing upon new opportunities provided by the presence of the Chinese Nationalist troops in the eastern Shan states.

In late 1949, Kuomintang (KMT) forces in Yunnan had given way before the Chinese Communist Fourth Army Group, and between January and March, 1950, some 2,000 KMT soldiers, with their families escaped into Burma, where they regrouped in the eastern reaches of the Shan state of Kengtung. There they proceeded to dig in and live off the countryside, where they had access to rice and opium (Fisher 1964:520n, Taylor 1973:11,13, Gutelman 1974:516). The most troublesome activity of the KMT was their continued assistance to ethnic insurgents, which unduly prolonged the struggle for

Burmese union. Moreover, it created an atmosphere, in which a black market could thrive, supported by international smuggling operations in the KMT-controlled Burma-Thai border area. Although difficult to prove, the present author, on the basis of fragments of interviews, has come to the conclusion, that a few Nyishangba were active in the Kengtung area up till 1953. They may have acted as itinerant small merchants who transported raw opium from the villages to the major Shan market towns (cf. McCoy 1973:131,247) but their involvement in trafficking opium across the Thai border is doubtful, as the opium trade was largely monopolized by Chinese Ho traders (Gutelman 1974:515).

Except for the Kengtung adventurers referred to above, and the few permanently settled gem-dealing Nyishangba in Mogok, Burma was a much less frequented area in the fifties than in the two preceding decades. Stricter border control but above all rising opportunities in Malaya and Singapore, made Burma a second choice for the majority of the traders. By 1960, however, persistent rumours of favourable 'market conditions' in Burma, made a group of thirty-five, mostly young Nyishangba decide to leave their villages:

The party first went to Calcutta, and subsequently moved on to Manipur, from where they proceeded on foot into Burmese territory. Via Kalewa, Pyingaing and Yeu they reached Mandalay, where they boarded the train to Rangoon. Only two days after having entered Burma illegally, they succeeded in convincing Burmese authorities that, like so many other Nepali immigrants, they had lived already for years in the country. Every member of the party was able to secure a Burmese identity card, which enabled them to travel freely around the country. After this 'coup' the group fell apart, and most of them stayed on in Burma for the next four years, engaging in various business ventures.

This renewed Nyishangba interest for Burma, or rather the whole Burma-Thai border area, should be seen in the light of the abolition of legalized opium trading in Thailand in 1959 and the so-called 'second KMT crisis' of 1961. This crisis was preceded by increasing Chinese Nationalist support to the Shan secessionist movement. The latter assistance was probably meant to safeguard the smuggling of opium into Thailand, a major source of KMT income (Taylor 1973:53). The actual crisis featured a concerted effort by Burmese and

Chinese troups to get rid of the Chinese Nationalists and drive them away from Burma.

The abolition of legalized opium trading in Thailand in 1959 precipitated a renewed attention for smuggling opium into the hills of northwest Thailand, a business much more accessible to outsiders than ten years before, while the 'second crisis' resulted in the move of the entire commercial apparatus of the KMT and its civilian adherents into northern Thailand (McCoy 1973:317). Gutelman (1974:518) points in this connection at the booming local economy at the western and southern fringes of the Golden Triangle in the period after 1960. Merchant capital, earned in the opium trade, was being transformed into shops and transport facilities, the goods and equipment for which were smuggled into Burma through northern Thailand. Most Nyishangba thrived in such a setting and became involved in the 'trade' of modern manufactured goods, including some arms.

The political soil, however, on which these activities flourished, increasingly showed signs of exhaustion, in particular on the Burmese side of the border. Already in 1958, a military caretaker government had tried to bring some order in the civil administration of Prime Minister U Nu. Temporarily allowed to return in 1960, U Nu faced a rise of insurrectional activity, particularly among the Shan and Karen, supported by remnants of the KMT still active in the Kengtung area. The wavering attitude of the civil administration towards the insurrectionist problem probably contributed much to its subsequent downfall. In March 1962 General Ne Win decided to bring to a close U Nu's crusade for democracy, and installed a Revolutionary Council (Trager 1966:190ff.).

As far as the Nyishangba were concerned, the 'Burmese Way to Socialism', as advocated by Ne Win and his followers, debouched into the promulgation of the 'Demonetizing Law' of May 17, 1964, through which bank notes of 50 and 100 *kyat* ceased to be legal tender. The Minister of Information explained the action in terms of eliminating a 'black market', and indeed, to those affected among whom were many Indian traders, it meant a serious financial blow. Foreign trade became exclusively a government monopoly. Most Nyishangba now left Burma, and the few traders staying behind were expelled from the country the next year, together with other

Nepali immigrants. Finally, the sun had set over the lucrative Burma adventures of the Nyishangba.

Malaya and North Borneo

The bell for the closing round in Burma triggered off an accelerated attention for business ventures in Thailand and the Malay Peninsula. Not that the field was entirely unknown - a few Nyishangba visited Singapore already before the war - but the major drive past the Salween river and across the Isthmus of Kra only occurred after mid-century. In time, these wider ventures proved to be a cornerstone development in the formation of a more inclusive Nyishangba trading network. In the course of the process, Bangkok and Singapore, as the regional poles of rapid postwar industrialization cum urbanization, came to provide the proverbial meat for the Nyishangba in terms of Van der Post's well-known dictum: 'where the lion feeds there is always meat for those who follow him'.

Once more, it seems appropriate to warn here against easy generalizations because trade ventures in the fifties were of an extremely diversified nature. Some Nyishangba, for example, although not specifically trans-Himalayan traders, temporarily pocketed the easy profits to be made in Lhasa and Gyantse as a result of the political upheavals of the time. The Chinese shadow over Tibet caused an outflow of things precious and beautiful. Silver wares, jewelry, turquoise and coral stone were an easy prey for the occasional Nyishangba venturing north. Profits as high as 700 per cent were realized on their return to Calcutta. Kathmandu too, proved to be an easy source of silver coins, plates and pots, where unseated Rana rulers panicked after the change of tide in 1951. It goes without saying that these loot-like trophies passed the Indian border unnoticed, but it should be kept in mind that only a tiny minority of the Nyishangba was involved in this chance trade, the vast majority being engaged in less sensitive business ventures covering Assam, Burma and, increasingly so, the Federation of Malaya.

Singapore had already attracted the attention of the Nyishangba before the Japanese invasion of Malaya. A few enterprising minds had found their way to Raffles' colonial capital by paying the sum of

32 rupees at Calcutta harbour to either the Arakan Flotilla Company or the Indian-owned Scindia Steam Navigation Company, both of whom operated a regular shipping service down the Burma and Malaya coasts. The former connected Calcutta, Chittagong, Akyab, Rangoon, Pinang and Singapore (Cook 1957:21), while the latter also touched at the Coromandel ports of Madras and Visakhapatnam.

A straight visit to Singapore before 1941 remained the exception rather than the rule, however. The much more frequent postwar calls on Singapore increasingly took place within a wider trading network, the bearings of which extended across the whole of the Malay peninsula. Thailand too, gained considerably in importance as an actual and potential Nyishangba trade field, especially so after 1953, when triangular forms of trade centring on Calcutta, Bangkok and Singapore emerged in the wake of the newly launched air service between the Bengal and Thai capitals. Also, in due time, Chiang Mai, in northern Thailand, which for centuries had contacts that extend north to Chiangrai, Kengtung and on to the Shan states of Burma (Donner 1978:732, who quotes Pendleton 1962:286-287, who cites Credner 1935:309) came to fulfil the complementary role that was to be expected in view of the booming Burma-Thai border trade in the late fifties and early sixties (see Figure 11).

All these new ventures were greatly facilitated by the Nyishangba's discovery of air travel after mid-century. Just as the extension of railway lines up to the Nepalese border shortly before 1900 greatly enhanced Nyishangba mobility in northern India, the undreamt possibility of reaching Bangkok or Singapore in a few hours flight from Calcutta or later on Kathmandu, implied a complete rethinking of existing and future trade opportunities. At the same time, however, the possibility of air travel tended to emphasize the by now apparent distinction between the better off and the less successful traders. Travelling by air was a costly affair and only those who had succeeded in amassing some capital could afford swifter means of transport. The resulting intra-group stratification, as well as diversification in trade fields, increasingly made for a heterogeneous and complex business situation, which defies description in terms of a single type of trade. In analysing such a state of affairs, the danger looms large of concentrating too heavily on the few success stories and presenting them as representative for the overall picture. A complementary danger rests in the temptation of interpreting the less spectacular and, therefore, more accessible cases, as the truth and nothing but the truth.

With regard to our analysis, I propose to highlight the regular Nyishangba ventures, yet occasionally to explore the more oblique side of their business. As the nature and direction of trade activities involved are partly a function of changes in the political economy of the Malayan region at large, due attention will also be given to the specific historical settings of the times and places mentioned.

Despite the disorganization of its economy, Singapore was quickly able to resume its accustomed commercial activities after the Japanese surrender. By 1947 the city's total trade exceeded the pre-war level but grew more slowly in 1948 and 1949 as the inception of communist guerrilla warfare made supplies uncertain (Geiger and Geiger 1975:154). Known as the Emergency, the insurrectional movement lasted for over ten years and substantially affected the country's weal and woe (see Short 1975, Clutterbuck 1973). Moreover, the Federation of Malaya as established in 1948, experienced all the birth pangs of young statehood, increasingly felt so through secessionist movements, racial strife and the conflict between Singapore and the Malayan mainland (Buchanan 1972:47-54, Sopiee 1973). For some time, Indonesia's policy of 'Confrontation' added an extra dimension to the difficulties experienced by the merger of Singapore and Malaya into the Federation of Malaysia (1963), but by 1966 both the 'merger' and 'Confrontation' were over and the Sarawak-Indonesian border insurgency was crushed by Malaysian and Indonesian forces alike (Van der Kroef 1968:255).

Generally speaking, the long period of political instability as referred to above, did not preclude regional economic growth and in some ways even stimulated it. Rapid urbanization and rising standards of living, at least for a growing urban middle class, provided new opportunities for the development of tertiary activities, regardless the social consequences. This again was the kind of milieu the Nyishangba so easily took advantage of. As long-distance traders in luxury goods, they found in Malaya the markets and the buying public they needed. In the course of the process, Singapore turned out to be an inexhaustible source of cheap manufactured goods, in particular ready-made cloth, vast quantities of which found their

Figure 11 Places visited by Nyishangba traders in the period 1950-1970

way to the Malayan countryside but even more so, to Calcutta and in the end Kathmandu:

In 1953, Shankar (a pseudonym), a trader from Tenki, went to explore the direct journey to Bangkok by air in the company of two friends. They did so on the bases of Indian passports, acquired by bribing a Shillong official in 1949. The merchandise the small party carried, consisted of the usual stones and rings, supplemented by some Kathmandu curiosities. After a two-week stay in Bangkok, the men set out on a southward-bound journey by train and by bus to Malaya and Singapore, visiting the major urban centres along the main railway lines in a manner not unlike that of the Assam days. Sitting down on the pavements of Georgetown (Pinang), Kuala Lumpur and Johor Baharu in the quality of specialized jewelry hawkers, they were able to secure a more than decent livelihood, the surplus money of which was invested in a variety of consumer goods once they reached Singapore. In fact, the latter place too, became an important market for stones, and an occasional trip back to Bangkok or even Rangoon sustained the necessary inflow of gems for a mainly Chinese buying public. Stones offered in Bangkok came from Chantabun and Bo Phloi in southeast Thailand (Donner 1978: 191-193). Returning fom Bangkok to Calcutta they brought with them some cloth, porcelain wares, a few wrist-watches and cameras, most of the stuff being sold in Kathmandu at great profit.

Once the basic patterns and possibilities of this triangular trade had been sufficiently explored, its volume and diversity greatly increased until it became the backbone of Nyishangba business for many years to come. The next decade and a half or so saw a proliferation of goods and places and the emergence of close-knit corporate groups specializing in one or two products or unspecified services.

Traders who in one way or another had acquired an Indian passport were of greatly privileged status. They crossed frontiers without the cumbersome palaver at customs and had easily extended their visa and other necessary permits. The longer some of them stayed, the more they came to know the local 'business environment'. Generally speaking, internal Malayan trade is characterized by a constant flow of products of land, sea and forest into the urban markets and a flow of locally manufactured articles into the rural markets (Ooi Jin-Bee 1963:333). One of these flows crystallized as the already mentioned postwar attention for rice transactions from across the Thai border. Although in line with the general pattern of import, these blurred dealings steadily decreased after the execution of the Emergency Regulations from 1948 onwards. Especially after 1952, when food denial techniques were introduced in order to trace the guerrillas (Clutterbuck 1973:211-219, Short 1975:375-379), few traders were prepared to take the risk of long imprisonment for smuggling food, not to speak of capital punishment when found active in the 'trade' of arms, ammunition and explosives. However, the several Gurkha regiments in the country (Short 1975:113) offered less sensitive trade opportunities, in particular with respect to culturally bound items for daily use and ornamentation of Nepalese origin. When by 1955 the high tide of the Emergency seemed over, growing numbers of Nyishangba ventured South. With the passing of time, Singapore and to a lesser extent Pinang, replaced Shillong as a winter abode. Quite a few young men made Singapore into their home basis for periods up to five years at a stretch. An exceptional thirteen years residence in Singapore was reported by a trader from Tenki. Also, women took increasingly part in less adventurous business ventures. In the late fifties the fact of whole families going down to Singapore for the winter months, had developed into a regular trait of the Nyishangba community. This state of affairs fits well in with some interesting observations made by Morris on his Kathmandu-Pokhara trek in 1960:

> Soon after leaving Sele we began to meet parties of Tibetans, not refugees from over the passes, but people who had long been living on the Nepalese side of the frontier ... (Morris 1963:78)

Another fragment from his journal may also refer to a group of Nyishangba:

> I once came across a large party of them on their way back to Tibet from Singapore. Their custom was to spend the summer wandering through the hills of Nepal collecting bears' pancreases and the powdered horns of rhinoceros (...) The money obtained from their sale was used to buy cheap turquoise, which is greatly prized in Tibet. Besides this, Singapore silver dollars, because of their size, could be sold at a large profit to the Gurkhas, who had them mounted as female ornaments. None of these Tibetans spoke a word of any language except their own and yet, so they told me, they somehow made the long journey to Singapore every year (Morris 1963:79)

The parties described possibly are the most representative for the average trade venture in the fifties. Some jewelry hawking combined with the sale of curio, herbs and whatever low weight for value items could be profitably carried, featured as the main package in these seasonal undertakings.

The more interesting side of Nyishangba trade in Malaya and Singapore was the way in which the younger and more permanently settled traders roved about the Malayan peninsula and its surrounding areas, especially so after 1960. In effect, the sixties saw a further diversification of trade, not in the least so on account of the liberal granting of passports to the Nyishangba after 1962 by the Nepalese government (see also the following chapter). Nevertheless, specialized jewelry hawking remained a key feature of the more lawful Nyishangba enterprise in Malaya, up till the late sixties (see Figure 12). The quiet pavement scene shown is characteristic for a stable period of reliable profit-making in the urban centres of the peninsula. Quite a few informants were able to recite without hesitation a long list of places in Malaya, which they had visited, as if it concerned an old-fashioned geography lesson forced down their throat by an ignorant teacher: Pinang, Taiping, Ipoh, Kuala Lumpur, Seremban, Melaka, Johor Baharu, Kota Baharu, Kuala Terengganu, Kuantan, Mersing (see Figure 11). Yet, it proved a shared experience, many of them had come to appreciate as a sure safety-valve in times of bad luck or outside disaster, even in 1981. Singapore featured as the geographical pivot of the system, but Pinang too, was a much frequented and highly functional place (for the economic position of post-war Pinang see: Courtenay 1972:208-211). The more daring traders seized upon all the opportunities of rising trade volumes in a politically fluctuating situation. For Indonesia's part, trade to or through Singapore was of considerable importance before 'Confrontation' and even greater importance after it. Estimates of the volumes concerned vary greatly, because major but inscrutable amounts of smuggling-trade distort the picture. As Buchanan writes:

> According to official statistics there has been no trade between Singapore and Indonesia since 1963. However, during the years of 'Confrontation' (1963-1966), there is no doubt that clandestine trade was of some importance to both countries. Smuggling, small-scale barter trade, and unofficial trade continued - both directly between the countries, and through 'third party' ports such as Labuan in Sabah (Buchanan 1972:112)

Figure 12 Nyishangba traders in Pinang (1970)

Indeed, several informants claimed to have visited North Borneo in the period between 1958 and 1968, mention being made of Kuching (Serawak), Seria (Brunei) and Jesselton (Kota Kinabalu) in Sabah, thereby proving that the political economy of the region had a clearly traceable influence on local variations in trade patterns and phasing of ventures. Labuan, a small island off the coast of Sabah, which acquired free port status in 1956 (Tregonning 1960:243), acted for some time as a relay for wider ventures. But the other places mentioned were as good as Labuan for the purpose of transit-smuggling. Mention should be made for example of Kuching which experienced a 'boom' around 1960 as a result of the immigration of Foochow businessmen, who founded a competitive bank and through it provided cheap credit (Lockard 1973:571-572). The transhipment to eastern Malaysia was made possible by the Straits Steam Company who operated a weekly service to the North Borneo towns through one of its diminutive vessels (ibid.:4). Increased trading in East Malaysia may also partly be explained by the marked shift of emphasis eastwards, following the 'Separation' of Singapore from the Federation of Malaysia in 1965 (Buchanan 1972:111).

Medan too, on Sumatra, was a port repeatedly mentioned by some middle-aged Nyishangba as a place where great profits could be made after 1966. At the same time, however, informants hinted at the dangers involved, two of them dropping the fact that they served short-term imprisonments in Singapore. Again the well-documented account of Buchanan seems to corroborate the information given by the traders:

> Smuggling and barter have greatly benefited Singapore traders since 1966. Imports of smallholders' crude rubber, handicrafts, batik sarongs, and so on are bought, and a variety of consumer goods - especially such 'luxury' items as transistor radios and watches - are sold. Petty traders in batik textiles alone, brought in some $10 to 20 million worth of sarongs in 1969 - until the Indonesian government suspended the thrice-weekly passenger service from Medan on which the traders were travelling, largely because of the growing problem of smuggling which accompanied this lawful trade (Buchanan 1972: 113)

The early sixties provided something of a breaking-point for Nyishangba enterprise. Indeed, from 1962 onwards, the liberal stance taken by the Nepalese government towards Nyishangba trade, made possible a scaling up of their business in almost every respect: number of traders involved, countries visited and volume of goods handled. To speak of a breaking-point invites recapitulation, as well as preliminary reflection on the two fundamental issues regarding the rise of the Nyishangba as international traders, those of capital accumulation and the role of the Nepalese state. This will be done in the following chapter.

7

POST-1962 DEVELOPMENTS

'one *lakh* of rupees is nothing for a Nyishangma'
(Tenki youth, 1981)

From the 1930s onward, money increasingly started to rule everyday life of the Nyishangba. Had a person's social status formerly been measured by descent or religious merit acquired, by the late fifties only the amount of capital owned counted as a sure sign of influence for the generation below 45 years of age. By that time too, great changes had already taken place within the larger Nyishangba community. An increasing number of households spent the winter months in Pokhara or Bhairawa at the expense of the one-time winter abode of Shillong, but more often in Kathmandu where permanent residence throughout the year became a general characteristic of the richer families. A gradual process of monetization, which had already begun by the second half of the nineteeth century, was nearly completed in 1962. By that date, international trade ventures had become of a highly capitalized nature, while regional exchanges with the middle hills followed suit the money-dominated trend at the expense of the number of barter transactions. In the course of the process, socio-economic stratification, e.g. in terms of landownership or cattle, became more pronounced, but soon lost its home-based expression in favour of real property in Pokhara or the Kathmandu Valley.

Although it is very difficult to get reliable data on prices and profits, an effort will be made here to sketch the broad outlines of capital accumulation through time in Nyishangba society. According to my information, one may safely assume that since the end of the nineteenth century *some* villagers from Manang and Braga were able to raise sums as high as 400 rupees a season, which had risen to net profits of 500-600 rupees by the early 1920s. Higher profits may have been at stake when involved in petty gold or opium smuggling. After 1920, the rise of the Assam trade frontier probably meant a secure yearly revenue of hundreds of rupees for the better traders, but the discovery of Mogok as a source of cheap precious stones undoubtedly accelerated the pace of capital accumulation and increased the possibility of windfall profits. By the mid-thirties, some traders must have had amassed quite substantial sums of capital, as a few of them had fixed shops in Burma and occasionally acted as moneylenders. A prudent guess might fix the profits involved at several thousands of rupees a year but only so for a tiny minority of traders. In the village of Braga in the late thirties, small amounts of land changed ownership already for 100-200 rupees, the actual sum depending on its location and quality. By 1939 traders easily paid fares up to 50 rupees for a one-way journey to Burma, another indication of the relative wealth of even the less financially strong. The war situation in the next decade certainly brought unprecedented gains to some Nyishangba, but others, like the ones who fled Burma in 1941, lost important sums of fixed and outstanding capital. The postwar Burma ventures, but more so the discovery of the Malayan Peninsula seem to have brought new assets to a by then established core of relatively wealthy businessmen, headed by the most successful traders from Manang, Braga and Pisang. The early fifties saw the rise of a group of four 'strong men' who dominated the valley economically and politically till at least 1962. Generally speaking, the fifties were a time of steadily increasing gains for the Nyishangba community as a whole and of windfall profits for some of its more cunning members.

As stated before, trade in the 1950s was of a highly diversified nature. Some traders were involved in the traditional musk trade, the speculative and partly illegal character of which could bring about a several hundred rupees gain or loss in one trip. Others pursued chance ventures like the trade in leopard skins, bought for five rupees in the Dhankuta area of East Nepal, to be sold in Calcutta for up to 100 rupees. A popular and not very risky trade was that of yaktails, which were brought down mainly from the Tibetan border markets and realized a steady one hundred per cent profit round 1960 on their sale in Indian urban markets. The quantities dealt in were at times quite substantial and mule trains of 12 to 20 pack animals carrying loads of yak tails down the Gandaki Valley were reported by some informants. The unstable political situation in Tibet offered additional opportunities for quick gains up to 700 per cent of the invested amounts. Substantial sums too, were earned beyond the Indian markets. Precious stones and other luxury items increasingly found their way to Bangkok, Malaya and Singapore. The latter place became a new wholesale link in the overall trading chain, a link that brought in net profits of over 1,000 per cent on return to Kathmandu. Annual turnovers started to surpass now and then the Rs 10,000 limit, another indication of the growing business.

Differential success in trade provided for a growing tendency towards economic stratification within the Nyishangba community, the roots of which may be traced way back into the 1930s. But although a trend towards greater inequality became noticeable, which, incidentally, tended to loosen the bonds among the Nyishangba as a closed corporate group, the community as a whole prospered. An indication of the relative wealth of the Nyishangba as a group is the virtual absence of *dhikur* associations (see Messerschmidt 1978, 1982), as most members had in one way or another access to the capital they required. A typical example in this respect is the story of a young man from Manang who received 1,100 rupees from his parents and Rs 400 from his wife's parents on the occasion of his wedding in 1962. And this was not an exceptional case.

The attitude of the Nepalese government towards the seven villages of Nyishang had remained virtually unchanged during the first half of the twentieth century. The *darbar* felt content with a fixed amount of *sirto*-tax, as a sign of loyalty to the Nepalese Crown, while the Nyishangba were at pains to convey the impression of a relatively poor and backward district to the authorities. The documental exchanges concerned (see e.g. Regmi 1983a, 1983c) confirm the policies followed by the respective parties. But if at all the *sirto*-tax of Rs 1,876 was a considerable sum of money in 1904, the slightly raised amount still paid by 1962 was certainly not. Yet, underlying motives of appeasement and control over an outlying area may have shaped the government's lenient attitude towards the Nyishangba. On the whole the 1950s may therefore be correctly interpreted as a period of incipient Nyishangba capitalist activity in the fullest sense of the word.

The role of the government

The years after 1962 saw an increased trade-off between the Nepalese government and the Nyishangba, the highlight being the visit of King Mahendra to Pokhara in 1954. On this occasion a petition was submitted by leading Nyishangba from Manang, Braga and Pisang supported by a Gurung clansman, because of his ability to read and write Nepali and his position as a power-broker in the upper Marsyangdi Khola region. The outcome of this appeal was the extension of the existing *lalmohar* rights, initially for a period of two years, and backed by the assurance that no customs duties would be charged (for the full text of these exchanges see Appendix 3). In 1966 the rights were extended indefinitely. This decision had far-reaching effects, not so much because of the privileges involved *per se* - for that would have been a mere continuation of the existing situation - but because they coincided with other facilities and circumstances such as the liberal granting of passports to the inhabitants of Manang District, the promulgation of a 'Foreign Exchange Entitlement Scheme' by the Ministry of Industry and Commerce from 1962 onward, the signing of the 1960 and 1963 Nepal-India Trade and Transit Treaties, and, finally, the rise of the so-called 'Gift Parcel System' that was in operation between 1967 and 1969. All these rules and regulations offered greatly increased opportunities for business transactions by traders having their home base in Nepal, a situation that temporarily earned Kathmandu the dubious name of 'the second Hong Kong'.

The 'planning' of trade on the part of the Nepalese government as exemplified by the above rules and regulations was a direct outcome of ideas developed in government circles in the early sixties: It can be said that a remarkable step on trade policy was taken in the plan holiday year 1961/1962. In that fiscal year, a 'Trade Development Policy' was strongly initiated and increasingly adopted. It mainly aimed at achieving both commodity and country-wise trade diversification. It also stressed to reduce consumer goods import, to increase capital goods import and to expand export business accordingly. This policy was formally incorporated in the Second Plan (1962/63-1964/65) (Pradhananga 1980:17) and supported by the government's monetary and financial policies of the day (Pant 1964:956).

The precise articulation between the government and the Nyishangba as a group have escaped scrutiny so far, but it is an established fact that the first Nepali passports were issued to leading Nyishangba already in 1962. This policy of liberally granting passports to the Nyishangba was continued in the following years, and formed a welcome addition to the Indian passports and Burmese identity cards that some traders possessed. Indeed, it opened the way for young traders to undertake long-distance ventures into Southeast Asian countries on a par with an older generation, that had more or less managed to monopolize international trade ventures beyond India up till then.

The Nyishangba also benefited from the Foreign Exchange Entitlement Scheme, popularly known as the Bonus Voucher Scheme. The Bonus Scheme was set up to encourage exports to convertible and hard currency areas, whereby foreign exchange earnings could be reclaimed by the exporter for importing goods of his own choice. The complex scheme included different percentage entitlements according to products, types of exporters and size of the transactions (Pradhananga 1980:22-25). Without going into all the technicalities involved, a few characteristics of the scheme may be outlined here. A key-reference in fixing the commencement of the scheme is a short notice which appeared in the *Nepal Gazette*, vol.11, no.42, Magh 23, 2018 V.S. (December 3, 1962) that reads as follows:

> *Ministry of Industry and Commerce*
>
> Merchants exporting the following commodities shall be allowed to import goods worth the following percentages of the foreign exchange thus earned by them;
>
> jute (raw or manufactured) - 40 %
> oil seeds - 50 %
> other goods - 60 %

The broad touch of the brush, so characteristic of the scheme when at first introduced, made way for finer configurations through a number of subsequent notifications. It concerns the following notifications all taken from the *Nepal Gazette*:

-vol.13, no.46, Falgun 19, 2020 V.S. (March 2, 1964)
-vol.17, no. 4, Baisakh 25, 2024 V.S. (May 8, 1967)
-vol.22, no.38, Poush 25, 2029 V.S. (January 8, 1973)
-vol.23, no.40, Magh 8, 2030 V.S. (January 21, 1974)
-vol.24, no.29, Kartik 19, 2031 V.S. (November 4, 1974)

-vol.24, no.43 (Extraordinary), Magh 16, 2031 V.S. (January 29,1975)
-vol.26, no.34, Marga 28, 2033 V.S. (December 13, 1976)

Ultimately, the aim of the scheme appears to have been:

> ...to encourage exports even at below cost prices and hence a feedback into the level of national economic activity by allowing exporters access to the relatively plentiful resource of convertible foreign exchange. Especially now that the vouchers were transferable this produced a situation in which non-Indian consumer goods could be relatively easily imported far in excess of local Nepalese demand. These goods which go to India convert potential convertible currency reserves into actual Indian rupees at rates very favourable to the Nepalese and thus help the problem of chronic Indian rupee shortages (Blaikie, Cameron and Seddon 1980:163)

In the course of the years, the Foreign Exchange Entitlement Scheme had to face mounting criticism from both within and outside Nepal (see Rawat 1974:250-251; Pradhananga 1980:24-25; Rose and Scholz 1980:108, and Banskota 1981:101). Finally, in 1978, after 16 years of operation of the system, the Nepalese government admitted the scheme to be a defective method of export promotion for a variety of reasons, not in the least the one related to problems of illegal trade, corrupt practices and smuggling in the country's foreign trade sector (on changes of the scheme over the years see: Banskota 1981:98-99).

The Bonus System almost certainly provided new chances for the bigger Nyishangba traders, but the wider Nyishangba community seems to have benefited in particular from the Gift Parcel Scheme with its very lucrative trade opportunities in the 1966-1969 interlude. Gift parcels, in the most literal sense, are the parcels sent by air or by surface mail either by one's relatives or friends. After 1966, no duties were due when the value of the parcel did not exceed the 1,000 rupees limit. However, the scheme quickly degenerated into a kind of import business. Banskota (1981:51) summarizes the episode as follows:

> The Gift Parcel System introduced in March 1966 took the form of import business in Nepal. The gifts imported under it were usually luxury goods and floated in Kathmandu and the Nepalese towns on the Indo-Nepalese border. The bulk of this trade was financed by a 'handful of Indian traders'. Thus Kathmandu became the centre of smuggling activity with links spread as far as Hong Kong, Bangkok, Singapore, Calcutta and Bombay. It was estimated that the average number of daily incoming parcels in the peak season 1968-69

amounted to 36,000 parcels. The recorded imports were approximately thirty-six million rupees and the average import duties on such imports were 50 per cent of its value. The system was abolished in 1969 following India's protest to it and in view of its notorious quality of permitting the export of luxury goods at the cost of genuine Nepalese goods (for a full treatment of the Gift Parcel Scheme see: Wagley 1969)

Although applicable, in theory at least, to any Nepali citizen, the Nyishangba, with their long-standing trading experience in Southeast Asian countries, were at a tremendous advantage in exploiting the Gift Parcel Scheme.

Through their collaboration with Indian traders resident in Kathmandu or the West-Central Nepal-Indian border towns, it proved possible to generate huge profits within a relatively short span of time. Blaikie, Cameron and Seddon (1977:92-93), for example, found 'a healthy balance of trade *surplus* with India in terms of local currency transactions at banks near the border (while on official current figures Nepal has a large deficit)'. This 'leaky' frontier situation has so far escaped critical investigation, though a number of authors have made preliminary remarks on trade and smuggling across the Nepal-India border: Donner 1972:409, Rawat 1974:236-258, Gaige 1975:49-55, Nath 1975:409-419, Blaikie, Cameron and Seddon 1977:92-96, 1980:162-165). However, it seems likely that the bulk of the trade was financed by Indian traders, while the Nyishangba with their Southeast Asian-wide commercial infrastructure, provided the indispensable supply lines. Several observations by different persons at Kathmandu airport in the period after 1966 bear witness to the Nyishangba's involvement in these large-scale international trade ventures. Altogether, the present author has come to the conclusion, that the crucial period for the rise of the Nyishangba as fully-fledged international traders has been the second half of the 1960s. Here we find the necessary combination of a long-established commercial infrastructure and government-induced trade policies, which goes to explain a period of unprecedented capital formation within some sections of the Nyishangba community.

It would be false, however, to conclude to a monolithic trade situation, exclusively geared towards exploiting the incentive schemes mentioned. Nyishangba trade has always been of a diversified nature, and some traders chose to develop lines of action in their own right, often linked to specific regional settings within the larger Southeast Asian framework. In the next section an effort will be made to provide a preliminary sketch of the actual development of Nyishangba trading activities in the period after 1962, especially with reference to the wider geopolitical situation of Southeast Asia.

The Golden Triangle and Indo-China

Apart from the Singapore and Bangkok-based wholesalers who were engaged in exploiting the opportunities mentioned in the previous section, a number of traders sought to renew and extend their business ventures beyond the Malayan peninsula and Greater Bangkok. With the useful help of newly acquired passports, a number of traders went to explore untrodden paths in the period after 1962. The cases of North Borneo and Medan have already been mentioned, but the specific context of the Indo-China milieu still needs to be discussed. At the outset it must be stated that the information for this particular period is scant, perhaps because only a limited number of traders was involved. Yet, an outline will be attempted here on the basis of some background literature and coloured in by the few cases available. Let us begin with a look at the 'Golden Triangle', that major opium-producing area along the tripartite borders of Burma, Thailand and Laos, contended by ethnic insurgents, political rebel armies and business warlords alike (Figure 11).

Despite the change of political tide in Burma in 1962 and the subsequent expulsion of foreign traders, the southern tracts of the Golden Triangle remained a business paradise for the more daring traders. General circumstances favourable to Nyishangba enterprise in northern Thailand were the economic boom Thailand experienced from 1960 onward, the growing number of tourists in the region (Donner 1978:202), but above all the wider geopolitical situation. The shift of the KMT commercial apparatus from Burma to Thailand in 1961, black market opportunities in Burma, and the opium-financed development urbanization of Chiang Mai (Noranitipadungkarn and Hagensick 1973), go a long way to explain the growing Nyishangba interest for northern Thailand after 1962. The main question here is:

to what extent were the Nyishangba involved in the local and regional business of the time?

For centuries, but especially so for the last hundred years, the forest-clad hill ranges in the Shan states of Burma, the South of Yunnan (China), northern Laos and Vietnam, and northern Thailand have acted as a place of refuge for migrating ethnic groups like Karen, Meo and Yao (Young 1962). Living at higher elevations than the plain-dwelling Tai, they have been able to retain bonds of cultural identity and economic solidarity that ignore political frontiers. In this sense it is impossible to separate the north of Thailand from a wider culture area, stretching across several frontiers (Bruneau 1980:966). Being shifting cultivators and in some cases skilled hunters, they have retained a way of life, that clearly sets them apart from the lowland people, contacts with whom remain restrained and occasional. In the 1930s these Indo-Chinese mountain areas offered much the same chances to traders as the tribal territories of Assam. As the local inhabitants hardly engaged in trade, there was ample opportunity for outsiders to sell the usual mix of old and new products. Non-essentials like silk, buttons, needles, mirrors and cowry-shells were bartered against ivory and rhinoceros-horn. Metals like iron, silver, copper and lead found their way into Meo and Akha territory and were exchanged for opium and cotton. Most of the trade was in the hands of itinerant Chinese Ho traders, some of whom became resident in the more receptive tribal communities (Bernatzik 1947:409-410, 423-424).

To the extent that some of these groups (like Meo, Yao, Lisu, Lahu and Akha) have developed into opium producers, it must be remembered that this was largely the result of the influence of foreign traders (Geddes 1973:213). In addition, the Karen were regularly hired by their Meo neighbours to assist in the cultivation of opium. The Meo paid them in cash or opium. Opium thus acquired was sometimes consumed by addicts but it was also used to pay off debts to traders (Cohen 1984:153). We may distinguish essentially between two categories of 'foreign' traders: resident and non-resident (itinerant). The first category comprise village-resident Ho traders of Chinese origin. The second refers to all those petty traders or commissioned buyers of opium, who operate from the towns of northern Thailand. The remaining group consists of 'real' itinerant traders of various origin. The presence of Ho traders holding the economic purse strings in some Lisu villages (Young 1962:32) probably inhibited itinerant traders from entering them, but in the more open and numerically dominant Meo communities, the chances of outsiders were better:

> The Meo may be seen frequently in and about the northern cities and towns, buying such luxury items as medicines, cloth, silver and other fancy items (...) they have many contacts with plainsmen who come to their villages with various wares, and if they have opium to sell, they trade through such visitors, rather than risk arrest by taking opium down to the towns (Young 1962:43)

Miles wrote of a Yao village:

> All Pulangka dwelling groups accept credit from these traders or their itinerant representatives. The hillmen purchase cloth, kerosene, lighting utensils, cooking and eating equipment as well as tools, horseshoes, nails, patent medicines, salt, dried fish and meats. All Yao clothing had such derivation. Male attire consists of ready-made black cotton 'pyjamas' or nylon slacks and shirts; women buy cloth and cotton which they manufacture into trousers, tunics and head-dresses diacritical of the ethnic group (Miles 1973:259)

It is hard to estimate the involvement of Nyishangba traders in the types of business as referred to by the above authors. Some Nyishangba mentioned Meo and Yao hillmen as their most frequent contacts, but Karen too featured occasionally in their reflections. In any case, the Australian anthropologist Paul Cohen strongly believes that traders involved were essentially opium dealers. Their appearance as inoffensive itinerant traders or shopkeepers belied the primary purpose of their business with the Karen and the Meo, which was to obtain opium as cheaply as possible through credit transactions (Cohen 1984:154). Some of the older traders have certainly been active along the Burma-Thai border in the early sixties (see chapter 6) but the younger traders and those active in the region after 1968, denied having ventured beyond the main urban centres of Chiang Mai, Lampang and Chiang Rai. This retreat may have had to do with the greater monopolization of the opium trade in the hands of a few warlords, who increasingly started to control sections of the Burma-Thai border area (Lamour and Lamberti 1972:108-123). Yet a much more important factor in explaining the shift towards the towns seems to have been the Meo insurrection as it developed between 1968 and 1974:

> At first a series of latent distributive conflicts between Thai and upland peoples, it soon developed in a full-scale war, mainly through a counterproductive suppressive response by the Thai government, which in turn led to a rapid escalation of violence in the North, and to a far greater number of armed opponents than had existed before (Race 1974:112)

In such circumstances the towns were the safer places to stay, but at the same time the open conflict boosted illegal forms of trade, not in the least place those of rice and arms. Payments for larger 'consignments' were invariably made in opium, the more so where the demand for the drug had steadily risen after 1965 in the wake of the escalating second Indo-China war (Gutelman 1974:17-51).

The period of retreat into the towns coincided with the development of tourism in Thailand as mentioned before, and offered fresh chances for legal participation in a growing tourist industry. A number of Nyishangba seized upon these new opportunities, transcending earlier specialist lines of jewelry hawking and the selling of cloth and ready-made garments in the villages through the establishment of more or less permanent shops, offering a wide range of 'fancy' goods, including tourist curio.

As it is hard to believe that traders abandoned the lucrative habit of buying up opium overnight, some shops may have acted as covers for a concealed petty opium business in which a few Nyishangba established themselves as secondary traffickers. This is a well-grounded possibility, as all opium-routes from the Golden Triangle converged in Chiang Mai and Lampang in the 1960s (Lamour and Lamberti 1972:125). Suggestive within the above described context are the stories as told by a 43-year-old trader from Manang and a 19-year-old trader from Tenki respectively:

The former used to visit the Chiang Mai region in the early sixties selling his wares on the pavements for periods not longer than one week at a stretch, the remaining time tramping through the villages nearby with newly acquired manufactured goods. The latter, at the time of the interview, was co-owner of a small shop in the city of Chiang Mai (cf. Barnard 1984:42-44), and, according to his own information, never ventured beyond the northern city limits. As a shopkeeper the young trader is exemplary of the more successful members of the younger generation, who combine access to capital, a notion of education (some of them finished the eighth class of a boarding school in Kathmandu, where English is the medium of instruction) and an accumulated trading experience of relatives and friends with the business opportunities Chiang Mai is offering. One may speculate on trade contacts with Burma - some of the older Nyishangba knew Burma very well after all - but no substantial proof is available through the traders themselves, except for an occasional confession.

Next to the development of individual retail lines in tourist centres like Chiang Mai and Pattaya (two hours South of Bangkok by train), traders increasingly developed wholesale operations. Some of them found their way to local craft-producers or small-scale industries in Bangkok and Chiang Mai, and started to supply retailers in curio and other shops throughout the country. It would be false, however, to think of these ventures as exclusive lines of action per individual trader. Rather they formed part of a wider mix of trade activities, locationally stretching across large parts of Southeast Asia and executed by bands of close-knit Nyishangba.

The above painted picture is well illustrated by the story of an experienced 40-year old trader from Tenki. Although the sequence of events is not always clear, the case is indicative for the multifarious ways of action of the younger Nyishangba generation. In 1954, at the age of 13, Karma (a pseudonym) went with his father and some friends for the first time to Calcutta where they sold their herb stocks, purchased unknown quantities of imitation stones and sold them in Bangkok where they had arrived by air. The Thai capital provided them with real precious stones from Burma (probably contraband) and indigenous gems from Chantabun. The stones were hawked about in the towns of peninsular Malaya in a way as has been described in the previous chapter. Between 1953 and 1966 he made Singapore and occasionally Kuala Lumpur into his permanent place of residence and together with some friends he tried to exploit supply lines down from Mogok to Rangoon (in the late fifties and early sixties), and from Bangkok via Ban Hat Yai near the Thai-Malay border. In 1962, at the age of 21, Karma tries to do a good stroke of business by 'bringing' a one lakh rupee lot of stones to Manila in the Philippines, which he had bought through a Rangoon middleman in Mogok. Something went wrong, however, and he lost some 40 per cent of the invested amount. Unable to return immediately, he is forced to spend more than a year in Luzon where he hangs on by means of unspecified activities in Manila, Quezon City, San Pablo and Tarlac. Back in Singapore, he explores the North Borneo connection, frequents Medan for some time, and visits Indonesia in an effort to check rumours about trade opportunities in relation to a developing tourist industry. To that end, Karma visits Jakarta, Semarang, Surabaya and Bali in 1966, but the experiment is not repeated. In the meantime, he has succeeded in establishing a lucrative wholesale trade in copper Buddha images of all sizes and qualities. Manufactured by a Bangkok-based industry, he sells right from the manufacturing plant to dealers in the tourist centres and the larger towns of Thailand and Malaysia. The initial 60,000 rupee loan - the origin of which could not be traced - is readily repaid as the direct result of a booming business. Lots of 500-700 images are smuggled across the Burmese border via the Chiang Rai-Taunggyi route to the Mandalay region, and even greater quantities pass the Malaysian border unnoticed. From 1966 onwards, our informant is drawn into the large-scale wholesale operations in 'ready-made' garments from Bangkok and Singapore to Kathmandu, thereby exploiting the government-induced trade opportunities as discussed in the previous section.

The wholesale activities as mentioned in the above example coincided with the American build-up in Indo-China during the 1960s. The secret war as fought in Laos from 1962 onwards (McCoy 1973:264-281; Lamour and Lamberti 1972:132-136), and the arrival of the first GI's in Vietnam in 1965, thoroughly changed the geo-political conditions of contraband trade, in particular that of opium. The general war situation in Indochina lured many a Thailand-based trader towards its eastern border. The Nyishangba too, were attracted by the black-market opportunities in the region. Cambodia was a popular venue between 1962 and 1968. Ventures into that country may be interpreted as more or less transitional lines of action that were close in character to the Malayan mainstream ventures.

As such, they involved the sale of semi-precious stones, but also of cloth and other manufactured goods, bought in Bangkok and sold in a yet undisturbed Phnom Penh and its rural hinterland. Most of the gold and opium smuggling, so characteristic of Laos in the 1960s, avoided the neutralist kingdom of Prince Sihanouk, however, so that it seems unlikely that Nyishangba activity in Cambodia went beyond the mere sale of innocuous articles. Yet, rice-smuggling along the Vietnamese border was mentioned by one informant from Manang, a state of affairs corroborated by observations of the French geographer Garry:

> The agricultural resources of Cambodia definitely played a certain role in the Vietnamese war. Up till the seizure of power by the Lon-Nol government, rice was the object of a general contraband trade to the profit of both the South Vietnamese and the Vietcong. On the one hand this smuggling was practised by individual traders, who transported the rice by bike or carrier-tricycle, on the other by private or even government organizations, using lorries (Garry 1972:177, author's translation)

Laos presents us with a different scene and probably with a different set of traders. Left behind after colonial partitioning of Indochina, it had hardly an economic base to rely on for future development. Unable to finance itself through corporate, mineral or personal taxes, the then Royal Laotian Government filled its coffers by tolerating the smuggling of gold, guns and opium. After 1962, the contraband paradise increasingly felt the reverberations of East-West rivalries:

The CIA's secret war in Laos effectively changed, but did not eradicate contraband trade flows. The heavy bombardments of Pathet Lao-held areas in northern Laos from 1964 onwards and the forced migration of hundreds of thousands of hill-dwellers to government-controlled areas, added substantially to the general confusion in the country. Opium production fell by some 80 per cent in a few years, the arms trade boomed and food shortages were acute. The opium vacuum was filled in by supplies from Burma, which reached northern Laos straight from the Golden Triangle. Part of these supplies ended up in Bangkok by crossing the Laotian-Thai border in exchange for arms and rice (Lamour and Lamberti 1972:156, 163, 174 and 179). From 1965 onwards, gold too, featured increasingly as a means of payment in the complex smuggling schemes (McCoy 1973:249-250).

The chaos in Laos seems to have attracted the more hardy Nyishangba traders. A Braga informant admitted that 'everything' in those days went through his hands... Also, the overall scarcity of

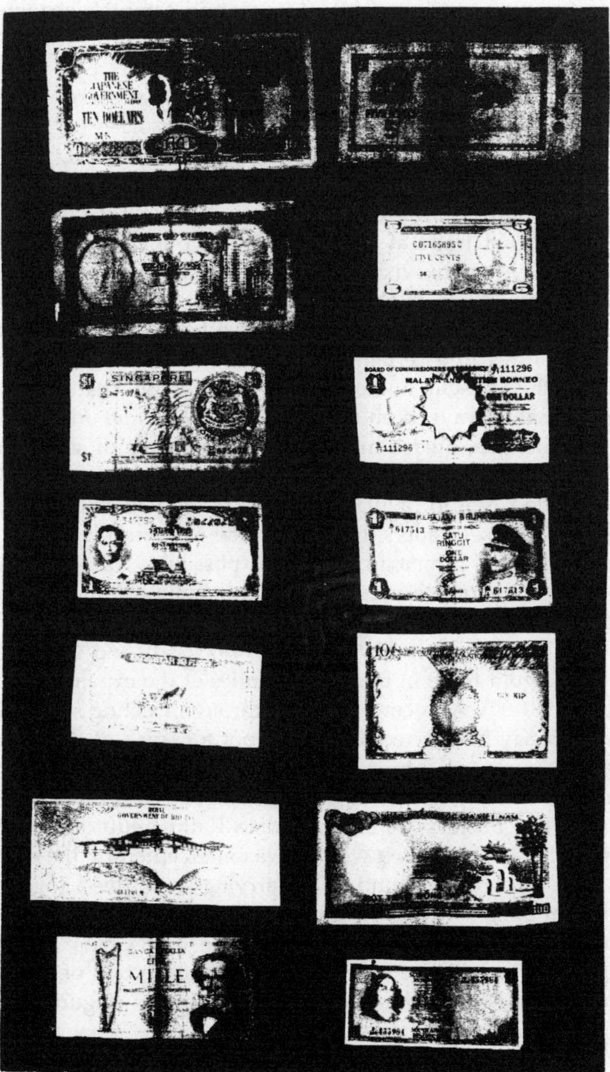

Figure 13 Collection of banknotes held by a Ngawal trader (1981)

commodities gave rise to exorbitant prices and some Nyishangba got away richer than they had ever been before.

Besides opium, gold may have been very much at stake, especially so where Laos' annual gold imports through licensed Vientiane brokers had shot up to seventy-two tons by 1967. In fact, Laos' low duty on imported gold made it into the major source of illicit gold for Thailand and South-Vietnam (McCoy 1973:250). Could the upsurge of the gold trade at least partially account for the increased number of Nyishangba visiting Laos between 1965 and 1968? It is difficult to say. When explicitly or indirectly asked about possible transactions in gold, the few informants who disclosed their Indo-China adventures to a certain extent, chose to remain silent on this point. Yet the present author holds the opinion that petty gold smuggling has always been an interesting side-line for the more daring Nyishangba. Burma may have been a source of small quantities of gold before the war (Coggin Brown 1935). Some informants also mentioned Macao, a place they had come to know after the exodus of Chinese traders from Calcutta as a result of the war between India and China in 1962. The possibility of a gold-racket after 1965 within some circles of the Nyishangba community should not be excluded beforehand, the more so where Singapore established a gold market in 1969 (McCoy 1973:250) and Hong Kong legalized the gold trade in the mid-seventies at the expense of Macao (Humlum 1981:90). As a corollary, and through existing supply lines, Kathmandu may have acted as an entrepôt for some of the gold that was legally imported into Asia through the regular gold markets. More recent events give rise to the belief that at least till the 1980s it was a lucrative business to bring gold to Kathmandu. For example, on August 11, 1983, a Dutch woman was intercepted by the police at Kathmandu airport and found to be carrying some five kilogrammes of gold from Bangkok to Kathmandu.

Clouded as the ways of the Nyishangba in Indo-China may be, a sure sign of their presence in the region is the collection of banknotes as photographed in the home of a Ngawal trader (Figure 13). The presence of Cambodian, Laotian and Vietnamese money tends to support the assumption of Nyishangba activity in Indo-China. In addition we have admissions of factual presence in Luang Prabang, Vientiane and Savannakhet (Laos) and Saigon (Vietnam) up till 1968 for a small number of traders. However, the interpretation of Nyishangba presence in these places for the period mentioned must await further scrutiny. It seems also clear, that after 1966 Indo-China lost much of its attraction. The escalation of the Vietnamese war, the establishment of the Singapore gold market and the rise of Kathmandu as a wholesale entrepôt after 1966, may all have had to do with the sudden break of interest in Indo-China on the part of the Nyishangba.

Hong Kong heyday

The post-1970 years confirmed the position of the Nyishangba as an international trading community. By then, the combined effects of several rules and regulations favouring Nyishangba enterprise had given rise to a booming Kathmandu market for fancy and other goods. Three types of business stand out in order of declining legality. First, the trade in curio for a growing number of tourists, second, the import of luxury goods for a restricted local market, and third, the import and re-export of large quantities of ready-made garments, and semi-luxury commodities like watches, radios and cameras. The first business type materialized as small Nyishangba-run curio-shops from 1968 onwards, some of them specializing in trekking equipment as well. Quite a few shops led a precarious existence resulting in untimely extinction due to high establishment costs. Others survived initial pressure through footloose manoeuvring and hawking practices, and have developed nowadays into an accepted feature of the Kathmandu retail-landscape. On the whole, however, the number of curio-shops declined after 1975, partly through a weeding-out of the weaker members of the family but more so on account of rapidly growing wholesale opportunities. The second, intermediate type of business, provides the Nepalese market with expensive luxury goods, often durable in nature and meant to be sold to a financially strong Nepalese upper class. This second type shades imperceptibly into the third, where some of the more expensive consumer goods are sold to visiting Indians and large quantities of ready-made garments find their way to India through the Nepalese border towns.

Supply lines for this wholesale trade invariably focus on Singapore, Bangkok and Hong Kong and were manned almost exclusively by Nyishangba, at least up till 1976. In the 1960s Singapore stood out as the uncrowned source of manufactured goods, be they ready-made garments or electrical appliances. But by 1970, Bangkok had partly superseded Singapore as a major wholesale market for cheap clothes, and from 1972 onwards, Hong Kong was considered a superior supply market for electronics. Moreover, a shift in the production of good quality wear from Singapore to Hong Kong after 1974, made the former into a less frequented place, as far as the Nyishangba were concerned. However, Singapore seems to have held her own as a source of first-class mechanical equipment.

The general tendencies noted above have been distilled from a number of interviews and checked against the economic realities of the Southeast Asian region. The shift of business from Singapore to Hong Kong, with Bangkok as a viable second, correlates with a decline in the number of small labour-intensive production units for light consumer goods in Singapore and the rise of comparable workshops in Bangkok and Hong Kong. As Geiger and Geiger (1975) noted:

> Initially, investment was concentrated in labor-intensive industries, such as textiles, wearing apparel and footwear and the assembly of electrical and electronic consumer goods from mainly imported components. But, as the city-state approached full employment in the early 1970s, the government ceased to grant pioneer status to labor-intensive activities and instead shifted its incentives to more capital-intensive industries requiring increasingly more advanced technologies and higher managerial, technical and labor skills (Geiger and Geiger 1975:16)

The concomitant rise in wages caused a subsequent shift of some of the less elaborate manufacturing processes to Bangkok and Hong Kong. Bangkok rose as a prime producer of cheap textiles (Donner 1978:195-196), while Hong Kong inherited for some time the assembly of cheap electrical goods. From 1974 onwards, the Hong Kong-based manufacture of apparel and clothing accessories made a tremendous leap both in quantity and quality:

> From 1974 to 1978 some 100,000 new jobs were created in the clothing industry, the exports rising from 8,752 to 15,709 million dollars. Today manufacturers

increasingly turn towards the production of better quality goods of original design (Denis 1980:62)

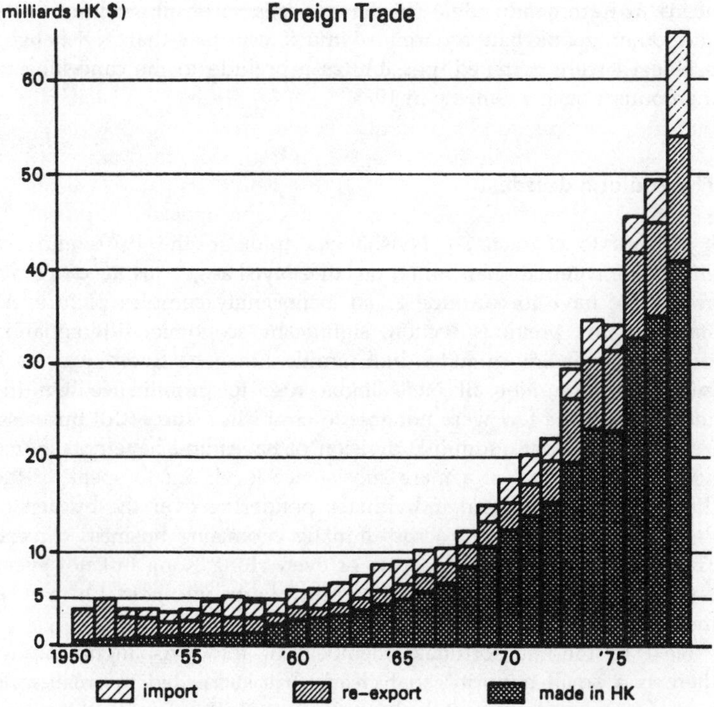

Figure 14 Development of foreign trade in Hong Kong After: Denis 1980

In addition, watches, cameras, transistors, stereo equipment, colour television sets and video-recorders are now being produced at high-quality levels, comparable to those of Japan, yet offered at a bare 20 per cent of current prices in western Europe (ibid.:64). Indeed, the attractive power of Hong Kong in terms of foreign trade can largely be explained by the booming industrial economy in the seventies based on cheap labour and liberal trade policies (see Figure 14).

The Nyishangba with their long-standing trading experience and their fine nose for quick gains, fully grasped the possibilities offered by the rise of Hong Kong as a major centre of industry and commerce. They did so even to the extent, that reverberations were heard in Kathmandu. By 1976 the free import of all kinds of fancy and other goods had aroused so much criticism that Nyishangba privileges were curtailed, possibly as a prelude to the cancelling of the Bonus Voucher Scheme in 1978.

The end of a decade

If we are to characterize Nyishangba trade in the 1970s and the effects of international trade on the Nyishangba as a corporate group, we have to conclude to an increasingly complex picture. As stated in the previous section, significant economic differentiation among households or individual families, may be traced way back into the 1930s. Not all Nyishangba rose to prominence. On the contrary, quite a few were not able to establish a successful business, resulting in a continuum-like division of haves and have-nots. Some households survive at a mere subsistence level, not to speak of the dire need of some aged individuals, pondering over the burden of debt, that may have cut across initially promising business careers. They may have been in Calcutta or even Hong Kong but not every Nyishangba has the innate ability to turn herbs into gold. Or may be they were just too honest.

Next to these unfortunate members of the Nyishangba family, there is a small minority, that clearly has succeeded in small-scale trade ventures but is still dependent on village agriculture and portered-in rice from the middle hills. This group in particular, felt the cancellation of Nyishangba privileges in 1976, while the herb traders among them had already been hard hit by the 1970 promulgation on the collection and export of herbs and drugs (*Nepal Gazette*, vol.20, no.36, Poush 13, 2027 V.S. (December 28, 1970). The traders in this group do not possess any houses beyond the Upper Valley, but occasionally rent a room in Kathmandu in times of relative prosperity. Most of them have not been able to secure a Nepali passport, which, in theory at least, limits the range of their trade ventures to Indian territory.

Then we come to a heterogeneous stratum of relatively successful traders, owning small second homes in the middle hills of Lamjung or in the Chitwan Terai, or are able to afford rented accommodation in Pokhara, Bhairawa or Kathmandu throughout the year. This group contains a number of younger traders, financially not yet too strong, but full of energy, trying to improve their economic status within the limits of the law. These traders often own passports, enabling them to deal with third-party countries. It is in this group that we find the first specimen of traders, specializing in so-called 'porterage' operations.

The phenomenon of 'porterage' rests in the legal possibility open to every Nepali citizen to import duty-free Rs 1,000 worth of goods once a year. The Nyishangba have been quick to use this customs rule to their advantage by designing schemes guaranteeing the legal import of goods worth up to Rs 15,000 in one journey. At the beginning of each fiscal year individual Nyishangba traders might group some 'acquaintances' together (not necessarily Nyishangba), who possess a Nepali passport and can afford a few days off. The trader who has an intimate knowledge of the trade environments of Singapore, Bangkok and Hong Kong pays the air fares for his 'friends' and buys them each a new set of clothes on arrival in the commercial capitals mentioned. In return, he expects each of them to carry goods worth 1,000 rupees back to Nepal for the benefit of the organizing trader. The trader and the 'porters' fly back together to Kathmandu airport, where the goods are legally cleared by customs officers. Current practice in the porterage system involves never less than two and never more than fifteen porters on one trip, the latter number usually being accompanied by two Nyishangba traders. The larger the numbers of porters, the better the prospects for the purchase of large quantities of goods at discount prices. According to a young trader from Tenki, profits range between 100 and 200 per cent of the amount invested, even after fares and sets of cloth for the porters have been deducted. Many of the traders in this group complain about the strictness of customs officers at Kathmandu airport and elsewhere. According to a trader from Braga: 'that used to be different' and, as he added unasked for 'if you really want to get rich nowadays, you should be prepared to take risks'. Some informants in this group stated that they were not prepared to run 'excessive' risks, an attitude which has some of them pushed back into the familiar pattern of mainstream Malayan ventures. The latter trips stand mainly for the sale of gems and petty curio, yet the complementary purchase of manufactured goods is the outcome of a successful venture rather than the preconceived projection of a fully capitalized trip to Bangkok or Hong Kong.

The traders or households in the previous group may be qualified as 'average' in terms of economic status and intra-group influence. It is beyond this stratum that it becomes increasingly difficult to obtain information that could be used for a further typification of the higher Nyishangba circles. To break into these rings and unravel the fabric of past and present trade ventures that bring the real wealth to the top strata of the Nyishangba community, would require another investigation, however. A few preliminary remarks may therefore suffice here.

It has been estimated that between 20 and 30 per cent of the world's trade is unspecified, that is beyond reach of statistical inventory (Bhagwati 1974:21). Trade to and through Nepal does not escape this general rule. Indeed, the highly lucrative Bonus Scheme may have encouraged a flow of goods beyond immediate government control, and consequently has been liable to the generation of 'unethical' business practices. A select group of Nyishangba, financially strong enough or otherwise having access to capital through Indian traders flooding Kathmandu especially after 1970, may have been instrumental in handling the greatly increased volume of foreign goods between 1972 and 1976. Having consolidated their position in the Nepalese political economy by the mid-seventies, it is hard to believe that the curtailment of their privileges in 1976 or the cancellation of the Bonus Scheme in 1978 substantially affected major Nyishangba enterprise. The changes may, however, have induced competition from rival trade groups.

In the meantime, accumulation of capital in some Nyishangba circles has moved apace: 'one *lakh* of rupees is nothing for a Nyishangma' confided a young Tenki trader to the present author. Real property in Kathmandu is now being acquired by Nyishangba for close to a million rupees according to another. And the fund that has been built up from fines imposed on local law-transgressing Nyishangba alone, is said to have passed the two million rupee mark (1981). As a result of this large-scale capital formation, quite a few traders have been able to afford smaller or bigger houses in

Kathmandu and elsewhere, and the general trend for this group seems to be one of increased future prosperity.

If, at the end of a decade of unprecedented gains in a booming trade, we are to characterize the Nyishangba community in terms of economic stratification, we have to conclude to a highly diversified picture. Some traders have remained inconspicuous, others have developed lucrative lines of trade, guaranteeing a stable average income without violating the law too much, while a minority increasingly stands on the slippery rope of international contraband 'trade'.

8

STRUCTURED FLUX AND HIDDEN VISTAS

This study has sought to account for the rise of the Nyishangba as international long-distance traders through a structured geohistorical description. In contrast to much formal theory, in which structure is thought of as given, and therefore determines the explanatory variables in advance, the structure of a particular geohistory only arises while unfolding. Structures in this perspective are not seen as static and durable, but as variable and concordant with historical change. They only acquire meaning through the particular geohistorical experience of human groups. Such an approach implies a long-term rather than a short-term perspective on societal change. The questions that arise are consequently less concerned with what society now is than with how society becomes or has become (Blok 1974:XXIX). Thus, geohistorical inquiry is the search for structure in societal flux, and in terms of regional geography, the identification of a particular regionality as defined in chapter 3. The gain of such an approach is that our fixation on particular would-be explanatory variables becomes less, that we appreciate more the continuous interplay of empirical observation and 'theoretical' structuration, and that hidden vistas are the reward for a certain openness of mind. However, the proof of the pudding remains the eating, and I will try to show in the following section that there is a surplus value in the approach as outlined above. To that end, I will briefly mention several explanations offered so far in the literature for the rise of a number of Tibeto-Himalayan trading communities. At the same time I will try to make it clear that these statements vary in explanatory force according to place and time. By extending our discussion into the realm of a geohistorically structured regionality, we come more fully to appreciate the contextual character of these explanatory variables. This will be briefly shown for the Nyishangba of Manang, which after all provided the *raison d'être* for this study. Finally, I will return to the two research questions as formulated in chapter 1 and see whether on the basis of the interpretation of the facts given in this study and the concepts used suitable answers can be provided.

Tibeto-Himalayan border trade, and the particular success of some of its traders, has been analysed in various ways, and it is interesting to see that the explanations offered generally vary with the scientific *Zeitgeist* and the lines of disciplinary inquiry along which they have been put forward. As the latter were mainly anthropological, and moreover coincided with a time when the cultural ecological point of view was fashionable, at least with a number of American anthropologists who were active in the field, it should come as no surprise that the problem of explaining Tibeto-Himalayan border trade was phrased in terms of ecological adaptation. This in a sense broad point of view, which at times also included attention to economic factors, became somewhat artificially contrasted by the cultural ecologist Andrew Manzardo with the socio-cultural position as taken up by the *éminence grise* of Himalayan anthropology, Christoph von Fürer-Haimendorf. Artificial, because the latter was fully aware of the role of ecological factors, but as a representative of a culturally-oriented generation of older ethnologists, ultimately preferred a socio-cultural explanation for a particular success in trade.

Let us begin with the ecological argument which at first sight provides the answer to a good many questions as far as traditional trade is concerned. According to Von Fürer-Haimendorf (1975:286), 'a self-contained peasant economy based on agriculture and animal husbandry cannot be sustained by the natural resources of valleys lying above 3,300 metres' (at least so in the Central Himalayas - WvS). There seems to be an element of necessity then in the occurrence of extra-local activities. The short growing season in combination with a shortage of labour as inherent to many traditional farming systems (see chapter 5), prevents the realization of a balanced subsistence budget, and thus provides an ecological stimulus to subsidiary income strategies. This may explain the winter exodus of many high-altitude dwelling groups to lower regions to find work as labourers or to engage in a little trade.

Commercial activities could gain in substance and importance if two further ecological factors were favourable. Firstly, and that applied to almost all Tibeto-Himalayan groups, was the circumstance of locational opportunity, that is the fact that most of them were located at the interstices of two culturally disparate but complementary ecozones. Secondly, there was the locational quality of nearness to natural channels of transport which favoured some of them beyond others. The Thakali of the Gandaki valley, for example, were extremely well located to control the exchange of basic products like salt, wool and grain between Tibet and the middle-ranges of Nepal.

Yet, in themselves, these ecological factors are of little explanatory value if considered unrelated to their particular geohistorical context. Ecological necessity, for instance, is not a constant factor over time. Populations may grow or decline, thereby altering the parameters of the agricultural labour question. Ecological complementarity too, only gains significance if in one way or another markets on the basis of surplus-producing populations can be brought into contact with each other. In addition, accessibility to transport routes may lose its importance as an explanatory variable if trade flows dry up or shift to other channels, as happened for example with the trade through the Gandaki corridor (see chapter 5). Whatever the precise influence of ecological factors may be, Von Fürer-Haimendorf, in my view, was very much aware of them when he made 'geographical' factors responsible for the rise of middlemen communities between the economies of two disparate ecozones (Von Fürer-Haimendorf 1975:286).

It is only where the above author starts looking beyond ecological factors, and makes the socio-cultural tradition, or a group's 'social outlook' as he termed it, into the ultimate ground for the trading success of particular Bhotia communities that anthropologists of cultural-ecological persuasion have nailed him on the cross, and not without a certain youthful zest for that matter (see in particular Manzardo 1977). Haimendorf emphasizes the wide scope for individual choice and concomitant ordering of social relations in a basically Buddhist Bhotia society, which in his view allows for relatively easy cross-cultural mobility and contact, and hence success in trade (Von Fürer-Haimendorf 1975:287). Manzardo, on the other hand, sticks to an ecological argument and maintains that 'the success of traders, and the size and nature of their enterprises, is *merely* (italics mine) a matter of access and control of good trade routes and good markets', and, as he adds two pages later, 'access to transport animals' (Manzardo 1977:74-76).

Without going into all the details of the argument involved, for which I should like to refer to the original texts (see Von Fürer-Haimendorf 1975:286-305, Manzardo 1977:63-81), it may be said that both views are infected by the virus of monocausality and a-historicity. Of course the ecological argument, including its locational connotation, is a powerful explanatory variable, but only so in combination with other factors. The 'social outlook' argument too may be viable, possibly if amended in terms of group cohesion and corporate organization. These may be articulated in the form of a specific religious tradition as Von Fürer-Haimendorf holds, but, as with Weber's interpretation of the protestant ethic and the rise of capitalism, it should be remembered that there is no implication whatsoever that a religious tradition *per se* (whether Christianity or Buddhism) is of any primary causal importance. As Trevor Ling in his thoughtful article demonstrates, it is 'only in conjunction with various other, non-religious factors, and in certain favourable situations' that the cultural factor in the guise of religion may explain a particular development (Ling 1985:239). Weber knew this already and argued for a multifactorial explanation of socio-economic change (ibid.:242). Moreover, we have instances from the Himalayan world in which trading groups deliberately adapted their religion in order to gain a stronger foothold in cultural environments differing from their own.

This cultural manipulation of a group's collective image, in order to suit changing social and economic conditions, has been aptly coined 'impression management' and worked out for the Thakali by Manzardo (1978:171-207, 1982). But there still looms the danger of monocausality in his analysis, and it is only with the work of Barbara Parker (1985) that we see something emerge of a multi-dimensional, partly historizing approach, in which the success of a particular group in trade is contextually interpreted. Again the Thakali serve as an example.

> Thakali entrepreneurial behavior emerges from a cultural orientation conditioned by religious and cosmological ideas and performances, while critical concepts and practices in the symbolic system have in turn been

> modified and recast in response to the history of social, political and especially economic relations between villages in the area, and between ethnic groups within Nepal as a nation (Parker 1985:6).

The above interpretive formulation is in my opinion a step in the right direction for the fruitful conceptualization of a particular group's success in trade. By hinting at the interplay of internal and external factors in a process of historical articulation, the tendency to reify single factors in an explanatory scheme is considerably reduced. Although Parker's thesis (1985) especially elaborates the cultural factor, her 'theoretical' openness of mind made her explore in a subsequent article (Parker 1988) the interface between culture as an internal factor and the wider political-economic universe as an external one. As I have pointed out in chapter 5 already, Parker sees Thakali wealth as a result of a 'fortuitous interaction between culture and circumstance' (Parker 1988:193). In essence, this is a Weberian position, in the sense that it reflects a willingness to take into consideration a variety of explanatory variables which at particular conjunctions produce an identifiable historical result. However, the external circumstance she mentions, that of a relative Thakali autonomy within a centralizing Nepalese state in combination with a collective cooperation in extra-local but non-world markets, stops short of the supranational perspective which in my opinion is a further necessary condition for understanding the rise of the Thakali or any other Tibeto-Himalayan trading community for that matter. Not that the status of trading groups as ethnic communities within the larger framework of the state would be analytically unimportant. Therefore 'ethnicity' has become too much entrenched in the perceptions of both the Bhotia communities themselves and the holders of power in a Kathmandu-based government. But to me, Bhotia identity seems as much a creation of culture in interaction with politics at the state level as of the complex interplay of the latter with factors of supranational economic opportunity and geopolitical change. In other words, a still higher level of analysis is involved.

Up till now I have deliberately refrained from using the concept of ethnic minority or trading minority. Instead I have used the more neutral term of community, because minorities and minority problems only seem to have risen with growing state power in shrinking geopolitical 'frontier areas', such as the Tibetan and Himalayan world as described in chapter 2. Growing state power refers to a dynamic historical process, and it was precisely this historical articulation which was emphasized by Wertheim as long ago as 1964 in his seminal article on the political economy of trading minorities in Southeast Asia (Wertheim 1964). He did so, because he felt that a focus on static social and cultural characteristics of ethnic groups could never in itself explain the rise of economically powerful minorities, but that it was necessary to make reference to political attempts at incorporation or assimilation of the groups concerned. By stressing a historical perspective, Wertheim, in a sense, was far ahead of his time. Together with his emphasis on the role of political and economic factors, especially in relation to the state, he provides us with another instance of a contextual and dynamic approach in the social sciences. We will come back to some of his arguments in relation to trading minorities when discussing the position of the economically powerful Nyishangba within the larger framework of the Nepalese state.

As far as the economics of success in trade are concerned two factors stand out: access to markets and the ability to control the means of exchange, which has been defined as 'an advantageous access to trade and a restriction of competition, both within groups and in relation to others' (Schrader 1988:303). Phrasing the problem of trade success in economic terms raises the question whether the emphasis on closed corporate or ethnic groups is fully justified. Schrader discusses this problem at some length and concludes that control over the means of exchange in traditional societies generally correlates with the socio-cultural hierarchy (ibid.:306-307). There may be some monocausality of reasoning then in the exposition of trade success in terms of group membership only. In fact, *intra*-group economic stratification is present in many Tibeto-Himalayan communities, and has been identified for the Nyishangba as well (see chapter 7). Thus the discussion on the control over the means of exchange becomes partly one of the historical articulation of 'big' people at the local level and the power holding élites at the national level. Yet, some groups as a whole did better than others and the question therefore remains one of the precise interaction of the central government and local populations. This brings us back to the first research question as posed towards the end of chapter 1, that of the particular geohistorical form of the Nyishangba trading experience. Although their meteoric rise as long-distance traders in South and Southeast Asia has been described in chapters 5, 6 and 7, the critical articulation between the Nyishangba and the Nepalese government still remains to be discussed.

With regard to the Central Himalayan region, the answer to the question of group excellence in trade is likely to be found in the special relationship between some of Nepal's northern border communities and a Kathmandu-based government, which from the very birth of the Nepalese state in the second half of the eighteenth century, sought to secure its territorial integrity by pursuing an active policy of containment relative to Tibet. Given the strategic location of certain communities near easy passages into Tibet (as in the case of Walongchung), or the nearness to petty principalities whose loyalty to the Nepalese crown was in doubt (as with Mustang), it was but a matter of time before the ruling élite in Kathmandu realized the potential benefits of an active containment policy. The often tense situation between Nepal and Tibet, aggravated by growing Chinese influence in Tibet since the end of the eighteenth century, led to a situation in which specific privileges were conferred on persons or groups that could positively contribute to the upholding of Nepalese territorial rights. Thus external factors of state articulation seem to have provided for favourable conditions of early capital formation among the Thakali and the inhabitants of Walongchung. The Nyishangba, whose peripheral location and 'Tibetan' cultural tradition preoccupied the élite in Kathmandu, also benefited from this containment policy, though at a low profile at first. The several written exchanges between the Nyishangba and the Nepalese government (see chapter 5), seem to support this point, but cannot hide the fact that the Bhotia from Walongchung and especially the Thakali were considered a superior instrument of containment in the period 1860-1930.

Yet, geopolitical containment alone does not seem to provide a sufficient explanation for increased government attention to the affairs of peripheral groups like the Thakali and the Nyishangba. Viewed from a different angle, growing interest from the political centre was also very likely shaped by considerations of state control over potential dissident or even separatist groups. Internal motives of power play seem to have guided as much the policy *vis-à-vis* peripheral groups as have external matters of geopolitical concern. Thus the rise of the Thakali in the first decades of the twentieth century, was viewed with growing anxiety by the central government. And apparently not without reason as Schrader notes, because they had the intention to form an autonomous state in the whole of the upper Kali Gandaki under their dominion (Schrader 1988:313). Growing government interest in Nyishangba affairs from the 1950s onwards may be viewed in the same light. The official attention had almost certainly to do with incipient claims for greater local autonomy based on the growing economic influence of the Nyishangba in the immediate postwar area. In order to control and if possible to co-opt a small but vigorous community in times of turbulent statehood and amidst a tense international geopolitical situation, the Nyishangba from the 1960s onwards, were lured into closer bonds of patronage with the Kathmandu power holders through economic privileges (see chapter 7). It may seem paradoxical, giving more economic power to those who already possess it, but this policy had the virtue of cutting both ways. The political strategists in Kathmandu hoped to weave the web of state more tightly around a peripheral group, while the economic technocrats saw potential hard currency earners in them. Both policies have met with considerable success. Nowadays, the Nyishangba are more closely tied to the political centre than ever before, but their economic power, extending beyond national borders, remains a source of anxiety within government circles. Their continued search for a strong group identity too, expressed in an ardent Buddhism, seems an attempt to avoid an all too close alliance with the Hindu-dominated core. Yet the same Nyishangba could not exist without the concentration of power in a national state and although their official privileges have been cut in 1976 - which they resent - it is the very Nepalese state they have to adhere to in order to survive. The articulation of their Buddhism in order to strengthen their ethnic identity as a Bhotia community is concordant with Wertheim's claim that minority groups tend to stress certain cultural traits by which they distinguish themselves from the (national) majority group (Wertheim 1964:79). However, the 'impression management' of the

Thakali in the direction of the Hindu core does not fit this thesis. Perhaps the Thakali recognized, earlier than similar groups, that the basic aim of the majority is to oust them in their position of economic power, and that in stressing a distinct identity they would still more endanger their position as a group (idem).

At first sight, many of the structural explanations offered for the rise of Tibeto-Himalayan trading communities in the foregoing pages seem valuable if not valid, and applied to specific cases within a Nepalese context may even generate a semblance of recognition and conviction. However, at the level of the single ethnic group, explanatory factors escape unambiguous interpretation. Locational opportunity, for example, in the case of the Nyishangba, does not play a significant role as they have no access to a through-going trans-Himalayan trade route. In addition, really effective government support in the form of economic privileges for the Nyishangba dates only from the 1960s, while that for the Thakali had already been withdrawn for more than three decades. What then, in the end, explains their differential but comparable rise as long-distance trading communities?

The above reasoning brings us right back to the second research question as formulated in chapter 1. The answer to that question can be found at a still higher level of analysis, that of a shared Tibetan regionality in terms of its external relations. In this connection, we must briefly revert to Braudel's concept of an *économie-monde* as an economically autonomous part of the world essentially capable of being self-sufficient, and enjoying a spatial and historical coherence of its movements (chapter 3). As has been pointed out earlier, China and India may be considered as two *économies-mondes,* and perhaps as the extreme poles of a *super-économie-monde* pivoting around the Malaysian world. Tibet, in this view, was a kind of neutral zone, which, though culturally speaking an *espace-mouvement,* cannot be considered the same in economic terms (chapter 3). Especially its regional population clusters in the eastern and northeastern provinces of Kham and Amdo looked towards the Chinese *économie-monde,* while the central and southwestern provinces of Ü, Tsang, and Ngari were economically linked to the Indian one. The latter orientation was emphasized by geopolitical developments in the first half of the twentieth century (chapter 2), and led to a partial, though by no means exclusive, reorientation of trade flows towards the South (chapter 4).

The pull of the Indian *économie-monde* made itself more clearly felt when the rise of a British colonial empire in India made possible an enhanced internal coherence of movements by a bout of road and railway building during the second half of the nineteenth century. China lagged behind in this respect, but after the revolution of 1911, transport networks in the latter country too, slowly improved. The increased mobility of goods and people which showed as a result, allowed for an intensification of old and new forms of economic activity, especially in the form of market places near zones of cultural and ecological transition, and at specific break-of-bulk points. It entailed the increased participation of border communities in traditional but widening networks of economic exchange, and made possible their experimentation with more extended forms of long-distance trade as conditioned by a particular *économie-monde*. However, it is the long-term dynamics of these *économies-mondes* in interaction with medium-term processes of state formation and boundary making in a contested and therefore shrinking geopolitical 'frontier' area, that ultimately provides a sufficient context for an interpretation of the rise (and subsequent decline) of the Bhotia communities concerned. Examples of the latter are to be found in a whole series of trading communities in the Himalayan border world. Here we find, at a critical 'time-space edge' (chapter 1, 4), the Bashahri, Kumaon Bhotia, Thakali, Sherpa, Walongchung Bhotia, Tromowa, and Monpa, that came to thrive as long-distance traders within a few generations. As such they structurally resemble a number of border communities in the Sino-Tibetan frontier area, like the Hui of western Kansu and the Sharba from the Sungpan region (chapter 4).

The extraordinary rise to prosperity of the Nyishangba too, as late as the 1960s, seems to fit in well with the preceding argument. When the Nepalese government granted economic privileges to them in 1962, the Nyishangba translated these advantages into an ever closer articulation of their trading activities with the *économie-monde* they were already embedded in for years (chapter 6). The reasons as to why the Nepalese government was so generous to one specific

Tibeto-Himalayan community at that particular time remains unclear, but it is my conviction that the tense international geopolitical situation along the Nepal-Tibet frontier, especially in Mustang and the neighbouring high valley of Nyishang, was largely responsible for that generosity (cf. Rose 1971:228-231, Peissel 1972:251-270, Mullin 1975:30-34, Ray 1983:28-30, Avedon 1984:122-129, Grunfeld 1987: 156-157).

The particular geohistorical form which the rise of the Nyishangba took after the wholesale granting of privileges in 1962, has been described in chapter 7 and need not be repeated here. It is interesting to see that their trading activities increasingly focused on the bigger manufacturing and commercial capitals of Southeast Asia, and that modern luxury goods largely came to replace traditional ones, now moreover transported by plane. Although by the early 1980s the Nyishangba still formed a strong business community, their intra-economic stratification and the rise of traders from other quarters constrained further autonomous growth. Their co-optation in the regular administrative system - they were formally represented in the Rastriya Pancayat - has freed the way for some of them to explore new highways and byways of mercantile development, now underscored by their conspicuous life-style in Kathmandu. All this has brought about the corrosion of the Nyishangba as a localized and functionally corporate group, and the future will probably see new societal alignments, in which Nyishangba corporate power, if it ever existed in this strong formulation, will only be a shadow of its past.

Thus the tale of the Nyishangba seems almost over, and along with it, similar tales of commercial structuration that gained their particular geohistorical form at critical interfaces of a shared Tibetan regionality. It is the latter which made these tales liable to structural comparison, but I hope to have shown that the ideal is a strait gate, not suited for the rash, the one-dimensional, and the a-historic. In time, new alignments will lead to new tales, featuring new regionalities. In the particular geohistorical conjunction of their multifaceted universes, new and perhaps unexpected phenomena will arise. It needs the structural imagination of the regional geographer to portray these in order that we may better understand the world in which we live.

APPENDIX 1

Authors, texts, and audiences

This study has made use of a wide variety of literary sources, both scientific and otherwise. The question therefore arises how they were selected, how they are valued, and what use has been made of them. In this connection we must ask what makes a text into a scientific one, as it would seem that it is only the authority of statements made in scientific books and articles that gives legitimacy to their quotation. What a scientific text distinguishes from an ordinary one is the fact that an explicit argumentation for a particular statement or observation is given. Both the credibility and convincing power of an argument give a particular text the authority for which its author may be cited or appealed to as an expert in future scientific debate. Such expert opinion or commentary is a necessary condition in any field of scientific enquiry. It is the thorough knowledge of a particular scientific domain in combination with a cogent argument, that makes true scholarship.

This all sounds pretty obvious, and in the literature on Tibet and its culturally related border worlds it is easy to point out instances of impeccable scholarship, as exemplified by a number of scholars in various academic settings around the world, including Tibetan refugee ones in northern India. Sailing on the compass of the above scholars, especially in the domains of linguistics, religious studies, cultural history and, more recently, anthropology, one can be assured of a safe arrival in the haven of accepted scholarship. But in the present study, sources used have by far not always scientific status. To reconstruct the geohistory of Tibetan trade and traders in the long century between 1850 and 1950, one has to rely on a variety of books and articles of widely differing scope and authority. The sources referred to fall within the category of travel literature, even those I would say, that fill the Geographical Journals in the golden age of exploration which roughly covers the same period.

Travel literature as a fountain of knowledge has its own problems of interpretation. The assumption here is that travel literature can be of assistance in the geohistorical enterprise of reconstructing a Tibetan regionality guiding further thematical elaborations. But as there are travel writers and travel liars it is important to argue the grounds on which a particular selection of texts takes place. This is a complicated affair, in which both the background of the authors and the lenses of the prospective reading audiences have to be kept in mind.

As regards the background of a whole generation of travellers who wrote down their experiences in one way or another, it has been argued that despite national and personal differences, they shared a common frame of reference, enhanced by the translation of quite a few foreign travel books into English. The literary critic Fussell (1980:73ff) even goes so far as to speak of 'the Englishness of it all', and Peter Bishop too, in his valuable study on travel writing regarding Tibet, notices a kind of British-inspired internationalism 'assisted by the similarities in class and gender among explorers and travellers, no matter what their nationality' (Bishop 1989:6-7). This may be true in a general sense, but I cannot fully agree on the harmonizing effect of the 'internationalist' frame of reference, as I find the range and quality of travel texts on Tibet still strongly marked by the personality and ability of the authors concerned, not to mention the contexts in which they made their observations.

With respect to the audience, it is necessary to point out the pitfalls of what has been labelled 'genre convention'. Genre convention as a set of time-specific rules and rhetorical means, answering dominant backgrounds and motives of an audience, has undoubtedly acted as a strait-jacket or even sieve for information and is therefore an important factor to be reckoned with in any assessment of a particular travel document (Kommers 1987:25ff.). British travel accounts from the turn of the century, for example, often fall in with utilitarian motives of audiences in an imperialistic Britain. The audience expects information about peoples, products and places, just as it expects a jingoistic exposition of 'the white man's burden' in faraway and 'uncivilized' countries. This being the case, certain facts may be emphasized or left out on doubtful grounds.

With regard to the context of observations made, we do well to realize that context is a function of both observer and the observed. The widely differing backgrounds of travel writers, as well as the specific geohistorical contexts they ran into - and in a way helped to mould - made observations greatly differing in scope and quality.

There were scientific-minded travellers and pseudo-scientific ones, hunters and pleasure-seekers, soldiers and missionaries, peripatetics and fast travellers, pilgrims and political agents, adventurers and diplomatic representatives, mountaineers and a few stray women. This carnivalesque procession of observers and prospective authors wound its way through Tibet under a great variety of circumstances. It makes the interpretation of and the inference from their written accounts a hazardous affair, which needs a judgement that only grows with experience. Considering the above and barring problems of selection on the side of the user, a comparative perspective on as many sources as possible seems to me the only way of deciding on the relative truth of an observation. Circumstantial evidence obtained in this way may lead to further insight, which in the end may yield an image with a certain degree of dependability and validity. This indeed is the procedure adopted for this study, and wherever available and accessible more than one source is quoted to substantiate a particular statement.

In a Tibetan application too, the above reflections boil down to the question of how reliable particular authors are, what bias can be pointed out in their work, but also what are their strong points. To begin with the latter, the fact that they were 'there', has often provided us with the one and only primary source about a particular region or event, which is an asset in itself. The Swedish explorer Sven Hedin, for example, saw many things that others never had the chance to see. Of course we lack corroborating evidence in such cases, but other parts or aspects of a particular *oeuvre* may be liable to comparison and on that basis it is possible to establish a measure of truthfulness with regard to the facts that go unchecked.

Accounts may also be strong on the ground that their authors are familiar with certain spheres of life, possess proven powers of observation, or speak the local language. Kawaguchi, for example, a Japanese Buddhist monk who visited Tibet from 1899 to 1902, has left us an interesting book on Tibetan society which is particularly detailed about the Tibetan clergy, because the author belonged to the same social category and had therefore easy access to the world of organized Tibetan Buddhism (Kawaguchi 1909). As regards the proven powers of observation, Hedin certainly was in possession of this great gift, but his knowledge of Tibetan remains debated. Not so Tucci, who had an extraordinary command of oriental languages, in particular Sanskrit and Tibetan. Hedin is therefore remembered as a geographer and explorer, Tucci rather as a linguist and culture historian of Tibet. This kind of contextual knowledge is helpful in deciding where the potential strength of an author and his work lies, and as such may contribute to a more subtle selection of facts.

With regard to the reliability of particular authors, we may mention Hedin again, who for one reason or another is considered suspect in a purely academic sense. He was refused a doctorate by Von Richthofen at the University of Berlin in 1890 (Kish 1984:32-33), and the 'Scientific Results' of his second Central Asian expedition were rated descriptive rather than analytical (review in the *Geographical Journal*, vol.27, 1906:613). His throughout pro-German stance in two world wars probably further detracted from his credibility in the eyes of his allied colleagues, as did his prolific popular writing. Yet his *oeuvre* stands as a grand record of exploration and if handled with care, remains in my view a mine of information.

Another instance of debated reliability may be found in the books of Ernst Schäfer, who visited Tibet several times in the 1930s (Gruber 1986). Schäfer's reputation is under a cloud as he was a staunch supporter of the Nazi regime. Gruber's praise of Schäfer's search for private money to finance his 1938/39 expedition to Tibet (1986:12) is seen in a different light when we realize that Schäfer was a protégé of the *SS-Reichsführer* Himmler, who personally paid the return tickets for the members of the expedition (Kater 1974:80). Are his books of no use then? I don't think so. If carefully handled and checked against other sources, they may still yield fruitful insight. Many more instances of debated reliability can be cited, and consequently, caution in using sources needs to be argued for always and everywhere. Even the unsuspected *oeuvre* of the great Italian orientalist Giuseppe Tucci (1894-1984) has recently been questioned as to its fascist antecedents (Benavides 1995). It is another warning against the creeping but perhaps inevitable social constructivist dangers in scientific knowledge.

Last but not least there is the question of hidden bias in travel accounts, the traces of which are not always easy to locate. In this respect, one can do no better than read *The myth of Shangri-La*, a book by Peter Bishop (1989), studded with insights about the ways in which reports on Tibet are slanted. According to Bishop, there are almost as many Tibets as there are authors, each structurally influenced by the dominant social and mental parameters of a particular era. It makes one wonder about one's own biases, and yet the position of the scientific author seems different to me from that of the travel writers. Bias can be reduced by adopting a comparative perspective. Sound argumentation does contribute to the production of less slanted accounts, 'truer' images, and higher degrees of validity. In that sense, the scientific enterprise differs from the storytelling one. The latter brings diversion, the former wants to ban ideology.

APPENDIX 2

Fieldwork and its burning questions

'Considerable physical and mental stamina are needed to make the transition from the predominantly sheltered intellectual environment of a university to the hardships inherent to mountain travel and work at high altitude' (Ward 1966:504). And indeed, fieldwork in Nyishang at an average altitude of 3,500 metres, as well as walking into that place in a seven-day trek across the main chain of the Himalaya, took more breath out of me than one wants to remember when back in Holland below sea level.

Nevertheless, I was there from June to September 1981 to carry out a descriptive and interpretive piece of research in order to get an insight, and possibly more, into the trading history of the Nyishangba of Manang. In addition to empirical fact-finding with regard to a community that was a virtual blank on the geographical and ethnographical map of Nepal, the fieldwork was planned in such a way as to find out more about the manner in which a rural community had greatly extended its external relations over the past century. As such it had a definite topical orientation.

To facilitate the generation of systematic-descriptive materials, a survey in the Nepali language was constructed, which however had to be burnt on the spot a few weeks later, because of the total non-response of the Nyishangba when confronted with a government-backed and paper-waving outsider, moreover accompanied by a 'Nepalese' interpreter, which some of them thought 'too smart' for his job anyway. The first weeks then of my stay in the village of Braga, a location chosen at the instigation of Dr. Von Fürer-Haimendorf whom I had met briefly in Kathmandu, were an outright disaster as far as the planned survey research was concerned.

With hindsight the non-response may be explained firstly by a false perception of the community involved on the part of the researcher and secondly by the use of the Nepali language in the questionnaire. The false perception effectively boiled down to not recognizing beforehand the Nyishangba as 'a community of smugglers' (Hagen 1972: caption plate 35), instead of a harmless batch of seasonal hawkers. To this day I consider my ignorance a mistake, for perhaps I could have known in advance by paying more attention to the context in which the fieldwork materialized (see my *Verslag van een studiereis naar Nepal*, 1981, unpublished), and by studying the available literature more closely. The use of the Nepali language, or perhaps the whole idea of a written survey, was another mistake, as quite a few Nyishangba traders had a history of crossing borders illegally, a fact they did not want to see advertised in Kathmandu government circles, let alone written down in a language they did not even bother to send their children to school for.

Given the situation of an allergic reaction to paper, my interpreter and I shifted to informal talks at whatever place and time was feasible. In the beginning this worked out quite well, but after a week the trickle of information coming down from the community tap suddenly dried up, and we were informed independently from two sides that the rumour had been spread in Braga that we were representatives of the 'Criminal Investigation Department'(CID), in other words, spies from the Kathmandu government with great executive powers. By burning the questionnaire, and by switching to the neighbouring villages of Manang and Tenki, we sought to defuse and circumvent the rumour, but we were only partly successful in doing so. Nevertheless, a number of villagers remained on friendly terms with us, and some of them even came to believe the story of a European researcher engaged in collecting information for a book on the history of Nyishangba trade. This measure of acceptance allowed a fresh research strategy to be introduced, based on orally conducted in-depth interviews through the medium of my interpreter. The latter proved moreover to be a Magar, a member of one of Nepal's Tibeto-Burman hill tribes and therefore not nearly considered so bad as a fully Hinduized Nepalese citizen.

Notwithstanding the above, interviews were conducted in Nepali, the *lingua franca* of Nepal. Altogether, twenty-eight in-depth interviews with traders were realized, ranging in length from one to three hours. As my own understanding of the Nepali language is limited, I had almost totally to depend on my interpreter. Together we worked out a strategy for covering as much selective ground as possible. The first three or so interviews were effected in a straight question and answer manner, partly following the contents of the burnt questionnaire. But this did not yield the expected results. With growing insight in Nyishangba trade history and by imaginatively using information already obtained, it proved possible to develop a kind of semi-structured interview which I thoroughly discussed with my interpreter, after which he was relatively free to proceed during an interview as he thought best. In this manner, much unsuspected information came to the fore. Every five minutes during an interview, my interpreter would summarize his findings in two or three English sentences, as well as a number of key-words, which I thoroughly memorized in the intervals. Towards the end of an interview I usually became more active in steering its course, especially with regard to the geographic context of trading ventures. Two Bartholomew Maps of the Indian subcontinent and South-East Asia (scale 1:4,000,000 and 1:5,800,000) worked wonders in this respect, and traders were generally very much interested in getting behind the secret of the many-coloured and folded device.

In time, it turned out that traders were generally more suspicious of each other than of a foreigner and his interpreter. They gave away, and they actually said so, more information to us than to their fellow traders, whom they saw as competitors. That is not to say that information was always easily obtained. Some interviews were long drawn-out and the informants had to be pumped for their reminiscences. A specimen of the latter-type discussion is the following.

Q. Did you ever visit Burma?
A. No.

Q. The Shwe Dagon Pagode is beautiful, isn't it?
A. Yes, yes.

Q. So you were in Rangoon?
A. Only once.

Q. Or twice?
A. Perhaps.

Q. Did you ever go to Mandalay?
A. Never seen the place.

Q. They do have a good gem market there, don't they?
A. Oh yes, it was a great market.

Q. So you were in Mandalay?
A. Yes.

Q. How many times?
A. Many times.

Q. Did your left-door neighbour ever visit Burma?
A. I doubt it, and when he says so he is lying.

Q. Maybe you are lying now too?
A. No, no. I am not a liar. I will tell you everything about my neighbour.

As all this had to be done without a scrap of paper, we hurried home after each interview, and tried to reconstruct the whole episode on the basis of my 'structured' memory and the detailed knowledge of my interpreter. Much, if not all, depends in such a set-up on the quality of the interpreter, and I think I was lucky in this respect. His Magar background, his university education, his pretty good English, his astounding memory, his natural ability to make contact with people of all walks of life, and above all his unembellished way of interpreting, go a long way to account for the relative success of the enterprise against all prevailing odds. Yet the question of the reliability of the material remains, and we may ask therefore by what possible sources of bias the above research strategy and its findings are contaminated.

First, there is the language question. As far as I could gather, most grown-up men in Nyishang had a good smattering of Nepali, and some of them were actually fluent in it, in particular the ones who lived in Kathmandu almost the whole year round. Women however, especially the elder ones, were proficient in the local language only. Together with the fact that it was difficult for a male outsider to approach women directly, the data are undoubtedly biased to the man's world. But as trade ventures were for the greater part a male monopoly, at least so according to the men, the distortion in this respect is probably slight. Another source of bias is the network strategy followed in gaining access to potential informants. At first, only family relations, friends, and neighbours of our landlord in Braga were willing to grant an interview, a stratum which had a mainly 'lower middle class' background, which in the context of Nyishangba society meant that they had been or actually were moderately successful in their trading schemes. Except for the cases of some former big bosses, 'middle class' bias is probably demonstrable in most of the interviews, as the contemporary big bosses were either not present or kept a low profile. Furthermore, the age group of traders between twenty and forty is underrepresented, as most of these were actively engaged in trade at the time. Consequently the material is most detailed but not necessarily strongest, for the period 1930-1960. The traders that did eventually talk, were probably telling the truth most of the time, as we were considered relative outsiders by them and therefore not particularly threatening to their position. Cross-checking between interview results confirms to a certain extent the assumption of truthfulness, as did the later contextual interpretation with the help of written sources. In fact, the latter is an essential and almost integral part of the research strategy followed, and is generally considered the touchstone of oral history writing (Vansina 1973:187). Although an oral historian must specify his informants, I have refrained from giving their real names in the text, as after all many of them are smugglers in one way or another and moreover I agreed not to reveal their identities in any way. A final source of bias which is far more difficult to trace, is the fact that undue attention may have been given to the extraordinary, the conspicuous and the particular, and that so from the side of both the interviewer and the interviewee. To what extent I have been able to redress this inclination lies largely hidden. I can only say that I was aware of the problem and that it has made me more prudent in interpreting the evidence when writing up my account of the Nyishangba of Manang as international long-distance traders. The reader may judge accordingly.

APPENDIX 3

Customs exemption for traders of Manang

On behalf of the inhabitants of the seven villages of Manang (Manang, Braga, Khangsar, Narme, Phugaun, Ngawal and Pisang), Pewa Tsering Gurung and others submitted the following petition to His Majesty's Government:

'We, inhabitants of seven villages in the Himalayan (Bhot) region, including Manang, have no lands, and depend on foreign trade for our livelihood. A royal order has been issued with the following provisions:

1. No customs duties shall be charged on goods imported or exported by us.
2. The inhabitants of these seven villages shall make a *sirto* payment amounting to Rs 1,797 every year, as well as a *salami* payment of 4.50 rupees to His Majesty.
3. They shall also supply the following goods every year:
   a) two pairs of *docha*
   b) one musk-deer
   c) one musk-pod
   d) two blue sheep skins

We had accordingly been fulfilling these obligations until the Vikrama year 2019 (A.D. 1962). The royal order also contained provision for payment of 50 rupees to us every year, as expenses for our journey (between Manang and Kathmandu). We have been receiving this payment regularly. When we visited Kathmandu in the Vikrama year 2020 (A.D. 1963) to make these payments and supplies, we were told that the rates of payments in money had been increased by 100 per cent under the 1963 Finance Act. Unable to make payment at the enhanced rate, we returned to Manang. Moreover, customs duties are now being collected from us. We, therefore, submitted a petition to His Majesty during the royal visit to Pokhara. On Shrawan 26, 2021 (August 10, 1964), we were informed that the following decisions had been taken:

1. The existing arrangements shall be retained for a period of two years

2. No customs duties shall be charged, but records of goods exported and imported (by the inhabitants of the seven villages) shall be maintained

Accordingly, we deposited the amount of the *sirto* payment at the Kunchha Revenue Office. Since we do not have any agricultural incomes, but depend on trade for our livelihood, we are unable to make the *sirto* payment at 100 per cent of the existing rate. Until, therefore, our lands are surveyed, and taxes assessed, we pray that we be allowed to pay the *sirto* and the *salami* levies, and supply the prescribed goods as usual, for the Vikrama years 2021-2022 (A.D. 1964/65 and 1965/66), and that the usual amount of expenses for our journey be paid to us.'

According to a decision taken on Baisakh 26, 2023 (May 8, 1966), His Majesty's Government decided:

1. To reconfirm the existing arrangements regarding customs exemption and payments
2. To direct the Commissioner of the Gandaki zone to make appropriate arrangements about land survey and tax assessment in consultation with the chairman of the local Panchayat
3. To continue payment of Rs 50 as travelling expenses every year

The decision to take action in respect to land survey and tax assessment in consultation with the chairman of the local Panchayat was prompted by the realization of the fact that '(these villages) are situated in Himalayan terrain and remain covered by snow. At some places which are not covered by snow, one crop of potato or barley is grown in a year. The petitioners say that the amount of payment assessed on such areas should not be increased by 100 per cent as elsewhere. It is, therefore, necessary to study the condition of the land and finalize arrangements which will be satisfactory to the local inhabitants.'

Source: M.C. Regmi (ed.) 1983a, *Regmi Research Series,* vol.15, no.5, May, 67-68.

GLOSSARY

Abbreviations

(Bur) - Burmese
(Chi) - Chinese
(Hin) - Hindi
(Nep) - Nepali
(Nyi) - Nyishangte
(San) - Sanskrit
(Tib) - Tibetan

amban (Chi)
: Manchu government representative at Lhasa before 1911

bhotia (Hin)
: Tibetan or Tibetanized ethnic groups in the Himalayan border region

bodhisattva (San)
: in Mahayana Buddhism a term that refers to a being that has attained the highest levels of purity and spiritual development immediately preceding Buddhahood, but for the moment refrains from entering this ultimate state of serenity in order to assist other beings subject to suffering in the cycle of birth, misery and death

bogyoke (Bur)
: senior officer, 'general'

Dalai Lama (Tib)
: the spiritual head of Tibetan Buddhism, formerly seated in the Potala palace at Lhasa in the central province of Ü; it is also the spiritual head of the Gelukpas, the predominant school in Tibetan Buddhism

darbar (Nep)
: palace, court, royal palace

dhaapa (Nyi)
: traditional village councils in Nyishang or rather their headmen

dhikur (Nep)
: rotating credit association in Nepalese society

duar (Hin)
: in this context a mountain pass leading from the Indian plains to the hills of Bhutan. In its plural form it is sometimes used to refer

to the entire strip of lowlands along the foot of the Bhutanese hills at the border with Bengal and Assam

dzo (Tib)
: cross between a yak and a cow

dzong (Tib)
: fort or fortified residence of a local aristocrat or governor

gompa (Tib)
: a Tibetan monastery

gurudvara (Hin)
: a Sikh temple

jagir (Nep)
: state-owned lands assigned to government employees and functionaries instead of their emoluments; abolished in Nepal in 1952

jimuwal, jimmawal, jimidar (Nep)
: a non-official functionary who collected taxes on *khet* (irrigated) lands before land reforms took place

kami (Nep)
: low sudra caste, the members of which are mainly specialized as blacksmiths

karma (San)
: the force generated by a person's actions, believed in Hinduism and Buddhism to determine his or her destiny in the next existence

khadganisana (Nep)
: during Rana rule a seal with the image of the *khadga* (royal sceptre)

khukri, khukuri (Nep)
: traditional Nepali knife

kyat (Bur)
: Burmese type of currency

lakh (Hin)
: a hundred thousand

lalmohar (Nep)
: the red seal His Majesty the King of Nepal customarily puts on documents concerning laws, special privileges or gifts

lama (Tib)
: a guru, or highly respected religious elder or teacher

mela (Hin)
: a seasonal, often religiously tinged fair

mukhiya (Nep)
: generic term for a local (village) headman, through which tax collecting was sometimes organized; lower post in government

bureaucracy below officer level during Rana times (1846-1950)

muri (Nep)
a volumetric unit ranging from some 48 kgs of paddy to approximately 68 kgs of wheat or maize; 20 *pathi* of foodgrains

nirkhi (Nep)
a sales tax in Nepal; was collected from the vendor when specified commodities were sold in the markets of the central hill region

nirvana (San)
the extinction of continual proces (Snellgrove 1987:13), liberation from the cycle of transmigration; the state of serenity that is the essential attribute of the Buddha

Panchen Lama (Tib)
the lama next to rank to the Dalai Lama, formerly based at Tashilunpo monastery near Shigatse in the province of Tsang

pandit (Hin)
a Hindu scholar of the Brahman caste; in a Himalayan and Tibetan context the term came to be used for the Indian undercover explorers sponsored by the Trigonometrical Survey of India in the second half of the nineteenth century

pathi (Nep)
a volumetric unit equivalent to some 3 kgs of grain; 20 *pathi* equals 1 *muri*

puja (San)
a general term referring to any act of worship, but usually comprising some sort of offering

raja (Hin)
king; the term also refers to leading persons of lesser authority

rastriya pancayat (Nep)
former Nepalese parliament under the *pancayat* system, abolished in 1990; now called *samsad*

sirto (Nep)
a tax payable through an *amali* (a regional tax collecting officer) by a few categories of feudatory states to the Nepalese government after 1852

subba (Nep)
a high government functionary; a title given to local revenue contractors

tantras (San)
a body of later Hindu and Buddhist scriptures strongly marked by mysticism and magic

thulo lama (Nyi)
see *tulku*

tola (Nep)
: a unit of weight equal to approximately ten grammes (0.01 kg), generally used for gold or silver

tulku (Tib)
: incarnated spiritual leader in a line of succession of supernatural beings, generally a Buddha or *bodhisattva*

ula (Tib)
: special privileges of government agents or traders, in particular the liberty to requisition yak and horses for carrying goods without payment; a kind of forced labour for the local population

REFERENCES

Addy, P. (1985)

Tibet on the imperial chessboard: the making of British policy towards Lhasa, 1899-1925. London: Sangam Books Limited.

Ahmad, Z. (1970)

Sino-Tibetan relations in the seventeenth century. Rome: IsMEO.

Aitchison, J.E.T. (1874)

Handbook of the trade products of Leh, with the statistics of the trade, from 1867 to 1872 inclusive. Calcutta: Wyman and Co., Publishers.

Alder, G. (1985)

Beyond Bokhara: the life of William Moorcroft, Asian explorer and pioneer veterinary surgeon, 1767-1825. London: Century Publishing.

Allix, A. (1922)

The geography of fairs. *Geographical Review,* vol.12: 532-569.

Andrugtsang, G.T. (1973)

Four rivers, six ranges. Reminiscences of the resistance movement in Tibet. Dharamsala: Information and Publicity Office of H.H. the Dalai Lama.

Anonymous (1907)

North and north-eastern frontier tribes of India (compiled in the Intelligence Branch Division of the Chief of Staff Army Headquarters India). Simla: Government Monotype Press 1907. Reprinted Delhi: Cultural Publishing House 1984.

Aris, M. (1980)

Notes on the history of the Mon-yul corridor. In: M. Aris and Aung San Suu Kyi (eds.), *Tibetan studies in honour of Hugh Richardson*: 9-20. Warminster: Aris and Phillips.

Aris, M. (1988)

Hidden treasures and secret lives. A study of Pemalinga (1450-1521) and the Sixth Dalai Lama (1683-1706). Delhi: Motilal Banarsidass/Shimla: Institute of Advanced Study.

Aris, M. (1994)

The raven crown. The origins of Buddhist monarchy in Bhutan. London: Serindia Publications

Asad, T. (1987)

Are there histories of peoples without Europe? A review article. *Comparative Studies in Society and History,* vol. 29, no.3: 594-607.

Avedon, J.F. (1984)

In exile of the land of snows. New York: Alfred A. Knopf.

Avedon, J.F. (1987)

Tibet today: current conditions and prospects. *Himalayan Research Bulletin,* vol.VII, nos.2-3: 1-10.

Aziz, B.N. (1978)
Tibetan frontier families. Reflections of three generations from D'ingri. New Delhi: Vikas Publishing House.

Baber, E.C. (1882)
Travels and researches in Western China. Royal Geographical Society, Supplementary Papers, vol.I, part 1. London: John Murray.

Bacot, J. (1908)
Le pèlerinage du Dokerla (Tibet oriental). *La Géographie*, tome XVII, I, 416-420.

Bacot, J. (1909)
Dans les marches tibétaines. Autour du Dokerla, novembre 1906 - janvier 1908. Paris: Plon-Nourrit et Cie.

Bailey, F.M. (1912)
Journey through a portion of South-Eastern Tibet and the Mishmi Hills. *The Geographical Journal*, vol.XXXIV, no.4, April: 334-347.

Bailey, F.M. (1914)
Exploration on the Tsangpo or upper Brahmaputra. *The Geographical Journal*, vol.XLIV, no.4, October: 341-364.

Bailey, F.M. (1945)
China - Tibet - Assam. A journey, 1911. London: Jonathan Cape.

Bailey, F.M. (1957)
No passport to Tibet. London: Rupert Hart-Davis.

Bailey, H.W. (1971)
The culture of the Iranian kingdom of ancient Khotan in Chinese Turkestan - the expansion of early Indian influence into Northern Asia. *Memoirs of the Research Department of the Toyo Bunko*, No.29: 17-29.

Bailey, H.W. (1979)
Dictionary of Khotan Saka. Cambridge: Cambridge University Press

Baker, A.R.H. (1984)
Reflections on the relations of historical geography and the Annales school of history. In: Baker, A.R.H. and D. Gregory (eds.), *Explorations in historical geography; interpretative essays*: 1-27. Cambridge: Cambridge University Press.

Bancaud, H. and Macdonald, A.W. (1982)
Haute route des Himalayas. Paris: Éditions Chaine Graphique.

Banskota, N.P. (1981)
Indo-Nepal trade and economic relations. Delhi: B.R. Publishing Corporation.

Barnard, B. (1984)
Part of life's rich tapestry for the hill tribes is commercialism. *Far Eastern Economic Review*, 30 August: 42-44.

Barnes, T. and M. Curry (1983)
Towards a contextualist approach to geographical knowledge. *Transactions of the Institute of British Geographers*, New Series, vol.8, no.4: 467-482.

REFERENCES

Barpujari, H.K. (1981)
Problem of the hill tribes, north-east frontier, vol.III: Inner Line to McMahon line. Gauhati, Assam: Spectrum Publications.

Barr, P. and R. Desmond (1978)
Simla, a hill station in British India. New York: Charles Scriber's Sons.

Basnet, L.B. (1974)
Sikkim: a short political history. New Delhi: S. Chand and Co.

Beckwith, C.I. (1977)
Tibet and the early medieval florissance in Eurasia. A preliminary note on the economic history of the Tibetan empire. *Central Asiatic Journal*, vol.XXI, no.2: 89-104.

Beckwith, C.I. (1987)
The Tibetan empire in Central Asia: a history of the struggle for great power among the Tibetans, Turks, Arabs, and Chinese during the early Middle Ages. Princeton, N.J.: Princeton University Press.

Bell, C. (1924a)
Tibet past and present. London: Oxford University Press. Reprinted 1968.

Bell, C. (1924b)
A year in Lhasa. *The Geographical Journal*, vol.LXIII, no.2, February: 89-105.

Bell, C. (1928)
The people of Tibet. London: Oxford University Press. Reprinted 1968.

Bell, C. (1931)
The religion of Tibet. London: Oxford University Press. Reprinted 1968.

Bell, C. (1946)
Portrait of the Dalai Lama. London: Collins. Reprinted London: Wisdom Publications 1987.

Benavides, G. (1995)
Giuseppe Tucci, or Buddhology in the age of fascism, D.S. Lopez Jr. (ed.), *Curators of the Buddha. The study of Buddhism under colonialism*: 161-196. Chicago and London: The University of Chicago Press.

Berdoulay, V. (1981)
La formation de l'école française de geographie (1870-1914). Paris: Bibliothèque Nationale.

Berdoulay, V. (1982)
La métaphore organiciste. Contribution à l'étude du langage des geographes. *Annales de Géographie*, Septembre-Octobre: 573-586.

Bernard, T. (1939)
Penthouse of the gods. New York: Charles Scribner's Sons.

Bernatzik, H.A. (1947)
Akha und Meau. Probleme der angewandten Völkerkunde in Hinterindien (two vols.). Innsbruck: Wagner'sche Universitäts-Buchdruckerei.

Berreman, G. (1960)
Cultural variability in the Himalayan hills. *American Anthropologist*, vol.62, 774-794.

Berreman, G. (1963)
Peoples and cultures of the Himalaya. *Asian Survey*, vol.3, no.6: 289-304.

Bhagwati, J.N. (1974)
Illegal transactions in international trade. Amsterdam: North Holland Publishing House.

Bhardwaj, S.M. (1973)
Hindu places of pilgrimage. A study in cultural geography. Berkeley: University of California Press.

Bhargava, G.S. (1964)
The battle of NEFA: the undeclared war. Bombay: Allied Publishers.

Bhatt, D.D. (1977)
Natural history and economic botany of Nepal. New Delhi: Orient Longman.

Bird, I. (1899)
The Yangtze valley and beyond: an account of journeys in China, chiefly in the province of Sze chuan and among the Man-tze of the Somo territory. London: John Murray. Reprinted London: Virago 1985.

Bishop, B.C. (1990)
Karnali under stress. Livelihood strategies and seasonal rhythms in a changing Nepal Himalaya. (Geography Research Paper Nos. 228-229). Chicago: University of Chicago.

Bishop, P. (1989)
The myth of Shangri-La. Tibet, travel writing and the western creation of sacred landscape. London: The Athlone Press.

Bista, D.B. (1971)
The political innovators of upper Kali Gandaki. *Man*, vol.6, no.l: 52-61.

Bista, D.B. (1980)
People of Nepal. Kathmandu: Ratna Pustak Bhandar.

Bjønness, I.-M. (1980)
Animal husbandry and grazing, a conservation and management problem in Sagarmatha (Mt.Everest) National Park. *Norsk Geografisk Tidsskrift*, vol.34, no.1: 59-76.

Bjønness, I.-M. (1983)
External economic dependency and changing human adjustment to marginal environment in the high Himalaya. *Mountain Research and Development*, vol.3, no.3: 263-272.

Blaikie, P., J. Cameron and J.D. Seddon (1977)
Centre, periphery and access in west central Nepal: approaches to social and spatial relations of inequality. Final Report to the Social Science Council (Monographs in Development Studies No.5). Norwich: School of Development Studies, University of East Anglia.

REFERENCES

Blaikie, P., J. Cameron and J.D. Seddon (1980)
Nepal in crisis. Growth and stagnation at the periphery. Oxford: Clarendon Press.

Bloch, M. (1978)
Feudal society (two vols.). London: Routledge and Kegan Paul (original French edition: Paris: Albin Michel 1939, 1940).

Blok, A. (1974)
The Mafia of a Sicilian village, 1860-1960. A study of violent peasant entrepreneurs. New York: Harper and Row.

Blok, A. (1977)
Clio en de antropoloog. In: Brunt, L. (ed.), *Anders bekeken. Wet en werkelijkheid in sociaal onderzoek*: 65-88. Amsterdam: Boom Meppel.

Blondeau, A.M. (1960)
Les pèlerinages tibétains. *Sources Orientales, vol.III - Les pèlerinages*: 203-245. Paris: Éditions du Seuil.

Blondeau, A.M. (1977)
Le Tibet. Aperçu historique et géographique. In: Macdonald, A. and Y.Imaeda (eds.), *Essais sur l'art du Tibet*: 1-22. Paris: Librairie d'Amérique et d'Orient, J. Maisonneuve.

Blunt, E.A.H. (1912)
Census of India 1911, Vol.XV, United Provinces of Agra and Oudh. Allahabad: Luker.

Boeck, K. (1903)
Durch Indien ins verschlossene Land Nepal. Ethnograpische und photographische Studien Blätter. Leipzig: Verlag von Ferdinand Hirt und Sohn.

Bogoslovskij, V.A. (1972)
Essai sur l'histoire du peuple tibétain ou la naissance d'une société de classes. (traduit du russe). Paris: Laboratoire d'Ethnologie et de Sociologie Comparative, Université de Paris X, Nanterre, Librairie C. Klincksieck.

Bonin, C.-E. (1911)
Les royaumes des neiges (états himalayens). Paris: Librairie Armand Colin.

Bonvalot, G. (1980)
De Paris au Tonkin à travers le Tibet inconnu. Paris: Hachette-Stock. Original edition: Paris: Librairie Hachette 1891.

Bosshard, W. (1929)
Politics and trade in Central Asia. *Journal of the Central Asian Society*, vol. XVI, part IV: 433-454.

Bosshard, W. (1950)
Kühles Grassland Mongolei. Zauber und Schönheit der Steppe. Frankfurt am Main: Büchergilde Gutenberg.

Boulnois, L. (1983)
Poudre d'or et monnaies d'argent au Tibet (principalement au XVIIIe siècle). Paris: CNRS.

Bourdé, G. et H. Martin (1983)
L'école des Annales. In: *Les écoles historiques*: 171-226. Paris: Éditions du Seuil.

Bower, H. (1894)
Diary of a journey across Tibet. London: Rivington, Percival. Reprinted Kathmandu: Ratna Pustak Bhandar 1976.

Braudel, F. (1958)
Histoire et sciences sociales: la longue durée. *Annales: Economies, Sociétés, Civilisations*, vol.13: 725-753.

Braudel, F. (1966)
La Méditerranée et le monde méditerranéen à l'époque de Philippe II, (two vols.). Paris: Librairie Armand Colin (seconde édition revue et augmentée).

Braudel, F. (1977)
Afterthoughts on material civilisation and capitalism. Baltimore and London: The Johns Hopkins University Press.

Braudel, F. (1979)
Civilisation matérielle, économie et capitalisme, XVe - XVIIIe siècle (three vols.). Paris: Armand Colin.

Brauen, M. (ed.) (1983)
Peter Aufschnaiter: sein Leben in Tibet. Innsbruck: Steiger Verlag.

Bray, J. (1990)
The Lapchak mission from Ladakh to Lhasa in British Indian foreign policy. *The Tibet Journal*, vol.XV, no.4, Winter: 75-96.

Brower, B. (1991)
Sherpa of Khumbu. Delhi: Oxford University Press.

Brown, C.W. (1984)
'The goat is mine, the load is yours'. Morphogenesis of 'Bhotiya-Shauka', U.P., India. Ph.D. dissertation, University of Lund (Lund Studies in Social Anthropology, No.l).

Bruijne, G.A. de (1976)
Het samenwoningssysteem. Enige geografische overwegingen (Bijdragen tot de Sociale Geografie, no.10). Amsterdam: Geografisch en Planologisch Instituut van de Vrije Universiteit.

Bruneau, M. (1980)
Recherches sur l'organisation de l'espace dans le Nord de la Thailande (two vols.). Thèse présentée devant l'Université de Paris IV, le 10 juin 1977. Atelier Reproduction des Thèses, Université de Lille III, Lille. Paris: Librairie Honoré Champion.

Buchanan, I. (1972)
Singapore in Southeast Asia. London: G. Bell and Sons.

REFERENCES

Burke, P. (1990)
The French historical revolution. The 'Annales' School, 1929-1989. Cambridge: Polity Press.

Burrard, S.G. (1915)
Records of the Survey of India, vol.VIII (in two parts). Dehra Dun: Office of the Trigonometrical Survey.

Buttimer, A. (1971)
Society and milieu in the French geographic tradition. Chicago: Rand McNally (published for the Association of American Geographers).

Buttimer, A. (1976)
Grasping the dynamism of life-world. *Annals of the Association of American Geographers,* vol. 66, no.2: 277-292.

Buttimer, A. (1978)
Charism and context: the challenge of *la géographie humaine.* In: Ley, D. and M. Samuels (eds.), *Humanistic geography: prospects and problems*: 58-76. London: Croom Helm.

Cable, M. et al. (1929)
The challenge of Central Asia. A brief survey of Tibet and its borderlands, Mongolia, North-West Kansu, Chinese Turkistan and Russian Central Asia. London: World Dominion Press.

Calhoun, A.B. (1929)
Burma - an important source of precious and semi-precious stones. *Engineering and Mining Journal,* vol.127, no.18, May 4: 708-712.

Cammann, S. (1951a)
The land of the camel: tents and temples of Inner Mongolia. New York: The Ronald Press Company.

Cammann, S. (1951b)
Trade through the Himalayas: the early attempts to open Tibet. Princeton, New Jersey: Princeton University Press.

Campbell, A. (1849)
Journal of a trip to Sikim. *Journal of the Asiatic Society of Bengal,* vol.XVIII, part I: 482-541.

Campbell, A. (1875)
Note on the Valley of Choombi. *Journal of the Royal Asiatic Society,* N.S., vol. 7: 135-139.

Candler, E. (1905)
The unveiling of Lhasa. London: Edward Arnold. Reprinted Berkeley-Hong Kong: Snow Lion Graphics 1987.

Cantwell, C. (1995)
Rewalsar: Tibetan refugees in a Buddhist sacred place. *The Tibet Journal,* vol.XX, no.1, 3-9.

Carey, A.D. (1887)
A journey round Chinese Turkistan and along the northern frontier of Tibet. *Proceedings of the Royal Geographical Society*, vol. 9, no.12: 731-752.

Carey, W. (1902)
Travel and adventure in Tibet. Including the diary of Miss Annie R. Taylor's remarkable journey from Tau-Chau to Tachienlu through the heart of the Forbidden Land. London: Hodder and Stoughton.

Carrasco, P. (1959)
Land and polity in Tibet. Seattle: University of Washington Press.

Cassinelli, C.W. and R.B. Ekvall (1969)
A Tibetan principality. The political system of Sa sKya. Ithaca, New York: Cornell University Press.

Chakrabarti, P.N. (1990)
Trans-Himalayan trade: a retrorespect, 1774-1914 (in quest of Tibet's identity). Delhi: Classics India Publications.

Chakrabarty, P.B. (1982)
The unknown country of Golok-Setas. *Tibetan Review*, vol. XVII, no.5: 18-20.

Chakravarti, S. (1976)
Overland routes to Tibet from Assam. *Geographical Review of India*, vol.38, no.4: 362-367.

Chandola, K. (1987)
Across the Himalayas. A study of relations between Central Himalayas and Western Tibet. Delhi: Patriot Publishers.

Chaudhuri, K.C. (1960)
Anglo-Nepalese relations. Calcutta: Modern Book Agency.

Chorlton, W. (1982)
Cloud dwellers of the Himalayas. The Bhotia. Amsterdam: Time-Life Books.

Choudhury, D.P. (1977)
British quest for trade routes from Assam to eastern Tibet: 1771-1914. *Asian Affairs*, vol.VIII, part II: 180-184.

Clarke, G.E. (1977)
The merchants of Mugu: a village in the Himalaya. *Journal of the Royal Society of Asian Affairs*, vol. VIII, part III, October: 299-305.

Clarke, G.E. (1980)
The temple and kinship among a Buddhist people of the Himalaya. Ph.D. dissertation, Lincoln College, University of Oxford.

Clarke, G.E. (1987)
China's reforms of Tibet, and their effects on pastoralism. Brighton: Institute of Development Studies. Discussion Paper, No.237.

Clarke, G.E. (1988)
Tibet today: propaganda, record and policy. *Himalayan Research Bulletin*, vol.VIII, no.l: 25-36.

REFERENCES

Claval, P. (1988)
Les géographes français et le monde méditerranéen. *Annales de Géographie*, No.542, Juillet-Août, 97e Année: 385-403.

Clifford, J. and G.E. Marcus (eds.) (1986)
Writing culture. The poetics and politics of ethnography. Berkeley: University of Califonia Press.

Clutterbuck, R. (1973)
Riot and revolution in Singapore and Malaya 1945-1963. London: Faber and Faber.

Coales, O. (1919a)
Eastern Tibet. *The Geographical Journal*, vol.LIII, no.4, April: 228-253.

Coales, O. (1919b)
Economic notes on Eastern Tibet. *The Geographical Journal*, vol.LIV, no.4, October: 242-247.

Coggin Brown, J. (1933)
Ruby mining in Upper Burma. *Far Eastern Review*, vol.XXIX, no.11, November: 512-517.

Coggin Brown, J. (1935)
Gold in Burma and the Shan states. *Far Eastern Review*, vol.XXXI, no.5: 183-188, no.6: 217-221.

Cohen, P.T. (1984)
Opium and the Karen: a study of indebtedness in Northern Thailand. *Journal of Southeast Asian Studies*, vol.XV, no.l: 150-165.

Combe, G.A. (1926)
A Tibetan on Tibet. London: T. Fisher Unwin. Reprinted Kathmandu: Ratna Pustak Bhandar 1975.

Consten, H. (1919-1920)
Weideplätze der Mongolen im Reiche der Chalcha (two vols.). Berlin: Dietrich Reimer.

Cook, B.C.A. (1957)
Burma. London: Her Majesty's Stationery Office.

Cooke, M.T. (1985a)
The people of Nyishang. Identity, tradition and change in the Nepal-Tibet borderland. Ph.D. thesis, University of California, Berkeley.

Cooke, M.T. (1985b)
Social change and status emulation among the Nyishangte of Manang. *Contributions to Nepalese Studies*, vol.13, no.1, Dec.: 45-56.

Cooke, M.T. (1986)
Outposts of trade: migration of the Nyishang traders of Nepal. *Kroeber Anthropological Society Papers*, nos. 65-66: 73-81.

Cooper, T.T. (1871)
Travels of a pioneer of commerce in pigtail and petticoats: Or, an overland journey from China towards India. London: John Murray.

Courtenay, P.P. (1972)
A geography of trade and development in Malaya. London: G. Bell and Sons.

Credner, W. (1935)
Siam. Das Land der Tai. Eine Landeskunde auf Grund eigener Reisen und Forschungen. Stuttgart: J. Engelhorns.

Crosby, O.T. (1904)
Turkestan and a corner of Tibet. *The Geographical Journal*, vol.XXIII, no.6, June: 705-722.

Curtin, P.D. (1984)
Cross-cultural trade in world history. Cambridge: Cambridge University Press.

Curzon, G. (1908)
Frontiers. (Romanes Lecture) Oxford: Clarendon Press.

Cutting, C.S. (1940)
The fire ox and other years. New York: Charles Scribner's Sons.

Dargyay, E. (1972)
Zur Interpretation der mythischen Urgeschichte in den tibetischen Historikern. *Central Asiatic Journal*, vol.XVI, no.3: 161-177.

Das, S.C. (1902)
Journey to Lhasa and Central Tibet. London: John Murray. Reprinted Kathmandu: Ratna Pustak Bhandar 1970.

Datta, C. (1970)
Significance of the shawl-wool trade in western Himalayan politics. *Bengal Past and Present*, vol.84, part I: 16-28.

Datta, C. (1973)
Ladakh and western Himalayan politics: 1819-1848. The Dogra conquest of Ladakh, Baltistan and West Tibet and reactions of other powers. New Delhi: Munshiram Manoharlal.

David-Néel, A. (1953)
Les marchands tibétains. *France-Asie*, vol.IX, no.83, avril: 284-293 (I), vol.IX, no.84, mai: 398-409 (II).

Deasy, H.H.P. (1901)
In Tibet and Chinese Turkestan. London: T. Fisher Unwin.

Deb, A. (1973)
Cooch Behar and Bhutan in the context of the Tibetan trade. *Kailash*, vol.I, no.l: 80-88.

Deb, A. (1976)
Bhutan and India. A study in frontier political relations (1772-1865). Calcutta: Firma KLM.

Denis, J. (1980)
Hong Kong. Paris: Presses Universitaires de France.

REFERENCES

De Rossi Filibeck (1990)
A guide-book to Tsari. In: L. Epstein and R.F. Sherburne (eds.), *Reflections on Tibetan culture*: 1-10. Lewiston: The Edwin Mellen Press.

Desgodins, C.H. (1885)
Le Thibet d'apres la correspondance des missionaires. Paris: Librairie Catholique de l'Oeuvre de Saint-Paul.

Dhondup, K. (1984)
The water-horse and other years. Dharamsala: The Library of Tibetan Works and Archives.

Dhondup, K. (1986)
The water-bird and other years. A history of the Thirteenth Dalai Lama and after. New Delhi: Rangwang Publishers.

Dobremez, J.-F. et al. (1986)
Sociétés, milieux et pratiques d'élévage en Himalaya. *Production Pastorale et Société*, no.19, automne, 2-3.

Dobremez, J.-F. and C. Jest (1969)
Carte écologique du Népal, no.1, Annapurna-Dhaulagiri. Paris-Grenoble: Centre National de la Recherche Scientifique.

Dobremez, J.-F. and C. Jest (1976)
Manaslu: hommes et milieux des vallées du Népal Central. Paris: Éditions du Centre National de la Recherche Scientifique.

Dollfus, P. (1989)
Lieu de neige et de genévriers: organisation sociale et religieuse des communeautés bouddhistes au Ladakh. Paris: Éditions du CNRS.

Donner, W. (1972)
Nepal. Raum, Mensch und Wirtschaft. Wiesbaden: Otto Harrassowitz.

Donner, W. (1978)
The five faces of Thailand. An economic geography. London: C. Hurst.

Doolaard, A. den (1962)
Prinsen, priesters en paria's. Reizen door India en Thailand. Amsterdam: Em. Querido's Uitgeverij.

Dowman, K. (1988)
The power-places of Central Tibet: the pilgrim's guide. London: Routledge and Kegan Paul.

Driver, F. (1988)
The historicity of human geography. *Progress in Human Geography*, vol.12, no.4: 497-506.

Dunbar, G.D.S. (1915)
Abors and Galongs: notes on certain hill tribes of the Indo-Tibetan border. *Memoirs of the Asiatic Society of Bengal*, vol. V, Extra Number. Calcutta: The Asiatic Society.

Duncan, M.H. (1929)
The mountain of silver snow. Cincinnati: Powell and White.

Duncan, M.H. (1952)
The Yangtze and the yak. Adventurous trails in and out of Tibet. Alexandria, Virginia/Ann Arbor, Michigan: Edwards Brothers.

Eberhard, W. (1942)
Kultur und Siedlung der Randvölker Chinas. Leiden: E.J. Brill.

Eden, A. et al. (1972)
Political missions to Bootan. New Delhi: Manjusri. Original edition: 1865.

Edgar, J.H. (1930-1931)
Notes on trade routes converging at Tachienlu. *Journal of the West China Border Research Society*, vol. IV: 5-8.

Edgar, J.W. (1874)
Report on a visit to Sikhim and the Thibetan frontier. Calcutta: Bengal Secretariat Press. Reprinted New Delhi: Manjusri Publishing House 1969.

Eekelen, W.F. van (1964)
Indian foreign policy and the border dispute with China. The Hague: Martinus Nijhoff.

Ekvall, R.B. (1939)
Cultural relations on the Kansu-Tibetan border. Chicago: University of Chicago Press. The University of Chicago Publications in Anthropology, Occasional Papers, No.1.

Ekvall, R.B. (1954)
Some differences in Tibetan land tenure and utilization. *Sinologica*, vol.IV, no.1: 39-48.

Elias, N. (1873)
Narrative of a journey through Western Mongolia, July 1872 to January 1873. *The Journal of the Royal Geographical Society*, vol.43: 108-157.

Ellen, R. (1988)
Persistence and change in the relationship between anthropology and human geography. *Progress in Human Geography*, vol.12, no.2: 229-262.

Elwin, V. (1958)
Myths of the North-East frontier of India. Shillong: North-East Frontier Agency.

Elwin, V. (1959)
India's North-East frontier in the nineteenth century. London: Oxford University Press.

Emmerick, R.E. (1967)
Tibetan texts concerning Khotan. London: Oxford University Press.

English, R. (1985)
Himalayan state formation and the impact of British rule in the nineteenth century. *Mountain Research and Development*, vol.5, no.l: 61-78.

Entrikin, J.N. (1991)
The betweenness of place. Towards a geography of modernity. Baltimore: The Johns Hopkins University Press.

Fairbank, J.K. and S.Y. Têng (1941)
On the Ch'ing tributary system. *Harvard Journal of Asiatic Studies*, vol.VI: 135-246.

Feng Han-yi and J.K. Shryock (1938)
The historical origins of the Lolo. *Harvard Journal of Asiatic Studies*, vol. III, no.1: 103-127.

Fergusson, W.N. (1911)
Adventures, sport and travel on the Tibetan steppes. London: Constable and Co.

Ferrari, A. (1958)
Mk'yen Brtse's guide to the holy places of Central Tibet. (Series Orientale Roma, vol.XVI) Roma: IsMEO.

Field, A.R. (1959)
Himalayan salt. A political barometer. *Modern Review*, vol.105, no.6, June: 460-465.

Filchner, W. (1906)
Das Kloster Kumbum in Tibet. Ein Beitrag zu seiner Geschichte. Berlin: Ernst Siegfried Mittler und Sohn.

Filchner, W. (1929)
Om mani padme hum: meine China und Tibet expedition 1925-28. Leipzig: F.A. Brockhaus.

Filchner, W. (1933)
Kumbum Dschamba Ling. Das Kloster der hunderttausend Bilder Maitreyas. Leipzig: F.A. Brockhaus.

Fisher, C.A. (1964)
Southeast Asia. A social, economic and political geography. London: Methuen.

Fisher, C.A. (1970)
Whither regional geography? *Geography*, vol.55: 373-389.

Fisher, J.F. (1986)
Trans-Himalayan traders. Economy, society and culture in northwest Nepal. Berkeley: University of California Press.

Fisher, J.F. (1990)
Sherpas. Reflections on change in Himalayan Nepal. Berkeley: University of California Press.

Fisher, W.F. (1987)
The re-creation of tradition. Ethnicity, migration, and social change among the Thakali of Central Nepal. Ph.D. dissertation, Columbia University, New York.

Fitzgerald, C.P. (1943)
The northern marches of Yunnan. *The Geographical Journal*, vol.CII, no.2, 1943: 49-56.

Fletcher, H.R. (1975)
A quest of flowers. The plant hunting explorations of Frank Ludlow and George

Sherriff told from their diaries and other occasional writings. Edinburgh: Edinburgh University Press.

Fletcher, J. (1979)
A brief history of the Chinese Northwestern frontier. In: M.E. Alonso (ed.), *China's Inner Asian frontier. Photographs of the Wulsin expedition to Northwest China in 1923*: 21-53. Cambridge, Mass.: The Peabody Museum of Archaeology and Ethnology, Harvard University.

Forbes, A.D.W. (1986)
Warlords and muslims in Chinese Central Asia. A political history of republican Sinkiang 1911-1949. Cambridge: Cambridge University Press.

Forde, C.D. (1934)
Habitat, economy and society. London: Methuen.

Frank, W.A. (1982)
Die 'Tamang'-Sherpa des Langtang-Tals. In: F.W. Funke (Hrsg.), *Die Sherpa und ihre Nachbarn*: 251-278 (Beiträge zur Sherpa-Forschung, Teil VI; Reihe Khumbu Himal 14). Innsbruck: Universitätsverlag Wagner.

Fürer-Haimendorf, C. von (1964)
The Sherpas of Nepal: Buddhist highlanders. London: John Murray.

Fürer-Haimendorf, C.von (1975)
Himalayan traders. Life in highland Nepal. London: John Murray.

Fürer-Haimendorf, C. von (1983)
Bhotia highlanders of Nar and Phu. *Kailash*, vol.10, no.1-2: 63-117.

Fürer-Haimendorf, C. von (1984)
The Sherpas transformed. Social change in a Buddhist society of Nepal. New Delhi: Sterling Publishers.

Fürholzer, E. (1942)
Arro! Arro! So sah ich Tibet. Berlin: Wilhelm Limpert-Verlag.

Fussell, P. (1980)
Abroad. New York: Oxford University Press.

Futterer, K. (1900)
Land und Leute in Nordost-Tibet. *Zeitschrift der Gesellschaft für Erdkunde, Berlin*, vol.35, part 5: 297-341.

Futterer, K. (1903)
Geographische Skizze von Nordost-Tibet. Ergänzungsheft No.143 zu Petermanns Mitteilungen. Gotha: Justus Perthes.

Gaborieau, M. (1973)
Récit d'un voyageur musulman au Tibet (1882-83). Paris: C. Klincksieck, Nanterre: Labethno, Université de Paris X.

Gaige, F.H. (1975)
Regionalism and national unity in Nepal. Berkeley: University of California Press.

REFERENCES

Ganguly, S. (1989)
The Sino-Indian border talks 1981-1989. *Asian Survey*, vol.XXIX, no.12, Dec.: 1123-1135.

Garry, R. (1972)
La géopolitique du Cambodge et la deuxième guerre d'Indochine. In: *Études de géographie tropicale offertes à Pierre Gourou*: 165-182. Paris-La Haye: Mouton.

Geddes, W.R. (1973)
The opium problem in Northern Thailand. In: Ho, R. and E.C. Chapman (eds.), *Studies of contemporary Thailand*: 213-234. Canberra: Australian National University.

Geertz, C. (1980)
Negara. The theatre state in nineteenth century Bali. Princeton: Princeton University Press.

Geiger, T. and F.M. Geiger (1975)
The development progress of Hong Kong and Singapore. London and Basingstoke: Macmillan.

Gerard, A. (1841)
An account of Koonawur, in the Himalaya, etc. London: James Madden and Co.

Ghosh, S. (1977)
Tibet in Sino-Indian relations, 1899-1914. New Delhi: Sterling.

Ghosh, S. (1979)
British penetration of intransigent Tibet. *The Tibet Journal*, vol.4, no.1: 7-16.

Giddens, A. (1979)
Central problems in social theory. London: Macmillan.

Giddens, A. (1984)
The constitution of society. Cambridge: Polity Press.

Gill, W. (1878)
Travels in Western China and on the Eastern border of Tibet. *The Journal of the Royal Geographical Society*, vol.48: 57-172.

Gill, W. (1880)
The river of golden sand. The narrative of a journey through China and Eastern Tibet to Burmah (two vols.). London: John Murray 1880.

Ginsburg, N. (1969)
On the Chinese perception of a world order. In: Kasperson, R.E. and J. Minghi (eds.), *The structure of political geography*: 330-340. London: University of London Press.

Glover, W.W. and J.K. Landon (1980)
Gurung dialects. In: Trail, R.L. et al., *Papers in South-east Asian Linguistics*, No.7: 29-77 (Pacific Linguistic Series, Series A, No.53). Canberra: The Australian National University.

Goldstein, M.C. (1974)
Tibetan speaking agro-pastoralists of Limi: a cultural ecological overview of high-altitude adaptation in the Northwest Himalaya. *Objets et Mondes*, tome XIV, no.4 (hiver): 259-268.

Goldstein, M.C. (1975)
A report on Limi panchayat, Humla District, Karnali Zone. *Contributions to Nepalese Studies*, vol.2, no.2: 89-101.

Goldstein, M.C. (1988)
On the political organization of nomadic pastoralists in Western Tibet: a rejoinder to Cox. *Himalaya Research Bulletin*, vol.VIII, no.3: 15-17.

Goldstein, M.C., with the help of Gelek Rimpoche (1989)
A history of modern Tibet, 1913-1951. Berkeley: University of California Press.

Goldstein, M.C. and C.M. Beall (1989)
Nomads of Western Tibet. The survival of a way of life. London: Serindia Publications.

Goswami, S. (1982)
The opium evil in nineteenth century Assam. *The Indian Economic and Social History Review*, vol. XIX, nos.3-4: 365-376.

Goullart, P. (1957)
Forgotten kingdom. London: RU-John Murray.

Gourou, P. (1953)
L'Asie. Paris: Hachette.

Gourou, P. (1973)
Pour une géographie humaine. Paris: Flammarion.

Graham, D.C. (1924-1925)
A trip to Tachienlu. *Journal of the West China Border Research Society*, vol.II: 33-37.

Greenhut II, F.A. (1982)
The Tibetan frontiers question from Curzon to the Colombo Conference. New Delhi: S. Chand and Co.

Gregory, D. (1981)
Human agency and human geography. *Transactions of the Institute of British Geographers*, New Series, vol.6, no.1: 1-18.

Gregory, J.W. and C.J. Gregory (1923)
To the Alps of Chinese Tibet. London: Seeley Service and Co.

Grenard, F. (1904)
Tibet. The country and its inhabitants. London: Hutchinson and Co. (translated from the original French edition 1904).

Grimshaw, A. (1983)
Celibacy, religion and economic activity in a monastic community of Ladakh. In: Kantowsky, D. and R. Sander (eds.), *Recent research on Ladakh*: 121-134. München: Weltforum Verlag.

REFERENCES

Gruber, U. (1986)
Die Tibetexpeditionen von Ernst Schäfer. *Tibet-Forum*, Vol.5, no.l: 9-12.

Grunfeld, A.T. (1987)
The making of modern Tibet. London: Zed Books.

Grünwedel, A. (1900)
Mythologie des Buddhismus in Tibet und der Mongolei. Leipzig: F.A. Brockhaus. Reprinted Osnabrück: Otto Zeller Verlag 1970.

Guibaut, A. (1947)
Ngolo-Setas, deuxième expedition Guibaut-Liotard au Tibet, 1940. Paris: J. Susse.

Gupta, R. (1975)
Sikkim: the merger with India. *Asian Survey*, vol.15, no.9: 786-799.

Gurung, H.B. (1980)
Vignettes of Nepal. Kathmandu: Sajha Prakashan.

Gurung, N.J. (1976)
An introduction to the socio-economic structure of Manang District. *Kailash*, vol.IV, no.3: 295-310.

Gurung, N.J. (1977a)
Socio-economic structure of Manang village. Unpublished M.A. thesis, Institute of Nepal and Asian Studies, Tribhuvan University, Kathmandu.

Gurung, N.J. (1977b)
An ethnographic note on Nar-Phu valley. *Kailash*, vol.V, no.3: 229-244.

Gurung, S.B. and Prodypto Roy (1980)
District and micro-regional planning: two case studies. In: *Strategic elements of rural development in Nepal*: 1-25. Kathmandu: Centre for Economic Development and Administration, Tribhuvan University.

Gutelman, M. (1974)
L'économie politique du pavot à opium dans le Triangle d'Or. *Études Rurales*, nos. 53-54-55-56: 513-525.

Haarh, E. (1969)
The Yar-Lun dynasty. A study with particular regard to the contribution by myths and legends to the history of Ancient Tibet and the origin and nature of its kings. Copenhagen: G.E.C. Gad's Forlag.

Hackmann, H. (1907)
Vom Omi bis Bhamo. Wanderungen an den Grenzen von China, Tibet und Birma. Berlin: Karl Curtius.

Haenisch, E. (1934-1935)
Die Eroberung des Goldstromlandes in Ost-Tibet. *Asia Major*, vol.X: 262-313.

Hagen, T. (1972)
Nepal. The kingdom in the Himalayas. London: Robert Hale and Company.

Hähnert, E. (1925)
Beiträge zur Siedelungskunde von Tibet. *Mitteilungen des Vereins für Erdkunde zu Dresden*, Band III, Heft 5 und 6: 94-216.

Hall, A.R. (1978)
Preliminary report on the Langtang region. *Contributions to Nepalese Studies*, vol.5, no.2: 51-68.

Hamilton, F.B. (1819)
An account of the kingdom of Nepal and the territories annexed to this dominion by the house of Gorkha. Edinburgh: Archibald Constable and Co. Reprinted New Delhi: Manjusri Publishing House 1971.

Hanbury-Tracy, J. (1938)
Black river of Tibet. London: Frederick Muller Ltd.

Handel-Mazzetti, H. (1927)
Naturbilder aus Südwest-China. Erlebnisse und Eindrücke eines österreichischen Forschers während des Weltkrieges. Wien und Leipzig: Oesterreichischer Bundesverlag.

Hanson-Lowe, J. (1940)
A journey along the Chinese-Tibetan border. *The Geographical Journal*, vol.95, no.5: 357-367.

Harcourt, A.F.P. (1871)
The Himalayan districts of Kooloo, Lahoul and Spiti. London: W.H. Allen. Reprinted Delhi: Vivek Publishing House 1972.

Harrer, H. (1952)
Sieben Jahre in Tibet. Wien: Ullstein.

Harris, C. (1978)
The historical mind and the practice of geography. In: Ley, D. and M. Samuels (eds.), *Humanistic geography: problems and prospects*: 123-137. London: Croom Helm.

Havnevik, H. (n.d., 1990)
Tibetan Buddhist nuns. History, cultural norms and social reality. Oslo: Norwegian University Press.

Hayden, H. and C. Cosson (1927)
Sport and travel in the highlands of Tibet. London: Richard Cobden-Sanderson.

Hedin, S. (1910-1913)
Trans-Himalaya. Discoveries and adventures in Tibet (three vols.). London: Macmillan and Co.

Hedin, S. (1917-1922)
Southern Tibet. Discoveries in former times compared with my own researches in 1906-08 (Band I-IX). Stockholm: Lithographic Institute of the General Staff of the Swedish Army.

Hedin, S. (1922-1923)
Tsangpo Lamas Wallfahrt (two vols.). Leipzig: F.A. Brockhaus.

Heide, S. von der (1988)
The Thakalis of North-Western Nepal. Kathmandu: Ratna Pustak Bhandar.

Heim, A. (1933)
Minya Gongkar. Forschungsreise ins Hochgebirge von Chinesisch Tibet. Bern-Berlin: Verlag Hans Huber.

Henss, M. (1981)
Tibet. Die Kulturdenkmäler. Zürich: Atlantis Verlag.

Hermanns, M. (1949)
Die Nomaden von Tibet. Die sozial-wirtschaftlichen Grundlagen der Hirtenkulturen in A mdo und von Innerasien; Ursprung und Entwicklung der Viehzucht. Wien: Verlag Herold.

Hermanns, M. (1965)
Das National-Epos der Tibeter: gLing König Gesar. Regensburg: Verlag Josef Habbel.

Heron, A.M. (1930)
The gem-stones of the Himalaya. *The Himalayan Journal*, vol.II, April: 21-28.

Heuberger, H. (1956)
Der Weg zum Tscho Oyu. Kulturgeographische Beobachtungen in Ostnepal. *Mitteilungen der Geographische Gesellschaft Wien*, vol.98, no.l: 3-28.

Hexter, J.H. (1972)
Fernand Braudel and the Monde Braudellien. *Journal of Modern History*, vol.44, no.4: 480-539.

Ho Ping-ti (1959)
Studies on the population of China 1368-1953. Cambridge, Mass.: Harvard University Press.

Hoffmann, H. (1950)
Tibets Eintritt in die Universalgeschichte. *Saeculum*, vol.l: 258-279.

Hoffmann, H. (1961)
The religions of Tibet. London: George Allen and Unwin.

Hollander, A.N.J. den (1967)
Social description. The problem of reliability and validity. In: Jongmans, D.G. and P.C. Gutkind (eds.), *Anthropologists in the field*: 1-34. Assen: Van Gorcum.

Hooker, J.D. (1855)
Himalayan journals. Notes of a naturalist in Bengal, the Sikkim and Nepal Himalayas, the Khasia mountains, etc. London: John Murray.

Hopkirk, P. (1990)
The Great Game. On secret service in High Asia. London: John Murray.

Hosie, A. (1890)
Three years in Western China. A narrative of three journeys in Ssu-ch'uan, Kuei-chow, and Yun-nan. New York: Dodd, Mead and Co.

Hosie, A. (1905)
Report on a journey to the eastern frontier of Thibet. London: His Majesty's Stationery Office.

Hoyanagi, M. (1975)
Natural changes of the region along the old Silk Road in the Tarim basin in historical times. *Memoirs of the Research Department of the Toyo Bunko*, vol.33: 85-113.

Huber, T. (1994)
Why can't women climb Pure Crystal Mountain? Remarks on gender, ritual and space at Tsari. In: P. Kvaerne (ed.), *Tibetan Studies*, vol.I: 350-371. Oslo: ICHRC.

Huber, T. (1997)
A guide to the La-phyi mandala. History, landscape and ritual in South-western Tibet. In: A.W. Macdonald (ed.), *Mandala and landscape*: 233-286. New Delhi: DK Printworld.

Huc, E.-R. and J.Gabet (1928)
Travels in Tartary, Thibet and China, 1844-1846. With a foreword by Paul Pelliot. London: George Routledge and Sons. Translated from the original French edition (1850). Reprinted New York: Dover Publications 1987.

Humlum, J. (1981)
Macao: the earliest European settlement in China. *Fennia*, no.159, 1: 85-91.

Huttenback, R.A. (1975)
The 'Great Game' in the Pamirs and the Hindu-Kush: the British conquest of Hunza and Nagar. *Modern Asian Studies*, vol.9, no.1: 1-29.

Iggers, G.G. (1975)
The Annales tradition - French historians in search of a science of history. In: Iggers, G.G., *New directions in European historiography*: 43-79. Middletown, Connecticut: Wesleyan University.

Iijima, S. (1977)
Ecology, economy, and cultural change among the Thakalis in the Himalayas of Central Nepal. In: S. Iijima (ed.), *Changing aspects of modern Nepal relating to ecology, agriculture and her people*: 69-92. Tokyo: Institute for the Study of Languages and Cultures of Asia and Africa.

Iijima, S. (1982)
The Thakalis: traditional and modern. In: D.B. Bista a.o., *Anthropological and linguistic studies of the Gandaki area in Nepal*: 21-39. Tokyo: Institute for the Study of Languages and Cultures of Asia and Africa.

Jackson, D.P. (1976)
The early history of Lo (Mustang) and Ngari. *Contributions to Nepalese Studies*, vol.4, no.l: 39-56

Jackson, D.P. (1978)
Notes on the history of Se-rib, and nearby places in the Upper Kali Gandaki. *Kailash*, vol.VI, no.3: 195-227.

Jackson, D.P. (1984)
The Mollas of Mustang. Dharamsala: Library of Tibetan Works and Archives.

Jacquemont, V. (1843)
Correspondance de V. Jacquemont avec sa famille et plusieurs de ses amis pendant son voyage dans l'Inde (1828-1832). Bruxelles: Wouters, Raspoet et Cie, Imprimeurs-Libraires (nouvelle édition).

Jest, C. (1964-1965)
Les Thakali. Note préliminaire concernant une ethnie du Nord-Ouest du Népal. *L'Ethnographie*, N.S., no.58-59: 26-49.

Jest, C. (1974)
Tarap. Une vallée dans l'Himalaya. Paris: Le Seuil.

Jest, C. (1975)
Dolpo. Communeautés de langue tibétaine du Nepal. Paris: Éditions du CNRS.

Jest, C. (1987)
Valeurs d'échange en Himalaya et au Tibet: l'ambre et le musc. In: *De la voûte céleste au terroir, du jardin au foyer*: 227-238. Paris: Éditions de l'Ecole des Hautes Études en Sciences Sociales.

Jones, S. (1996)
Tibetan nomads. Environment, pastoral economy, and material culture. London: Thames and Hudson.

Jong, M. de (1995)
Carolingian monasticism: the power of prayer. In: *The New Cambridge Medieval History*, vol. II, 622-653. Cambridge: Cambridge University Press.

Karan, P.P. (1976)
The changing face of Tibet. The impact of Chinese communist ideology on the landscape. Lexington: The University Press of Kentucky.

Kater, M.H. (1974)
Das 'Ahnenerbe' der SS 1935-1945. Ein Beitrag zur Kulturpolitik des Dritten Reiches. Stuttgart: Deutsche Verlags-Anstalt.

Kaulback, R. (1937)
Eighteen months in south-eastern Tibet. *Journal of the Royal Central Asian Society*, vol.24, part 4: 551-566.

Kaulback, R. (1939)
Salween. Expedition into South Eastern Tibet. New York: Harcourt, Brace and Co.

Kawaguchi, E. (1909)
Three years in Tibet. Madras: The Theosophist Office. Reprinted Kathmandu: Ratna Pustak Bhandar 1979.

Kawakita, J. (1957)
Peoples of Nepal Himalaya. In: Kihara, H. (ed.), *Scientific results of the Japanese expeditions to Nepal Himalaya*, vol.III. Kyoto: Fauna and Flora Research Society.

Kearns, G. (1988)
History, geography and world-systems theory. *Journal of Historical Geography*, vol.14, no.3: 281-292.

Kessler, P. (1983)
Die historischen Königreiche Ling und Derge. (Laufende Arbeiten zu einem ethnohistorischen Atlas Tibets (EAT), Lieferung 40.1). Rikon, Zürich: Tibet Institut.

Khazanov, A.M. (1984)
Nomads and the outside world. Cambridge: Cambridge University Press.

Kim, H. (1986)
The Muslim rebellion and the Kashgar emirate in Chinese Central Asia, 1864-1877. Ph.D. dissertation, Harvard University, Cambridge, Massachusetts.

Kingdon Ward, F. (1913)
The land of the blue poppy. Travels of a naturalist in Eastern Tibet. Cambridge: Cambridge University Press. Reprinted with an introduction by Geoffrey Smith: London: Cadogan Books 1986.

Kingdon Ward, F. (1927)
The overland route from China to India. *Journal of the Central Asian Society*, vol.XIV, part III: 213-226.

Kingdon Ward, F. (1936)
Botanical and geographical exploration in Tibet, 1935. *The Geographical Journal*, vol.LXXXVIII, no.5, November: 385-413.

Kingdon Ward, F. (1938)
The Assam Himalaya. Travels in Balipara. *Journal of the Royal Central Asian Society*, vol.XXV: 610-619.

Kingdon Ward, F. (1948)
Tibet as a grazing land. *The Geographical Journal*, vol.CX, nos.1-3: 60-75.

Kinser, S. (1981)
'Annaliste' paradigm? The geohistorical structuralism of Fernand Braudel. *American Historical Review*, vol.86: 63-105.

Kirby, A.M. (1986)
Le monde braudellien. *Society and Space*, vol.4: 211-219.

Kirk, W. (1962)
The Inner Asian frontier of India. *Transactions and Papers of the Institute of British Geographers*, vol.31: 131-168.

REFERENCES

Kish, G. (1984)
To the heart of Asia: the life of Sven Hedin. Ann Arbor: The University of Michigan Press.

Klieger, P.C. (1989)
Ideology and the framing of Tibetan history. *The Tibet Journal*, vol.XIV, no.4: 3-16.

Klimberg, M. (1982)
The setting. The Western Trans-Himalayan crossroads. In: D.E. Klimberg-Salter (ed.), *The silk route and the diamond path. Esoteric Buddhist art on the Trans-Himalayan trade routes*: 24-37. Los Angeles: UCLA Art Council.

Köhler, G. (1952)
Die Bedeutung des Huang Ho innerhalb des nordwest-chinesischen Verkehrsnetzes. *Petermanns Geographische Mitteilungen*, vol.96: 85-89.

Koirala, T.P. (1981)
Manang: an introduction (in Nepali). Kathmandu: The Royal Nepal Academy.

Kolmas, J. (1967)
Tibet and imperial China. A survey of Sino-Tibetan relations up to the end of the Manchu dynasty in 1912. Canberra: The Australian National University, Centre of oriental Studies.

Kommers, J. (1987)
Antropologie en reisliteratuur. *Focaal. Tijdschrift voor Antropologie*, Februari: 15-50.

Kouwenhoven, A.O. (1979)
Perspectief op de cultuur van de geografie. Amsterdam: Vrije Universiteit.

Kozlow, P.K. (1925)
Mongolei, Amdo und die tote Stadt Chara-choto. Die Expedition der Russischen Geographischen Gesellschaft 1907-1909 (autorisierte Uebersetzung aus dem Russischen). Berlin: Verlag Neufeld und Henius.

Kreitner, G. (1881)
Im fernen Osten. Reisen des Grafen Bela Szechenyi in Indien, Japan, China, Tibet und Birma in den Jahren 1877-1880. Wien: Alfred Holder.

Kristof, L.K.D. (1959)
The nature of frontiers and boundaries. *Annals of the Association of American Geographers*, vol.49: 269-282.

Kroef, J.M. van der (1968)
The Sarawak-Indonesian border insurgency. *Journal of Modern Asian Studies*, vol.II, no.3: 245-265.

Kuo, T. (1941)
A brief history of the trade routes between Burma, Indochina, and Yunnan. *T'ien Hsia Monthly*, vol.12: 9-32.

Kvaerne, P. (1987)
The beggar from Amdo (book review). *The Tibet Journal*, vol.XII, no.3: 68-74.

Lamb, A. (1960)
Britain and Chinese Central Asia. The road to Lhasa (1767-1905). London: Routledge and Kegan Paul.

Lamb, A. (1964)
The China-India border. The origins of the disputed boundaries. London: Oxford University Press.

Lamb, A. (1986)
British India and Tibet, 1766-1910. London and New York: Routledge and Kegan Paul.

Lamb, A. (1989)
Tibet, China and India 1914-1950. A history of imperial diplomacy. Hertingfordbury, Hertfordshire: Roxford Books.

Lambert, E.T.D. (1937)
From the Brahmaputra to the Chindwin. *The Geographical Journal*, vol. LXXXVIII, no.4, April: 309-326.

Lamour, C. and M.R. Lamberti (1972)
Les grandes manoeuvres de l'opium. Paris: Éditions du Seuil.

Lattimore, O. (1928)
Caravan routes of Inner Asia. *The Geographical Journal*, vol.LXXII, no.6, December (reprinted in : 0. Lattimore, Studies in frontier history. Collected papers 1928-1958: 37-72. London: Oxford University Press 1962).

Lattimore, O. (1951)
Inner Asian frontiers of China. (American Geographical Society Research Series, no.21). Irvington-on-Hudson: Capitol Publishing Comp., and New York: American Geographical Society (original edition: 1940).

Lawrence, C.H. (1989)
Medieval monasticism. Forms of religious life in Western Europe in the Middle Ages. London: Longman (second edition).

Learner, F.D. (1933)
Rusty hinges. A story of closed doors beginning to open in North-East Tibet. London: China Inland Mission.

Legendre, A.-F. (1910)
Le far-west chinois. Vol.II - Kientchang et Lolotie (chinois, lolos, sifans). Paris: Librairie Plon.

Leur, J.C. van (1955)
Indonesian trade and society. Essays in Asian social and economic history. The Hague/Bandung: W. van Hoeve.

Lévi, S. (1905-1908)
Le Népal. Etude historique d'un royaume hindou. Paris: Ernest Leroux (Annales du Musée Guimet, tomes 17,18,19).

Levine, N.E. (1988)
The dynamics of polyandry. Kinship, domesticity, and population on the Tibetan border. Chicago and London: The University of Chicago Press.

Lewin, T.H. (1879)
The trade routes from Bengal to Tibet. *Proceedings of the Royal Geographical Society*, vol.I, no.10, October: 680-682.

Lewis, T.T. (1984)
The Tuladhars of Kathmandu: a study of Buddhist tradition in a Newar merchant community. Ph.D. dissertation, Columbia University, New York.

Ley, D. and M. Samuels (eds.) (1978)
Humanistic geography: prospects and problems. London: Croom Helm.

Li, T.T. (1956)
The historical status of Tibet. New York: Columbia University Press.

Li An-che (1948)
Our pilgrimage to a Tibetan sacred mountain. *Asian Horizon*, vol.2, summer: 39-48.

Li An-che (1982)
Labrang. A study in the field (edited by Chie Nakane). Tokyo: Institute of Oriental Culture, the University of Tokyo.

Limberg, W. (1982)
Untersuchungen über Siedlung, Landbesitz und Feldbau in Solu-Khumbu (Beiträge zur Sherpa-Forschung, Teil V, Khumbu Himal, Band 12). Innsbruck: Universitätsverlag Wagner.

Limpricht, W. (1922)
Botanische Reisen in den Hochgebirgen Chinas und Osttibet. Dahlem bei Berlin: Verlag des Repertorium.

Lindegger, P. (1982)
Griechische und Römische Quellen zum peripheren Tibet. Band II 'Ueberlieferungen von Herodot bis zu den Alexanderhistorikern. (Die nördlichsten Grenzregionen Indiens). (Opuscula Tibetana: Fasc.14). Rikon, Zürich: Tibet-Institut.

Ling, T. (1985)
Max Weber and the relation of religious to social change: some considerations from Sikkim and Nepal. *Journal of Developing Studies*, vol.I, fasc.2, Dec.: 237-250.

Lipman, J.N. (1981)
The border world of Gansu, 1895-1935. Ph.D. dissertation, Stanford University.

Lockard, C.A. (1973)
The Southeast Asian town in historical perspective: a social history of Kuching,

Malaysia, 1820-1970. Ph.D. dissertation, University of Wisconsin, Madison, Wisconsin.

Longman Dictionary (1988)
Longman dictionary of the English language. London: Longman.

Louis, J.A.H. (1894)
The gates of Thibet. Calcutta: Catholic Orphan Press. Reprinted Delhi: Vivek Publishing House 1972.

Loup, R. (1953)
Martyr au Thibet: Maurice Tornay, chanoine régulier du Grand-StBernard 1910-1949. Fribourg: Éditions Grand-St-Bernard-Thibet.

Ludlow, F. (1938)
The sources of the Subansiri and Siyom. *The Himalayan Journal*, vol.X, no.1: 1-21.

Maanen, J. van (1988)
Tales of the field. On writing ethnography. Chicago and London: The University of Chicago Press.

Macaulay, C. (1885)
Report of a mission to Sikkim and the Tibetan frontier. Calcutta: Bengal Secretariat Press. Reprinted Kathmandu: Ratna Pustak Bhandar 1977.

Macdonald, A. (1971)
Une lecture des P.T. 1286, 1287, 1038, 1047, 1290. Essai sur la formation et l'emploi des mythes politiques dans la religion royale de Sron Bcan sgampo. In: *Études tibétaines dédiées à la mémoire de Marcelle Lalou*: 190-391. Paris: Adrien Maisonneuve.

Macdonald, A.W. (1974)
Sociology and anthropology in Nepal. In: Sharma, P.R. (ed.), *Social science in Nepal*: 27-38. Kathmandu: Institute of Nepal and Asian Studies, Tribhuvan University.

Macdonald, A.W. (ed.) (1982)
Les royaumes de l'Himâlaya; histoire et civilisation. Paris: Imprimerie Nationale.

Macdonald, A.W. (1985)
Points of view on Halase, a holy place in East Nepal. *The Tibet Journal*, vol.X, no.3: 3-13.

Macdonald, A.W. (1987)
Remarks on the manipulation of power and authority in the High Himalaya. *The Tibet Journal*, vol.XII, no.1: 3-16.

Macdonald, A.W. (1990)
Hindu-isation, Buddha-isation, then Lama-isation or: what happened at La-phyi? In: T.Skorupski (ed.), *Indo-Tibetan studies*: 199-208. Tring: Institute of Buddhist Studies.

Macdonald, A.W. (ed.) (1997)
Mandala and landscape. New Delhi: DK Printworld.

REFERENCES

Macdonald, A.W. et al. (1982)
Les royaumes de l'Himalaya. Histoire et civilisation. Paris: Imprimerie Nationale.

Macdonald, D. (1929)
The land of the lama. London: Seeley Service and Co.

Macfarlane, A. (1976)
Resources and population. A study of the Gurungs of Nepal. Cambridge: Cambridge University Press.

Mackenzie, A. (1884)
A history of the relations of the Government with the hills tribes of the North-East frontier of Bengal. Calcutta: Home Department Press. Reprinted New Delhi: Mittal Publications 1979.

McCoy, A.W. (1973)
The politics of heroin in Southeast Asia. New York: Harper and Row.

McKay, A.C. (1992)
The establishment of the British trade agencies in Tibet: a survey. *Journal of the Royal Asiatic Society*, Series 3, vol.2, no.3, 399-421.

McKay, A.C. (1997)
Tibet and the British Raj. The frontier cadre 1904-1947. London: Curzon Press.

McKay, A.C. (ed.) (1998)
Pilgrimage in Tibet. London: Curzon Press.

Maillart, E. (1937)
Oasis interdites. De Pékin au Cachemire. Paris: Éditions Bernard Grasset.

Manandhar, N.P. (1980)
Medicinal plants of Nepal Himalaya. Kathmandu: Ratna Pustak Bhandar.

Mansier, P. (1990)
La guerre du Jinchuan (rGyal-rong): son contexte politico-religieux. In: *Tibet: civilisation et société*: 125-142. Paris: Éditions de la Fondation Singer-Polignac, Éditions de la Maison des Sciences de l'Homme.

Manzardo, A.E. (1977)
Ecological constraints on Trans-Himalayan trade in Nepal. *Contributions to Nepalese Studies*, vol.4, no.2: 63-81.

Manzardo, A.E. (1978)
To be kings of the north: community, adaptation and impression management in the Thakali of Western Nepal. Ph.D. dissertation, University of Wisconsin, Madison.

Manzardo, A.E. (1982)
Impression management and economic growth: the case of the Thakalis of Dhaulagiri zone. *Kailash*, vol.IX, no.1, 45-60.

Manzardo, A.E., D.R. Dahal and K. Rai (1976)
The Byanshi: an ethnographic note on a trading group in Far Western Nepal. *Contributions to Nepalese Studies*, vol.3, no.2: 84-118.

Maraini, F. (1954)
Secret Tibet. London: Readers Union-Hutchinson (translated from the Italian).

Marco Polo (1982)
The travels of Marco Polo (translated and with an introduction by Ronald Latham). Harmondsworth: Penguin Books.

Markham, C.R. (1875)
Travels in Great Tibet, and trade between Tibet and Bengal. *The Journal of the Royal Geographical Society*, vol.45: 299-315.

Markham, C.R. (1876)
Narratives of the mission of George Bogle to Tibet and of the journey of Thomas Manning to Lhasa. London: Trübner and Co. Reprinted New Delhi: Manjusri Publishing House 1971.

Martin, D. (1990)
Bonpo canons and Jesuit cannons: on sectarian factors involved in the Ch'ien-lung emperor's second goldstream expedition of 1771-1776 based primarily on some Tibetan sources. *The Tibet Journal*, vol. XV, no.2, 3-28.

Mazaudon, M. (1978)
Consonantal mutation and tonal split in the Tamang sub-family of Tibeto-Burman. *Kailash*, vol.VI, no.3: 157-179.

Mead, W.R. (1963)
The adoption of other lands. *Geography*, vol.48: 241-254.

Mehra, P. (1958)
Tibet and Russian intrigue. *Journal of the Royal Central Asian Society*, vol.45, no.l: 28-42.

Mehra, P. (1968a)
The Younghusband expedition: an interpretation. London: Asia Publishing House.

Mehra, P. (1968b)
Sikkim and Bhutan: an historical conspectus. *Journal of Indian History*, vol.46: 89-124.

Mehra, P. (1969)
The Mongol-Tibetan treaty of January 11, 1913. *Journal of Asian History*, vol.III, no.l: 1-2.

Mehra, P. (1974)
The McMahon line and after. A study of the triangular contest on India's North-eastern frontier between Britain, China and Tibet, 1904-47. Delhi: Macmillan.

Mehra, P. (1976)
Tibetan polity, 1904-37. The conflict between the 13th Dalai Lama and the 9th Panchen. Wiesbaden: Otto Harrassowitz.

Mehra, P. (1979-80)
The North-Eastern frontier: a documentary study of the internecine rivalry between India, Tibet and China (two vols.). Delhi: Oxford University Press.

Messerschmidt, D.A. (1978)
Dhikurs: rotating credit associations in Nepal. In: J.F.Fisher (ed.), *Himalayan anthropology*: 141-165. The Hague-Paris: Mouton.

Messerschmidt, D.A. (1982)
Miteri in Nepal: fictive kin ties that bind. *Kailash*, vol.IX, no.1: 5-43.

Messerschmidt, D.A. and N.J. Gurung (1974)
Parallel trade and innovation in Central Nepal: the cases of the Gurung and Thakali subbas compared. In: C. von Fürer-Haimendorf (ed.), *Contributions to the anthropology of Nepal*: 197-221. Warminster: Aris and Phillips.

Middleton, R. (1989)
Alexandra David-Neel. Portrait of an adventurer. Boston and Shaftesbury: Shambhala.

Migot, A. (no date)
Caravane vers Bouddha. Un français à travers la Haute-Asie mystique. Paris: CAL (1961). Édition revue par l'auteur.

Mikesell, M.W. (1978)
Tradition and innovation in cultural geography. *Annals of the Association of American Geographers*, vol.68, no.1: 1-16.

Miles, D. (1973)
Some demographic implications of regional commerce: the case of North Thailand's Yao minority. In: Ho, R. and E.C. Chapman (eds.), *Studies of contemporary Thailand*: 253-272. Canberra: Australian National University.

Miller, B.D. (1961)
The web of Tibetan monasticism. *Journal of Asian Studies*, vol.20, no.2: 197-203.

Miller, R.J. (1961)
Buddhist monastic economy and the Jisa mechanism. *Comparative Studies in Society and History*, vol.3: 427-438, Comment 439-442.

Miller, R.J. (1965)
High altitude mountaineering, cash economy and the Sherpa. *Human Organization*, vol.24, no.3: 244-249.

Mills, J.P. (1950)
Problems of the Assam-Tibet frontier. *Journal of the Royal Central Asian Society*: 152-161.

Moorcroft, W. (1818)
A journey to Lake Mánasaróvara in Un-dés, a province of little Tibet. *Asiatick Researches*, vol.12: 380-536.

Moorcroft, W. and G. Trebeck (1841)
Travels in the Himalayan provinces of Hindustan and the Panjab, in Ladakh

and Kashmir, in Peshawar, Kabul, Kunduz and Bokhara (two vols.). London: John Murray. Reprinted Karachi: Oxford University Press, 1979.

Morgan, G. (1981)
Anglo-Russian rivalry in Central Asia, 1810-95. London: Frank Cass.

Morris, C.J. (1923)
The gorge of the Arun. *The Geographical Journal,* vol.LXII: 161-173.

Morris, C.J. (1935)
A journey to Bhutan. *The Geographical Journal,* vol.LXXXVI, no.3: 201-217.

Morris, C.J. (1963)
A winter in Nepal. London: Rupert Hart-Davis.

Mortari Vergara, P. et G. Béguin (eds.) (1987)
Demeures des hommes, sanctuaires des dieux. Sources, développement et rayonnement de l'architecture tibétaine. Roma: Università di Roma 'La Sapienza', Dipartimento di Studi Orientali.

Mullin, C. (1975)
Tibetan conspiracy. *Far Eastern Economic Review,* September 5: 30-34.

Mumford, L. (1961)
The city in history. New York and London: Harcourt, Brace, Jovanovich.

Mumford, S.R. (1989)
Himalayan dialogue. Tibetan lamas and Gurung shamans in Nepal. Madison: The University of Wisconsin Press.

Mus, P. (1977)
L'angle de l'Asie. Paris: Hermann (Collection Savoir).

National Planning Commission (1975)
Population Census 1971. Kathmandu: Central Bureau of Statistics.

National Planning Commission (1988)
Statistical Pocket Book Nepal 1988. Kathmandu: Central Bureau of Statistics.

Narzounof, O. (1904)
Trois voyages à Lhassa (1898-1901). Présentés par J. Deniker. *Le Tour du Monde,* vol.10, 1904, no.19: 217-228, no.20: 229-240.

Nath, T. (1975)
The Nepalese dilemma, 1960-1974. New Delhi: Sterling Publishers.

Neyroud, M. (1985)
Organisation de l'espace, isolement et changement dans le domaine transhimalayen: le Zanskar. *L'Espace Géographique,* vol., no.4: 271-284.

Nishi, Y. (1982)
Five Swadesh l00-word lists for the Ghale language: a report on the trek in the Ghale speaking area in Nepal. In: Bista, D.B., S. Iijima, H. Ishii, Y. Nagano, Y. Nishi, *Anthropological and linguistic studies of the Gandaki area in Nepal*: 158-194. Tokyo: Institute for the Study of Languages and Cultures of Asia and Africa.

Noranitipadungkarn, C. and Hagensick, A.C. (1973)
Modernizing Chiengmai: a study of community elites in urban development. Bangkok: National Institute of Development Administration.

Norbu, D. (1985)
An analysis of Sino-Tibetan relationships, 1245-1911: imperial power, noncoercive regime and military dependency. In: Aziz, B.N. and M. Kapstein, *Soundings in Tibetan civilization*: 176-195. New Delhi: Manohar.

Norbu, D. (1990)
The Europeanization of Sino-Tibetan relations, 1775-1907: the genesis of Chinese 'suzerainty' and Tibetan 'autonomy'. *The Tibet Journal*, vol.XV, no.4, Winter: 28-74.

Norbu, J. (1986)
Warriors of Tibet. The story of Aten and the Khampas' fight for the freedom of their country. London: Wisdom Publications.

Norbu, N. (1983)
A journey into the culture of Tibetan nomads (Tibetan text; a translation is being made at the Library of Tibetan Works and Archives). Arcidosso: ShangShung Edizioni.

Nyman, L.E. (1976)
Tawang - a case study of British frontier policy in the Himalayas. *Journal of Asian History*, vol.10, no.2: 151-171.

Nyman, L.E. (1977)
Great Britain and Chinese, Russian and Japanese interests in Sinkiang, 1918-1934. Malmö: Lund Studies in International History, no. 8.

Nyman, L.E. (1983)
Modernisierungsversuche in Tibet während der Zwischenkriegszeit. *Central Asiatic Journal*, vol.27, no.1-2: 101-111.

Oldfield, H.A. (1880)
Sketches from Nipal (two vols.). London: W.H. Allen. Reprinted Delhi: Cosmo Publications 1974.

Onon, U. and D. Pritchatt (1989)
Asia's first modern revolution. Mongolia proclaims its independence in 1911. Leiden: E.J. Brill.

Ooi Jin-Bee (1963)
Land, people and economy in Malaya. London: Longmans.

Oppitz, M. (1968)
Geschichte und Sozialordnung der Sherpa (Beiträge zur Sherpa-Forschung, Teil I, Khumbu Himal, Band 8). Innsbruck-München: Universitätsverlag Wagner.

d'Ollone, H.M.G. (1911)
Les derniers barbares. Chine - Tibet - Mongolie (Mission d'Ollone 1906-1909). Paris: Pierre Lafitte. Reprinted Paris: Éditions You-feng 1988.

d'Orléans, H. (1898)
Du Tonkin aux Indes, janvier 1895-janvier 1896. Paris: Calmann Lévy.

Ortner, S.B. (1978)
The Sherpas through their rituals. Cambridge: Cambridge University Press.

Ortner, S.B. (1989)
High religion: a cultural study and political history of Sherpa Buddhism. Princeton, New Jersey: Princeton University Press.

Ossendowski, F. (1922)
Beasts, men and gods. London: Edward Arnold.

Paassen, C. van (1957)
The classical tradition of geography. Groningen: J.B. Wolters.

Paassen, C. van (1976)
Human geography in terms of existential anthropology. *Tijdschrift voor Economische en Sociale Geografie*, vol, 67, no.6: 324-341.

Paassen, C. van (1981)
The philosophy of geography. From Vidal to Hägerstrand. In: Pred, A. (ed.), *Space and time in geography. Essays dedicated to Torsten Hägerstrand*: 17-29. Lund: Gleerup.

Paassen, C. van (1982)
Het begin van 75 jaar sociale geografie in Nederland. Amsterdam: Sociaal-Geografisch Insituut, Universiteit van Amsterdam.

Paassen, C. van (1991)
Some points for discussion about 'Regional Geography' (unpublished note).

Pallis, M. (1949)
Peaks and lamas. New York: Alfred A. Knopf (3rd and definitive edition).

Pant, M.R. and P.H. Pierce (eds.) (1989)
Administrative documents of the Shah dynasty concerning Mustang and its periphery (1789-1844 A.D.). Bonn: VGH Wissenschafts-verlag.

Pant, S.D. (1935)
The social economy of the Himalayans. London: George Allen and Unwin.

Pant, Y.P. (1964)
Nepal's recent trade policy. *Asian Survey*, vol.IV, no.7: 947-957.

Parker, B. (1985)
The spirit of wealth: culture of entrepreneurship among the Thakali of Nepal. Ph.D. dissertation, University of Michigan.

Parker, B. (1988)
Moral economy, political economy, and the culture of entrepreneurship in highland Nepal. *Ethnology*, vol.XXVII, no.2: 181-194.

Paterson, J.H. (1974)
Writing regional geography. *Progress in Geography*, vol.6, no.1: 1-27.

Patterson, G.N. (1990)
Requiem for Tibet. London: Aurum Press

REFERENCES

Peissel, M. (1972)
Les cavaliers de Kham. Paris: Éditions Robert Laffont.

Pelliot, P. (1904)
Deux itinéraires de Chine en Inde à la fin du VIIIe siècle. *Bulletin de l'École Française d'Extrême-Orient*, tome IV, janvier-juin, 131-413. Hanoi: F.H. Schneider.

Pendleton, R.L. (1962)
Thailand: aspects of landscape and life. New York: Duell, Sloane and Pearce.

Petech, L. (1950)
The missions of Bogle and Turner according to the Tibetan texts. *T'oung Pao*, vol.39, no.4-5: 330-346.

Petech, L. (1972)
China and Tibet in the early XVIIIth century. History of the establishment of Chinese protectorate in Tibet. Leiden: E.J. Brill (second, revised edition).

Petech, L. (1976)
China and the European travellers to Tibet, 1860-1880. *T'oung Pao*, vol.LXII, no. 4-5: 219-252.

Petech, L. (1977)
The kingdom of Ladakh, c.950-1842 A.D. Rome: IsMEO.

Petech, L. (1983)
Tibetan relations with Sung China and with the Mongols. In: Rossabi, M. (ed.), *China among equals*. Berkeley and Los Angeles: University of California Press.

Petech, L. (1984)
Mediaeval history of Nepal (c. 750-1482). Roma: IsMEO (second, thoroughly revised edition).

Petech, L. (1990)
Central Tibet and the Mongols. The Yüan-Sa-skya period of Tibetan history. Rome: IsMEO.

Pickles, J. (1985)
Phenomenology, science and geography. Cambridge: Cambridge University Press.

Pignède, B. (1966)
Les Gurungs. Une population himalayenne du Népal. Paris-La Haye: Mouton. Annotated English translation by S. Harrison and A. Macfarlane: *The Gurungs. A Himalayan population of Nepal*. Kathmandu: Ratna Pustak Bhandar 1993.

Pirenne, H. (1969)
Histoire économique et sociale du moyen âge. Paris: Presses Universitaires de France (original edition 1933).

Pohle, P. (1986)
High altitude populations of the remote Nepal-Himalaya. Environmental knowledge and adaptive mechanisms (a study of Manang District. In: K.

Seeland (ed.), *Recent research on Nepal*: 113-139. München-Köln: Weltforum Verlag.

Pohle, P. (1988)
The adaptation of house and settlement to high mountain environment. A study of the Manang District in the Nepal Himalaya. *Journal of the Nepal Research Centre*, vol. VIII: 67-103.

Pohle, P. (1990)
Useful plants of Manang District. A contribution to the ethnobotany of the Nepal Himalaya (Nepal Research Centre Publications, No.16). Stuttgart: Franz Steiner Verlag Wiesbaden.

Polanyi, K. (1957)
The economy as instituted process. In: Polanyi, K. (ed.), *Trade and market in early empires*, 243-270. Glencoe: The Free Press.

Pradhan, K. (1991)
The Gorkha Conquests. The process and consequences of the unification of Nepal, with particular reference to Eastern Nepal. Calcutta: Oxford University Press.

Pradhananga, U.B. (1980)
An overview of Nepal's foreign trade. *Management Dynamics*, vol.I, no.1: 15-30.

Pranavananda, Swami (1950)
Exploration in Tibet. Calcutta: University of Calcutta.

Prasad, R.R. (1989)
Bhotia tribals of India. Dynamics of economic transformation. New Delhi: Gian Publishing House.

Pratt, A.E. (1892)
To the snows of Tibet through China. London: Longmans Green. Reprinted New Delhi: Mittal 1987.

Pred, A. (1984)
Place as a historically contingent process: structuration and time-geography. *Annals of the Association of American Geographers*, vol.74, no.3: 279-297.

Pred, A. (1990)
Making histories and constructing human geographies. Boulder, Co.: Westview Press.

Prince Peter (1963)
A study of polyandry. The Hague: Mouton and Co.

Prejevalsky, N.M. (1876)
Mongolia, the Tangut country and the solitudes of Northern Tibet (two vols.). London: S.Low, Marston, Searle and Rivington.

Pudup, M.B. (1988)
Arguments within regional geography. *Progress in Human Geography*, vol.12, no.3: 369-390.

REFERENCES

Race, J. (1974)
The war in Northern Thailand. *Modern Asian Studies*, vol.8, no.1: 85-112.

Radhu, A.W. (1981)
Caravane tibétaine. Paris: Fayard (adapté en français par Roger Du Pasquier d'après les mémoires inédits de l'auteur).

Rana, N.R.L. (1970)
The Anglo-Gorkha War 1814-1816. Naxal: N.R.L. Rana.

Rankin, R. (1930)
A tour in the Himalayas and beyond. London: John Lane, the Bodley Head.

Rauber, H. (1987a)
Trade in far west Nepal: the economic adaptation of the peripatetic Humli-Khyampa. In: Rao, A. (ed.), *The other nomads. Peripatetic minorities in cross-cultural perspective*: 65-87. Köln-Wien: Böhlau Verlag.

Rauber, H. (1987b)
Stages of women's life among Tibetan nomadic traders: the Humli-Khyampa of far western Nepal. *Ethnos*, vol.52, no.1-2: 200-228.

Raverty, H.G. (1895)
Tibbat three hundred and sixty-five years ago. *Journal of the Asiatic Society of Bengal*, vol.64, no.2: 82-122.

Rawat, P.C. (1974)
Indo-Nepal economic relations. Delhi: National Publishing House.

Rawling, C.G. (1905a)
Exploration of Western Tibet and Rudok. *The Geographical Journal*, vol.XXV, no.4, April: 414-428.

Rawling, C.G. (1905b)
The Great Plateau. Being an account of exploration in Central Tibet, 1903, and of the Gartok expedition, 1904-1905. London: Edward Arnold.

Ray, H. (1983)
China's strategy in Nepal. New Delhi: Radiant Publishers.

Reck, G.G. (1983)
Narrative anthropology. *Anthropology and Humanism Quarterly*, vol.8, no.1: 8-12.

Redfield, R. (1956)
Peasant society and culture. An anthropological approach to civilization. Chicago: The University of Chicago Press.

Regmi, D.R. (1975)
Modern Nepal. Rise and growth in the eighteenth century (two vols.). Calcutta: Firma K.L. Mukhopadhyay (original edition: 1961).

Regmi, M.C. (ed.) (1983a)
Customs exemption for traders of Manang. In: *Regmi Research Series*, vol.15, no.5 , May, 67-68.

Regmi, M.C. (ed.) (1983b)
The impact of India's railway system on Nepal's economy during the closing years of the 19th century. In: *Regmi Research Series*, vol.15, no.5, May, 72-76.

Regmi, M.C. (ed.) (1983c)
Revenue collection in Manang and other villages. In: *Regmi Research Series*, vol.15, no.9, September, 138-139.

Rennie, S. (1866)
Bhotan and the story of the Doar war. London: John Murray. Reprinted New Delhi: Manjusri Publishing House 1970.

Richardson, H.E. (1984)
Tibet and its history. London and Boulder: Shambhala Press (second edition, revised and updated).

Richardus, P. (1989)
The Dutch orientalist Johan van Manen: his life and work. Leiden: Kern Institute.

Rijnhart, S.C. (1901)
With the Tibetans in tent and temple. Narrative of four years' residence on the Tibetan border, and of a journey into the far interior. Edinburgh and London: Oliphant, Anderson and Ferrier.

Rock, J.F. (1930)
Seeking the mountains of mystery. An expedition on the China-Tibet frontier to the unexplored Amnyi Machen Range. *The National Geographic Magazine*, vol. LVII, no.2, February: 131-185.

Rock, J.F. (1956)
The Amnye Ma-Chen range and adjacent regions. A monographic study. Roma: IsMEO (Serie Orientale Roma, XII).

Rockhill, W.W. (1891a)
Tibet. A geographical, ethnographical and historical sketch, derived from Chinese sources. *Journal of the Royal Asiatic Society*, N.S., vol. XXIII, no.1: 1-133, no.2: 185-291.

Rockhill, W.W. (1891b)
The land of the lamas. Notes of a journey through China, Mongolia and Tibet. London: Longmans, Green and Co.

Rockhill, W.W. (1894)
Diary of a journey through Mongolia and Tibet in 1891 and 1892. Washington: Smithsonian Institution.

Roerich, G.N. (1967)
Trails to inmost Asia. Five years of exploration with the Roerich Central Asian Expedition. Reprinted in: *Izbrannye trudy*: 35-149. Moscow: Izdatel'stvo, Nauka. Original edition New Haven: Yale University Press 1931.

Rose, L.E. (1971)
Nepal. Strategy for survival. Bombay: Oxford University Press.

Rose, L.E. and J.T. Scholz (1980)
Nepal. Profile of a Himalayan kingdom. Boulder, Colorado: Westview Press.
Rosthorn, A. von (1895a)
Eine Reise im westlichen China. *Mitteilungen der Geographische Gesellschaft Wien*, vol.38, 285-320.
Rosthorn, A. von (1895b)
On the tea cultivation in Western Ssuch'uan and the tea trade with Tibet via Tachienlu. London: Luzac.
Rudolph, S.H. (1987)
State formation in Asia - prolegomena to a comparative study. *The Journal of Asian Studies*, vol. 46, no. 4, 731-746.
Ryall, E.C. (1879)
Explorations in western Tibet, by the trans-Himalayan parties of the Indian Trigonometrical Survey. *Proceedings of the Royal Geographical Society*, vol.I: 444-452.
Ryder, C.H.D. (1905)
Exploration and survey with the Tibet frontier commission, and from Gyangtse to Simla via Gartok. *The Geographical Journal*, vol.XXVI, no.4, October: 369-395.
Sacherer, J. (1977)
The Sherpas of Rolwaling, North Nepal: a study in cultural ecology. Ph.D. dissertation, Paris: École des Hautes Études en Sciences Sociales.
Sagant,P. (1968-1969)
Les marchés en pays Limbu (notes sur trois hat bajar des districts de Taplejung et de Terathum. *l'Ethnographie*, Nouvelle Série, nos.62-63: 90-118.
Sagant,P. (1978)
Ampleur et profondeur historique des migrations népalaises. *l'Ethnographie*, vol.120, nos.77-78: 93-119.
Sagant, P. (1990)
Les tambours de Nyi-shang (Nepal). Rituel et centralisation politique. In: *Tibet, civilisation et société*: 151-170. Paris: Éditions de la Fondation Singer-Polignac; Éditions de la Maison des Sciences de l'Homme.
Saguchi, T. (1965)
The eastern trade of the Khoquand khanate. *Memoirs of the Research Department of the Toyo Bunko*, No.24: 47-114.
Sahlins, M. (1974)
Stone age economics. London: Tavistock Publications.
Sahlins, M. (1985)
Islands of history. London and New York: Tavistock Publications.
Samuel, G. (1978)
Religion in Tibetan society: a new approach. Part one: a structural model. *Kailash*, vol.VI, no.1: 45-67.

Samuel, G. (1982)
Tibet as a stateless society and some Islamic parallels. *Journal of Asian Studies*, vol.XLI, no.2: 215-229.

Samuel, G. (1992)
Ge sar of Ling. The origins and meaning of the East Tibetan epic. In: *Tibetan Studies, Narita 1989*, vol.2: 711-721. Narita: Naritasan Shinshoji.

Samuel, G. (1993)
Civilized shamans. Buddhism in Tibetan societies. Washington and London: Smithsonian Institution Press.

Samuel, G. (1994)
Ge sar of gLing. Shamanic power and popular religion. In: G. Samuel, H. Gregor and E. Stutchbury (eds.), *Tantra and popular religion in Tibet*: 53-78. New Delhi: Aditya Prakashan.

Sanguin, A.-L. (1981)
La géographie humaniste ou l'approche phénoménologique des lieux, des paysages et des espace. *Annales de Géographie*, Septembre-Octobre: 560-587.

Sanwal, B.D. (1965)
Nepal and the East India Company. New York: Asia Publishing House.

Sato, H. (1975)
The route from Kokonor to Lhasa during the T'ang period. *Acta Asiatica*, vol.29: 1-19 (Bulletin of the Institute of Eastern Culture, Tokyo).

Sautter, G. (1961)
L'étude régionale: réflexion sur la formule monographique en géographie humaine. *L'Homme*, vol.I: 77-89.

Schäfer, E. (1938)
Dach der Erde. Durch das Wunderland Hochtibet. Berlin: Paul Parey Verlag.

Schafer, E.H. (1963)
The golden peaches of Samarkand. A study of T'ang exotics. Berkeley and Los Angeles: University of California Press.

Schrader, H. (1988)
Trading patterns in the Nepal Himalayas. Saarbrücken - Fort Lauderdale: Verlag Breitenbach (Bielefelder Studien zur Entwicklungssoziologie, Band 39).

Schuler, S.R. (1983)
Fraternal polyandry and single women: a study of marriage, social stratification and property in Chumik, a Tibetan society of the Nepal Himalayas.
Ph.D. dissertation, Harvard University, Cambridge, Massachusetts.

Scott, J. (1934)
A short journey through northwestern Kansu and the Tibetan border country. *Journal of the Royal Central Asian Society*, vol.XXI, part I, January: 18-37.

REFERENCES

Sen, J. (1971)
India's trade with Central Asia via Nepal. *Bulletin of Tibetology*, vol.VIII, no.2: 21-40.

Sen, J. (1977)
Indo-Nepal trade in the nineteenth century. Calcutta: Firma KLM.

Serruys, H. (1975)
Sino-Mongol relations during the Ming. Vol.III - Trade relations: the horsefairs (1400-1600). Bruxelles: Institut Belge des Hautes Études Chinoises.

Shakabpa, T.W.D. (1967)
Tibet, a political history. New Haven and London: Yale University Press. Reprinted New York: Potala Publishers 1984 (Tibetan edition (two vols.): Kalimpong, West-Bengal: Shakabpa House 1976).

Shakya, T.W. (1990)
1948 Tibetan trade mission to United Kingdom. *The Tibet Journal*, vol.XV, no.4, Winter: 97-114.

Shelton, F. Beal (1923)
Shelton of Tibet. New York: George H. Doran Company.

Sherring, C.A. (1906)
Western Tibet and the Indian borderland. London: Edward Arnold. Reprinted Delhi: Cosmo Publications 1974.

Shi-yang, G. and L. Bing-xiao (1981)
Borate minerals on the Qinghai-Xizang plateau. In: *Geological and ecological studies of Qinghai-Xizang plateau*: 1723-1731. Beijing: Science Press, New York: Gordon and Breach.

Short, A. (1975)
The communist insurrection in Malaya. London: Frederick Muller Ltd.

Shukla, S.R. (1976)
Sikkim. The story of integration. New Delhi: S. Chand and Co.

Shuttleworth, H.L. (1922)
Border countries of the Punjab Himalaya. *The Geographical Journal*, vol.LX, no.4, October: 241-268.

Shuttleworth, H.L. (1923)
A wool mart of the Indo-Tibetan borderland. *The Geographical Review*, vol.XIII, no.4: 552-558.

Silcock, T.H. (1967)
The rice-premium and agricultural diversification. In: T.H. Silcock (ed.), *Thailand: social and economic studies in development*: 231-257. Canberra: Australian National University Press.

Singh, A.K.J. (1988a)
The history of Tibet, Sikkim and Bhutan 1765-1950. A guide to source material in the India Office Library and Records. London: The British Library.

Singh, A.K.J. (1988b)
Himalayan triangle. A historical survey of British India's relations with Tibet, Sikkim and Bhutan 1765-1950. London: The British Library.

Singh, H. (1977)
Territorial organisation of gompas in Ladakh. In: *Himalaya - écologie, ethnologie*: 351-370. Paris: CNRS.

Singh, J. (1990)
A brief survey of village gods and their moneylending operations in Kinnaur district of Himachal Pradesh; along with earlier importance of trade with Tibet. In: *Wissenschaftsgeschichte und gegenwärtige Forschungen in Nordwest-Indien*: 244-258. Dresden: Staatliches Museum für Völkerkunde.

Singh, O.P. (1985)
Strategic Sikkim. Delhi: B.R. Publishing Corporation.

Sion, J. (1925)
La 'Géographie Humaine' de M. Jean Brunhes. *Bulletin de la Société Languedocienne de Géographie,* tome XLVIII, no.1-2: 138-143.

Skrine, C.P. (1926)
Chinese Central Asia. An account of travels in Northern Kashmir and Chinese Turkestan. London: Methuen. Reprinted Hong Kong: Oxford University Press 1986.

Skrine, C.P. and P. Nightingale (1987)
Macartney at Kashgar. New light on British, Chinese and Russian activities in Sinkiang, 1890-1918. Oxford: Oxford University Press (original edition London: Methuen and Co. 1973).

Slusser, M.S. (1982)
Nepal Mandala. A cultural study of the Kathmandu Valley (two vols.). Princeton, N.J.: Princeton University Press.

Snellgrove, D.L. (1981)
Himalayan pilgrimage. A study of Tibetan religion. Boulder, Col.: Prajna Press (original edition Oxford: Bruno Cassirer 1961).

Snellgrove, D.L. (1987)
Indo-Tibetan Buddhism: Indian Buddhists and their Tibetan successors. London: Serindia Publications.

Snellgrove, D. and H. Richardson (1980)
A cultural history of Tibet. Boulder: Prajna Press (original edition: London: Weidenfeld and Nicolson 1968).

Snelling, J. (1983)
The sacred mountain. Travellers and pilgrims at Mount Kailas in Western Tibet, and the great universal symbol of the sacred mountain. London and The Hague: East West Publications.

Snelling, J. (1993)
Buddhism in Russia. The story of Agvan Dorzhiev, Lhasa's emissary to the tsar. Shaftesbury, Dorset: Element.

Sopiee, M.N. (1973)
The Penang Secession Movement, 1948-1951. *Journal of Southeast Asian Studies*, vol.IV, no.l: 52-71.

Sorre, M. (1948)
La notion de genre de vie et sa valeur actuelle. *Annales de Géographie*, vol.LVII: 97-108, 193-204.

Southern, R.W. (1993)
Saint Anselm. A portrait in a landscape. Cambridge: Cambridge University Press.

Spate, D.H.K., A. Learmonth and B.H. Farmer (1972)
India, Pakistan and Ceylon: the regions. London: Methuen.

Spence, H. (1991)
Tsarong II, the hero of Chaksam, and the modernisation struggle in Tibet 1912-1931. *The Tibet Journal*, vol. XVI, no.l, spring: 34-57.

Spengen, W.van (1987)
The Nyishangba of Manang: geographical perspectives on the rise of a Nepalese trading community. *Kailash*, vol.XIII, nos.3-4: 131-277.

Spengen, W. van (1988)
Jules Sion, 1879-1940. *Geographers: Biobibliographical Studies*, vol.12: 159-165.

Sperling, E. (1976)
The Chinese venture in K'am, 1904-1911, and the role of Chao Erh-feng. *The Tibet Journal*, vol.l, no.2: 10-36.

Steensgaard, N. (1973)
Carracks, caravans, and companies: the structural crisis in the European-Asian trade in the early 17th century. (Monograph Series, Vol.17). Copenhagen: Scandinavian Institute of Asian Studies.

Stein, A. (1918)
Routes from the Panjab to Turkestan and China recorded by William Finch (1611). *The Geographical Journal*, vol.LI, no.l, January: 172-175.

Stein, M.A. (1907)
Ancient Khotan: detailed report of archaeological explorations in Chinese Turkestan. London: Oxford University Press.

Stein, R.A. (1959)
Recherches sur l'épopée et le barde au Tibet. Paris: Presses Universitaires de France.

Stein, R.A. (1961)
Les tribus anciennes des marches sino-tibétains: légendes, classifications et histoire. Paris: Presses Universitaires de France.

Stein, R.A. (1987)
La civilisation tibétaine. Paris: l'Asiathèque (édition définitive) (réédition revue et augmentée de l'édition de 1962. Paris: Dunod).

Steinmann, B. (1988)
Les marches tibétaines du Népal: état, chefferie et société traditionnels à travers le récit d'un notable népalais. Paris: L'Harmattan.

Stevens, S.F. (1993)
Claiming the high ground. Sherpas, subsistence, and environmental change in the higher Himalaya. Berkeley: University of California Press.

Stevenson, P.H. (1932)
Notes on the human geography of the Chinese-Tibetan borderland. *The Geographical Review*, vol.XXII, no.4, October: 599-616.

Stiller, L.F., S.J. (1968)
Prithwinarayan Shah in the light of Dibya Upadesh. Ranchi, Bihar: The Catholic Press.

Stiller, L.F., S.J. (1972)
A note on Himalayan trade. *Journal of the Tribhuvan University*, No.7: 1-34

Stiller, L.F., S.J. (1973)
The rise of the house of Gorkha: a study in the unification of Nepal 1768-1816. New Delhi: Manjusri Publishing House. Reprinted Patna: Patna Jesuit Society 1975.

Stoddard, H. (1985)
Le mendiant de l'Amdo. (Recherches sur la Haute Asie, vol.9). Paris: Société d'Ethnographie, Nanterre: Labethno, Université de Paris X.

Stoll, E. (1966)
Ti-se, der heilige Berg in Tibet. *Geographica Helvetica*, vol.21: 162-167.

Stötzner, W. (1924)
Ins unerforschte Tibet: Tagebuch der deutschen Expedition Stötzner 1914. Leipzig: Verlag von K.F. Koehler.

Tafel, A. (1914)
Meine Tibetreise. Eine Studienfahrt durch das nordwestliche China und durch die innere Mongolei in das östliche Tibet (two vols.). Stuttgart, Berlin, Leipzig: Union Deutsche Verlagsgesellschaft.

Taylor, R.H. (1973)
Foreign and domestic consequences of the KMT intervention in Burma. Data Paper No.93, Southeast Asia Program, Department of Asian Studies, Cornell University, Ithaca, New York.

Teichman, E. (1922)
Travels of a consular officer in Eastern Tibet; together with a history of the relations between China, Tibet and India. Cambridge: Cambridge University Press.

Thomas, F.W. (1948)
Nam: an ancient language of the Sino-Tibetan borderland. London: Oxford University Press.

Thomas, L., Jr. (1959)
The silent war in Tibet. New York: Doubleday and Co.

Thomson, T. (1852)
Western Himalaya and Tibet: a narrative of a journey through the mountains of Northern India, during the years 1847-8. London: Reeve and Co. Reprinted Kathmandu: Ratna Pustak Bhandar 1979.

Thurston, A.F. (1988)
The Chinese view of Tibet - is dialogue possible? *Cultural Survival Quarterly*, vol.12, no.l: 70-73.

Tilly, C. (1984)
Big structures, large processes, huge comparisons. New York: Russell Sage Foundations.

Tilman, H.W. (1951)
Explorations in the Nepal Himalaya. *The Geographical Journal*, vol.CIV, no.3: 263-274.

Tilman, H.W. (1952)
Nepal Himalaya. Cambridge: Cambridge University Press.

Tinker, H. (1975)
A forgotten long march: the Indian exodus from Burma, 1942. *Journal of Southeast Asian Studies*, vol.6, no.l: 1-16.

Toffin, G. (1976)
The peoples of the Upper Ankhu Khola Valley. *Contributions to Nepalese Studies*, vol.3, no.l: 34-46.

Tolstoy, I. (1946)
Across Tibet from India to China. *The National Geographic Magazine*, vol.XC, no.2, August: 169-222.

Tonkin, E., M. Mcdonald and M. Chapman (eds.) (1989)
History and ethnicity. London: Routledge (ASA Monograph 27).

Trager, F.N. (1966)
Burma, from kingdom to republic: a historical and political analysis. London: Pall Mall Press.

Traill, G.W. (1832)
Statistical report on the Bhotia Mehals of Kamaon. *Asiatic Researches*, vol. XVII: 1-50.

Tregonning, K.G. (1960)
North Borneo. London: Her Majesty's Stationery Office.

Tsarong, P. (1987)
Economy and ideology on a Tibetan monastic estate in Ladakh: processes of production, reproduction and transformation. Ph.D. dissertation, University of Wisconsin.

Tsybikoff, G. (1904)
Lhasa and Central Tibet (Annual Report of the Board of Regents of the Smithsonian Institution). Washington: Government Printing Office.

Tsybikoff, G. (1904)
Journey to Lhasa. *The Geographical Journal*, vol.23: 92-97.

Tsybikov, G.T. (1992)
Un pèlerin bouddhiste dans les sanctuaires du Tibet. D'après les journaux de voyage tenus entre 1899 et 1902. Paris: Éditions Peuples du Monde. Translated from the original Russian edition of 1919 by Bernard Kreise.

Tucci, G. (1949)
Tibetan painted scrolls (three vols.). Rome: La Libreria della Stato. Reprinted Kyoto: Rinsen Book Company 1980.

Tucci, G. (1956)
To Lhasa and beyond. Diary of the expedition to Tibet in the year MCMXLVIII. Roma: Libreria della Stato.

Tucci, G. (1967)
Tibet: Land of Snows. New York: Stein and Day (French translation: Tibet, Pays des Neiges. Paris: Éditions Albin Michel 1969).

Tucci, G. (1980)
The religions of Tibet. London: Routledge and Kegan Paul.

Tucci, G. (1989)
Sadhus et brigands du Kailash. Mon voyage au Tibet occidental (translated from the Italian). Paris: Éditions Raymond Chabaud - Peuples du Monde (original edition Milan: Casa Editrice Ulrico Hoepli 1937).

Tucci, G. and E. Ghersi (1935)
Secrets of Tibet. Being the chronicle of the Tucci scientific expedition to Western Tibet (1933). London and Glasgow: Blackie and Son. Translated by Mary A. Johnstone from the original Italian edition published in Rome (1934).

Turner, S. (1800)
An account of an embassy to the court of the Teshoo Lama in Tibet, containing a narrative of a journey through Bootan, and part of Tibet. London: G.W. Nichol. Reprinted New Delhi: Manjusri Publishing House 1971.

Turrell, R.V. (1988)
Conquest and concession: the case of the Burma ruby mines. *Modern Asian Studies*, vol.22, no.1: 141-163.

Tyson, J. (1953)
Himalayan traders. *The Geographical Magazine*, vol.26, no.10, July: 139-146.

Uprety, P.R. (1980)
Nepal-Tibet relations, 1850-1930. Kathmandu: Puga Nara.

Vansina, J. (1973)
Oral tradition. A study in historical methodology. Harmondsworth: Penguin Books.

REFERENCES

Vansittart, E. (1890)
The Goorkha's. Calcutta: Superintendent of Government Printing. Reprinted Delhi: Ariana Publishing House 1980.

Varadarajan, L. (1988)
Silk in Northeastern and Eastern India: the indigenous tradition. *Modern Asian Studies*, vol.22, no.3: 561-570.

Vaurie, C. (1972)
Tibet and its birds. London: H.F. and G. Witherby Ltd.

Vidal de la Blache, P. (1911a)
Les genres de vie dans la géographie humaine (premier article). *Annales de Géographie*, vol.XX, no.111, 15 mai: 193-212.

Vidal de la Blache, P. (1911b)
Les genres de vie dans la géographie humaine (second article). *Annales de Géographie*, vol.XX, no.112, 15 juillet: 289-304.

Vidal de la Blache, P. (1913)
Des caractères distinctifs de la géographie. *Annales de Géographie*, vol.XXII, no.124, 15 juillet: 289-299.

Vinding, M. (1984)
Making a living in the Nepal Himalayas: the case of the Thakalis of Mustang District. *Contributions to Nepalese Studies*, vol. XII, no.l, December: 51-105.

Vinding, M. and K.B. Bhattachan (1985)
An annotated bibliography on the Thakalis. *Contributions to Nepalese Studies*, vol.12, no.3, August: 1-23.

Wagley, S.P. (1969)
The gift parcel system in Nepal. In: *Trade and transit: Nepal's problem with her southern neighbour*: 31-35 (CEDA Occasional Paper No. l). Kathmandu: Centre for Economic Development and Administration.

Wagner, P.L. (1972)
Environments and peoples. Englewood Cliffs, N.J.: Prentice Hall.

Wagner, P.L. and M.W. Mikesell (1962)
The themes of cultural geography. In: *Readings in cultural geography*: 1-24. Chicago: University of Chicago Press.

Walker-Watson, M.N. (1983)
Turquoise - the gemstone of Tibet. *Tibetan Review*, vol.XVIII, no.6-7: 16-18.

Wallace, B.A.(ed.) (1980)
The life and teaching of Geshé Rabten. London: George Allen and Unwin.

Waller, D. (1990)
The pundits: British exploration of Tibet and Central Asia. Lexington, Kentucky: University of Kentucky Press.

Wallerstein, I. (1974a)
The modern world-system: capitalist agriculture and the origins of the European world- economy in the sixteenth century. New York: Academic Press.

Wallerstein, I. (1974b)
The capitalist world-economy. Cambridge: Cambridge University Press.

Walsh, E. H. (1906)
Elective government in the Chumbi Valley. *Journal and Proceedings of the Asiatic Society of Bengal,* N.S., vol.2, no.7: 303-308.

Walt van Praag, M.C. van (1985)
Whose game? Records of the India Office concerning events leading up to the Simla Conference. In: Aziz, B.N. and M. Kapstein, *Soundings in Tibetan civilization*: 215-230. New Delhi: Manohar.

Walt van Praag, M.C. van (1987)
The status of Tibet: history, rights, and prospects in international law. London: Wisdom Publications.

Ward, M. (1966)
Some geographical and medical observations in North Bhutan. *The Geographical Journal,* vol.132, part 4: 491-506.

Warikoo, K. (1988)
Central Asia and Kashmir: a study in political and cultural contacts during the 19th and early 20th centuries. *Central Asian Survey,* vol.7, no.1: 63-83.

Warikoo, K. (1989)
Central Asia and Kashmir: a study in the context of Anglo-Russian rivalry. New Delhi: Gian Publishing House 1989.

Watkins, J.C. (1996)
Spirited women. Gender, religion and cultural identity in the Nepal Himalaya. New York: Columbia University Press.

Weber, M. (1978)
Gesammelte Aufsätze zur Religionssoziologie, Vol. II, Hinduismus und Buddhismus. Tübingen: J.C.B. Mohr (original edition 1921).

Weigold, H. (1935)
Südost-Tibet als Lebensraum. *Jahrbuch der Geographischen Gesellschaft zu Hannover für 1934 und 1935*: 203-247.

Weiss, F. (1912)
Die Provinz Yünnan, ihre Handels- und Verkehrsverhältnisse. *Mitteilungen des Seminars für Orientalische Sprachen,* vol. XV: 1-57.

Wertheim, W.F. (1964)
The trading minorities in Southeast Asia. In: *East-West parallels. Sociological approaches to modern Asia*: 39-82. The Hague: W. van Hoeve.

Wesseling, H.L. (1981)
Fernand Braudel. In: A.H. Huussen Jr., E.H. Kossmann, H. Renner (eds.), *Historici van de twintigste eeuw*: 229-245. Amsterdam: Intermediair.

Wessels, C. (1924)
Early Jesuit travellers in Central Asia, 1603-1721. The Hague: Martinus Nijhoff. Reprinted New Delhi: Asian Educational Services 1992.

Wheatley, P. (1971)
The pivot of the four quarters. A preliminary enquiry into the origins and character of the ancient Chinese city. Chicago: Aldine.

White, H. (1984)
The question of narrative in contemporary historical theory. *History and Theory*, vol.23: 1-33.

Wiley, T.W. (1986)
Macro exchanges: Tibetan economics and the roles of politics and religion. *The Tibet Journal*, vol.XI, no.l: 3-20.

Winnington, A. (1957)
Tibet. Record of a journey. London: Lawrence and Wishart.

Wissler, C. (1917)
The American Indian. An introduction to the anthropology of the new world. New York: D.C. McMurtrie.

Wolf, E. (1982)
Europe and the people without history. Berkeley: University of California Press.

Wollaston, A.F.R. (1922)
The natural history of South-Western Tibet. *The Geographical Journal*, vol.LX, no.l, July: 5-20.

Woodman, D. (1969)
Himalayan frontiers: a political review of British, Chinese, Indian and Russian rivalries. London: Barrie and Rockliff, The Cresset Press.

Wright, D. (1877)
History of Nepal. Cambridge: Cambridge University Press. Reprinted Kathmandu: Nepal Antiquated Book Publishers 1972.

Wylie, T.V. (1978)
Reincarnation: a political innovation in Tibetan Buddhism. In: Ligeti, L. (ed.), *Proceedings of the Csoma de Körös Memorial Symposium*: 579-586. Budapest: Akadémiai Kiadó.

Yoshinobu, S. (1983)
Sung foreign trade: its scope and organization. In: Rossabi, M. (ed.), *China among equals*: 89-115. Berkeley and Los Angeles: University of California Press.

Young, G. (1962)
The hill tribes of Northern Thailand. Bangkok: Siam Society.

INDEX

Page numbers referring to Figures are written in **bold**